2.9/

THE IMPACT OF THE CIVIL WAR
A SERIES PLANNED BY
THE CIVIL WAR CENTENNIAL COMMISSION

AGRICULTURE AND THE CIVIL WAR
by Paul W. Gates (1965)

BONNET BRIGADES
by Mary Elizabeth Massey (1966)

Among the Volumes in Preparation

THE MILITARY THOUGHT AND PRACTICES OF EUROPE
by Cyril Falls

ON PHILANTHROPY AND WELFARE
by Robert H. Bremner

THE NORTH TO POSTERITY
by James I. Robertson, Jr.

ON MEDICINE AND SURGERY
by William F. Norwood

ON CONSTITUTIONAL AND STATUTORY LAW
AND INTERPRETATION
by Harold Hyman

Heard Round the World

THE IMPACT OF THE CIVIL WAR

[THE CIVIL WAR CENTENNIAL COMMISSION SERIES]

Edited by Allan Nevins

HEARD ROUND THE WORLD

THE IMPACT ABROAD OF THE CIVIL WAR

H. C. Allen David H. Pinkney John Hawgood
Hans Rogger John A. Williams Harry Bernstein

Edited by *Harold Hyman*

William Hobby Professor of
American History at Rice University

New York: Alfred · A · Knopf

1969

973.714
H

FIRST EDITION

Introduction

Ninety years ago, as the centennial of the American Revolution approached, a would-be writer of a history of the United States, Mrs. Martha J. Lamb, advised a friend, the nation's Chief Justice Morrison R. Waite, that her publisher was ". . . extremely anxious that my history should have the precedence of all other enterprises, in order to catch the centennial penny." But the publisher's financial backer was balking. According to Mrs. Lamb the backer was ". . . a business dummy, [who] knows nothing at all about the subject in question, stares aghast at the outlay involved, and is afraid he will not get his money back." She and the publisher were attempting to convince him that a history "cannot fail to sell, particularly in this centennial hubbub."[1]

Readers should be assured at once that the contributors to *Heard Round the World* responded to imperatives other than the ones that moved Mrs. Lamb. They have created an essentially different sort of commemoration than those of 1876 which celebrated the Declaration of Independence,[2] or those beginning in 1961 which commenced the "centennial hubbub" about the Civil War and Reconstuction. In place of the latter's battlefield pageants, now ended, *Heard Round the World* is one of many ongoing private confrontations with the past that are being fought in research archives and libraries, and in book reviews, learned journal articles, and book-length monographs.

Which is to say that the historian's Civil War and Reconstruction remains unfinished business. It moves ahead at a quick march, and gives no evidence of slowdown, much less of a halt. This forward motion is taking place on several research fronts

---

[1] Oct. 13, 1875, Waite Papers, Manuscripts Division, Library of Congress.

[2] Dee Brown: *The Year of the Century: 1876* (New York, 1966) suggests impressionistically the spirit of the first centennial.

at once. Currently partisans on campuses argue warmly the allegedly superior illumination of the past which their favored investigative methods make possible. Some strong voices praise interdisciplinary and cross-cultural approaches, psychological insights, especially for biography, and quantitative constructions. Others debate the adequacy of techniques traditional since Tacitus. Few scholars are absolutists, however, altogether accepting or rejecting either the old ways or the newer, scientifically oriented attitudes. Meanwhile, the broad-gauged research—and arguments over methodological viability—continues into the Civil War and Reconstruction as into other significant segments of the American heritage.[3]

Probably makeweights of the Civil War generation would have found amusing or, worse, irrelevant, today's continuing campus concern over interconnections. For the age of Lincoln required no proofs that the affairs of men and nations were a tangle of internal goads and external wants, economic pressures and selfless passions, inextricably involving societies with each other. Lincoln's reference to the Union as the world's last, best hope presented this workaday understanding in engaging imagery. Similar concepts were widely expressed by his contemporaries. In the following retrospection of 1868, the historian John Lothrop Motley provided a fair example of this innately pluralistic view. Motley believed as Lincoln did that "The effect of the triumph of freedom in this country on the causes of progress in Europe is plain." Referring specifically to England, Motley asserted that the Union army's 1865 successes had made certain the passage of Britain's 1867 Reform Act. "Who can doubt," he asked rhetorically, "that . . . the English household suffrage bill is the fruit of the Appomattox apple-tree [?] Who imagined in 1862 that [political] power would be transferred in England, so soon from land to people, without bloodshed, and that it would be done by Tories?"[4]

Although a fair number of informed Englishmen also believed that their dramatic democratization in politics in 1867 was

---

[3] A summary of research crosscurrents is found in John Higham et al.: *History* (Englewood Cliffs, N.J., 1965), pp. 82–232.

[4] John Lothrop Motley: *Historic Progress and American Democracy: Address to the New-York Historical Society, December 16, 1868* (New York, 1869), pp. 39, 62–3.

a direct consequence of Union victory in 1865,[5] many historians have come to doubt the validity of the proposition that Motley advanced so confidently. Although scholarship more thoroughgoing than any Motley knew makes his ebullient judgment less supportable, there has been no radical swing from his position to the opposite extreme, that the Anglo-American interaction was unimportant. Motley's premise that American events strongly affected affairs in Britain and vice versa, and that such reciprocal influence was not confined to conventional diplomatic intercourse, has been upheld. Vital transoceanic interchange took place not only between Washington and Whitehall but also between America's and Britain's aesthetic, economic, and intellectual communities.

Obviously it is a difficult and subtle task to evaluate such complex interactions even with respect to England, where most of the research has centered, and where it is facilitated by the presence of familiar institutions.[6] Equally obviously, the difficulties increase as one moves to other lands and strays from the traditional trails of diplomatic history. Most scholarship has understandably followed familiar pathways of diplomatic history involving Britain, and to a slightly lesser degree, France. In the field of aesthetics and ideas the stress has been on how we in this country received and adopted insights and outlooks, rather than the other way around.[7]

• • •

---

[5] See as an example Leslie Stephen: *Life of Henry Fawcett* (London, 1886), pp. 215, 222.

[6] Cf. David Paul Crook: *American Democracy in English Politics, 1815–1850* (Oxford, 1965); Henry Pelling: *America and the British Left: from Bright to Bevan* (London, 1956); G. D. Lillibridge: *Beacon of Freedom: The Impact of American Democracy upon Great Britain, 1830–1870* (Philadelphia, 1954). Outstanding is H. C. Allen: *Conflict and Concord; The Anglo-American Relationship since 1783* (New York, 1959); and see his current thinking on the 1867 Act, in his essay below, pp. 3–96.

[7] Despite its title, Philip Van Doren Stern: *When the Guns Roared: World Aspects of the American Civil War* (Garden City, N.Y., 1965), deals primarily with Lincoln's carpet-slipper diplomacy with England and France. On the one-way direction of studies of intellectual interaction, see Howard Mumford Jones: "The Influence of European Ideas in Nineteenth-Century America," *American Literature*, VII (Nov. 1935), 241–73; Daniel J. Boorstin: *America and the Image of Europe: Reflections on American Thought* (New York, 1960); Cushing Strout: *The American Image of the Old World* (New York, 1963), especially Chap. vii.

Lincoln's American contemporaries proudly believed that there *was* a reverse current. A common proposition had it that the Union's unanticipated stiffening after Sumter, its surprising strength during the long war years, and its stability during Reconstruction proved the desirability to foreigners of American constitutional-political arrangements. It appeared obvious that America's impact abroad began during the Civil War because foreigners could ignore no longer what was going on here. Sometime between Sumter and Appomattox, this despised New World society graduated in Europe's estimation from a provincial backwater destined to collapse from the centrifugal strains set up by its inner contradictions to a higher place among nations.[8]

Although Americans boasted about making an impact abroad, some were aware that the impression was as various as Joseph's coat. "We must not miscalculate our influence," warned one July Fourth orator in 1870:

> The great principles that underly our polity, as a nation, do not yet express themselves by giving rise in Europe to forms of government like our own. But in the latest [1867] advance of English reform, in the formal recognition of the sovereignty of the people by the Emperor of the French, in the latest assertion of the right of the people to hold the reigns of government by the people of Spain; and, in fine, in the general awakening of the people throughout Europe, we see the principles of our own government, giving the promise of a better future, and the first faint manifestations of its coming. . . . The people of Europe have learned from the new world that they have rights.[9]

Perhaps the proud Independence Day speaker may be pardoned some exaggeration. It was true that many Europeans had begun to pay attention to American affairs. Heads of state and diplomats such as Russia's Baron Edouard de Stoeckl, France's

---

[8] Samuel Osgood: *American Leaves: Familiar Notes of Thought and Life* (New York, 1867), pp. 168–71, is a typical statement of this view. Osgood was a *Harper's* correspondent.

[9] Edward Ames: *The Historical Importance of the Day: An Oration . . . July 4, 1870* (Providence, R.I., 1870), p. 23.

Introduction

Prince Louis Napoleon, and England's Lord Palmerston were concerned as a matter of course. Less predictably, John Bright, Robert Browning, Georges Clemenceau, Charles Darwin, Friedrich Engels, Giuseppe Garibaldi, Count Agénor de Gasparin, Karl Marx, and John Stuart Mill, among many other leading lights in European letters, thought, and politics, weighed and worried over the past and future of the un-United States during the Civil War and Reconstruction.[1] Many of these observers were very keen indeed. Marx and Engels, for example, understood quite early in the course of the war its revolutionary potentialities in matters of race. They clearly saw that America's destiny involved a global audience.[2]

Although a century ago foreigners across the world showed interest in the outcome of America's Civil War, it is only recently that scholars have expanded their research horizons beyond western Europe and beyond traditional diplomatic questions.

Had western European nations besides Britain and France experienced serious concern or involvements with America's Civil War and Reconstruction? With some significant exceptions, this question had hardly been asked at all about eastern European regions, Asia, Canada, or Latin America. In those rare instances when scholars did contemplate continental rather than narrowly national and traditionally diplomatic concepts in their efforts to gauge the Civil War's meaning abroad, the wider angle involved resulted in hasty, generalized surveys rather than convincing delineations in depth.[3]

• • •

---

[1] A convenient recent compilation is Belle Becker Sideman and Lillian Friedman, eds.: *Europe Looks at the Civil War* (New York, 1962). For a recent insight into a little-noted part of Europe, see Joseph W. Wieczerzak: *A Polish Chapter in Civil War America* (New York: Twayne; 1967).

[2] See Gerard Runkle: "Karl Marx and the American Civil War," *Comparative Studies in Society and History*, VI (Jan. 1964), 117–41; *The Civil War in the United States: Karl Marx and Frederick Engels* (New York, 1937).

[3] Compare Halvdan Koht: *The American Spirit in Europe: A Survey of Transatlantic Influences* (Philadelphia, 1949), Chap. viii, with Heinz K. Meier: *The United States and Switzerland in the Nineteenth Century* (The Hague, 1963).

Introduction

Nor did such studies tend to include the Reconstruction. The dramatic ending of the war with the nearly simultaneous surrender of Lee and assassination of Lincoln seems to have put a firm dividing line between the war and the peace that followed in the minds of historians. As the able English historian and friend of the Union Goldwin Smith said in a lecture given in London in 1866 on his return from an extended tour of the conquered South and the victorious North: "The curtain has fallen upon the great drama of the war." But Smith took care to note what has subsequently been largely forgotten—that history's curtain is in constant motion: "It rises for a political drama almost as great [as the war]," he stated. "The work of reconstruction presents problems which will tax to the utmost the practical sagacity of the American people . . ."[4] What impressed Smith and other commentators abroad was that Americans should approach the complex tasks of Reconstruction so confidently and moderately. Many foreign observers were struck by what Americans wrought while the guns roared, and with what they tried to accomplish afterward.[5] Certainly America's impacts upon foreign lives did not end on the day Lee surrendered. As a horrible example of democracy's allegedly corrupting excesses, or as the world's shining, unique symbol of democracy's rich promises and ennobling rewards, the American nation was frequently a center of foreign attention.

With the elimination of slavery, the world had lost its main incitement to partisanship with either side in America's civil conflict. After Appomattox, nationalism remained as the aspect of American life that attracted continuing interest abroad, and its meaning for the rest of the world aroused great uncertainties in such widely divergent types as English novelists, Irish secular

---

4 Goldwin Smith: *The Civil War in America: An Address Read at the Last Meeting of the Manchester Union and Emancipation Society* (London, 1866), pp. 67–8. A recent interpretation of the Civil War, for Italian readers, is Raimondo Luraghi's *Storia della guerra civile Americana* (Torino, 1966). Luraghi pays relatively little attention to post-Appomattox events, although he does offer comparisons between America's experiences of the 1860's and those of European nations caught up in unification and industrialization.

5 See Harold M. Hyman, ed.: *The Radical Republicans and Reconstruction, 1861–1870* (Indianapolis, 1967), pp. lxii–lxiv.

and church leaders, Hapsburg princelings, Mexican insurrectionists, and Canadian newspaper editors.[6]

Naturally, foreign interest in American affairs was by then not as intense or as consistent as it had been while the nation's and the Negro's fates were daily in the balance, but it continued. Often, it took the form of fear. Among conservatives, concern increased after Appomattox that America's transoceanic thrust would be greater than ever now that the will of majorities was no longer checkreined by slavery. America, "a republic in action," excited every republican "in theory" from Scandinavia to the Mediterranean, according to a correspondent of the Massachusetts Senator Charles Sumner. Every standpat or reactionary advocate was on alert.[7] Of the dour latter breed, the important English political writer J. Arthur Partridge deserves mention. He feared that Appomattox marked ". . . the beginning of an Americanizing process in England. The new Democratic ideas are gradually to find embodiment. The separation of Church and State, a complete secularisation of politics, . . . [and] a popular system of education apart from all associations with creed or Church."[8]

In short, whether they aroused joy or dismay, American affairs after Appomattox demanded attention abroad because America was too vigorous and compelling to be ignored. Once the encumbrance of slavery and the threat of secession were gone, unparalleled progress marked the American scene. The fundamental adventure was the attempt to reconstruct through law the states' federal and racial relationships—and not only of the defeated former Confederate states, it should be noted. Numerous

---

[6] Donaldson Jordan and Edwin J. Pratt: *Europe and the American Civil War* (Boston, 1931), pp. 11–12; Charles E. Shain: "The English Novelists and the American Civil War," *American Quarterly*, XIV (Fall 1962), 399–421; Joseph M. Hernon, Jr.: "Irish Religious Opinion on the American Civil War," *Catholic Historical Review*, XLIX (Jan. 1964), 508–523; Robert A. Naylor, ed.: "A Mexican Conspirator Views the Civil War," *Civil War History*, IX (Mar. 1963), 67–73; Helen G. MacDonald: *Canadian Public Opinion on the American Civil War* (New York, 1926).

[7] See W. R. Brimmer to Sumner, Dec. 30, 1866, Sumner Papers, Houghton Library, Harvard University.

[8] J. Arthur Partridge: *On Democracy* (London, 1866), p. ix.

other exciting innovations were under way in a dozen different reform arenas in as many states. It all moved the editor of Britain's most prestigious law journal to comment in 1868 that America had become "the great transatlantic workshop" where the world might find "models in good working order of all our projected reforms." With the American experience to illuminate the unknown and the theoretical, Europeans could avoid blind "leaps in the dark." The Englishman suggested that Parliament establish as a rule for Commons and Lords that "whenever any novelty is proposed, let them at once inquire diligently—'Have they tried it in America? How does it work?' " Appomattox had made progress possible in America, he continued:

> The United States are generally the vile corpus out of which by dint of many an experiment, essay, and strange vagary, the good comes by which we tardily profit. The American loves to dabble in those subjects which are somewhat vaguely known as "Social Science," and we believe that in one State or another of the Union, . . . education, criminology, legal reforms, sanitary reforms, and so on, [have] been further sifted than [they have] at home.[9]

Some Americans also understood this. "Our European foes are watching the wranglings in our Union [party] ranks with an interest similar to that which they exhibited in the progress of the war," noted John Jay, a partisan Republican New Yorker, during the critical congressional elections of 1866. Two years later, as the nation lurched through the impeachment of President Andrew Johnson and prepared simultaneously to nominate presidential candidates for both parties, now restored as national institutions, some European friends were amazed at the sturdy strength that American institutions were displaying. John Bright marveled that in the "progressing revolution" represented by the war and Reconstruction, "it is wonderful that your government securities remain unshaken whilst your Congress and Executive are almost at open war!"[1]

---

[9] "Americans and Their Prisons," *Law Magazine and Law Review* (London), XXV (1868), 51–2, 57–8. The idea that Appomattox allowed social "science" to commence enjoyed many supporters. The American Social Science Association dates from the autumn of 1865. See on this subject Boston's *Round Table*, III (Nov. 21, 1865), 105.

[1] John Jay: *The Political Situation in the United States, A Letter to the Union League Club of New York* (London, 1866), pp. 18–19; Bright to

Introduction

There is an impressive amount of similar testimony. New York merchant William T. Blodgett, a major organizer and an originator of the Loyal Publication Society, was one of a large stream of Americans who toured Europe during the first peacetime summer. Home again, Blodgett reported jubilantly that Europeans ". . . cannot understand us, and wonder to see the first steps being taken toward Reconstruction, & stocks advancing daily—and the [common] people [of Europe] . . . notice every detail."[2]

Common or not, a great many people abroad noticed that emancipation was not rescinded, that the Union army dissolved out of existence without even a hint of a *coup d' état*; that unobstructed elections, in which even soldiers voted, continued throughout the war in the North and resumed in the South very soon after the surrender; that Reconstruction involved no mass blood bath, property confiscations, or disfranchisements; and that schools surged southward as soon as bluecoats opened the way, becoming a basic element in the Reconstruction effort. All of this was a sharp departure from the sad history of civil wars and their aftermaths as less blessed peoples had experienced it.[3] An extensive traveler here and a careful observer of America's first year after Appomattox, the Englishman Laurence Oliphant, a member of Parliament, wrote that these departures from the predictable made America difficult for foreigners to understand:

> There is no country in the world in which it is so difficult to arrive at authentic information upon any point as in America, or in which all one's preconceived ideas are likely to be more completely at fault. It is impossible to judge of it by any historical parallel, because no historical parallel exists. Every political experience through which it passes is novel and unique; and whereas the political convulsions of

Sumner, Mar. 7, 1868, in "Bright-Sumner Letters, 1861–1872," *Massachusetts Historical Society Proceedings* (Oct. 1912), p. 159.

[2] Quoted in W. W. Broom (alias Eboracus): *Great and Grave Questions for American Politicians, with a Topic for America's Statesmen* (New York, 1865), p. 67; and see John W. Forney: *Letters from Europe* (Philadelphia, 1867), pp. 145–6.

[3] See Hyman: *Radical Republicans,* pp. liii–lxviii.

Europe are almost monotonous from their uniformity, those of America are quite original, and, I may add, highly sensational.[4]

The impact abroad of America's Civil War and Reconstruction was "sensational" enough to spread into Parliament's debates on Irish Home Rule during the 1880's; into French left-wing radical thinking from 1870 on into the next century; into educational practices in Argentina, introduced there by Yankee veterans of Civil War pedagogical innovations; into the abortive attempts of Dom Pedro II, Emperor of Brazil, to import American-style judicial review into his troubled land; and, more recently, into distortions of Civil War and Reconstruction history fostered by Adolph Hitler on the one hand and Soviet scholars on the other.[5]

But these are only a thin course in the moveable feast that the Civil War and Reconstruction America has provided for an audience more dispersed around the globe and more attentive to American events than has been supposed. The contributors to *Heard Round the World* have tried to look into some obscure areas both of geography and of interest, as well as the more familiar ones, and to make a substantial, original contribution to a subject of unending interest.

Harold M. Hyman
Champaign, Illinois
March 1968

---

[4] Laurence Oliphant: *On the Present State of Political Parties in America: Lecture in Stirling, Burghs, . . .* (London, 1866), pp. 6–7.

[5] Joseph M. Hernon, Jr.: "The Use of the American Civil War in the Debate over Irish Home Rule," *American Historical Review*, LXIX (July 1964); Leo A. Loubère: "French Left-Wing Radicals and the Law as a Social Force, 1870–1900," *American Journal of Legal History*, VIII (1964), 54–71; Alice Houston Luiggi: *65 Valiants* (Gainesville, Fla., 1965); Percy Alvin Martin: "Causes of the Collapse of the Brazilian Empire," *Hispanic American Historical Review*, IV (1921), 23; Gerhard L. Weinberg: "Hitler's Image of the United States," *American Historical Review*, LXIX (July 1964), 1006–20; Wilbur R. Jacobs and Edmond E. Masson: "History and Propaganda: Soviet Image of the American Past," *Mid-America*, XLVI (Apr. 1964), 77.

Contents

Heard Round the World

Civil War, Reconstruction, and Great Britain

H. C. Allen

*W*hat . . . *has the political economy of England to do with that of America, or that of America with England?"* Ed-*ward Gibbon Wakefield asked in 1834. Replying in a 376-page book to his own question, he set the scheme for this large effort in the prefatory statement, "Comparison is the easiest way to truth."*[1]

Englishmen have consistently been attracted to this allegedly easy road, although the trip did not always result in happy con-clusions about America—Dickens's Martin Chuzzlewit has many companions.

The Civil War both inspired and rendered more complicated such comparisons. The war and its aftermath involved both nations, both societies, both histories in complex ways that de-serve continuing, competent examinations from both shores. A mere mention of Lord Bryce and Sir Denis Brogan suggests the weight of talent that Britain has invested. Professor H. C. Allen

---

[1] Edward Gibbon Wakefield: *England and America: A Comparison of the Social and Political State of Both Nations* (New York: Harper; 1834), p. 2.

is another in this pride of transatlantic scholars who has centered his intersts on the British-American interaction. Professor of history at the University of London and director of its Institute of United States Studies, Professor Allen's Great Britain and the United States: A History of Anglo-American Relations (1783– 1952) *(New York, St. Martin's; 1955), as well as others among his publications, led him to consider the effects of the American Civil War in his homeland. The result follows.*

*T*he *Economist* of London (which was edited, during a period almost exactly coterminous with the Civil War and Reconstruction, by Walter Bagehot) stated on January 12, 1861:

> The tidings from what we can no longer call the United States bid fair, for some time to come, to surpass all others in interest and importance. The relations of this country with America, commercial and political, are so intimate, that every transaction on the other side of the Atlantic has its echo and vibration here. Nothing that passes beyond our shores can affect us so powerfully or concern us so much as the proceedings and condition of the great Federal Republic.[1]

This concern did not cease with the war but continued until the settlement of the *Alabama* dispute seven years after it was over. The *Saturday Review* had written in 1866, "The memory of that unfortunate ship rankles still in the breasts of the Americans,"[2] and on the eve of the Geneva award, which brought about the settlement in September 1872, *The Economist* wrote, "While it rancours in the minds of both nations . . . there can be no real peace between the two countries. And till there is . . . the vast monetary transactions which are natural between two such countries and which are so profitable to both, will be throughout hampered and in part suspended."[3]

According to the authors of *Europe and the American Civil War,* the effects that *The Economist* had predicted just before its outbreak did in fact follow:

> It is impossible here to give an accurate impression of the place of British interest in America in the life of the time.

I wish to pay a very warm tribute to the invaluable assistance of Mrs. Christine Bolt in the preparation of this chapter. I also wish to acknowledge with sincere thanks the permission to use certain materials which were unearthed by Mrs. Mary Jones. I should like, too, most gratefully to thank Charlotte Erickson, Jack Pole, Jim Potter, and Michael Thompson for their very helpful comments on the manuscript. For the weaknesses and errors (both of commission and omission) in the final product, I am entirely responsible.

[1] Pp. 29–30.
[2] Nov. 24, 1866, p. 627.
[3] May 25, 1872, pp. 637–8.

But there is no question of the magnitude of that interest which ensured that literally every one outside the ranks of agricultural labor had opinions of some sort on trans-Atlantic affairs. To judge by the press, from the penny weekly of the working man to the half-crown quarterly, the Civil War occupied a place which for a year and a half had not even temporary rivals.[4]

This peak period of eighteen months followed the crisis that arose from the high-handed seizure by Captain Wilkes (U.S.N.) of two Confederate envoys from the British ship *Trent* in November 1861, and the fact that it was the peak period of British concern goes to show that the primary impact of the war and its aftermath on Britain was the direct, diplomatic one. In other words, the effects of the Civil War and Reconstruction in Britain must be studied within the fundamental and indispensable framework of foreign policy, which is not our principal concern here and the history of which has in any case been very fully told and analyzed already.[5]

With the main outlines of this frequently recounted story we are already familiar. We know how, at first after the secession of the deep South, traditional British antislavery sentiment led to a vague but perceptible and widespread sympathy for the North, but how, after Sumter, Lincoln's emphasis on the preservation of the Union as the central cause of the war led to a growing feeling in Britain that the federal government could not and should not try to restore the Union by force of arms. We know, too, how in fact after its recognition of the belligerent status— but not the independence—of the Confederacy, the British government endeavored, sincerely if sometimes incompetently, to pursue a policy of strict neutrality, whatever the conflicting opinions of different statesmen and sections of public opinion in Britain. We also know how the two countries were brought to the very brink of war in the *Trent* case and to its threshold in

---

[4] Donaldson Jordan and Edwin J. Pratt: *Europe and the American Civil War* (Cambridge, Mass., 1931), p. 123. "Literally every one" is no doubt an overstatement.

[5] See especially E. D. Adams: *Great Britain and the American Civil War* (London, 1925), and H. C. Allen: *Great Britain and the United States: A History of Anglo-American Relations (1783–1952)* (London, 1954), Chap. xiii.

the case of the escape of the British-built Confederate commerce raider *Alabama* in July 1862 and the near escape, in analogous circumstances, of the Laird rams fifteen months later. We know how, after this, the danger of Anglo-American conflict waned, as the gradually increasing success of Northern arms convinced even those unsympathetic to the Union that the cause of the South was lost, and as the Emancipation Proclamation began to exercise its full sway over a British public opinion still deeply moved by the slavery question.

The tale of the acrimonious legacy left by the war has also been told, although it is less familiar. We are aware that when the fighting was over ill-feeling in the North toward Britain (and sentiment in the South was no more sympathetic) found diplomatic expression in the complex of grievances that centered on the claim for damages (both "direct" and "indirect") against the British government for the depredations of the *Alabama* on Union shipping. We are aware, finally, how all efforts to settle these questions, including the Johnson-Clarendon Convention of 1869 (which was summarily rejected by the Senate), came to nothing until the signature of the Treaty of Washington of 1871. This treaty, once the Geneva arbitration award, made under its terms, was accepted by Britain, laid the basis for twenty-five years of quiet in Anglo-American relations.

These events in foreign policy provided the practical and emotional precondition of all the other facets of the influence of the Civil War and Reconstruction on Britain, but obviously their impact was felt on a much wider front than the merely diplomatic.

In the first place, the passions produced by the struggle in American hearts and minds evoked consequential feelings in those of Britons. Charles Sumner, for instance, early became convinced (and the conviction was to carry over from war into peace) that the British government was fundamentally hostile to the Union cause; *The Economist* greeted his first great speech in 1863, which accused Britain of this animus, with the words, "When men in Mr. Sumner's position can write and speak as he has done, we may well begin to despond as to the possibility of maintaining either a good understanding or even mere peace between the countries."[6] Many elements in British public opinion

---

[6] Oct. 3, 1863, p. 1094.

took this American resentment, of which Sumner's passion was not unrepresentative, very hard, because a great majority of Britons really felt as Sir George Grey, then home secretary, expressed it on May 1, 1865:

> In the Civil War, the existence and long continuance of which we have so sincerely deplored, it is well known that the Government of this country, acting, as I believe, in accordance with the almost unanimous feeling of this country, has maintained a strict and impartial neutrality.

"But," he felt bound to continue, "it is notorious, and it could not in a great country like this be otherwise, that different opinions have been entertained by different persons with regard to the question at issue between the Northern and Southern States of America."[7] This division of opinion continued to exist up to and even beyond the *Alabama* arbitration. Sir Charles Dilke strongly believed, as he wrote in 1869, that "It would be to the eternal disgrace of civilization" if "we should set to work to cut our brothers' throats upon a point of etiquette," by refusing to go to arbitration on the claims, but he pointed out that

> All nations commit at times the error of acting as though they think that every people on earth except themselves are unanimous in their policy. Neglecting the race distinctions and the class distinctions which in England are added to the universal essential differences of minds, the Americans are convinced that, during the late war, we thought as one man, and that, in this present matter of the Alabama claims, we stand out and act as a united people.[8]

Bagehot in *The Economist* had, during the course of the war, pointed out the importance of distinguishing between "English[9] *opinion*" and "English *action* on American questions," for "The truth is that though singularly divided in our *sympathies* on this

---

[7] *Hansard's Parliamentary Debates, Third Series, commencing with the Accession of William IV* (hereafter *Hansard*), Vol. 178, p. 1242.

[8] Charles Wentworth Dilke: *Greater Britain: A Record of Travel in English-Speaking Countries during 1866 and 1867* (New York, 1869), p. 217.

[9] We may notice that contemporaries frequently used the word "English" to mean "British." This piece of strictly English arrogance is nowhere better illustrated than in Disraeli's frequent phrase the "Empire of England." I follow this rather loose contemporary practice.

matter, we are singularly united in our *intentions* and decision. We all of us know so distinctly what we shall *do,* that we feel no scruple in expressing with equal distinctness what we *think*."[1] And as he was to note seven years later, very little in the press of either Britain or America is lost upon the other, because there is no filter of language as in the case of France or Germany.[2] The directness of contact between the two public opinions, exemplified especially in the press, was to become much more pronounced and powerful during this period with the final coming into operation, on July 28, 1866 (after a number of abortive attempts stretching back over nine years), of the transatlantic telegraph cable, while the volume of Anglo-American mail almost doubled between 1863 and 1868. This immediacy of impact often added to the tensions and difficulties, but in the case of the assassination of Lincoln it had the opposite effect.

Over this first of four public murders of American Presidents in less than a century, there was a remarkable unity of British opinion and, seemingly, more than surface compassion. It was perhaps the earliest of those surges of British sympathy for an American tragedy that were occasionally to manifest themselves later. In 1966, only three years after another American assassination, we cannot write as Halvdan Koht did in 1949 about that of Lincoln: "At the present date it is difficult to conceive that a political murder could arouse such general commotion."[3]

Even *The Times,* whose officials had consistently blackguarded the members of the Lincoln administration and which had, on the occasion of the Emancipation Proclamation, "violently attacked Lincoln as 'a sort of moral American Pope,' "[4] had now changed its tune and declared that the news "will be received throughout Europe with sorrow as sincere and profound as it awoke even in the United States themselves."[5] *The Economist,* which had never in any case been quite so hostile to the North,

---

[1] *The Economist,* Oct. 31, 1863, p. 1209. Though unsigned, this article, like most others of this kind during these years, seems plainly to be from the masterly pen of Bagehot.

[2] Ibid., Dec. 10, 1870, p. 1482.

[3] Halvdan Koht: *The American Spirit in Europe* (Philadelphia, 1949), p. 144.

[4] *The History of The Times: The Tradition Established, 1841–1884* (London, 1939), p. 381.

[5] *The Times,* Apr. 27, 1865.

altered its coloring more deliberately. It had once, in a moment of vexation, castigated the President as one who "means well, but . . . does nothing else well"[6] (and in another, even rashly derided his "feeble and ungrammatical prolixity"),[7] but it had welcomed his re-election in 1864. This it did because, as it declared, "Mr Lincoln said, 'I wish to maintain the Union by destroying slavery': General McClellan said, 'I wish to maintain the Union by maintaining slavery.' " But it still declared, in the same article, that "Mr Lincoln has been honest, but he has been vulgar" and that he is "a person whose words are mean even when his actions are important."[8] After his death it had no reservations left:

> Mr. Lincoln, by a rare combination of qualities—patience, sagacity and honesty—by a still more rare sympathy, . . . and by a moderation rarest of all, had attained such vast moral authority that he could make all the hundred wheels of the Constitution move in one direction without exciting any physical force . . . That despotism . . . was exercized by a man whose brain was a very great one. We do not know in history [Bagehot justified his change of opinion] such an example of the growth of a ruler in wisdom as was exhibited by Mr. Lincoln. Power and responsibility visibly widened his mind and elevated his character.[9]

Most of those more in sympathy with the Northern cause had little to recant, though Lord John Russell, who had left an unhappy diplomatic legacy (for which he was in 1868 to make a handsome public apology[1]), said in the House of Lords on May 1, 1865, that

---

6 Apr. 25, 1863, p. 450.

7 Oct. 31, 1863, p. 1209.

8 Nov. 26, 1864, p. 1454.

9 *The Economist*, Apr. 29, 1865, p. 495.

1 "Well, I have my own faults to acknowledge in this respect, because I certainly thought, when the Slave States of America endeavored to establish their independence, and at the same time to continue and perpetuate the institution of slavery, that the Northern States ought at once to have proclaimed not only their own abhorrence, but the abolition and destruction, of slavery. Distance and want of knowledge of the circumstances of America made me fall into error in that respect. . . . I did not do justice to the efforts made by the United States; . . ." See report of a breakfast in honor of W. L. Garrison in W. P. and F. J. Garrison: *William Lloyd Garrison, 1805–79. The Story of His Life* (4 vols.; New York, 1885–9) Vol. 4, p. 210.

President Lincoln . . . displayed a character of so much integrity, so much sincerity and straightforwardness, and at the same time so much kindness, that if any one could have been able to alleviate the pain and animosities which prevailed during the period of civil war, I believe that President Lincoln was that person.[2]

In other tributes from those further to the left, one can even detect perhaps the first signs of that process of secular canonization which was soon to produce the Lincoln legend. As Professor Beesly of University College, London, a positivist and advocate of working-class rights, affirmed on April 28, 1865:

The one fact that the wise and good man who has so firmly, yet so temperately guided his country through her difficulties, was a working man raised by universal suffrage to the highest office in her State, will never be forgotten by the working men of England. It has come home to their hearts as no foreign event ever did before.[3]

It was, however, the Tory Disraeli, with that understanding of the human heart which made him a match even for the moral force of Gladstone, who perhaps best expressed the popular feeling:

There are rare instances when the sympathy of a nation approaches those tenderer feelings that generally speaking, are supposed to be peculiar to the individual, and to form the happy privilege of private life; and this is one. . . . [I]n the character of the victim, and even in the accessories of his last moments there is something so homely and so innocent that it takes as it were the subject out of all the pomp of history and the ceremonial of diplomacy; it touches the heart of nations, and appeals to the domestic sentiment of mankind. . . . Nor is it possible for the people of England, at such a moment, to forget that he sprang from the same fatherland, and spoke the same mother tongue.[4]

---

[2] *Hansard*, Vol. 178, p. 1220.

[3] *Beehive*, Apr. 29, 1865.

[4] Quoted in G. M. Trevelyan: *The Life of John Bright* (London, 1925), p. 326.

Few, if any, other events of the war and its diplomatic sequel had a direct impact on the individual feelings of Britons equal to that of Lincoln's death. And after the settlement of the *Alabama* claims, the influence of the United States upon Britain was not to be exercised in any great degree through diplomatic disputes, but through the broader and in general more beneficent channels of ideas, policies, and practices, in the manner depicted for a later period by R. H. Heindel.[5] And even in the years immediately after the Civil War the American impact was not confined to the war and its aftermath proper, for Reconstruction itself had a very considerable effect on British political and social ideas. But the skeletal structure of the relationship in these years from 1861 to 1877 is still provided by foreign policy.

Nor must the actual diplomatic achievement of avoiding war between the two countries be underestimated. The Geneva award was a great triumph, and well might Charles Francis Adams, Jr., say of his father:

> When he landed in New York on November 13, 1872, he had a right to exclaim, as he did, "Io Triumphe!" for every issue between Great Britain and the United States growing out of the great civil war either was definitely settled, or was in course of early settlement.[6]

This, perhaps the greatest of international arbitrations, decisively strengthened the Anglo-American arbitral tradition first tentatively established in the Jay Treaty of 1794; it was a fitting sequel to the emotion this wartime American minister had felt at the funeral, seven years before, of Richard Cobden, a foremost British apostle of the arbitration movement and a friend of the United States.

Bagehot in 1870 quoted an American, who replied to his protest that America had not equally resented the wartime conduct of France, as saying, "The fact is, that in America we think only of England, and only care for England"; on this Bagehot himself commented, "We are like two brothers, intimate in infancy but separated in life, who cannot help thinking of one another,

---

5 *The American Impact on Great Britain, 1898–1914* (London, 1940).
6 Charles Francis Adams, [Jr.]: *Charles Francis Adams* (Boston and New York, 1900), pp. 399–400.

but yet can hardly with the utmost difficulty understand one an-other."[7] The Treaty of Washington of the following year was, indeed, a vital turning point in the history of Anglo-American relations. It was not merely that, as Gladstone—himself far from blameless in the matter—was to express the hope in 1878, the "political controversies . . . are happily, as I trust, at an end,"[8] but that a fresh spirit was in the making in Britain. It was fully expressed by the Duke of Argyll, secretary of state for India from 1868 to 1874, one of the North's most ardent supporters in the war, at a public breakfast held in honor of William Lloyd Garrison in 1868:

> This country desires to maintain with the American people not merely relations of amity and peace; it desires to have their friendship and affection. (Cheers.) It is not merely that that country has sprung from us in former times. It is that it is still to a great extent springing from England. (Hear, hear.) . . . I think we ought to feel, every one of us, that in going to America we are going only to a second home. (Cheers.) Such are the relations which I trust we shall see established between the two countries. (Hear, hear.) Surely it is time to forget ancient differences (loud cheers) . . . I maintain that . . . there is no one in this room—who is not almost as proud of Washington as he is of Wellington—(cheers)—the memory of both belonging indeed to the common heritage of our race.[9]

The analysis in depth of international influences is in itself a formidable task, for international relations are of immense complexity and operate at many levels and in many ways. The extent to which the investigatory techniques of modern social science (even where they do not confuse rather than clarify through the huge mass of data that they present) can be applied by a single student to events a century ago is strictly limited, and he who generalizes on the vastly complex impact of one nation upon an-

---

[7] *The Economist*, Dec. 10, 1870, p. 1482.

[8] W. E. Gladstone: "Kin Beyond Sea," *North American Review*, CXXVII. (Sept.–Oct. 1878), p. 179.

[9] *Proceedings at the Public Breakfast Held in Honour of William Lloyd Garrison* (London, 1868), pp. 28–9.

other takes his scholarly life in his hands. But in this case there is an added difficulty, for how are we to distinguish (or even to define the terms in which we do so) the impact of the American Civil War and Reconstruction upon life and liberalism in Britain from the influence that the United States had exercised upon the United Kingdom before 1861 and was to continue to exert in even greater measure after 1877?

Thus the mere existence of a study such as G. D. Lillibridge's *Beacon of Freedom: The Impact of American Democracy upon Great Britain, 1830–70*[1] clearly indicates that British liberalism was already subject to American influence long before the war. Richard Cobden, to take one example, had declared in his *England, Ireland and America,* published in 1835, "We believe the government of the United States to be at this moment the best in the world; but then the Americans are the best people,"[2] and more than fifty years later James Bryce could write ". . . altho' the U.S. is very far from being ideal, still its *social* and moral state— apart from politics— is an advance . . . on anything yet attained elsewhere."[3] Although British liberal and radical opinion tended to be favorable to the American "experiment" through most of the nineteenth century, there were also persistent strains of criticism. In either case, to disentangle the specific effects of the war from this general and continuing influence is an exceedingly delicate task.

The same is true of more specific cases, such as that of the Irish in America: here, too, (as frequently on other issues) the war exacerbated but did not fundamentally alter the situation. All Ireland was still a part of the United Kingdom, and the Fenian movement in the United States was able to use Northern mistrust of Britain to good effect in this period, when a number of raids upon Canada from Union territory were carried out by what were in effect Irish guerrillas. As Dilke succinctly expressed it in 1869:

> The Fenians would be as absolutely without strength in America as they are without credit, were it not for the anti-

---

[1] (Philadelphia, 1955).

[2] Quoted in Frank Thistlethwaite: *The Anglo-American Connection in the Early Nineteenth Century* (Philadelphia, 1959), p. 43.

[3] Quoted in Henry Pelling: *America and the British Left from Bright to Bevan* (London, 1956), p. 54.

British traditions of the Democratic party, and the rankling of the Alabama question, or, rather, of the remembrance of our general conduct during the rebellion, in the hearts of the republicans.[4]

The impact of the Fenian activities on Anglo-American relations would have been far worse but for the basically strict and sober propriety, in actual practice, of the federal government's actions. And ultimately American Fenianism was to have considerable effects on English policy toward Ireland. The *Saturday Review* wrote in 1868, "In their encouragement of the Fenian Conspiracy, and in habitual professions of enmity to England, both parties are equally culpable, and both are equally entitled to the apology that they are probably insane."[5] *The Economist*'s prophecy of 1868, however, was in the long run to be to a considerable extent fulfilled:

> . . . the *natural* sympathies of the popular party in America must go with the popular party in England, which is almost certain to triumph in the approaching elections . . . In making "justice to Ireland" the great issue . . . , he [Mr. Gladstone] will do an immense amount to paralyse the Fenian influence in the United States, and to retain all the wise and instructed public opinion in America in favour of any Government which turns a deaf ear to their mad and impotent schemes for wresting Ireland from British hands.[6]

Here the war years seem to have reinforced and accelerated a pre-existing trend.

On the other hand, even where the immediate impact of the war in a particular sphere was fairly unmistakable, the long-term results were not necessarily quite so clear. Thus the initial effect of hostilities on emigration to the United States from Great Britain (excluding Ireland) was that, according to the United States immigration figures, uncertain and ambiguous as they are, it dropped from 29,737 in 1860 to 19,675 in 1861, and then rose to 24,639 in 1862. In 1863, however, it leaped up to 66,882, even higher than the peak-year figure for the immediate prewar period

---

[4] *Greater Britain*, p. 216.
[5] July 11, 1868, p. 41.
[6] Sept. 12, p. 1046.

—58,479 in 1857. In 1864 it dropped a little once more, to 53,428, but in 1865 and 1866 rose to 82,465 and 94,924 respectively. It declined again in 1867 to 52,641, and in the American depression year, 1868, sank to the very low total of 24,127, but with economic recovery it rose to a plateau of over 80,000 a year for the five years beginning in 1869, with a peak of 103,677 in 1870. Then, as the long and grueling depression of 1873 set in, it decreased year by year to a new low of 22,150 in 1878. Then an upward climb in the figures set in once more, although the proportion of American immigration constituted by the British was never again to be so high; indeed, it was never as high after the war as it had been before it began.[7] There seems to be no reason for assuming that this relative ultimate decline was in any significant sense a result of the war and of Reconstruction, but it is apparent that the war, with the uncertainties and fears it aroused, at first checked but then soon stimulated British emigration by its insatiable demand for men. This effect spilled over into the two years of immediate postwar boom, but after that recession checked and then depression seriously reduced the flow. During the war some Britons had welcomed emigration as a means of diminishing the numbers dependent on relief, but others —and they increased in number and strength with the coming of peace—deplored the loss of skilled labor to America, suggesting that the United States during Reconstruction did not present a very attractive picture to the would-be immigrant. But, from the early 1870's, the specific effects of the war and its aftermath must have waned rapidly, and a long-term trend toward a reduction in the British content of American immigration seems to have asserted itself.

However, the immediate impact of the war on a continuing trend could be slight, whereas its ultimate effect could be considerable. Thus the Northern system of free public schools, essentially based on "the Massachusetts plan," had long been the model much of British radical opinion had wished to follow in educational reform. In 1850 Cobden, although his view had not always been so favorable, had written, "I call for the American

---

[7] *Historical Statistics of the United States: Colonial Times to 1957* (Washington, D.C.: U.S. Bureau of the Census; 1960), p. 57.

system; I am for the American system precisely as it stands."[8] Forster's Education Act of 1870 in fact diverged from the American theory—which separated church and state—by allowing the teaching of the Bible on a nondenominational basis, but although the Act probably did not borrow consciously from the example of the United States, "Within limits . . . , with its elected school boards, its finance from the local rates and its compulsory powers," it "bears a great resemblance to the Massachusetts System."[9] In 1870 one sympathetic British visitor could write:

> Nothing in America excited my admiration more than the system of common schools . . . It is a magnificent development of the old Scottish system of parochial schools and endowed colleges.[1]

That the Act was passed in 1870, five years after the war, owed something to the fact that ultimately the North's victory greatly strengthened the prestige of the American example, in education as in other spheres, such as the widening of the franchise in 1867, which will be described below. The Act was the first comprehensive legislative enactment that pointed toward compulsory universal education in Britain.

The ultimate effects of the war probably had a considerable impact on feminism also, to take another reform movement, but it was much more indirect and remote. Before 1861 the United States had been the heart of the movement for women's rights, and the American example long continued to be a vital influence on British feminism. Although the organized movement for women's rights in the United States was seriously weakened by the Civil War and Reconstruction and failed effectively to use the radical demand for the Negro vote as a lever for getting votes for women, the war taught professional women in America to organize and to work out of the home; the huge growth of women's clubs after 1865 owed much to the training of tens of thousands of them in Sanitary Commission work during the war. The founding of the National Woman Suffrage Association and

---

[8] Quoted in Lillibridge: *Beacon of Freedom*, p. 101.

[9] Thistlethwaite: *The Anglo-American Connection*, p. 146.

[1] The Reverend David Macrae: *The Americans at Home* (first publ. 1870; Glasgow, 1908), II, 358.

the American Woman Suffrage Association and the enfranchisement of women in Wyoming, all occurring in 1869, gave a great
fillip to the few British feminists, helping to keep the movement
alive in the United Kingdom until, nearly half a century later,
the circumstances for reform became more auspicious, largely as
a result of developments similar to those in the American Civil
War appearing in Britain during World War I.[2]

In sharp contrast to these mild and distant effects by way
of emulation, the war and Reconstruction had marked results of
a wholly different kind in Britain, for it brought out much that
was bad as well as much that was good in American life. There
had always been conservative British criticisms of the extent of
corruption in American politics (though the charges were re-
butted with equal vigor from the Left, and countercharges made
of undoubted corruption, though of a somewhat different kind,
in England). Thus the *Spectator* wrote in 1867, under the title
"The Anglo-Saxon Canker-Worm":

> Every race has its own special political vice, and ours is a
> peculiarly dirty one . . . In America, as in England, honest
> politicians are at this moment confessing to each other that
> the one dangerous canker in the body politic is pecuniary
> corruption, and are looking round almost in despair for an
> effective remedy.[3]

But there is no doubt that American political and financial corruption increased sharply in the postwar era. How much of this
growth can be ascribed to the war cannot be accurately assessed,
but it would not be surprising if it was in considerable degree due,
after this as after other wars of history, to an outburst of materialism and hedonism, thoroughly understandable when following upon years of blood, toil, tears, and sweat. Nor can it be
doubted that, however noble its motives partly were, radical Reconstruction provided an unhappy stimulus to corrupt practices.
This produced a revulsion in Britain that grew stronger as time
passed. It was not sufficient to check the democratic tendency
there, but in the end it was to make even radical British opinion
increasingly skeptical of the American type of democracy and in-

---

[2] For this information I am indebted to my colleague Andrew Sinclair.
[3] *Spectator*, Apr. 27, 1867, p. 465.

creasingly susceptible to the arguments of socialism and Marxism.

Thus in the House of Commons in 1866 Mr. W. H. Gregory, Liberal, from Galway, said that

> if there were one thing more notorious than another it was the prevalence of corruption at the American elections. In England the corruption was only retail—in America it was wholesale as well as retail; and the worst of the corruption there was, that it extended from the constituency to the representative.[4]

Parliamentary reform passed through Parliament nonetheless, after many vicissitudes, in 1867, but five years later, at the beginning of the presidential election campaign of that year in which the corruption of General Grant's administration was the central issue, *The Economist* wrote:

> That two or three swindlers should be able to get into their hands an immense undertaking like the Erie railway, . . . and . . . that they should be unchecked by any controlling power, . . . is a peril which the framers of the American Constitution never dreamed of, but which we may be certain, if they had been able to foresee it, Jefferson and Hamilton would have agreed to guard against.[5]

The *Spectator* put it this way: "Where is the proof . . . in all that has occurred that New York institutions, which are in theory perfect examples of the democratic ideal, may not at any moment be manipulated for the purposes of plunder?"[6]

This wave of corruption added force to the customary European criticism of the American pursuit of the Almighty Dollar; as the *Saturday Review* declared: "No nation is more liberal of money, but the absence of other social distinctions gives extraordinary importance to wealth."[7] The *Spectator* saw it thus:

> On the other side of the Atlantic the evil has reached further, as was natural, wealth there gratifying two pas-

---

4 *Hansard*, Vol. 182, p. 1792.
5 *The Economist*, Jan. 13, 1872, p. 35.
6 *Spectator*, Mar. 30, 1872, p. 397.
7 *Saturday Review*, Aug. 5, 1865, p. 163.

sions instead of one, the passion for distinction, as well as the passion for luxury and ease. Bribery there, avoiding the polling booths, has invaded the Legislatures, and from Congress downward is in all declared to be the master evil which threatens the country, and must be extirpated.[8]

As the historian of America and the British left was to write of the late 1870's: "It was not easy for the Radicals to maintain, after a decade of startling news about the corruption of American politics, that all was well in the Republic they still so much admired."[9] By 1880 H. M. Hyndman, one of the pioneers of British socialism, could write in an article on "The Chicago Riots and the Class War in the United States":

> The corruption of the state legislatures and the munici-
> palities, the hopelessness of getting any matters attended
> to which affect the welfare of great masses of men, but
> which conflict with the interests of the great monopolies,
> are steadily driving the intelligent workers to the convic-
> tion that, if the present attitude is maintained, an appeal
> to downright force is the only solution of the question.[1]

The American example, among other things, helped to increase the existing British mistrust of corruption and apprehension of anything resembling the spoils system; these fears took practical form in such measures as the Corrupt Practices Act of 1883 and continued improvements in the selection and working of the Civil Service.

All these cases illustrate the fact that the Union victory ensured the continuation, and in the end the increase, of the power of the United States to influence other nations, including Britain. In some respects it also altered the character of that influence. Thus there had long been a trend in international affairs toward the ultimate commercial, industrial, and financial supremacy of the United States, but there is no doubt that in economic matters

---

[8] *Spectator*, Apr. 27, 1867, p. 465.
[9] Pelling: *America and the British Left*, p. 48.
[1] Quoted in ibid., p. 62.

the Civil War had great and varying effects upon the character and intensity of America's influence on Britain.

Cotton, for approximately half a century the essential core of the Anglo-American economic relationship, is in many respects the key, and it nicely illustrates many aspects of the question. Some estimates of the proportion of the English population that lived directly or indirectly off the cotton industry in 1861 have been as high as the extraordinary figure of 20 per cent, and the South provided about four fifths of the raw material. The Confederacy proved mistaken in its belief that "King Cotton" would force the British government to intervene in the war, but its initial embargo on the export of cotton and, later, the increasing efficacy of the Northern blockade produced a cotton famine that had an exceedingly heavy direct impact upon British life, especially in Lancashire, where the cotton industry was centered. In that area, nearly half a million persons accepted relief in December 1862,[2] the peak period, which was some ten times as many as in normal circumstances, while *The Economist* had estimated in July that there were over 35,000 paupers as a result of the cotton shortage—more than a third of those who were employed directly in the cotton trade. The impact was not worse only because it was cushioned by the abundant stocks on hand in Britain as a result of the bumper harvest of 1860, by the million and a half bales that got through the blockade (three quarters of a normal year's supply), and by the new sources of supply that were rapidly developed in India, Egypt, and elsewhere.

The British economy as a whole did not suffer greatly, because there was a compensating war boom in some other industries, such as wool, linen, iron, shipbuilding, and munitions, while an early increase in the exports of American wheat to Britain at first helped the United States to buy these British exports. Thus the very severe impact of the war was chiefly confined to Lancashire, but here the situation was slow to return to normal. The American cotton crop in 1859–60 had been 4,669,770 bales, and it was not until 1875–6 that this was almost equaled once more—with a crop of 4,669,288 bales—and not until 1877–8 that it was actually surpassed, with 4,759,000. Exports to Britain

---

[2] John Watts: *The Facts of the Cotton Famine* (London, 1866), p. 129.

were to pick up in due course, for, as *The Economist* had pointed out in 1864, only North America produces good *"moderately-stapled cotton,"* so that "the importance to Lancashire of *American* cotton has diminished in a far less degree"[3] than many Englishmen believe. But despite this process of revival (which in any case was a slow one), the British textile industry never again became so uniquely dependent upon American cotton exports as it had been before the war. Certainly this trend might have developed in any case, but there can be no doubt that the war and its aftermath hastened the process by which Britain found other sources of supply to augment the American.

Another aspect of the war's economic influence on Britain was the financial, and here too there was a powerful immediate impact, but a far more pronounced long-term effect. There had long been a strong British tradition of investment in America (it was, of course, older than the Republic itself), so that it has been estimated that there was between £50,000,000 and £60,000,000 of British investment in the United States in 1854.[4] The Civil War naturally administered a sharp check to this flow of capital. Added to the general concern for the solvency of the Union government if the North should fail to win, there was a real fear, which persisted long after the war, that the debts of the federal government might be repaid in debased paper currency. Under the influence of the so-called Ohio idea, the Democratic platform of 1868 advocated payment of the debts of the United States in U.S. government bonds except where payment in coin was expressly stipulated; thus "public dishonour," Bagehot pronounced in 1868, is "the corner-stone of the new policy."[5] Similarly, John Stuart Mill wrote to the New York *Nation* in the same year to protest against a Democratic proposal to pay off the federal debt in greenbacks.

An immediate practical effect of the war and the consequent disruption of trade was the transfer of much American gold to Europe, and this, especially in Britain, "became the basis for considerable monetary expansion supporting a new wave of

---

[3] *The Economist*, May 7, 1864, pp. 574, 575.
[4] L. H. Jenks: *The Migration of British Capital to 1875* (New York and London, 1927), p. 413.
[5] *The Economist*, July 11, 1868, p. 786.

speculation."[6] The failure on May 10, 1866, of Overend, Gurney and Company, an old and respected discounting and bill-broking house that had transformed itself into a finance company after the French fashion and then become overstretched by speculation, led to the collapse of the boom and a hysterical run on the banks the next day, one of a number of days in history known as "Black Friday." It would be going much too far to ascribe this boom and slump wholly or even preponderantly to the Civil War, for the speculative fever was nearly as chronic in Britain as in America and it conformed closely to the almost regular cycle of financial crises in the mid-nineteenth century (1825, 1837, 1847, 1857). But it may perhaps have been exacerbated by the monetary consequences of the struggle. We may note in passing that it had little backlash in the United States, which remained in a phase of postwar prosperity from 1865 to 1868, when there was a minor recession: it was not until 1873 that America felt the full blast of what perhaps may, even then, be regarded as a postwar depression.

However, despite all these setbacks and such shocks to investors' confidence as the American "Black Friday" gold corner attempt of 1869 and the revelations of the Tweed Ring's corruption in New York City in 1871 (as well as the Erie Railroad and the Whisky Ring scandals), there was a remarkable resurgence of British investment in the United States in the postwar era. Between 1870 and 1880 the total market value of British investment in American government bonds was approximately £160,000,000 and in American railroad securities some £40,000,000. But in the end, by the beginning of the twentieth century, there was to be a relative decline in British investment in the United States, largely as a result of the increasing availability of American funds, which was in no small measure due to the development of a domestic American money market (although as late as 1899 there was still more than £550,000,000 of British investment in the United States). This development partly resulted from the stimulus of the federal government's need for funds in the Civil War, but once again other factors were at work to pro-

---

[6] Judd Polk: *Sterling, Its Meaning in World Finance* (New York, 1956), p. 37.

duce this contraction of British investment in America, such as the increasing attractions of the Empire as an outlet for British capital, as well as the natural processes of United States financial development, which were already far advanced in this era of the American economic "take-off." However, there can be little doubt that the war accelerated the process.

Certainly the impact on Britain of the American currency question, as such, which first arose in its modern form out of the Civil War, was very important. As one British observer, Sir George Campbell (then a member of the Council of India), wrote in 1879: "The Currency question is so burning and important in the United States, and of so much interest on this side of the Atlantic."[7] Britain, after going off gold in the French wars, had returned to the gold standard in 1821, and had, despite difficulties for a number of years, become increasingly wedded to it as the century advanced. This marriage had particular convenience for a free-trade country with an unprecedented spread of commerce throughout the world and a consequent need for international monetary stability. Accordingly, by the outbreak of the Civil War the marriage had become a veritable love match, and by 1878 the English feeling for gold had approached idolatry, so that Gladstone could even write of the American "proposal to tamper with the true monetary creed, which the Tempter lately presented to the nation in the Silver Bill."[8]

The Americans, by contrast, had been in some senses the governmental inventors of paper currency, the use of which had deep roots in the Colonial period. What is more, until 1873 the United States was technically on a bimetallic standard— silver as well as gold. In that year "the Crime of '73" demonetized silver and thus prepared the way for the growth of the whole violent bimetallism controversy as silver depreciated in value in terms of gold. In 1869 the government had pledged itself ultimately to pay its obligations in coin, and by 1875, after a number of vicissitudes, especially as a result of the depression of 1873, the resumption of specie payments (that is to say, now, gold payments) was finally enacted. (And if the British thought

---

[7] Sir George Campbell, M.P.: *White and Black: The Outcome of a Visit to the United States* (London, 1879), p. 89.
[8] "Kin Beyond Sea," pp. 211–12.

that only the Devil could tempt a nation away from the gold standard, Anglophobic bimetallists were later to reciprocate by regarding the American return to gold as the result of a deep-laid British conspiracy.) The contrast may perhaps be seen as that between the needs of a nation that was the world's greatest creditor and those of one that was still a debtor, though an increasingly mature one; between an industrialized and a still industrializing country; and between a people dependent to an almost unprecedented degree on foreign trade and one of increasing, and ultimately remarkable, economic self-sufficiency. The need to finance the Civil War had resulted in the drastic step of the issue of $450,000,000 of inconvertible paper money, the greenbacks, which had helped to produce a severe inflation, though not a runaway one as in the Revolutionary period. Despite the fact that they had followed the same course half a century earlier, the British were critical of the greenbacks even during the war, and when peace came they indignantly mounted their hobby-horse against this monetary inflation, long before the end of six years, the period it had taken the British government to return to gold after 1815.

Thus on December 14, 1867, *The Economist* pontifically, if ironically, declared:

> The Secretary of the Treasury, Mr McCulloch . . . holds "sound" views upon currency questions, . . . that a Government can no more create money by its bare fiat, than it can create coals. . . . A very large section of the House of Representatives thinks otherwise, . . . that when Governments order coal sacks to be called sacks of coal, it creates coals.[9]

The shock to British susceptibilities was most severe at the time noted above, when it was proposed to keep the greenbacks as legal tender for the payment of debts but not to make them convertible into gold. The *Saturday Review* wrote of this "Ohio idea":

> . . . the payment of the principal in greenbacks, or renewed promises to pay, would be a direct violation of the understanding on which the loans were contracted . . . The Democratic repudiators and their Republican accomplices have

---

[9] *The Economist,* Dec. 14, 1867, p. 1407.

no desire to be honest, and they are indifferent to any theories which might supply a plausible excuse for their policy.

It continued, in its customary High-Tory vein:

The American people have been for many generations sedulously taught by their political instructors that their own will is the paramount rule of right, and their own interest a sufficient apology for the exercise of irresponsible power. The characteristic lawlessness of all American declarations on foreign politics is explained by the belief in popular sovereignty which dictates the proposed repudiation of the debt.[1]

But even to those at the other end of the political spectrum, the proposal was equally unwelcome; the *Spectator* wrote on the same day:

Something like a fifth of the American Debt is believed to be held in Europe, the second greatest party in the Union resolves in solemn conclave that it will, if it can, plunder the holders of that debt ... But the attempt to pay in paper instead of gold is neither more nor less than confiscation ... They, in fact, reduce their debts one-third by a sheer act of force. Indeed we are not sure that the limit is one-third. It is part of their plan to pay off the debt in currency, and the enormous consequent increase in the circulation of paper will probably make the ultimate loss to the holders fifty or sixty per cent.[2]

The Ohio idea and its later successor, the bimetallism doctrine, served to air new monetary ideas that were to come into their own under various guises in our day, even though at the time the greenback movement had only a limited success and bimetallism was to fail altogether. The *Spectator* in 1876 welcomed the success of the Americans in progressively reducing their national debt, as the announcement of the return to specie payments had been widely welcomed in the previous year, in commenting on a recent funding operation:

---

[1] *Saturday Review*, July 11, 1868, p. 40.
[2] Pp. 813–14.

How Mr. Gladstone must yearn for the management of American finance! . . . If the operation succeeds, as seems probable, it will follow that the Americans . . . have reduced the burden of their Debt one-third since the war . . .

The Americans . . . were not going to submit . . . to such a permanent imposition upon their national energies. The reduction of the Debt became one of the principal and most popular elements of the Republican policy . . . the Washington Treasury has unflinchingly and doggedly quarried away, and with the most notable results . . . This is a magnificent result of persistence in a fixed purpose . . .[3]

The Greenback party had polled a million votes in the congressional elections of 1878. Largely as a result of this showing, when in the next year the greenbacks became convertible into gold, no more of them were retired from circulation, so that over $300,000,000 of paper money remained a permanent part of the national currency. This constituted a by no means inconsiderable success. In fact the greenbacks had pretty steadily risen in value since the war (as had Bank of England notes in the analogous circumstances of 1815–21), so that Bagehot observed in December 1871, "It will be very singular if the United States, by its natural power of expansion, should bring about the restoration of its paper to a condition in which it would be easier to make it convertible." This did indeed tend to happen, and the greenbacks might even have come to equal gold in value without any need for the formal step of making them convertible; in this event the experiment might have had more effect than it did upon the development of paper currency in the next century, for it is uncertain how much direct influence it—or, in a way, bimetallism— had upon the financial policies of, for example, the New Deal. Britain was able in the event gradually to lose her sense of uneasiness at America's paper-money proclivities, although even as late as the Presidential election of 1876 *The Economist* could write that "This question of the currency, indeed, is the only issue involved in the present contest that has any immediate interest for Englishmen."[4]

---

[3] *Spectator*, Sept. 2, 1876, pp. 1086, 1093.
[4] *The Economist*, Dec. 16, 1871, p. 1525; Jan. 10, 1876, p. 681.

In fact, the long-term economic influence of America on Britain was to lie in the economic growth associated with the industrialization of the United States. Between 1870 and 1885 the industrial leadership of mankind passed to the United States. In 1870, it has been claimed, the United Kingdom led the nations with 31.8 per cent of the world's manufacturing production as compared with 23.3 per cent for the United States: in the period 1881–5 the U.S. had 28.6 per cent and the U.K. 26.6 per cent.[5] This world-wide ascendancy America was to maintain until the present day. But, once again, for those with eyes to see, the extreme likelihood of this development had been apparent well before the war.

Thus the impact of American economic growth upon British life was clearly foreseen by Cobden as early as 1835, when he pointed out that it was not the fashionable Russian bogey that his countrymen should fear:

> . . . it is to the industry, the economy and peaceful policy of America and not to the growth of Russia that our statesmen . . . ought to direct their anxious study; for it is by these, and not by the efforts of barbarian force, that the power and greatness of England are in danger of being superseded; yes, by the successful rivalry of America, shall we, in all probability, be placed second in the rank of nations. The New World is destined to become the arbiter of the commercial policy in the old.[6]

In 1878 Gladstone was to write in very similar terms of

> the menace which . . . America offers to the commercial preëminence of England . . . On this subject I will only say that it is she alone who, at a coming time, can and probably will wrest from us our commercial supremacy . . . We have no more title against her than Venice or Genoa or Holland has had against us.[7]

Here once more the problem arises as to how much this process was accelerated by the Civil War and its aftermath. Sir George

---

[5] Brinley Thomas: *Migration and Economic Growth: A Study of Great Britain and the Atlantic Economy* (Cambridge, 1954), p. 120.
[6] Quoted in Thistlethwaite: *The Anglo-American Connection*, p. 168.
[7] "Kin Beyond Sea," p. 180.

Campbell, however, put the matter in its proper perspective, war or no war, in this same year, when he wrote of Britain:

> I won't say that this country has culminated and begun to go down—we have not, I hope, come to that—but there is no doubt that, with very limited land and immense foreign competition in manufactures, we can hardly hope to hold a place *relatively* so far in advance of the world as we have in past generations. We shall, I hope, still progress in many ways, but it is almost in the nature of things that America must progress faster.[8]

Yet not all men, even the highly intelligent who were well versed in economics and politics, used their eyes to see. Bagehot himself, in *The Economist,* failed to draw the proper conclusion from his observations: he saw the wealth of the United States, but not the power and effectiveness of its economic competition. He did grasp, as early as 1865, the actual and potential scale of American wealth:

> The truth is, we have absolutely *no idea* in England of the wealth of a population whose average means are probably over £100 a year for every family in the land. With a very wealthy upper class and a very comfortable middle class, we are yet quite unable to realise the condition of a people, the great masses of whose labourers are all as comfortable as our best paid operatives in Manchester.[9]

However, even though he saw one of the vital reasons for the growth of this wealth in industry, he did not understand the overwhelming competitive advantage it was to confer on the United States; he correctly wrote, twelve years later in 1877, "Americans . . . excelled by the rapidity which they showed in inventing and adopting labour-saving machinery," but he was not so correct in writing "American competition with British industries is a subject about which there exists a good deal of baseless apprehension." A year earlier he had expressed himself even more strongly:

---

[8] *White and Black,* p. 106. This view was confirmed, to cite another instance, by Sir Samuel Morton Peto, a well-known building and railway contractor (and subsequently bankrupt!) who was a Liberal M.P., in his book *Resources and Prospects of America* (London and New York, 1866).

[9] *The Economist,* Nov. 18, 1865, p. 1399.

As yet the Americans have never been able to stand up before us in the open field of competition, and the conclusion that they will be able to do so, because under Protection they have improved production and got the command of their own markets, is a wholly illegitimate inference.[1]

Here, however, Bagehot reveals the *idée fixe* that distorted his judgment. *The Economist* had been founded by James Wilson (financial secretary to treasury from 1853 to 1859) as a free-trade journal during the Corn Laws agitation, and its editor, Bagehot, was committed, emotionally as well as intellectually (he married Wilson's daughter), to the pure doctrine of free trade. Throughout these years he not only denounces the aberration of American protectionism, but he also constantly predicts an American return to free trade; from the real fact that protection was enacted at the expense of the American farmer (before long to be relatively a waning force in American life), he drew the false conclusion that the farmer would still be strong enough politically to overthrow it. Indeed, he was so passionately devoted to the undiluted free-trade spirit of the classical economists that when, at the height of the cotton famine in the war, he noted that raw cotton was actually being *exported* from Liverpool, he quite clearly felt that nothing could be done about it by the government. Only toward the end of his life did he begin to doubt the imminence of an American abandonment of protection; the return of the United States to free trade, he wrote in 1873, "will be, it is feared, the labour of years."[2]

In this addiction to free trade he was, of course, far from alone. For example, Viscount Cranbourne [*sic*], the future Lord Salisbury, declared that "in Australia, the United States, Canada, and France . . . you have a much wider suffrage than you have here, in each free trade doctrines are scorned"[3]—thus closely associating these two, to him, evil forces. Others were even more passionate, such as Barham Zincke, a chaplain to Queen Victoria but a radical in politics, who wrote in 1868, after a visit to the United States, of "the degree to which they are crippled and im-

---

[1] Ibid., Feb. 3, 1877, p. 124; Sept. 16, 1876, p. 1083.
[2] *The Economist*, May 24, 1873, p. 620.
[3] *Hansard*, Mar. 12, 1866, Vol. 182, pp. 231–2.

poverished by the pestilent heresy of protection."[4] Robert Somers, economic journalist and editor of the Glasgow *North British Daily Mail,* in similar circumstances, launched a violent diatribe against protection, which included the arguments that sugar production in Louisiana was protected and that it was the only thing in the South that had not progressed since the war, and also that, as a result of protection, the quality of American manufactures was very poor.[5] Gladstone, now the accepted high priest of free trade, was being studiously moderate when he wrote in 1878 of "the leanings of America to protectionism, and the more daring reliance of the old country upon free and unrestricted intercourse with all the world."[6] Even Disraeli, who had risen to the leadership of the Conservative party in the House of Commons by his bitter attacks upon Peel for his repeal of the Corn Laws, had now fully accepted free trade. There was to be no significant revival of protectionist sentiment in Britain for many years. Powerful as its impact on them was ultimately to be, almost all Britons were slow to realize the drastic and fundamental change which was to overcome the structure of the Atlantic economy in the last years of the nineteenth century, and which was heralded by the growth of American protectionism.

Certainly this change would have come in any case, but there can be no doubt that the raising of the American tariff in 1861 was made possible by Secession and the consequent departure from Congress of the Southern senators, who were the chief opponents of protection. The dubious constitutionality of direct-taxation methods, suitable for raising the revenue that would be needed if hostilities began, added strength to the arm of those who wanted protection in any case and thus led to the Morrill tariff of 1861. The level of these import duties continued to rise throughout the war and had drastic effects on Britain, as, for example, in Lancashire. By the time peace came the industrial interests who favored protection had the bit between their teeth, and could in any event argue that the revenue was still needed

---

[4] F. Barham Zincke: *Last Winter in the United States* (London, 1868), p. 101.

[5] Robert Somers: *The Southern States Since the War, 1870–1* (London, 1871), pp. 204–13.

[6] "Kin Beyond Sea," p. 179.

to pay off the nation's huge debt. The *Saturday Review* was to write in 1867:

> American astuteness has always known how to profit by patriotic excitement. Before a dollar had been spent in the war, Mr. Morrill took the opportunity of the withdrawal of the Southern members to carry a protective tariff through Congress; and at every stage of the subsequent contest manufacturers and dealers have used the public necessities as an opportunity for placing additional restrictions on the liberty of consumers.[7]

By 1879 Sir George Campbell could write, "Free trade is no longer a question between North and South—in fact, if the truth must be told, it is not now a question in the United States at all."[8] But the adverse effects that the high tariff was to have on Britain's economic future can plainly be in large part ascribed to the war.

Not all the economic effects of the war, however, were so unfavorable to Britain as this. One case in point was closely associated with the tariff question—the relative decline of American shipping. The ascendancy of the United States merchant marine, which reached its apogee in the clipper ship before the Civil War, was not to be restored until very recent times. Doubtless even a clipper (which might on occasion cover as much as four hundred miles in twenty-four hours) would never have been a match for the steam vessels that had begun to make their appearance by the 1840's, and even for the iron sailing ships of the 1860's and 1870's, so that this phase of Atlantic commerce was doomed in any case. But certainly, too, the war gave American shipping a *coup de grâce*, if only because of the war losses and the utilization for naval vessels of such shipbuilding resources as were in production. The decline was hastened by the high level of taxation on shipbuilding under the tariff and by the passing, largely coincidental, of the wooden ship, for the building of which the United States had such great natural assets. In the construction of iron vessels propelled by steam, on the other hand, Britain was still to have for many years very substantial com-

---

[7] *Saturday Review*, June 8, 1867, p. 713.
[8] *White and Black*, p. 192.

petitive advantages. In this development the war played no small part.

How much the growth of American economic strength—which was to have deep, lasting effects upon British life (and also upon British liberalism, which was, partly as a result of it, ultimately to lose faith in its cherished doctrine of free trade)—was accelerated by the Civil War is a question too broad for real analysis here. The long-held traditional view was, of course, that the war greatly stimulated American industrialization, but Thomas C. Cochran, in leading a revisionist trend in interpretation, has recently gone so far as to suggest that the war may actually have retarded industrial growth. One may suspect that, like many historiographical revisions, this goes a good deal too far, but the war clearly cannot again be given the overwhelmingly prominent role in this process that it once had. But at the very least it may be claimed with assurance that, in the event, the victory of the North in the Civil War had here—as in other spheres—a decisively negative effect. The establishment of Confederate independence might well have been followed by a neocolonial relationship between the raw-material producing South and industrial Britain: the preservation of the economic as well as political integrity of the Union unquestionably made possible in the end the unique world ascendancy of the United States.

This same difficulty, however, of disentangling the effects of the war and Reconstruction from those that resulted from independent long-term trends exists, perhaps in equal measure, when we turn from the economic to the political aspects of the subject. Thus there can be no question that once the United States had, under the Treaty of Guadalupe Hidalgo in 1848, attained virtually her present contiguous continental limits, she was destined to become a very great power—provided only (and the proviso is plainly of profound importance) that she was able to preserve the Union. Indeed, in this political sphere, the negative effect of the war—which ensured that a truly United States would continue to exist—is more clear-cut and dramatic than in economic matters. In other words, the political effects of the war are in a number of cases clearly distinguishable from long-term processes.

Thus in another maritime matter, naval power, the impact of the war on Britain was plain—and quite opposite to its effect in the case of the merchant marine. Whereas the war gravely weakened American commercial shipping interests *vis à vis* those of Britain, it greatly strengthened the American navy, where American maritime efforts were naturally concentrated while hostilities lasted. That the war came at the crucial point in the technical revolution which was to replace the traditional wooden man-of-war with the steam ironclad vastly increased its impact. The British, whose long naval ascendancy had been built on wooden walls (as well, no doubt, as hearts of oak), had been, as the leading industrial power, aware of these developments, but, with economy dominant among government policies and pacifism a considerable force in the country, they had actually lagged behind France in ironclad design and construction. But France was at peace with Britain, and nations in the throes of war advance with incomparably more speed in military technology than those which are not. It was, therefore, the shock of the development of American ironclads, graphically illustrated by the encounter of the *Monitor* and the *Merrimac* in 1862, that sharply jolted British opinion into an awareness of this potential threat to her naval supremacy.

In 1862 *The Economist* wrote, "It is clear that to maintain the relative naval power of England we must, as quickly *as our means will permit*, transform our wooden fleet into an iron fleet."[9] This in due course happened, and Britain, for much the same reasons that her merchant marine flourished, very soon realized, and rightly, that she had, as the most highly industrialized nation, the capacity to outbuild any other naval power. This was to remain true until the twentieth century, but then the long-term result of United States economic growth as it affected naval affairs was the establishment of an American ocean supremacy even greater relatively than that of Britain in the nineteenth century.

The American military force generated by the war, in fact, did not assume a predominantly maritime form, and her naval strength did not attain great-power levels until after 1905. But

---

[9] *The Economist*, Apr. 5, 1862, p. 367.

on land, the forces the Union had at the time of Appomattox, and even after demobilization, were so large that they not only gave the United States the status of a great power but almost made her "practically sovereign on this continent,"[1] as Secretary of State Richard Olney said thirty years later. This was clearly demonstrated by the way in which the forces of Napoleon III were ignominiously bundled, bag and baggage, out of Mexico as soon as the Civil War was over, and by the decisive consequent strengthening of the Monroe Doctrine. The *Saturday Review* wrote in 1865, "It was almost impossible to exaggerate the material prosperity of the United States, or to overrate the practical energy which has been displayed both in war and peace";[2] the *Spectator* also wrote, "Nobody doubts any more that the Union is a power of the first class, a nation which it is very dangerous to offend and almost impossible to attack."[3]

This power was being wielded by an administration whose diplomatic tone, even when its hands were tied by the war, was to the editor of *The Economist* highly unpleasant and abrasive. In 1863, in a typical vein of recurrent irritation, he had declared that

> the Government of the Federal States has fallen into the hands of the smallest, weakest, and meanest set of men who ever presided over the policy of a great nation at the critical epoch of its affairs.[4]

And the administration was, as *The Times* had pointed out in 1862, under the control of an even more passionate (and, in *The Times*'s view, plebeian) public opinion: "The American Government is not able to rule of itself, but must seek its direction, not from the wise and prudent, but from the ignorant and violent."[5] This ill-feeling did not subside after the war (whose restraints on American opinion and policy toward foreign powers were then removed), but persisted until it was finally exorcised by the settlement of the *Alabama* claims. This postwar resentment on the

---

[1] R. J. Bartlett, ed.: *The Record of American Diplomacy* (New York, 1947), p. 345.
[2] Nov. 18, 1865, p. 626.
[3] Feb. 17, 1866, p. 177.
[4] *The Economist,* Apr. 25, 1863, p. 450.
[5] Jan. 13, 1862.

part of a triumphant North—and the defeated South felt an almost equal, if different, sense of disillusion with Britain—had its chief impact on British North America; there, because of the revival of the American desire for annexation, it was probably the chief cause of Canadian confederation. But it could not fail to have also a considerable impact, direct as well as indirect, on the mother country. Only the uneventful twenty years that followed the Treaty of Washington of 1871 were finally to see a clear improvement in the climate of Anglo-American relations.

This growth in the actual and potential world power of the United States—which was demonstrated by the fact that, in reality, the terms of the *Alabama* settlement accepted the American view of the duties of neutrals in time of war—was not only the result of increasing American strength, but also of the great growth of the federal government's effective powers. Thus the *Spectator* wrote in 1866:

> The American Revolution[6] marches fast towards its goal—the change of a Federal Commonwealth into a Democratic Republic, one and indivisible. Congress, which only five years ago was little more powerful than a debating club, . . . has suddenly become the Sovereign power, begins even to be conscious that it is Sovereign.[7]

The United States had more strength, and its government was able to use it much more fully. This process of internal constitutional change enthralled politically conscious Britons: they were in a general sense aware that the federal government, as a result of the nationalizing tendency (so to speak) that the victory of the Union produced, was greatly extending its strength and jurisdiction. In 1867 W. H. Dixon, author and editor of the weekly journal *Athenaeum*, wrote:

> In the great contest now going forward in every part of this Republic . . . as to the principle and plan on which the New America may be built up—every party seems to have put the Union in its front.[8]

---

[6] The *Spectator* here anticipates by a great many years Beard's description of the Civil War era as the Second American Revolution.

[7] Dec. 22, 1866, p. 1420.

[8] William Hepworth Dixon: *New America* (London, 1869), p. 430.

In 1866 in the House of Commons Lord Robert Montagu, advocate of plurality voters, noted that in the United States "the extension of the franchise had given overwhelming power to the Government." But Britons were greatly confused—as were many Americans—about the manner in which this new power would be exercised.

Lord Montagu saw this power as presidential. He went on: "Congress offered an idle opposition to the President."[9] During the second year of the Johnson administration, this—seen in the light of Lincoln's great wartime power as Chief Executive—was a not unreasonable judgment. But with the assertion of congressional authority, which was entailed in radical Reconstruction, most Englishmen believed that the new centralizing tendency would increase the power of the legislature. Bagehot, who was probably the most acute constitutional observer in Britain (although even he could be mistaken in coping with the complexities of the American Constitution, as when he supposed that the President could veto a constitutional admendment[1]), declared in 1868, "All that is clear is, that Congress is desperately intent— we think wisely intent—on asserting for itself, *in some way or other,* the supreme power, both legislative and executive."[2] The *Saturday Review* had written a year earlier:

> This purpose would be formally defeated if President Johnson were successfully impeached and deposed on the ground that he has followed a policy opposite to that of Congress. Such a precedent would establish, once for all, the rule that the Administration is dependent on the Legislature, and must either change its course or resign upon a vote of censure. In other words, the American Constitution would be assimilated to that of England.[3]

Since the situation was both complicated and fluid, and since many Americans believed, probably with reason, that in fact the development of a long-term American trend toward legislative sovereignty was possible and even likely, it is scarcely surprising

---

9 *Hansard,* Vol. 182, p. 1285.
1 *The Economist,* Apr.. 21, 1866, p. 472.
2 Ibid., Jan. 18, 1868, p. 59.
3 Jan. 5, 1867, p. 14.

that many British observers mistook for a fundamental constitutional change what was to turn out to be a passing and exceptional phase.

In fact, however, Bagehot and others tended to believe this because they wanted to believe it. Tightly in the grip of the nineteenth-century belief in national sovereignty, they felt that the lack of a legal sovereign was a fundamental deficiency in the American Constitution; the *Saturday Review* wrote of the founding fathers:

> Partly to avoid dissensions in their own body, and partly perhaps because they did not discern the vast practical consequences that turned on the point they left unsettled, they forbore to determine in express words where that sovereignty was to reside, which in every political society must have a fixed place, or must find one.[4]

Bagehot similarly deplored the lack of sovereignty in either branch of the government: "The splitting of sovereignty into many parts amounts to there being no sovereign."[5] Even more than at present (after America's twentieth-century displays of matchless military and political power) and especially so soon after the near-final disruption of the Union, Britons had grave reservations about the efficiency of the American system of government, and about the document on which it was based. The *Saturday Review* declared in 1867, "The proceedings of Congress inspire spectators with little confidence in its fitness for the sovereignty which it is rapidly assuming."[6]

Most of them recognized, however, what the *Saturday Review* called Americans' "superstitious faith in the Constitution."[7] A year earlier the same journal had noted the advantages of this faith at a time when it had been weakened by Secession and the Civil War:

> The curious reverence of Americans for their Constitution appears to be at least temporarily shaken . . . Foreign

---

[4] Jan. 5, 1867, p. 13.
[5] *The English Constitution* (London, 1963), p. 219.
[6] Jan. 26, p. 97, n. 98.
[7] Apr. 27, 1867, p. 516.

critics have often smiled at the unbounded faith of the American nation in a document which could by no possibility have provided for all future contingencies; but the Constitution is undoubtedly a remarkable monument of political ability; and it is a first condition of national greatness that there should be a common and unquestioning belief in some symbol of unity, whether it be a King, a flag, or a Constitution.[8]

The aspect of this reverence Britons found most difficult to understand was that for the Supreme Court, which the *Spectator* called "a constitutional god whose worship has even survived the Civil War, and who *cannot* be constitutionally overruled."[9] Bagehot did not believe that this ascendancy of the Supreme Court could be maintained: "The end of the revolution which has been in progress since 1860 . . . is this. The will of the nation as a whole . . . is to be the ultimate law of the United States . . .," for "a Court of Justice can no longer remain the ultimate political arbiter." On another occasion he summed it up:

> To us, the great lesson of the constitutional difficulties in America is the mischief of attempting to get an Executive which is not really and openly dependent on the Legislature . . . This kind of thing *cannot* last with a people as shrewd as the Yankees.[1]

Indeed, Englishmen, even those sympathetic to American democracy, tended to believe in the superiority of the *mechanics* of the British cabinet system, and to expect the Americans to follow their example and alter the presidential system. As W. H. Dixon put it:

> If any human effort of the pen is sacred in the eyes of these people it is their Constitution. Indeed, a stranger in the land can hardly comprehend the reverence—sometimes rising into awe—with which brave Virginians, practical Pennsylvanians, bright New Englanders, always speak of their Organic law . . . On the day of its adoption it was no

---

[8] Mar. 10, 1866, p. 283.
[9] Mar. 23, 1867, p. 315.
[1] *The Economist*, Feb. 16, 1867, p. 176; Dec. 7, 1867, p. 1379.

more than a compromise, and ever since that day it has stood in the way of progress in the United States . . . How can a progressive country pretend to limit its power of future growth?[2]

Or as Bagehot put it in *The English Constitution*:

> The English Constitution, in a word, is framed on the principle of choosing a single sovereign authority, and making it good; the American, upon the principle of having many sovereign authorities, and hoping that their multitude may atone for their inferiority. The Americans now extol their institutions, and so defraud themselves of their due praise. But if they had not a genius for politics; if they had not a moderation in action singularly curious where superficial speech is so violent; if they had not a regard for law, such as no great people have yet evinced, and infinitely surpassing ours,—the multiplicity of authorities in the American Constitution would long ago have brought it to a bad end.[3]

There were, of course, ardent admirers of the American egalitarian and republican system, with its separation of church and state; one such man was John Bright, who declared on March 26, 1863:

> Privilege thinks it has a great interest in this contest, and every morning, with blatant voice, it comes into your streets and curses the American Republic. Privilege has beheld an afflicting spectacle for many years past. It has beheld thirty millions of men, happy and prosperous, without emperor, without king, without the surroundings of a court, without nobles, except such as are made by eminence, in intellect and virtue, without State bishops and State priests . . . without great armies and great navies, without great debt and without great taxes.[4]

But even he was more deeply moved, one may judge, by the degree of American freedom and democracy than by constitu-

---

2 *New America*, pp. 439–40.
3 *The English Constitution*, p. 220.
4 Quoted in Trevelyan: *The Life of John Bright*, p. 307.

tional mechanisms, and this was what he was primarily thinking of when on December 18, 1862, he spoke of "the most free government and the noblest constitution the world has ever seen." He showed understanding of the immense scale of the great American experiment, and comprehended far better, one may suspect, than almost all his countrymen the need in America for a complex federal system, as, for instance, when he declared on the same occasion:

> I see one vast confederation stretching from the frozen North in unbroken line to the glowing South, and from the wild billows of the Atlantic westward to the calmer waters of the Pacific main—and I see one people and one language, and one law and one faith, and over all that wide continent, the home of freedom and a refuge to the oppressed of every race and of every clime.[5]

But although Bright's fervent admiration for American democracy was to be of immense importance, as we shall see, even he was not blind to American faults, as when, in 1867, in the House of Commons, he opposed a detailed proposal for reform, which was similar to an American practice, on the grounds that it had resulted there in "positively appalling"[6] corruption.

Those Englishmen who did admire the American system to any great degree would probably have expressed their praise in the relatively faint fashion of Gladstone in 1878:

> But, as the British Constitution is the most subtile organism which has proceeded from the womb and the long gestation of progressive history, so the American Constitution is, so far as I can see, the most wonderful work ever struck off at a given time by the brain and purpose of man.[7]

Most British observers, however, believed that their form of government represented "progressive history," and that "America will be on the high road towards . . . a practical identity between

---

[5] Quoted in Lillibridge: *Beacon of Freedom,* pp. 119–20.

[6] *Hansard,* Vol. 189, p. 1191.

[7] "Kin Beyond Sea," p. 185.

the legislative and executive powers . . . which in England we have already secured." During the development of the struggle between President Johnson and the radicals, *The Times*, although sympathetic to the President, frequently reproached him for clinging to what it regarded as a quite outmoded, outdated view of the Constitution. After the dismissal of Secretary of War Stanton, Bagehot declared, Congress will become (in the French meaning of the term) "an absolute Convention."[8] At the time of the impeachment, it was often thought that this would be effected by Congress imposing its will forcibly on the President; later that it might be effected by a constitutional compromise. As the *Spectator* wrote of the man who was to be the next President, General Grant: "Just at this juncture, however, a man turns up who offers the nation a means of reconciling its two desires— of retaining the Constitution inviolate, yet of making the nation visibly Sovereign, through its representatives."[9] Not that Bagehot expected it to be an easy process "to revise that sacred document which they have learned to revere, with an accumulating power of reverence, for eighty years."[1]

In fact, he constantly comments upon the extreme political conservatism of Americans—what he called on one occasion, in a striking phrase, "the constitutional prudery that is rooted in the American mind."[2] At another time he observed that "of all people, Americans most dislike plunges into the unknown,"[3] a view so contrary to the traditional view of the New World that it is perhaps desirable to quote an earlier observation of his as a counterbalance: "One of the most curious modifications effected in our character by the transfer of the Anglo-Saxon race to the American continent is a certain wonderful flexibility and adaptability to new circumstances"—which comes a good deal closer to the orthodox frontier theory of the historians. But by 1877 *The Economist* was beginning to have doubts as to whether profound constitutional changes were in fact going to take place in America, and with a certain air of approbation wrote:

---

[8] *The Economist*, Aug. 24, 1867, p. 955.

[9] Jan. 4, 1868, p. 8.

[1] *The Economist*, Dec. 7, 1867, p. 1379.

[2] Ibid., Feb. 6, 1875, p. 148.

[3] Ibid., Oct. 19, 1867, p. 1184.

However, we cannot deny that the American people are showing their usual sobriety in this difficult emergency. . . . They are too Conservative, too conventional, too much wedded to use, to propose what would amount to a Constitutional revolution.[4]

Bagehot, indeed, was sensible of the virtues of this conservatism, when compared, for example, with the flightiness of the French in constitutional matters (he had actually been in France in 1851 during Napoleon III's *coup d'état*), but he did not see the vital relationship between it and the now axiomatic democracy of America, largely because he did not himself believe in democracy. He apprehended in theory, as the arch antidemocrat Robert Lowe (in 1868 the first M.P. for the University of London) put it in the House of Commons in 1866, that "The great men who founded the constitution of America . . . knew that democracy required checks, and they sought to check it by various means."[5] They in fact checked democracy both by cleaving to the federal system, which divided power between states and central government, and by dividing even that degree of power which was left to the national government between the legislature and executive. But Bagehot was, as the leading exponent of the virtues of the English system of responsible legislative sovereignty, impatient of the seeming, and often (at the time) real inefficiency of the separation of powers, writing that "in America the dread of democratic passion has contrived expedients" for thwarting the nation "even in its clearest and most emphatic expression of a new resolve. . . . It would be well for America if there were fewer obstacles interposed between the good sense and will of the nation and the action of the Government."[6]

He did not see how illogical it was for an antidemocrat to demand the free and uninhibited exercise of popular power in a democracy at the same time that he pronounced the clear failure of universal suffrage in New York City, owing to the problems of mass immigration. Nor did he see the connection between this constitutional caution and the fact that, as he himself had written

---

[4] Ibid., Nov. 18, 1865, p. 1399; Jan. 27, 1877, p. 91.

[5] *Hansard*, Vol. 182, p. 2109.

[6] *The Economist*, Apr. 27, 1872, p. 511.

at the peak period of feeling over the Trent affair, "It is true that American rage even at its highest pitch usually manages to stop short where policy would direct, and that we in England are exceedingly liable to be deceived by its effervescent symptoms."[7] Few Englishmen saw the wisdom of Americans holding fast to their Constitution, pretty much as it was, under the strains imposed on it during this first great and hectic experiment in mass democracy.

Yet Britons could not but be increasingly aware of the American political example as the power of the government of the United States was strengthened by the Civil War. This power was apparent even in the techniques of administration, and we shall see later its profound effect upon the general principles of political life. Our period, after all, stands midway between Alexis de Tocqueville's *Democracy in America* (1835) and James Bryce's *The American Commonwealth* (1888). Indeed, attempts were made in the late 1870's and 1880's to "Americanize" certain procedures of the Liberal party, under the leadership of Joseph Chamberlain, but these efforts, especially that to introduce the caucus system, did not radically affect British constitutional development and indeed produced a reaction against American ideas that was an important factor in the disillusion of the British left with the example of the capitalist United States.[8] Thus, among the British press, *The Times*, the *Daily Telegraph*, *Manchester Courier*, *Scotsman*, and *Dublin Evening Mail* all consistently deplored the application of the American constitutional example in Britain.

By and large British opinion, pragmatic as it was, still agreed with Disraeli, who said in a characteristically perceptive speech against Gladstone's Reform Bill of 1866:

> Are we to consider this subject in the spirit of the English Constitution, or are we to meet it in the spirit of the American Constitution? I prefer to consider the question in the spirit of our own Constitution. In what I say I do not intend to undervalue American institutions, quite the reverse. I approve of American institutions, for they are

---

[7] Ibid., Apr. 27, 1861, p. 450.
[8] Pelling: *America and the British Left*, Chap. iii *passim*.

adopted in the country in which they exist. The point I would always consider is, whether the institutions of a country are adapted to the country where they are established. But I say none of the conditions exist in England which exist in America, and make those institutions flourish so eminently there. If I see a great body of educated men in possession of a vast expanse of cultivated land, and behind them an illimitable region where the landless might become landowners, then I should recognize a race to whom might be intrusted the responsibility of sovereign power. The blot of the American political system is not essential to it, but accidental: it is those turbulent and demoralized mobs which exist in the cities of the sea coast which constitute so great a reproach to American institutions. If, however, you introduce those institutions into England, I believe the effect would be disastrous. You would not gain that which is excellent in the American system, but that which is not an essential quality . . . You would have the rule of mobs in great towns, and the sway of turbulent multitudes.[9]

The example of actual American institutions, as distinct from the example of the democratic spirit that underlay them, was not to be important for Britain, save in the direct adaptation of the American federal system to the needs of her emergent self-governing dominions overseas, especially Canada in 1867 and Australia at the beginning of the twentieth century. Here, where the lands were vast and the problems closely analogous, the experience of the United States was deeply drawn upon, and was of the first importance.

Where the influence of the now vindicated self-confidence and growing strength of the American people upon the United Kingdom did show itself unmistakably was in the first steps the United States took in the direction of world power. Despite the fact that Britain's great colonies were now beginning to achieve self-government in domestic matters, London was still the center of a vast, and growing, Empire; indeed, Great Britain was about to enter a renewed phase of imperialist vigor, symbolized by Disraeli's success in persuading Parliament to confer upon Queen Victoria the title Empress of India in 1876. Such a unique, world-

---

[9] *Hansard*, Vol. 183, p. 103.

wide organization could not help being in some degree sensitive to the emergence of a new great power on the international scene. This development was dramatized by the United States' acquisition of Alaska in 1867 and by such signs of increasing interest in the Pacific area as her growing domination of Hawaii. Some Britons saw more clearly than others the importance of this fact; one was Disraeli, who made one of his penetrating observations about the issue when he said in 1872 that America was "throwing lengthening shades over the Atlantic" and creating "vast and novel elements in the distribution of power."[1] Others expressed it more explicitly: one British visitor to the United States wrote on his return in 1868, with deep insight into the future, that the Atlantic had replaced the North Sea as the great maritime area of Anglo-Saxon activity: "And so it comes to pass that America is peopled with that which is most enterprising and progressive in that race in which these qualities had been most highly developed. It is the main stream of the history of man." We "look upon American events as fraught with a greater amount of good and of evil to ourselves, than what is happening in all the world besides." Compared with what occurs in France or Italy, "Everybody . . . feels that the future of humanity will be greatly influenced by, and in no small degree depend upon, what is going on in America."[2]

The fact that there were already premonitory rumblings of the sudden upheaval in American political tradition constituted by the outburst of imperialism toward the end of the century makes it possible to see these developments on both sides of the Atlantic as part of a single achievement. Thus W. H. Dixon wrote in 1876:

> The great draws, annexes and absorbs the less. Some months ago, Lord Dufferin, Governor-General of Canada, annexed the whole region . . . stretching towards the North Pole; and some months hence, either President Grant or his successor at the White House, will annex the great provinces of Lower California, Sonora, and Chihuahua, with parts of Cinaloa, Cohahuila, and Neuva Leon, to the United States.

---

[1] Quoted in Allen: *Great Britain and the United States*, pp. 522–3.
[2] Zincke: *Last Winter in the United States*, pp. 28–30.

In the end, of course, it did not turn out that way because more orthodox anticolonial traditions reasserted themselves in American affairs.

Nevertheless, one aspect of these parallel imperialisms in Britain and America long remained of importance—that indicated by a later sentence of Dixon's: "The surface of the earth is passing into Anglo-Saxon hands."[3] Or as he put it elsewhere, "The tale of a Hundred Years of White Progress is a marvellous history. The European races are spreading over every continent, and mastering the isles and islets of every sea."[4] He was, as we shall see when we discuss the effect of Reconstruction upon the idea of race in Britain (with which the imperial idea has very close links), quite rabid on this issue—

> Disaster in the past, menace in the future, warn us to stand by our common race; our blood, law, language, science. We are strong but we are not immortal. A house divided against itself must fall. . . . So many foes are still afield that every White man's cry should be "Close ranks!"[5]

Yet those much less possessed by the notion of Anglo-Saxon superiority were prepared to see the Anglo-American world as a unit, so that the spirit of realpolitik (which might have made Britain welcome what Palmerston thought of as the "diminution of a dangerous power" by the "severance"[6] of North and South, and which might even have made her fight a bitter and inevitably losing battle to prevent the emergence of this immensely powerful new rival) never gained control of British policy. Just the reverse happened, as Admiral Alfred Thayer Mahan pointed out:

> The same tendency is shown in the undeniable disposition of the British people and of British statesmen to cultivate the good-will of the United States, and to draw closer the relations between the two countries. For the disposition underlying such a tendency Mr. Balfour has used an expression, "race patriotism" . . . When we begin really to

---

[3] W. H. Dixon: *White Conquest* (London, 1876), II, 371–2.
[4] Ibid., p. 368.
[5] Ibid., p. 372.
[6] Quoted in Allen: *Great Britain and the United States*, p. 456.

look abroad, and to busy ourselves with our duties to the
world at large in our generation—and not before—we shall
stretch out our hands to Great Britain, realizing that in
unity of heart among the English-speaking races lies the
best hope of humanity in the doubtful days ahead.[7]

The new power of the United States would not have been
possible without the preservation of the Union in the Civil War,
and this power was to be of decisive importance to the future
of mankind, both because of its magnitude and because of its
direction. Before long Bryce was to write of its magnitude:

In this age, more than any preceding, wealth means power,
offensive power in war as well as financial power in peace
. . . The Republic is as wealthy as any two of the greatest
European nations, and is capable, if she chooses, of quickly
calling into being a vast fleet and a vast army. Her wealth
and power has in it something almost alarming.[8]

Its direction after the victory of the North was to be decisively
democratic. Lincoln had fully realized this in the course of the
war; indeed, he spelled it out as early as his Message to Congress
in Special Session on July 4, 1861:

And this issue embraces more than the fate of these United
States. It presents to the whole family of man the question
whether a constitutional republic or democracy—a government of the people by the same people—can or cannot
maintain its territorial integrity against its own domestic
foes.

More than that, he said later, it was

essentially a people's contest . . . a struggle for maintaining
in the world that form and substance of government whose
leading object is to elevate the condition of men—to lift
artificial weights from all shoulders; to clear the paths of

---

[7] Quoted in Allen: *Great Britain and the United States*, p. 562.
[8] Quoted in Allan Nevins: *America through British Eyes* (New York,
1948), p. 539.

laudable pursuit for all; to afford all an unfettered start, and a fair chance in the race of life.[9]

Lincoln had thus set the aims of the North in the war as high as they could well be set: they consisted not merely of preserving the Union but of ensuring the future of free democratic government, not only in America but throughout the world.

The effect of the war upon Britain can only be understood in the context of this broad stream of development. As we shall see, its effect upon the democratization of the British political system was perhaps decisive, and in 1865 Britain was probably at the peak of her international power. That both Britain and the United States were henceforth to struggle, at first independently but in due course jointly, for the promotion of democratic institutions in the world was of first importance for the future of mankind. What came in the mid-twentieth century to be called the free world has been in a special but real sense an Anglo-American creation; historically, neither power could have achieved it alone, but the victory of the North in the Civil War meant that by the twentieth century it really would be possible to call the New World into existence to redress the balance of the Old. Bismarck was thinking of the potential strength of this Anglo-American combination when he said that the supreme fact of the nineteenth century was that Britain and the United States spoke the same language.

That the world would have been a very different place without this rise of Anglo-American friendship can be seen from an examination of the general prospects of democracy at the time when Lincoln made his most moving plea, that there should be "a new birth of freedom; and that government of the people, by the people, for the people, shall not perish from the earth."[1]

In 1863 the technological supremacy of Europe and the West in the world was overwhelming, and politically, although the flood of the new imperialism had not yet made itself felt, the same was true. Three years before in the Far East, the Treaty of

---

[9] Abraham Lincoln: *Complete Works, Comprising His Speeches, Letters, State Papers and Miscellaneous Writings,* ed. by John G. Nicolay and John Hay (New York, 1920), II, 57, 64.

[1] *Works,* II, 439.

Pekin had made clear the impotence of the Chinese imperial government, while Japan had only just sent her very first envoys overseas—to Washington. In India five years before, the suppression of the Indian Mutiny had led to the final transfer of power from the East India Company to the Crown, but "darkest Africa" had still not aroused the serious competitive instincts of the great colonial powers. The fact of Europe's hegemony of the globe in the mid-nineteenth century can scarcely be disputed.

Even in Britain in 1863, as we shall see, the future of democracy, if not of free institutions, was far from hopeful. Elsewhere in Europe, despite the revolts in Greece and Spain, and the emancipation of the Russian serfs in 1861, the prospects for any real political liberty were decidedly gloomy. The year before, Bismarck had come to power in Prussia, and, the year after, he was to go to war over Schleswig-Holstein. In 1863 itself the insurrection of the Polish nation was effectively crushed, and the future of the relatively liberal Austrian constitution of 1861 was already highly uncertain. The year before, the cause of Italian freedom had received a setback with the capture of Garibaldi at Aspromonte. Finally, Napoleon III seemed so confident of his destiny that his troops entered far-off Mexico City in this year, 1863.

Thus the future of free government and, even more, of democracy, was to depend in remarkable degree during and after the Civil War on the influence of Britain and the survival of the United States. As we have noted, America was to attain new heights of power after 1865, and we shall see also that the Northern victory was to give a marked impetus to the democratic movement in the United Kingdom. This was to be the most potent impact of the Civil War upon life and liberalism in Britain.

But before we finally scrutinize this crucial question in detail, we must examine the not unimportant influence that Reconstruction, as distinct from the war itself, had upon British life and liberalism. The most seminal work, in the historiographical revolution that has occurred in the interpretation of Reconstruction during the last thirty years, contains the words:

A great political scientist [John W. Burgess: *Reconstruction and the Constitution*, p. 133] in one of the oldest and largest of American universities wrote and taught thousands of youths and readers that "There is no question, now, that Congress did a monstrous thing, and committed a great political error, if not a sin, in the creation of this new electorate. It was a great wrong to civilization to put the white race of the South under the domination of the Negro race. The claim that there is nothing in the color of the skin from the point of view of political ethics is a great sophism. A black skin means membership in a race of men which has never of itself succeeded in subjecting passion to reason; has never, therefore, created any civilization of any kind." Here is the crux of all national discussion and study of Reconstruction.[2]

Few, if any, historians would now disagree with this contention of W. E. B. Du Bois, that the fundamental issue in Reconstruction was that of race.

And race was to become one of the dominant themes in British history in the quarter-century after Reconstruction. National attention had already been focused on what Thomas Carlyle was to call "The Nigger Question" by Governor Edward Eyre's bloody suppression of a Negro revolt that broke out in Jamaica on October 11, 1865. As Dr. George Ford has pointed out:

> For almost two years, England was split into two camps over an issue which engaged the passions of many men who otherwise spurned active politics . . . Why was it that the Eyre case aroused such bitter feelings? The division of opinion in England during the American Civil War had perhaps prepared the ground [as had the horror at the Indian Mutiny only eight years before], but more important was the fact that, between 1865 and 1867, agitation for the passing of a new Reform Bill was at its height. In the same period there was also constant dread of Fenian uprisings.[3]

Nor was Jamaica the only colony that could be a source of trouble; as Christine Bolt notes, "During the 1850's and 60's, as

---

[2] W. E. Burghardt Du Bois: *Black Reconstruction: An Essay toward a History of the Part which Black Folk played in the attempt to Reconstruct Democracy in America, 1860–80* (New York, 1935), p. 381.

[3] "The Governor Eyre Case in England," *University of Toronto Quarterly* (Apr. 1948), pp. 222–3.

Britain's colonial possessions in South Africa and New Zealand became increasingly troublesome, there was a perceptible hardening of middle and upper class attitudes towards the Negro. The old, somewhat patronising view of the peaceful 'child of nature' was now disturbed by fear."[4] (Hence the ironic title of Dickens's essay in almost the Carlyle vein, *The Noble Savage*.) Among the British press for example, only the *Daily News* and the *Spectator* supported radical Reconstruction, and all that it meant to the Negro, with any real consistency.

In the Eyre case, a group of liberals, led by John Stuart Mill, formed a Jamaica Committee; its executive committee included Thomas Huxley, Goldwin Smith, Thomas Hughes, Herbert Spencer, and John Bright, and its supporters numbered among them Charles Darwin, A. R. Wallace, Leslie Stephen, John Morley, and Sir Charles Lyell. Its opponents formed the Eyre Defence Committee, and included John Ruskin, Charles Kingsley, Henry Kingsley, Tennyson, J. A. Froude, and possibly even Matthew Arnold. Honors on the Eyre issue were about even, but to a remarkable degree it foreshadowed the later polarization of opinion in Britain on the race question, between the "two types" of men "represented by Mill and Carlyle respectively," as *The Times* put it.[5] As Mill said in his *Autobiography*, "There was much more at stake than only justice to the negroes, imperative as was that consideration. The question was, whether the British dependencies, and eventually, perhaps, Great Britain itself, were to be under the government of law or of military licence."[6] To Carlyle, on the other hand, the Jamaica Committee was "a small loud group, small as now appears, and nothing but a group or knot of rabid Nigger-Philanthropists, barking furiously in the gutter."[7]

The Eyre case terminated with the governor's acquittal in 1868, by which time radical Reconstruction had begun, and something of the same British interest was aroused by this vastly greater problem in America. By no means the only concern was

---

[4] C. A. Bolt: *British Attitudes to Reconstruction in the United States, 1863–77* (MS of Ph.D. Thesis, University of London).

[5] Dec. 6, 1901.

[6] Quoted in Bolt: *British Attitudes to Reconstruction*.

[7] Quoted in ibid.

the Negro: as we have seen, there was also deep interest in the constitutional aspects of Reconstruction. Nor was all the attention focused on the racial aspect of the Negro question. The deep roots of the prewar British antislavery movement were in fact brought to flower again in the form of the widespread and remarkably successful work done by British freedmen's aid societies on behalf of the Southern Negro.[8] As Sir George Campbell put it, "The Negro has been to some extent under the protection of a powerful philanthropic party in this country [Britain],"[9] despite, in his view, the often malign influence in some colonies of local white-planter oligarchies. But it is symptomatic that, in fact, a number of the freedmen's aid societies were badly split by opposite feelings as to the wisdom of aiding Jamaican Negroes in the circumstances following the Jamaica rebellion.

Britons were greatly prone to compare the problems of imperial government of subject races with those that America was struggling with in Reconstruction; there is clear evidence of this concern in all sections of the British press.[1] Campbell, one of the wisest of British observers, stated in the introduction to his *White and Black* in 1879, "I had . . . a special desire . . . to learn something of the present position of 'the nigger question'—a subject on which very little has been written in this country." As he put it more fully later in the book:

> I was . . . led to look particularly into the relations between the black and white races in the Southern States, for the sake of the lessons that might be learned as bearing on our management of British possessions where white and black races are intermingled.
>
> I do not here speak of our great dependency, India, where our system has been to rule both races by a Government avowedly absolute and despotic. In regard to that system I am one of those to be judged rather than to judge others; but this at least I may claim, that the Indian administration of the past cannot be accused of any habitual

---

[8] For a detailed treatment of the British freedmen's aid societies, see C. A. Bolt: *British Attitudes to Reconstruction.*

[9] *White and Black*, p. 114.

[1] For example, *The Times*, the *Daily Telegraph*, *Beehive*, *Daily News*, *Spectator*, and *Pall Mall Gazette*.

subordination of the rights and interests of the coloured races to those of the whites.[2]

He continues, in a vein somewhat hostile to non-Indian British colonial administration, to be critical of the Redeemers and the White South. As he wrote in one place, "There is no excuse whatever for the lengths to which the triumph of the Democrats has been pushed"; in another he wrote, "It is the struggle for political power, and the question whether the coloured people are to be allowed to vote freely, which has caused all the trouble. It is . . . absolutely necessary that the South should honestly accept the 15th Amendment," and not insist on a completely "solid South."[3]

Campbell not only felt warm toward the American people as a whole (they "are really and truly our kin. This is not a mere phrase"), but he also held that their "manners . . . are our manners, their ways are our ways, and their hearts and sympathies are the hearts and sympathies to which we are accustomed."[4] Furthermore, he sympathized with what was really the fundamental approach of the enlightened Northerner to the whole problem: "I . . . incline [in our colonies] to a system which may lead us towards the state of things now found in America, where Africans have been converted in manners, religion, language, and clothing, and assimilated to the white man's standard."[5]

By no means all Britons, of course, took so kindly a view of the radical Republicans' attempts to handle the problem of the Negro race in the South. Bagehot, for example, reacted very differently to the idea of immediate Negro suffrage, which is not surprising in one with deep doubts about the electoral franchise even for the English workingman. In 1867 he wrote, "It is, indeed, a deplorable political position, when the entrusting of large political power to a thoroughly ignorant and half-barbarous though loyal class seems the only practicable remedy for social and political anarchy."[6] He felt this way, however, not from any prejudice against the Negro as such, but from his deep doubts as

---

[2] Campbell: *White and Black*, p. 111.
[3] Ibid., pp. 186, x–xii.
[4] Ibid., pp. 2, 97.
[5] Ibid., p. 124.
[6] *The Economist*, Mar. 30, 1867, p. 352.

to the fitness of any uneducated and propertyless class for the franchise. Furthermore, he could see the advantages that could possibly be extracted from so difficult a situation: "The expedient of impartial suffrage may have this effect, that by putting so much political power into the hands of the negroes, it will make it in their former masters' interests to treat them with decent humanity, if not, indeed, to court their support."[7]

Nevertheless, five years later Bagehot had not really changed his view, despite the opening sentence of the article in which he wrote of the presidential election of 1872—"But by far the most important and gratifying result of the election is the negro vote" —for he continued, "There never was in the history of democracy so dangerous an experiment as that of entrusting full electoral power to nearly four millions of black persons, but just emancipated from actual slavery, totally uneducated and hungry for material advantages." Not surprisingly, we find him writing, again five years later (in 1877), of the great American compromise over Reconstruction in that year: "We shall be disappointed if the State [South Carolina] does not settle down peacefully and labour with success to recover its lost credit under General Hampton's rule." Somewhat optimistically, he was to conclude all his observations on Civil War and Reconstruction with the words "The liberties of the negroes will not be touched, though they will no longer have an opportunity of despoiling the public Treasury."[8]

Indeed, far from agreeing with radical Republican policies, Bagehot believed that, as in a number of political matters, the boot was on the other foot and that the United States had much to learn from Britain in this affair of what was, after all, the ruling of an empire. Here he did put his finger on a great American dilemma (which is far from resolved even now, in the mid-twentieth century). He pointed out in 1874 that

> the public sentiment of the United States is rigorously opposed to anything approaching to the rule of dependencies. It was resolved, therefore, to give back the right of self-government to the Southern States, but to maintain the dis-

---

[7] Ibid., p. 351.
[8] Ibid., Nov. 9, 1872, p. 1367; Apr. 7, 1877, p. 385.

abilities of the "rebels," that is, of all the white population with a very few insignificant exceptions, and to enfranchise the whole of the negroes.[9]

The *Spectator* had put it another way in 1868: "The United States have shown an almost nervous horror of open military occupation even of rebellious States."[1] Yet no one could pretend, Bagehot argued, that the Negroes were fit for self-government; to him the root of the evil was the American fixation on the Declaration of Independence and its assumption that all men are ready for instant political rights and duties.

> In short, the rights of man asserted in the declaration of Independence, are rights to which all men may in time be trained, but into which it is simply impossible to enter without a training. And yet American prejudices will not admit of suspending for any time the political privileges of the multitude in a large group of the States, and governing them on principles like those applied to our great Indian dependency.[2]

To him, as to other British observers, the solution was simple, although "the Radicals shrink" from it "because it sounds arbitrary":

> The true policy is, then, to dispense with self-government, to keep strict order, to form and protect institutions administering impartial justice *and imparting impartial education*, and to trust to the healing influence of time gradually to build up a society in which self-government would again become possible.[3]

There could not be a clearer contrast between British gradualism and American immediacy.

Many of the Britons who were interested in the problem, of course, did not take either of these two decisive points of view,

---

[9] Ibid., Aug. 22, 1874, p. 1020.

[1] Nov. 7, 1868, p. 1302.

[2] *The Economist*, Nov. 14, 1874, p. 1366. There are in many journals constant comparisons, also, between Ireland and the ex-Confederate States.

[3] Ibid., Dec. 21, 1867, p. 1443.

that of Campbell or that of Bagehot. The Reverend David Macrae, for example, at this time paid a long visit to America, including South Carolina, whose Negro secretary of state, Francis L. Cardozo, he remembered as a fellow university student in Scotland —"a well-read man, with a clear head, and . . . an excellent argumentative speaker, a first-rate organizer and man of business."[4] He took a middle position in his book, which was published in 1870, after his return. He sympathetically reported Cardozo as saying that "the coloured people would have a long struggle before they could overcome the prejudice against them. That prejudice was strong both in the North and in the South." Macrae also pointed out that the lessons from experience constituted a two-way traffic: "It must be admitted . . . that the results of emancipation in the West Indies [where most ". . . of the white people have gone back to Britain, and most of the black people have gone back to the bush"] have fallen far short of what was anticipated; and this is the aspect of the case which was constantly looked at by the people of the Southern States"[5] before the war. (The *Daily News*, we may note, still argued at the time that America should benefit from the example of Britain's mishandling and neglect of Jamaica's problems, for which the Negro could not really be blamed.) However, Macrae wrote at another time:

> . . . even in the places where the black population may slightly preponderate, it seems to me that the fears of the white population are not creditable to themselves. Where is the boasted superiority of the Anglo-Saxon if he cannot rule without being in a majority? . . . the world is not governed by votes. It is governed by ideas. Majorities never rule.

But even he was not unmoved by current racial ideas; as he declares, "The idea of the Negro ruling the South is preposterous," and elsewhere "Anglo-Saxon ideas are moulding America from Canada to the Gulf, and from the Atlantic to the Pacific."[6]

Like most British observers of the American scene, Macrae

---

[4] Macrae: *The Americans at Home*, I, 326.
[5] Ibid., I, 327, 374 *n.*, 370.
[6] Ibid., I, 360, 361.

was at bottom most fascinated by the racial question as such, although no doubt his time in the mission field had given him a special interest. He pointed out that the apparently widespread assumption "that the negro is dying out is, to say the least of it, premature."[7] He also saw clearly the degrading legacy of slavery, which "now hangs like a millstone round the neck of the emancipated race, and makes the present crisis so full of difficulty and peril."[8] He showed, as was fitting in a minister, a truly Christian charity in his understanding of the Negro problem, and it is apparent that he really mixed with and liked the colored man; he asserts that the Negro is not shiftless, but will work and is capable of saving, as well as having a deep desire for education. On innate capacities, he makes what is, given his period, a balanced judgment; "Whether the negro is capable of as high culture as the white man is a question which I do not pretend to settle . . . But . . . there are great possibilities that lie waiting for development in the negro brain."[9] He even contemplates racial intermixture, fear of which, he believes, is the fundamental issue in the South; here again he notes the corrupting influence of slavery, which had resulted in so many mulattoes. But he believed that barrenness inevitably overtakes mixed bloods in four or five generations, so that social admixture could only continue if there was constant intermarriage between whites and blacks, and this, he declares (with something which seems not far from an air of relief), Northern experience has shown to be pretty unlikely.

Rather similar in its relative moderation is the view of Dilke, who is studiously fair to the Negro. Quoting the opinion of Alexander H. Stephens that "slavery is the natural and moral condition of the negro," he observes that its

> effects . . . upon the slave are less terrible than its effects upon the master . . . In no direction can the matter be followed out to its conclusions without bringing us face to face with the sad fact, that the faults of the plantation negro are every one of them traceable to the vices of the slavery system.

---

[7] Ibid., I, 360.
[8] Ibid., II, 7 et seq.
[9] Ibid., II, 42, 44.

Nor are we British, he points out, without blame in the matter nor able to be unconcerned about it: we no longer believe in slavery, but "as long as we possess Jamaica, and are masters upon the African west coast, the negro question is one of moment to ourselves." On the question of racial capacities, he judges that "there is reason to believe that the American negroes will justify the hopes of their best friends; they have made the best of every chance that has been given them yet; they made good soldiers, they are eager to learn their letters, they are steady at their work."[1]

Yet Dilke, too, cannot doubt the superiority of the Anglo-Saxon race, although he gives the term a somewhat wider and more sensitive meaning than it often came to bear later. In the Preface to *Greater Britain* he writes:

> In 1866 and 1867 I followed England round the world; everywhere I was in English-speaking, or in English-governed lands. If I remarked that climate, soil, manners of life, that mixture with other peoples had modified the blood, I saw, too, that in essentials the race was always one.
>
> The idea which in all the lengths of my travels has been at once my fellow and my guide . . . is a conception, however imperfect, of the grandeur of our race, already girdling the earth, which it is destined, perhaps, eventually to overspread.
>
> In America, the peoples of the world are being fused together, but they are run into an English mould: Alfred's laws and Chaucer's tongue are theirs whether they would or no. . . . Through America England is speaking to the world.
>
> Sketches of Saxondom may be of interest even upon humbler grounds: the development of the England of Elizabeth is to be found, not in the Britain of Victoria, but in half the habitable globe. If two small islands are by courtesy styled "Great," America, Australia, India, must form a Greater Britain.[2]

To others, however, Anglo-Saxon superiority went much more obviously with Negro inferiority. Thus another Briton, Barham Zincke, laid it down in 1868 after his American visit

---

[1] Dilke: *Greater Britain*, pp. 28–31.
[2] Ibid., pp. ix–x.

that no one, not even a radical Republican, who knows anything of the history of the black race "abstractedly"[3] [sic] believes them capable of participating in government, though he thinks that they will certainly get the franchise because, as Dilke put it, "Government through the negroes is the only way to avoid government through an army, which would be dangerous to the freedom of the North. It is safer for America to trust her slaves than to trust her rebels—safer to enfranchise than to pardon."[4] As to "the fusion of the two races," Zincke continues, "history assures us that nothing of the kind has ever been accomplished, and that it is physically impossible."[5]

Yet others, like W. H. Dixon, are, or become, positively obsessed with the racial problem. (There is a striking difference of tone between his two books, one published in 1867 after journeying in America with Dilke, the other in 1876.) The dedication of the second, *White Conquest,* runs "To Marian These Pictures of the Great Conflict of Races on the American Soil as seen in 1875 are Affectionately Inscribed." (Bagehot was more cautious, asking in 1874, "Is there really a 'war of races' in the South, and, if so, of what kind is it?"[6] The extraordinary degree of this frenzied interest on the part of the Englishman is clearly illustrated in the following passage, with its marked psychosexual overtones. The township of Caddo, Dixon relates, is inhabited

by the new race of mixed bloods known to science as Zambos—the offspring of Negro bucks and Indian squaws.

According to Tschudi's List of Half-castes, a White father and a Negro mother produce a Mulatto; a White father and an Indian mother produce a Mestizo; an Indian father and a Negro mother produce a Chino; a Negro father and an Indian mother produce a Zambo. These four hybrids are the primary mixed breeds of America.

A Mulatto is coffee-coloured; a Mestizo is ruddy-gold; a Chino is dirty-red; a Zambo is dirty-brown.

A White father and Mulatta mother produce the Quadroon; a White father and Mestiza mother the Creole. Quad-

---

[3] *Last Winter in the United States,* p. 99 et seq.
[4] *Greater Britain,* p. 34.
[5] *Last Winter in the United States,* p. 107.
[6] *The Economist,* Oct. 31, 1874, p. 1308.

roons and Creoles, though dark and coarse, are sometimes beautiful, and in a state of servitude young females of these families always fetched more money than a Turkish pasha gave for his Georgian slave. A Negro father and Mulatta mother produce a Cubra, and a Cubra is an ugly mongrel. In another generation the original Negro-type returns. Not so with the Indian family. An Indian father and a Mestiza mother produce the Mestizo-claro—often a handsome specimen of the human animal. But Indian blood appears to mix imperfectly with Black. The Chino is a lanky and ungainly fellow, and his half-brother, the Zambo, is uglier still. Nature, one imagines, never meant these families to mix. A breed so droll in figure and complexion as the Zambo imps who sprawl and wallow in these huts is hardly to be matched on earth.

Yet these ugly creatures are said to be prolific. Every cabin in Caddo shows a brood of imps; and if the new school of ethnologists are right, they may increase more rapidly than the ordinary Blacks. What sort of mongrels shall we find at Caddo in a hundred years?

It is not surprising, then, to find Dixon laying it down that "The African brain is limited in range"[7] and that "A Negro cannot stand the impact of free life." He quotes with approval a Southern view: "Nature has given the White man brain and strength, invention, courage, and endurance of a higher quality, on a larger scale, than she has given these elements to the Black."[8] (It is interesting to observe that he takes the antithesis seriously enough to capitalize both White and Negro in his writing, which was unusual at that date.) He carries this principle into the depths of nature:

A colony of black ants usually settles near a colony of red. Does Nature mean her duskier children to be seized and made to labour for the fairer kinds? . . . Who knows the mystery of colour? By consent of every age and country black has been adopted as a sign of woe and servitude . . . Are the shades of colour, grades of power? . . . In every part of Europe people in the upper ranks are fairer than people in the lower ranks.

---

[7] *White Conquest*, I, 273–4, 333.
[8] Ibid., II, 143, 134 et seq.

It is, perhaps, not too fanciful to see in his British view of Texas, whose "calendar of crime . . . is a fearful record," an echo of the Southern idealization of Scott, which went hand in hand with slavery: "A Texan is a mounted man; a knight, who rides and carries arms. The air is hot and swells in mortal veins."[9]

His feeling, we may note in passing, is not confined to the Negro. He quotes, again with approval, an American senator's remark that "The Yellow Question is more menacing to republican institutions than the Black." The problem is, he says, "Shall European civilization or Asiatic barbarism prevail on the Pacific Slope?" Somewhat more bizarrely, he declares, "The Mongol's advent in America has brought into the front the great struggle for existence between eaters of beef and eaters of rice." This is, of course, in his view a world problem: "An English broadside smashed the gates of this paradise of tea drinkers and opium smokers. Through the breach . . . the natives came pouring forth . . . Who can assure us that these streams will ever stop?"[1]

The roots of these excesses of racialism in the nineteenth century are plainly very tangled and complex, and a study of the effect of Reconstruction upon British notions is no place for a lengthy consideration of them. Obviously they had indigenous origins in both countries—and other origins elsewhere, such as Germany (in a case like that of Houston Stewart Chamberlain, a forerunner of Nazism). Darwinian ideas were plainly one source, and another may well have been the unusual psychological repressions of the Victorian era, which it took the genius of Freud to explain. Yet another was the actual technological, material, and politico-organizational superiority of the West, although this was combined with a considerable sense of insecurity, and hence an assertiveness, which arose from the sudden contraction of that still largely closed world as a result of this very technical development. But, above all, the excesses in racial ideas must have been due to the new and sudden interaction of the world's peoples that accompanied the enormous acceleration of communications in the first half of the nineteenth century.

The strangeness of this sudden contact is brought out in

---

[9] Ibid., I, 279–80, 330, 325.
[1] Ibid., II, 197, 216, 236, 210.

Dilke's remark that "it is easy . . . to set down negroes as a monster class of which nothing is yet known, and, like the compilers of the Catalan map, say of places of which we have no knowledge, 'Here be giants, cannibals, and negroes' ";[2] the feeling of sudden and uncomfortable proximity is similarly evoked by Zincke's characteristic comment on the fact (in this context very familiar) that one man, although "theoretically he was a strong Negrophilist . . . liked him [the Negro] best at a distance."[3] Even in the South the experience of near-integrated living was in some respects new, and, to the extent that it was not, accounted for the greater ease of the Southerner in the presence of the Negro. This meant that to an unprecedented degree a phenomenon like Reconstruction could in its racial aspect strike Britons as relevant to their own experience in their colonial Empire, and no doubt played its part in the development of the new British imperialism in the late nineteenth century.

Before leaving this topic, it is perhaps comforting to see how very sane and balanced could be the judgment of one Briton (who had had long practical and personal experience with the color question, in India) on the lessons that Britain could draw with profit from the American experience with the Negro race problem.

Campbell's cautious and realistic assessment of the fundamental problem is characteristic:

> The first and most difficult question is the capacity of the negro as compared with other races. In one sense all men are born equal before God; but no one supposes that the capacities of all men are equal, or that the capacities of all races are equal, any more than the capacities of all breeds of cattle or dogs, which we know differ widely. There is, therefore, no *primâ facie* improbability of a difference of capacity between white Aryan and the negro race, though I believe there is no ground for presuming that white races *must be* better than black.

Today, however, we would probably disagree sharply with a further judgment of his: "It is unnecessary to try to distinguish between differences due to unassisted nature and those due to

---

2 *Greater Britain*, p. 28.
3 *Last Winter in the United States*, p. 6.

domestication and education . . . It is enough to take the negro as he is."

Campbell's other judgments seem essentially sound. He remarks that "in the New Orleans country, under the French practice (which has not our Anglo-Saxon antipathy to intimacy with coloured races), many creoles of mixed blood attain a far higher position than in other parts of the United States." Elsewhere, "even in the North . . . the free negroes were subjected to a social ostracism which made their success in commerce and the professions almost impossible." The Negroes "are certainly not a race remarkable for energy and force under difficulties," but on "the other hand, they have a very remarkable good nature and good temper." Furthermore, the "allegation against the negro character" that it prefers "to squat down in idleness . . . seems to me quite disproved by experience." He confesses that "even an English Radical is a little taken aback at first" by riding with Negroes in public conveyances, though "like separate Hindoo castes, they do not intermarry, or worship or eat together." Joseph Crosfield, a prominent English Quaker of very liberal sympathies who visited America at this time, did not object to the segregation of races imposed during mealtimes at the American meetings he attended. But even recent revisionist historians could scarcely differ much from Campbell's judgment that "On the whole . . . I am inclined to believe that the period of Carpet-bag rule was rather a scandal than a very permanent injury," while his object in passing judgment seems impeccable—we "must deal with them [the American Negroes] as a single, English-speaking people." Finally, wise Britons might well have reflected with him that "the white serfs of European countries took hundreds of years to rise to the level which these negroes have attained in a dozen."[4]

All of these effects of the Civil War and Reconstruction on Britain, however, were subsidiary to its main impact, which was on the fundamentals (rather than the mechanics) of political life—that is to say, the part it played in the progress of democracy in the United Kingdom. In a republication, in 1908, of his original book of 1870 David Macrae wrote, with the advantage

---

[4] *White and Black*, pp. 128–9, 131, 135–42, 180, 195.

of hindsight, that it was necessary for Britons to study America, since she

> is now exercising a powerful influence on this country . . .
> North and South [in the Civil War] were felt to be but
> names for two great principles, contending not only in
> America but here. On those battle-fields of Virginia British
> conservatism and British liberalism fought by proxy . . .
> The triumph of the North meant British reform, John
> Bright in the Cabinet, Free Schools, and justice to Ireland.[5]

Cobden had rightly observed in a letter to Sumner more than forty years before, on January 11, 1865, "I agree with a remark in the concluding passage of your last letter—that you are fighting the battle of Liberalism in Europe as well as the battle of freedom in America."[6]

We have seen that, in this era, despite the American Union's emerging power and dedication to democracy (which were to be so important in the twentieth century), the influence of Britain in Europe and elsewhere was still very great, and that, for this reason, the success of fully representative government in the world, for the foreseeable future, depended in considerable degree upon its fate in the United Kingdom. The extent to which the victory of the North was responsible for the triumph of democracy in Britain has long been a disputed question. The American historian E. D. Adams, for example, in his *Great Britain and the American Civil War*, rates the importance of the American influence very high, and by implication plainly considers it the prime factor in the passage of the Parliamentary Reform Bill of 1867, the most decisive step in the progress of British democracy. On the other hand, Charles Seymour, another distinguished American diplomatic historian, in his study *Electoral Reform in England and Wales*, published in New Haven in 1915, simply does not mention America or the victory of the North at all as a reason for the passage of the bill. More recent historians, British and American, have taken a middle position. G. D. Lillibridge

---

[5] Macrae: *The Americans at Home*, pp. 13–14.
[6] Quoted in J. A. Hobson: *Richard Cobden: The International Man* (London, 1918), p. 382.

concludes his study entitled *Beacon of Freedom: The Impact of American Democracy upon Great Britain, 1830–1870* with the words (British in their understatement, American though he is), "Though there were many forces and factors leading to this long-awaited day in 1867, who will now deny that the role of the American destiny was not a humble one in this decisive triumph of the democratic movement in England in the nineteenth century?"[7] Similarly, in *America and the British Left* Henry Pelling writes, "And since the Civil War had ended in the triumph of the Union, the American example, being a rallying-point for the forces of British Radicalism, played its part in setting Britain further and more decisively upon the path that led to full democracy."[8]

There can be no doubt at all that during the course of the war itself the cause of the Union was, generally speaking, a rallying point for the forces seeking democracy in Britain. Nor is there any doubt that those who disliked democracy feared the triumph of the North; the Earl of Shrewsbury, for example, in the well-known words quoted by E. D. Adams, declared, "I see in America the trial of Democracy and its failure. I believe that the dissolution of the Union is inevitable, and that men now before me will live to see an aristocracy established in America."[9] Though much less openly and theoretically oligarchical than this, Lord Palmerston, too, certainly mistrusted the idea of democracy (and even of limited parliamentary reform) in the middle-class Britain that he had so long and so successfully dominated. Privately, he hoped for the success of the Confederacy, because it would gravely weaken a potential rival of Britain's—and a democratic one. But, realist that he was, he kept his personal opinions to himself and consistently adapted his public policy to the military situation. Thus, as Gladstone later said, "Lord Palmerston desired the severance as a diminution of a dangerous power, but prudently held his tongue."[1]

Others were much less restrained, indeed extraordinarily

---

7 *Beacon of Freedom*, p. 122.

8 Pelling: *America and the British Left*, p. 29.

9 *Great Britain and the American Civil War*, II, 282.

1 John Morley: *The Life of William Ewart Gladstone* (London, 1908), I, 535.

passionate. John Thadeus Delane, for example, the influential
editor of *The Times*, who was close to Palmerston, was positively
vitriolic, and this goes a long way to account for the attitude of
the paper; he wrote to W. H. Russell, *The Times* correspondent
in America, on December 11, 1861, at the time of the *Trent*
affair:

> It is real, downright, honest desire to avenge old
> scores; not the paltry disasters of Baltimore and New Or-
> leans, but the foul and incessant abuse of the Americans,
> statesmen, orators and press, and if we are foiled by a sur-
> render of the prisoners, there will be an universal feeling of
> disappointment. We expect, however, that they will show
> fight—and *hope* it, for we trust we will give them such a
> dusting this time that even Everett, Bancroft and Co won't
> be able to coin victories out of their defeats.[2]

This was a common theme; thus William Aitken, who had visited
America in 1842, lecturing at the time on "The American Crisis"
in Ashton-under-Lyme, a cotton industry area, declared that "the
Americans hated the English with a deadly hatred; they envied
our greatness."[3] There were vocal Americophobe elements in
Britain, and they tended to center in those parts of the population that disliked democracy.

It is often asserted also, but is by no means so clear, that
there was widespread sympathy in certain English circles for the
Southern cause, as being an aristocratic one: such positive feeling toward the Confederate planter oligarchy is, in fact, not
easy to find. For one thing it was inhibited by the deeply ingrained antislavery sentiment of almost all Britons (which was
general despite the profits that many of them indirectly made
from the institution). Other factors, too, were probably much
more important than aristocratic fellow-feeling in arousing
sympathy for the South. One was the military skill and gallantry
of this outnumbered people. Another was the coincidental cross-
current of feeling for the low-tariff, free-trade views and interests
of the South, especially as protectionism became increasingly
dominant in the North. (Even Cobden had had initial doubts on

---

[2] *The History of The Times*, p. 373.
[3] *Ashton Standard*, Dec. 7, 1861.

this score: "In your case we observe a mighty quarrel: on one side protectionists, on the other slave owners. The protectionists say they do not seek to put down slavery. The slave owners say they want Free Trade. Need you wonder at the confusion in John Bull's poor head?"[4])

Finally, and perhaps most important, the European liberal's close association of nationality with freedom, which derived from events (for example) in Greece and Italy and Poland, led to a real muddle in the views of many Britons, even ones as enlightened as Lord Acton; he wrote to Robert E. Lee in 1866,

> I saw in State Rights the only availing check upon the absolutism of the sovereign will, and secession filled me with hope, not as the destruction but as the redemption of Democracy. . . . Therefore I deemed that you were fighting the battles of our liberty, our progress, and our civilization.[5]

Many pro-Southern voices were raised among cotton workers in the Lancashire area, contrary to the general impression created by the tale of the Manchester workingmen's missive to President Lincoln in January 1863.[6] As a speaker in Ashton, the Reverend H. F. Williams (vicar of Christ Church, Ashton-under-Lyme, from 1858 to 1865) put it, he took

> that opportunity of avowing without the slightest hesitation that his own sympathies were irresistibly enlisted in behalf of that brave nation which, with all their faults, were fighting a desperate and uphill battle in a war of independence . . . —a war for hearts and homes.[7]

In the end, after Lincoln's Emancipation Proclamation, the mass of public opinion in the country as a whole probably allowed its antislavery sentiments full rein and came to agree with Mr. G. L. Ashworth, when he declared in Rochdale, in the very heart of Lancashire,

---

[4] Quoted in F. J. Klingberg: "Harriet Beecher Stowe and Social Reform in England," *American Historical Review*, XLIII (1938), 543.

[5] D. S. Freeman: *R. E. Lee* (New York, 1935), IV, 516–17.

[6] Mary Arfon Jones: MS of thesis for the University of London.

[7] *Ashton and Stalybridge Reporter*, Jan. 31, 1863.

But they were quite willing, however long the struggle might last, to submit with patience to all the privations which the struggle might impose upon them believing, as they did, that sooner or later the freedom of the slave must be the final result of the struggle (cheers) . . . Nay, . . . better for the cotton trade of this country to perish, and to perish for ever, than that its future prosperity should be restored with slavery as its basis and foundation.[8]

The major motive of those who remained consistently hostile to the North was generally their antipathy to democracy. C. F. Adams, the American minister in London, was not without some justification for the view he expressed to Secretary of State Seward in 1864:

There is no longer any sort of disguise maintained as to the wishes of the privileged classes. Very little genuine sympathy is entertained for the rebels. The true motive is apparent enough. It is the fear of the spread of democratic feeling at home in the event of our success.[9]

As Jordan and Pratt put it, "The prevalent current among the English upper classes was far more definitely anti-Northern than pro-Southern."[1] On the other hand there were supporters of the South who were also ardent democrats, most notable among them being John Arthur Roebuck, an M.P. for Bath and then Sheffield, and a member of the Reform Club.

The press, of course, was deeply divided. Foremost among the opponents of the North was *The Times*, but, as Cobden put it in 1861, "Do not overrate the power of *The Times*. Seven years ago it had a monopoly of publicity. Now its circulation is not perhaps one-tenth of the daily Press."[2] The "Thunderer" was in fact in the process of losing its unique voice, as a result of the

---

[8] For a fuller treatment of the detailed make-up of public opinion, see Jordan and Pratt: *Europe and the American Civil War*, *passim*. Ashworth was one-time mayor of Rochdale and a vice president of the Manchester Union and Emancipation Society. He was a close friend of John Bright; *Rochdale Spectator*, Apr. 2, 1864.

[9] Quoted in E. D. Adams: *Great Britain and the American Civil War*, p. 300.

[1] *Europe and the American Civil War*, p. 87.

[2] Hobson: *Richard Cobden*, p. 350.

competition, especially from the local press, that resulted from the repeal in 1855 of the penny stamp-duty on newspapers. But its consistently anti-Northern and antidemocratic line still had an influence that must not be underestimated, for its prestige was still exceedingly high throughout the 1860's and 1870's.[3] The *Daily Telegraph*, too, although it "began its career by attacking the animosity shown by the high-priced papers to America",[4] was in fact, on the whole, hostile to the North, as was the *Morning Post*. *John Bull* was the fullest embodiment of Tory feeling, referring frequently to "The Untied States," and the *Saturday Review* was also unsympathetic to the federal government; the *Quarterly Review* carried many articles by Lord Robert Cecil, later Lord Cranborne, which were markedly antidemocratic. The *Index* was frankly a Confederate organ.

These views were also reflected in the local press. The *Ashton Standard*, to quote but one example, was quite capable of outdoing *The Times*. It wrote in an editorial about an address by what it called a pro-Northern "mob orator," Mr. Mason Jones:

> He sees not . . . any beauty in our balanced constitution. . . . All his hopes of liberty, all his aspirations after a higher social and political position, all his visions of the future are wrapped up in the contemplation of a huge, bloated, bullying Union of Democratic States, covering the area of North America. . . . They insanely imagine that if the democracy or republicanism of the North suffers a check in its onward advance, that, therefore, the cause of freedom and the advance of the human race to their natural rights will be thrown back for ages. . . . , the liberties of the working classes in England and on the Continent be crushed by a landed aristocracy. Now every thinking man knows this to be arrant nonsense. The liberties of Englishmen depend not on the success of the demand for liberty elsewhere; their own right arm and sense of justice is their salvation. . . . And should the Southern states of America separate from those they despise, and assert an independent position, what is there in that to endanger the cause of political freedom? . . . There is not in England a Southern sym-

---

[3] James Grant: *History of the Newspaper Press* (London, 1871–2), II, 36–7.
[4] *The History of The Times*, p. 359.

pathiser who does not abhor the traffic in human flesh as much as Mason Jones does. . . . We sympathise with the South, not because they are slaveholders, but because they are standing up manfully for the right of self-government. . . . But Mr. Jones warns us that when the dis-United States [comes] out of this crisis as an United States, she will have a navy which will be a match for England and France together. It will cost us 100 millions to be the equal of the re-United States, on the waves we have ruled too long. We don't believe Mr. Mason Jones. But if we did, we should say that this argument alone was sufficient to induce every Englishman . . . to use every effort to strengthen the South, that in the western hemisphere one power might counterbalance another, so that the peace of the world should not be at the mercy of a rabid and rampant democracy, whose love of glory and hatred of real personal liberty is less excusable than that of France or Russia.[5]

Some of the press, even in deeply involved Lancashire, did attempt to maintain impartiality as well as neutrality. *The Economist* declared that it was accused equally of being pro-Union and pro-Confederate, but, as we have seen, Bagehot meant by his version of impartiality acceptance of the inevitable fact of separation.[6] Jordan and Pratt sum up his attitude fairly: he was "thoroughly independent, but dominated by commercial considerations and by a steady distrust of democracy of the American variety."[7] On the other hand, there were individuals, such as Gladstone and Russell, who wished well to the cause of the Union, but who seemed on occasion to court the risk of doing that cause more harm than the unsympathetic but realistic Palmerston—Russell as foreign secretary (especially over the *Alabama*), and Gladstone in his ill-fated speech on October 7, 1862, proclaiming the nationhood of the South, which he later admitted to be an error of "incredible grossness."[8] Cobden, however, had written to Sumner in July of that same year, "I *know* that Gladstone would restore your Union tomorrow if he could, and yet he has steadily maintained . . . that . . . it is impossible that the

---

[5] *Ashton Standard*, Mar. 5, 1864.
[6] Aug. 1, 1863, p. 841.
[7] *Europe and the Civil War*, p. 87.
[8] Morley: *The Life of William Ewart Gladstone*, p. 535.

South can be subdued."[9] As Gladstone himself confessed on a subsequent occasion, the statesman who most scrupulously maintained his impartiality was Disraeli, whose "course of forbearance and prudence"[1] during the conflict entitled him, in Gladstone's view, to speak out strongly in justification of Britain's policy during the final stages of the *Alabama* dispute in 1871.

There was, however, a pro-Northern press quite equal in vigor to its opponents. The *Spectator* and the *Daily News* both remained firm supporters of the Union and, needless to say, John Bright's paper the *Morning Star* was strongly radical and democratic. But the "most widely-circulated radical paper of the day" was *Reynold's Weekly Newspaper*, and, except for some irritation at the administration's delay in grasping the nettle of emancipation, it stuck strongly to its opinion of March 1861 that, "The great democracy will come out of the present ordeal, even though civil war should be one of its stages, purified, regenerated, and more powerful for the promotion of human freedom than ever."[2] The *Beehive*, established in 1861 to represent the rights of the industrial classes, was, from the end of the following year, just as resolute. On April 29, 1865, one of its most eloquent contributors, Professor Beesly, wrote:

> The time has come when those who have unswervingly supported the Republican cause . . . at length find themselves in possession of the field, their opinions vindicated, their predictions verified, and their opponents silenced and abashed. . . . America is a standing rebuke to England. Her free institutions, her prosperity, the education of her people, the absence of a privileged class, are in too glaring contrast with our condition to be forgiven. The working men of England may not aspire themselves to political careers—they may even care very little for the right of giving a vote—but they sicken of a land where property and rank seem perpetually standing on guard against them; where they cannot open a newspaper—Tory or Liberal—without being insulted with the tedious controversy as to their vices and virtues; where the whole atmosphere

---

[9] Hobson: *Richard Cobden*, p. 365.
[1] G. E. Buckle: *The Life of Benjamin Disraeli, Earl of Beaconsfield* (London, 1920), V, 137.
[2] Quoted in Lillibridge: *Beacon of Freedom*, pp. 113–14.

is heavy with the blight of privilege, and the taint of a servile origin still clings to the man who lives by the labour of his hands. Unless a reform, not merely political, but social and industrial, be soon inaugurated, it seems likely that we shall see an emigration from England in the next few years no less remarkable than that from Ireland, where the national life is being slowly crushed out by laws and institutions modelled on our own.

But in the presence of the glorious triumph of our principles on the other side of the Atlantic let us take heart. Our opponents told us that Republicanism was on its trial. They insisted on our watching what they called its break-down. They told us plainly that it was for ever discredited in England. Well, we accepted the challenge. We staked our hopes boldly on the result. We forced them to keep their hands off when they wanted to break into the ring. We cheered on our Republican friends to their work, bidding them remember that the eyes of Europe were upon them. They have not disappointed us. Under a strain such as no aristocracy, no monarchy, no empire could have supported, Republican institutions have stood firm. It is we, now, who call upon the privileged classes to mark the result. They may rely upon it that a vast impetus has been given to Republican sentiments in England, and that they will have to reckon with it before long.[3]

So, too, the local press could provide radical and prodemocratic material to match that of the national journals (as well as pro-Southern yet also prodemocratic journals like the *Oldham Chronicle*). The *Rochdale Spectator,* Rochdale being the constituency of Cobden and the home of Bright, was, as might be expected, consistently prodemocracy and pro-Union. In 1861 it quoted with approval Cobden's message to a local dinner in honor of Bright:

We endeavoured to impose our laws, by force, on the Americans when they were three millions of colonists, and we know the result. Again, in 1812, . . . a war broke out on this very question of belligerent rights at sea, which, after

---

[3] Until George Potter and George Troup were ousted from control of the paper at that time, the *Beehive* contained articles strongly favoring the Confederacy. See J. R. Pole: *Abraham Lincoln and the Working Classes of Britain* (London, 1959), pp. 11, 15–16.

two years of mutual slaughter and pillage, was terminated by a treaty of peace in which, by tacit agreement, no allusion was made to the original cause of the war. With these examples, can we reasonably hope by force of arms to compel twenty millions of Americans . . . to accept our exclusive interpretation of the law of nations? . . .

An opinion seems to be entertained . . . that it is in the power of the governments of England and France to control if not put an end to the conflict. I entertain the strongest conviction, on the contrary, that any act of intervention . . . can have no other effect but to aggravate and protract the quarrel.[4]

But the radical, democratic, pro-Union cause gained a great deal, compared with that of its opponents, from the fact that it had a much greater degree of unity: this resulted from the ascendancy in it of John Bright. He had long been the leading advocate of drastic parliamentary reform, he continued to advocate it during the war, and he, more than any other single man, was responsible for the accomplishment of reform shortly after the coming of peace. The restraining effect that he exercised on any interventionist tendencies that Palmerston, for instance, might have developed are well known; as Henry Adams said of himself in his autobiography, he "felt peace in his much troubled mind, for he knew how careful the Ministry would be once they saw Bright talk republican principles before Trades Unions."[5] This renewed influence of Bright, which had been at a low ebb in the late 1850's, was to carry over from the war years into those that followed. The way it was exercised is best seen in a typical wartime speech, which he delivered in December 1861. He said in the course of the speech—and I quote it at great length in order to give the full flavor of the words of perhaps the greatest English-speaking orator in the nineteenth century[6] and the greatest British friend America has ever known:

---

[4] Dec. 7, 1861.

[5] *The Education of Henry Adams, An Autobiography* (Boston, 1918), p. 190.

[6] Although Bright did not perhaps equal the greatest passages of Lincoln, he possibly maintained a consistently higher standard. Both, in the full flood of mid-nineteenth oratory, spoke with the simpler tongue of the mid-twentieth century.

Now, . . . we look to the west. There we see a struggle in progress of the very highest interest to England and to humanity at large. . . . England is the living mother of great nations, on the American and on the Australian continents, and she promises to belt the world with her knowledge and her civilisation, and even with something more than the freedom which she herself enjoys. . . .

We know that in agriculture and manufactures, with the exception of this kingdom, there is no country in the world . . . in advance of the United States. (Applause.) With regard to inventions, I believe, within the last 30 years, we have received more useful inventions from the United States than we have received from all the other countries of the earth. (Hear, hear.) In that country there are probably ten times as many miles of telegraph as there are in this country, and there are at least five or six times as many miles of railway. The tonnage of its shipping is at least equal to ours, if it does not exceed ours. The prisons of that country—for even in the countries most favoured prisons are needful—have been models for other nations of Europe; and many European nations have sent missions at different times to inquire into the admirable system of education so universally adopted in their free schools throughout the Northern States. If I were to speak of this country in a religious aspect, I should say that, considering the short space of time to which their history goes back, there is nothing on the face of the earth besides, and never has been, to equal the magnificent arrangement of churches and ministries, and of all the appliances which are thought necessary for a nation to teach Christianity and morality to its people. (Cheers.) . . . I need not perhaps say further, that there has existed amongst all the population an amount of comfort and prosperity and abounding plenty such as I believe no other country in the world, in any age, has displayed. (Applause.) . . .

There is a most extensive suffrage, and there is the ballot box. . . . Every four years there springs from the vote created by the whole people a President over that great nation. I think the world offers no finer spectacle than this; . . . You may point, if you will, to hereditary royalty, . . . but to my mind there is nothing so worthy of reverence and obedience, and nothing more sacred, than the authority and the freely chosen magistrate of a great and free people (applause); and if there be on earth amongst men any right divine to govern, surely it rests with a ruler so chosen and so appointed. . . .

The free states in the North now stand before the world the advocates and defenders of freedom and civilisation. The slave states offer themselves for the recognition of Christian nations, based upon the foundation—the unchangeable foundation in their eyes—of slavery and barbarism. (Cheers.) . . .

I want to know whether it has ever been admitted by politicians, or statesmen, or people, that any great nation can be broken up at any time by the will of any particular section of that nation. It has been tried occasionally in Ireland, and if it had succeeded history would have said that it was with very good cause. But if anybody tried now to get up a secession . . . in Ireland . . . I am quite sure the *Times* . . . would describe with all . . . glee . . . the manner in which the Irish insurrectionists were cut down and made an end of. (Cheers.) . . . It has been said, "How much better it would be"—not for the United States, but—"for us, that these states should be divided." . . . There cannot be a meaner motive than this . . . that it is "better for us." For whom? The people of England, or the government of England?—that the United States should be severed, and that the continent should be as the continent of Europe is, in many states, and subject to all the contentions and disasters which have accompanied the history of the States of Europe. (Applause.)

I should say that if a man had a great heart within him, he would rather look forward to the day when, from . . . the Pole, to the shores of the great Gulf, the whole of that vast continent might become one great confederation of states—that without great army, and without great navy, not mixing itself up with the entanglements of European politics—without a Custom House inside, through the whole length and breadth of its territory—and with freedom everywhere, equality everywhere, law everywhere, peace everywhere—would afford at least some hope that man is not forsaken of Heaven, and that the future of our race might be better than the past. (Loud cheers.) . . .

Since 1815 . . . more than three millions of persons have emigrated from the United Kingdom to the United States. . . . At this very moment . . . there are millions in the United States who personally, or whose immediate parents, have at one time been citizens of this country, . . . They found a home in the far west; they subdued the wilderness; they met with plenty there, which was not afforded them in their native country; and they became a great people.

There may be those persons in England who are jealous of the States. There may be men who dislike democracy, and who hate a republic; there may be even those whose sympathies warm towards the slave oligarchy of the South. But of this I am certain, that only misrepresentation the most gross, or calumny the most wicked, can sever the tie which unites the great mass of the people of this country with their friends and brethren beyond the Atlantic. (Loud cheers.)

Now, . . . in a few years . . . the 20 millions of free men in the North will be 30 millions, or even 50 millions— a population equal to or exceeding that of this kingdom. (Hear, hear.) When that time comes, I pray that it may not be said among them that in the darkest hour of their country's trials, England, the land of their fathers, looked on with icy coldness and saw unmoved the perils and calamities of her children. (Cheers.) As for me, . . . I am . . . but one in the citizenship of this country; but if all other tongues are silent, mine shall speak for that policy which gives hope to the bondsmen of the South, and tends to generous thoughts, and generous words, and generous deeds, between the two great nations who speak the English language, and from their origin are alike entitled to the English name. (Loud cheers; during which the hon. member resumed his seat, having spoken for an hour and forty minutes.)[7]

But how important was the victory of the Union in facilitating or promoting the passage of the Reform Bill of 1867, the crucial measure for the democratic movement, which Dr. Gertrude Himmelfarb describes as "one of the decisive, perhaps *the* decisive event, in modern English history"? In this article her ably argued thesis expresses doubt as to the full validity of any of the causes usually given for the passage of the bill, including the influence of the American Civil War, which was in her view "more often the occasion for a debater's point than a genuine change of heart towards democracy."[8] By contrast she calls attention, with some justice (carrying further, it seems,

---

[7] *Rochdale Spectator*, Dec. 7, 1861.
[8] "Politics and Ideology: The Reform Act of 1867," in *Victorian Minds* (New York: Alfred A. Knopf; 1968), pp. 333, 348.

the ideas of Francis H. Herrick[9]), to the curiously indecisive, indeed meandering, manner in which Parliament actually dealt with the reform issue, and to what she considers, less justifiably, the apathy of the country. Plainly, such a view would make the significance of the Civil War to the British reform movement minimal, and would considerably reduce the importance that the historian must ascribe to its impact on life and liberalism in Britain.

The parliamentary proceedings were indeed muddled. They began with the House of Commons' rejection in 1866 of a substantial measure of reform introduced by Gladstone, as chancellor of the exchequer in Earl Russell's administration, and ended with the passage in 1867, under the hand of his successor Disraeli, of a much more sweeping measure, embodying urban household suffrage, which was far beyond the apparent original intentions of the government. Sir E. Bulwer-Lytton, M.P., and secretary of state for the colonies in 1858–9, described the latter bill as "the inevitable step to democracy."[1] But it seems a fundamental error of interpretation to divorce these proceedings from events outside Parliament—to declare, as Dr. Himmelfarb does, that "it was not the reformers inside or outside the House who forced up the price of reform, but rather the party leaders themselves." It may be true that the radicals, and even Bright himself, had occasional qualms of doubt about household suffrage, which, after all, did in actual fact constitute what Derby called it in 1867, "a great experiment . . . 'a leap in the dark,'" but it is equally probable that Bright was displaying moderation for tactical reasons, for his strange, almost intimate, relationship with Disraeli may well have convinced him that the leader of the House of Commons was, for whatever reasons, agreeable to a decisive degree of reform.[2]

The crux of the question seems to be the degree of public

---

[9] F. H. Herrick: "The Second Reform Movement in Britain, 1850–65," *Journal of the History of Ideas*, IX (Apr. 1948), 174–92; and "The Reform Bill of 1867 and the British Party System," *Pacific Historical Review*, III (June 1934), 216–33.

[1] *Hansard*, Vol. 182, p. 1245.

[2] Ibid., Vol. 189, p. 952; and see Trevelyan: *The Life of John Bright*, pp. 370–2.

apathy, and this is exceedingly difficult to gauge. Dr. Himmelfarb, for example, considerably writes down the importance usually given to the Hyde Park demonstrations of July 1866. She cites Karl Marx as evidence for the calmness of the Hyde Park meeting; he remarked that if only a few policemen had been killed, "there would have been some fun," but it may plausibly be argued that he had rather exceptional standards as to what constitutes a riotous meeting. There was a deep, conservative middle-class fear of violence in Britain that went back to the Gordon riots and Peterloo, but there had also been, since the failure of Chartism nearly twenty years before, an increasingly powerful tradition of public order. In a sense it was the relative lack of violence in the Hyde Park incident that made it so impressive a protest. It calls to mind the sentiments of Cobden in 1861: "We are, in ordinary times, *two* nations [Disraeli's phrase, be it remembered]: a busy toiling multitude, and a governing class. . . . But when a sufficient motive is presented to induce the busy millions to exert their power, they can always bring the aristocracy into subjection to their will."[3]

Looked at through the eyes of Bright, who was, despite working-class mistrust of his middle-class commercial and industrial interests and ideas, the central figure in the drama, the picture is vastly different. There were a number of public meetings in favor of reform at which many tens of thousands were present; one at Birmingham (Bright's own constituency) on August 27, 1866, was conservatively estimated at 150,000, well over one half of one per cent of the entire population of the country.[4] And, as Trevelyan points out, we must not judge the activity of political campaigns by the standard of a later age, when the degree of public participation possibly became greater, nor by an unconsciously different—for example, American— standard.

Certainly some of the speeches inside the House are far

_____

[3] Hobson: *Richard Cobden*, p. 353.

[4] J. T. Bunce, in the *History of the Corporation of Birmingham* (Birmingham, 1885), II, 110, gives the total population of the city as 319,932, although this no doubt excludes the inhabitants of greater Birmingham, since otherwise the attendance at the meeting would nearly have equaled half the entire city population.

from giving the impression that their authors did not think persons outside it had any views, or that those views were of little account. Indeed they clearly show the influence of popular pressure. In the debate on the first reading of Gladstone's bill, on March 12, 1866, Mr. Edward Horsman declared that the radicals, under "the leadership of the hon. Member for Birmingham," who was a revolutionary rather than a reformer and the evil genius of the movement, had passed out the word to

> agitate! agitate! agitate! . . . at simultaneous meetings in every district—monster gatherings in every town, petitions, addresses, deputations, leagues, placards, and all the machinery of uproar. The hon. Member for Birmingham was himself to rush through the provinces, to ride on the whirlwind and direct the storm . . . during those two months of democratic delirium . . . Democracy was upon us.

In the final debate on the 1867 Act in the House of Lords, on August 6, 1867, the prime minister, Lord Derby, said:

> I have felt strongly the necessity and the importance of passing this Bill—first of all because, after being accepted by the House of Commons, its rejection by your Lordships would have been fraught with imminent peril; and next, because I indulged a hope . . . that in the adoption of this Bill we may find the means of putting a stop to the continual agitation of a question which, as long as it remained unsettled, only stood in the way of all useful legislation.[5]

Outside the House the sort of language used by Bright was, equally certainly, not directed at merely notional supporters:

> I speak out of no hostility to any class or any institution. That man who proposes to exclude permanently five millions of his countrymen from the right which the constitution of his country makes sacred in his eyes, I say that is the man that separates Englishmen into two nations and makes it impossible that we should be wholly or perma-

---

[5] Horsman was a Liberal M.P. from 1836. By the 1860's, however, he acted with increasing independence in the House; and with Lowe he opposed Gladstone's Reform Bill of March 1866. His speech is in *Hansard*, Vol. 182, pp. 107–8. Lord Derby's is in Ibid., Vol. 189, p. 952.

nently a contented people. . . . Who is there that . . . will
dare to say, in the hearing of an open meeting of his countrymen, that these millions . . . are too degraded, too
vicious, and too destructive to be entrusted with the elective
franchise?

This he called on another occasion "the Botany Bay view" of the
workingman, and he continued, certainly not mincing his words:

And if there was more knowledge of the people there would
assuredly be more sympathy with them. . . . The class
which has hitherto ruled in this country has failed miserably. It revels in power and wealth, whilst at its feet, a
terrible peril for its future, lies the multitude which it has
neglected. *If a class has failed, let us try the nation.*[6]

The clearest proof that the 1867 decision was in effect taken
outside the walls of Parliament seems to lie not merely in the
activities of such bodies as the National Reform League and the
National Reform Union but also in the general acceptance of
the idea of Lowe (the great opponent of the bill) that "both our
political parties will bid for the support of the working-man,"
and therefore that they had inaugurated a "ruinous game of
see-saw." For whose support, if the country was not interested,
were the parties bidding, and how? In fact they were clearly
bidding in a democratic fashion for the support of Bright's five
million unenfranchised; the Act of 1867 at one blow increased
the electorate by 88 per cent, adding nearly one million men to
the voting registers. Both parties were in the end to have their
fair share of the support of *demos*, the Liberals first in 1867,
the Conservatives later in 1874. Indeed, as W. D. Jones has
cogently pointed out,[7] the Tory party had already, during the
actual course of the war itself, made a decisive practical move
in the direction of reform and democracy by seeking to pursue
a policy that would be popular with the people in the forth-

---

[6] G. B. Smith: *The Life and Speeches of the Right Honourable John
Bright, M.P.* (London, 1881), pp. 113–14, has the first quotation; Trevelyan:
The Life of John Bright, pp. 367–8, the second.

[7] "The British Conservatives and the American Civil War," *American
Historical Review* (Apr. 1953).

coming election. Once conservative political leaders had plainly
begun to seek, by the policies they pursued, to win votes in elections, parliamentary reform was not far away. Henceforth, as
the debates of 1867 in Parliament themselves illustrate, it was
precisely outside Parliament that governments had to look for
support. As *The Economist* put it in 1867, "the Conservative
metamorphosis is only a single instance, though, doubtless, the
strongest and most conspicuous, of the great change which has
come over the public opinion of England."[8] Parliament in the
forthcoming heyday of Gladstone and Disraeli remained the
central arena, but it was the spectators who increasingly influenced events by putting thumbs up or down.

But how important were the various influences upon the
popular mind compared with the American example? There had,
after all, been reform bills proposed before the Civil War, by
Russell in 1852, 1854, and 1860, and one proposed by Disraeli
in 1859, but all had failed, and there followed a period when
things remained "immobile"—indeed, Seymour talks of the
question being "submerged."[9] Bright's forceful campaign for reform culminating in 1859 had failed, and his reputation was at
a low ebb. It is possible that the reforming movement would have
remained in the doldrums, but with the outbreak of the Civil
War, Bright, as we have seen, was able to associate indelibly
in the public mind the cause of reform with the victory of the
Union. But as long as Palmerston lived and was prime minister,
he was a formidable, and in the view of some, an insuperable,
obstacle to the passage of a Parliamentary Reform Bill, as Russell had discovered. Derby put it this way on July 22, 1867:
"During the latter period of Lord Palmerton's protracted life,
no question of Parliamentary reform was raised in Parliament."[1]
When he died on October 18, 1865, however, Russell succeeded
him as prime minister and the way was opened for reform—or,
as Mr. Horsman described it five months later in the Commons,
the "downward movement in the direction of government by
numbers" which had been resisted by the "masculine, English

---

[8] Apr. 20, p. 439.
[9] Charles Seymour: *Electoral Reform in England and Wales* (New
Haven, 1915), pp. 246–7.
[1] *Hansard*, Vol. 188, p. 1779.

common sense"[2] of Palmerston, but which was now to be accomplished through the evil spell that Bright had cast over Russell. It is possible that in the final stages of the long parliamentary struggle that began with the introduction of Gladstone's abortive bill on March 12, 1866, and ended with the final passage of Disraeli's Act on August 15, 1867, the acute economic slump may have accelerated the pace of proceedings.

The sequence and logic of events, as originally suggested by Francis Herrick, would seem to be that from, say, the 1852 bill, parliamentary reform had become a sort of shuttlecock of domestic politics *within* the House of Commons, with bills proposed occasionally to entice or confirm the support for the administration of groups of M.P.s who favored reform. In the very different atmosphere of the years after the American Civil War, the rejection of the Russell-Gladstone Bill led to extensive and passionate *outside* agitation. This meant, as Disraeli realized, that the issue now had to be settled by some kind of reform Act, and he was resolved (he had after all himself proposed reform much earlier) that, whatever measure emerged, it should be passed by a Tory government. In this profoundly important popular agitation, the American example was, however, only one factor.[3]

How are we to assess the importance of the American example? It is argued[4] that the proceedings in Parliament "can hardly be associated with an event so far removed in time and place," but this ignores the fact that although the war was more than two years away, the United States was still very much there (more so, indeed, than ever)—a living witness to the victory of democracy. (Bright even said on one occasion that among working people there was "a much stronger interest in American politics than in the politics of their own country."[5]) And an analysis of the parliamentary debates on reform in these sixteen months certainly does not bear out the contention that the victory of the Union had little influence on them.

In the whole range of debates, on both bills in both houses,

---

[2] Ibid., Vol. 182, p. 102.

[3] For advice on this passage I am greatly indebted to my colleague, Michael Thompson.

[4] Gertrude Himmelfarb: "Politics and Ideology."

[5] *Hansard*, Vol. 184, p. 612.

some 3 per cent of the speeches contained references, often long ones, to the United States. This may not seem a high figure, but the number of speeches in Committee of the whole House, frequently exceedingly short and purely domestic or technical in character, make up a large proportion of the total. In the debates on the 1867 bill (which, of course, since it was the only one that passed, was the only one that went through all its stages) under 2 per cent of the speeches referred to America. But a much fairer gauge is the first bill, which only went through two readings, both, under British parliamentary procedure, of a general character; here no less than 10 per cent of the speakers cited the American example—a very substantial proportion in the circumstances. And, though references to the experience of other countries, especially Australia and France, also occur quite often, they do not do so with anything like the same frequency.

It is also argued, on the subject of Henry Pelling's "conventional thesis"[6] on this topic, that what he succeeds in showing is that both proponents and opponents of reform invoked America to support their prior prejudices and positions—not that they were influenced by America to change their opinions. In Parliament, it is true, the speeches that can be classified as anti-American and antireform were approximately twice as numerous as those that invoked the example of the United States as an argument in favor of the bills. (Only about one tenth of the total—including Disraeli's—could really be classified as impartial in their attitude to America.)

But what exactly does this demonstrate, if we bear in mind that the Act was, after all, passed? In the first place, there is ground for thinking that supporters of reform deliberately eschewed the American argument in the House of Commons (which was, of course, by definition still unrepresentative) lest it unnecessarily alienate some members; in the second place, that the pressure from outside, against which anti-American members were reacting so strongly, was not only powerful but decisively motivated by the example of the United States. Gladstone himself, for instance, in the course of his several parliamentary speeches, only mentions the United States three times, twice

---

6 Gertrude Himmelfarb: "Politics and Ideology."

briefly in passing, and once, on April 12, 1866, merely to refute most emphatically (but perhaps not too convincingly) the *Quarterly Review*'s explanation of how he came to introduce his bill:

> . . . the reforming zeal of the Radicals . . . was appeased by the sacrifice of the gallant Confederacy. But with the fall of Richmond Mr. Bright's heart was set at ease concerning the fate of the Government to which his true allegiance is given . . . And the moment Lord Palmerston was removed by death the Government instinctively felt that the time had again come round for buying off once more their insatiable ally. This time there was nothing for it but to reproduce a Reform Bill.[7]

Thereafter Gladstone seems deliberately to have avoided the charge of being pro-American by the simple expedient of not mentioning the United States in the House at all.

But outside Parliament, at Liverpool only five days before this speech, at a Reform meeting in the Amphitheatre, he devoted a substantial portion of his speech to

> another illustration which I can't refrain from mentioning, although it is possible that I may expose myself and others to some misunderstanding. I mean an illustration from the civil war in America . . . The point I ask you to look at is this: not the comparative merits of American institutions, but the one single and important point of the effect that has been produced in America by a largely-extended population franchise, by a widely-spread participation on the part of the people in the choice of their governors; the wonderful, the unexampled, the almost incredible effect that has been produced by that system of giving expression to the national will. . . . I say that . . . we ought . . . to appropriate the lessons which may be gathered from the experience of other portions of the human family.[8]

In other words, he talked a very different language in and out of the House of Commons. As Disraeli taunted him, he "made one of those pilgrimages of passion of which we have largely

---

[7] *Quarterly Review*, quoted by Gladstone in *Hansard*, Vol. 182, p. 1130.
[8] *Daily Telegraph*, April 7, 1866.

had a specimen . . . "—"he goes to Liverpool and confesses to American principles in their widest sense . . . Remember the speech he made a year and a half ago, which confounded his Colleagues, confused the House, and perplexed and agitated the country, when he based the title of admission to the suffrage on the rights of man," for the vote "was a moral right, and ought to be so considered."[9]

Even Bright himself did not mention America more than five times in the course of the Commons debates, and only one of those references was substantial (and in fact it was not directly apposite). He at any rate had no need to advert to the American example in the House—he, along with Cobden, had long been known as the "Members for the United States." On the contrary, he had every reason to play it down, because national chauvinism could easily be aroused in these upper-class, parliamentary circles, as he had discovered, by excessively frequent references to what one member called "his usual topic . . . America."[1] Here already is, in embryo, that fear of the increasingly overwhelming influence—social, political, and economic—of the United States on Britain, that concern for British national independence and even identity, which was to be a persistent theme of the next century; as Sir Hugh Cairns, attorney general in 1866, lord justice of appeal from 1866 to 1868, predicted with dismay, "This is the beginning of an Americanizing process in England."[2]

The range of arguments presented in the debates and the extent of knowledge of America and its institutions (even on the part of its enemies) are in themselves also evidence of the American impact, which would have been very different without the war.[3] The hostile references covered many topics, a number of which we have discussed already. Some saw a connection be-

---

[9] *Hansard*, Vol. 183, pp. 108, 111, 112.
[1] Ibid., Vol. 182, p. 1907.
[2] Ibid., Vol. 182, p. 1476.
[3] The author, who has himself lived his adult life during the thirty years from 1935 to date, feels impelled to judge the knowledge of American politics shown by British politicians then considerably superior to that shown by their successors a century later—at least till about 1950.

tween high protective tariffs and democracy, and opposed it on that account; as Lowe said, "America out-protects protection." Others feared, with Sir Thomas Bateson, that "when the Constitution of Old England had been Americanized . . . an attack upon the monarchy of this country would very soon follow." Many believed, again with Lowe, that "Bribery is every day making progress in America . . . and . . . if you pass this Bill . . . we are about to plunge into a sea of corruption," albeit Mr. W. E. Baxter, a Radical M.P. and from 1871 to 1873 joint secretary of the Treasury, declared, to many skeptical ears, that "there was nothing like bribery in American elections" and that (although he admitted some American corruption) "no systematic corruption such as prevailed here was known" there.[4] Similarly, there was a widespread belief that the independence of the judiciary would be weakened by democracy; as Lowe once more put it, "In the great State of New York the Judges are appointed for six years only, and further west the term decreases, until in Mississippi two years is the maximum. And why? In order that they may be able to administer the law not in accordance with the law, but in accordance with the popular sentiment." Viscount Cranborne correctly predicted a future issue in British politics when he said, "We were in danger of drifting into a system of nomination caucuses such as were to be seen in operation in America . . . [of falling] into the hands of the party managers, men . . . not usually . . . of the purest motives or highest character . . . ," concerned with "the hard machinery of local party organization."

More weighty was the criticism from history that "even in America . . . ," as Sir E. Bulwer-Lytton pointed out, "the true fathers of the future republic made a period of 150 years of education . . . precede the establishment of a democracy, the action of which is even now qualified by checks on the Representative Chamber . . . unknown to the English House of Commons." This was hard to distinguish from the argument for caution in any reform—or indeed the belief, in the famous words of a

---

[4] *Hansard*, Vol. 182, p. 2106 (Lowe); Vol. 183, p. 1857 (Bateson); Vol. 187, p. 793 (Lowe, on bribery); Vol. 182, p. 1235; Vol. 183, p. 1602 (Baxter).

parliamentarian of an earlier day, "Single-speech" Hamilton, that when it is not necessary to change, it is necessary not to change. Mr. Horsman expressed the specific fear that "that old tree of English liberty which had been the slow growth of ages and the admiration of nations should be transformed into the brazen image of ignorance and intolerance which the worshippers of Trans-Atlantic equality wanted to set up."[5]

This argument could, however, be turned on its head, as it was by Mr. Baxter:

> Those who studied the history of . . . events in Europe from 1789 to 1848, and those who had had, like himself, an opportunity of studying politics in the south-western States of America, where no admirable school system, as in the North, fitted the people for the possession of political power, might well be alive to the great perils of universal suffrage . . .

But this, he continued, was all the more argument for *moderate*[6] change like the 1867 bill. "It was the policy of determined resistance to all changes, and the persistent refusal to grant reasonable popular demands, which in the end endangered the constitution."[7] Lowe, by contrast, put a different gloss from some critics on the intentions of the Founding Fathers but came to the same conclusion as many of them as far as Britain was concerned when he warned the House that it must "beware of putting itself on too democratic a foundation." "You are aware," Lowe said,

> that the wise men who founded the Constitution of America knew that, with its democratic foundation, it would be absolutely impossible to have the English system, so they established a system under which the executive government and the Legislature . . . might have no point of contact with each other. The feebleness which that . . . imparted . . . may be seen in the discord which has broken out between the head of the Executive and the Legislature.[8]

---

[5] Ibid., Vol. 182, p. 2113 (Lowe); Vol. 187, p. 1357 (Cranborne); **Vol.** 182, p. 1245 (Bulwer-Lytton); Vol. 182, p. 99 (Horsman).

[6] My italics.

[7] *Hansard*, Vol. 182, pp. 1229–30.

[8] Ibid., Vol. 182, pp. 159, 158.

After all, some Britons asked, had not the American system recently come near to collapse in the greatest of civil wars, and were they not now (in the throes of the 1866 struggle between the President and Congress) once more on the threshold of disunion?

The fear of democracy went much further than the conviction that it was unsuited to the British Constitution, the feeling of Sir Thomas Bateson "'Nolumus leges Anglice mutare' . . . the laws of this country should be English and not American": it involved, in many British minds, a deep suspicion of the common people. As Lowe put it, on a theme already familiar to us, "We have inaugurated a new era in English politics this Session . . . We have . . . two parties of competition, who . . . are both bidding for the support of Demos . . . This will be the permanent condition of things. It is the condition of things in America." Behind this, embryonic but soon to become of the first importance, lay an even deeper fear of the effects of democracy on property rights; this was the threshold of the age when the specter of socialism was beginning to haunt the middle and upper classes. Even one so deeply concerned for the welfare of the oppressed as the Earl of Shaftesbury could point out that Mr. [Ben] Wade, the "President of the Senate," had been arguing in the Western United States for greater equality of property, and went on, "With the strong resemblance between the two countries, the frequent intercourse and interchange of ideas, and the fraternization which takes place between the two peoples, may we not expect that what is going on in America will be imitated here . . . ?"[9] As Lowe put it:

Look at America. There the working classes . . . have come to the conclusion that their political influence can be turned to account in other ways, and you see by this morning's papers that in the State of Pennsylvania—and I believe the same attempt is being made in several other States—they have arbitrarily fixed the day's labour at eight hours. . . . Imagine anything in the proceedings of this House at all analogous to what we are familiar with as every-day occur-

---

[9] Ibid., Vol. 183, p. 1857 (Bateson); Vol. 187, p. 797 (Lowe); Vol. 188, p. 1927 (Shaftesbury).

rences in America . . . Imagine such things as wild words
spoken even by a minority of the House about the Debt,
about shifting the incidence of taxation, removing it from
labour and placing it on capital. What would be the effect
on our credit in our mercantile and industrial position?

As he and other members pointed out, there was a fundamental difference in the geographical and economic positions of
the two countries (quite apart from the isolation of America,
which others noted), for the United States was still seen as the
rural nation she had been and not as the industrial giant she
was to become:

> And what remedy have we? We have nowhere to go to—
> no backwoods in which to found a new State out of the
> *débris* of the old one . . . [for] the chief property of America
> is the gift of nature. It is fertile land, noble rivers, bound-
> less extent of territory. But property in England is the work
> of art and of time. It has been piled up century after cen-
> tury by the industry of successive generations of English-
> men. The thing is artificial, it depends upon moral causes,
> upon a feeling of confidence and credit.[1]

Disraeli, in opposing Gladstone's bill, attacked Bright and the
idea of universal suffrage on the same lines:

> I think that this House should remain a House of Com-
> mons, and not become a House of the People, the House of
> a mere indiscriminate multitude, devoid of any definite
> character, and not responsible to society, and having no
> duties and no privileges under the Constitution. . . . If a
> dominant multitude were to succeed in bringing the land
> of England into the condition of the land in America, they
> would after all get but a limited area, and that only after a
> long struggle, in the course of which the great elements of
> our civilization would disappear, and England, from being
> a first-rate Kingdom, would become a third-rate Republic.

But the greatest, and perhaps most sincere, doubts were
felt on purely political grounds—especially that apprehension
which John Stuart Mill had expressed in his essay *On Liberty*

---

[1] Ibid., Vol. 187, pp. 791, 795.

(published in 1859) about the effect of majority rule upon the essential rights and liberties of minorities. He himself, strongly in favor of reform, came out on the whole in favor of the American example:

> Let me refer hon. Gentlemen to Tocqueville, who is so continually quoted when he says anything uncomplimentary to democracy [and whom Mill knew probably much better than any of his hearers], that those who have not read him might mistake him for an enemy of it, instead of its discriminating but sincere friend. Tocqueville says that, though the various American Legislatures are perpetually making mistakes, they are perpetually correcting them too.[2]

But others accused Mill of inconsistency; on one particular question, the virtual exclusion of the upper or cultivated minority from American politics, Mr. James Whiteside, M.P., and chief justice of Queen's Bench in Ireland from 1866 to his death, paraphrased Mill as saying of the United States "that that false democracy places the enlightened few at the mercy of the ignorant majority."[3] Earl Grey, from 1846 to 1852 secretary of state for the colonies, framed the accusation (which was to be put in its classic form later by Bryce) in his own forceful words:

> These fears, my Lords, can hardly be considered chimerical by those who have looked with any attention at what goes on in our Australian colonies, and on the other side of the Atlantic. It was long ago said, by Tocqueville, and the fact has since become far more evident, that the extremely democratic system of representation has utterly deprived the higher and more cultivated classes of society of all influence in the Government of the United States.[4]

There were those who defended the United States against the charge of majority tyranny, like Bright, or Mr. Shaw Lefevre,[5] who said that, "There was no country where the position and

---

[2] Ibid., Vol. 183, pp. 103–4 (Disraeli); Vol. 182, p. 1261 (Mill).

[3] Ibid., Vol. 183, p. 1866.

[4] Ibid., Vol. 188, p. 1779.

[5] It seems very probable that the Shaw Lefevre in question was secretary to the Board of Trade and then to the Admiralty, and from 1880 to 1884 first commissioner of works.

numbers of a minority were so closely studied, and where, even when unrepresented in Congress, it carried more weight in proportion to its numbers." But even he thought that in America it was "much less likely that a minority would be represented in proportion to its numbers than in our House of Commons."[6] And the majority of members clearly seemed to believe with Earl Grey that the House of Representatives was greatly inferior to the House of Commons, "partly . . . because in America the natural tendency of giving unlimited power to the numerical majority of the population is developing itself more and more. An assembly representing the numerical majority of the population is by its very nature intolerant of contradiction, and we know that a system of not only outvoting, but of silencing the minority, has been adopted in Congress by means of the 'previous question.' "[7] The Earl of Carnarvon, twice undersecretary of state for the colonial department, put it pungently, "In the United States, where all questions are pushed to an extreme, we have seen how a not excessive majority is able not only to disfranchise but absolutely to silence the minority."[8] But, as was his wont, Mr. Horsman expressed it most ferociously in declaring that any of the reform bills would be "fatal to the growth of liberty—that they were the creed of a small and noisy section of politicians of extreme opinions . . . and . . . that the two great political parties in the State were so evenly balanced that rival chiefs vied with one another in bidding for the support of that extreme minority."[9]

Not all Conservative opinion, inside or outside the House, was so immoderate or so hostile to America, or in fact the 1867 bill would never have passed at all. Thus Mr. Seymour Fitzgerald said to a meeting at Horsham in December 1865, talking of Bright:

> In his speeches he is constantly quoting to us the example of America. I am one of those who regard with the greatest admiration the system which has been pursued in America, the efforts they have made in the direction of self-govern-

---

6 *Hansard*, Vol. 188, pp. 1070–1.
7 Ibid., Vol. 185, p. 1906.
8 Ibid., Vol. 189, p. 460.
9 Ibid., Vol. 182, p. 98.

ment, the enormous extension of education, and the position which that Republic has been enabled to take in the
councils of the world. (Cheers.) There is no man more
willing to tender a meed of admiration to the course
pursued by the American nation than I am—Tory as I
am, and as Mr. Bright chooses to call me. But what will
suit a new country, with new institutions, . . . will not
suit a country where the interests are so complicated . . .
as in this country . . . What suits the one will not suit
the other; and it is impossible to reason, by any method
of analogy whatever, from the success of the institutions
of America that the same success would attend similar in-
stitions here. (Cheers.)[1]

In the House of Commons Disraeli showed the same caution in
using the American example, urging that precedents should not
be disregarded "in a country so practical in its politics as England." But he goes out of his way to avoid any tinge of that
arrogance in the English attitude to the United States which had
so long infuriated Americans:

Well, then take the case of the United States of America.
There you have a House of Representatives, framed by the
children of our loins, and certainly under the inspiration
of as pure a patriotism as ever existed. That also is elected
by universal suffrage. But does anyone contend that the
House of Representatives at Washington can equal in authority the House of Commons? And what is the cause of
this? Why, no doubt the American nation is inferior to us
in no point; it is of the same blood, the same brains, the
same intelligence, of equal energy, perhaps of more enter-
prize; but the House is elected by one class; there is no
variety in it.[2]

As he had said on Gladstone's bill, the late Sir George Cornewall
Lewis (Gladstone's former colleague)

would not have intrusted the destiny of this country to the
judgment of a numerical majority; he would not have coun-
selled the Whig party to re-construct their famous institu-

[1] *Daily Telegraph*, Dec. 16, 1865.
[2] *Hansard*, Vol. 183, p. 75; Vol. 185, p. 233.

tions on the American model. . . . Sir, it is because I wish to
avert from this country such calamities and disasters that
I shall vote for the Amendment of the noble Lord.

Disraeli changed his mind, or rather, accepted changes that
ultimately ended in democracy, but he was not persuaded to
do so by speeches and events inside the House of Commons. It
was the result of his realization that, in the state of public
opinion at that time, reform which "has been a Parliamentary
question for fifteen years"[3] had now to be effected in such a way
as to lay the agitation at rest. He would have preferred, perhaps,
to keep the decision insulated in Parliament, but he was essentially a realist in these matters and came to understand that it
was not possible, and so he accepted household suffrage in the
boroughs (though it may be noted that he effected only a very
limited redistribution of seats, so that the large constituencies
still remained relatively underrepresented). As Gladstone also
understood, once the idea of household suffrage entered the popular mind, there was no alternative to it: Bright wrote, "Wonderful conversions to Household Suffrage on every side. I begin to
be an authority with the Tory party! What next?"[4]

But, although it was the public view that prevailed, despite
the fact that those in Parliament who cited the American example
adversely outnumbered the others, the latter did make their
voices heard. Some spoke, for instance, in favor of such devices
as the secret ballot, as used in the United States, although others
denied its success or utility in determining the popular will.
The Duke of Argyll (one of the strongest supporters of reform),
however, pointed out in 1867 how relatively unimportant mere
constitutional differences were, since they arose from different
circumstances: "Last year we heard a great deal about 'Americanizing' our institutions . . . As regards American institutions and
our own, what is the essential difference between them? Has it
not been this—that ours have been a growth, theirs have been
emphatically a device—a device admirably contrived, indeed, by
some of the greatest Statesmen and politicians that ever spoke
the English tongue, but necessarily adapted to the circumstances
of a new country." But Mr. Butler-Johnstone cut even more ruth-

---

[3] Ibid., Vol. 183, p. 113; Vol. 185, p. 220.
[4] Trevelyan: *The Life of John Bright,* p. 372.

lessly through these mechanistic ideas, and declared them of less importance in Britain than America; he called for trust in the British people: "They would never very widely diverge from the magnetic currents of society, and . . . consequently they would be able safely to do in England what would be unsafe in America and in Australia. In these states of society they required checks and counterpoises, but in England he believed that they would be utterly vain and pusillanimous."

This theme, indeed, dominates the liberal arguments in Parliament and is justified by the actual facts of the matter in the country as a whole. Bright pointed out that without a truly popular electorate, "during the late war, the United States Government never could have been borne up, as they were, by the entire people."[5] Mr. Charles Villiers, president of the Poor Law Board and chairman of the Reform Club political committee, argued that the workingman had in the war already proved his fitness to vote:

> Are we not fresh from admitting the patience and fortitude with which the people in Lancashire bore their recent suffering . . . upon the occasion of the cotton famine? . . . I believe that much of the patience referred to arose from the decided and distinct opinions which they have formed respecting that great struggle . . . and I believe that everything which was done to induce them to clamour for a departure by this country from a policy of strict neutrality and non-interference completely failed; and they could not be shaken in their steadfast conviction that it was an unrighteous war . . . provoked for their own purposes by the Southern or Slave States.

Bright characteristically sought to bring the issue home to the House by moving the American example forward from war to Reconstruction:

> I ask Gentlemen opposite whether they mean to stop the working men of this country exactly where the 4,000,000 of negroes in the United States are stopped. Well . . . the negroes ask for further rights—and though it has been resolved not to give them the right of voting, I don't think in

---

[5] *Hansard*, Vol. 188, p. 1957 (Duke of Argyll); Vol. 186, p. 574 (Butler-Johnstone); Vol. 188, p. 1093 (Bright).

the United States that position can be long sustained. I am quite sure in this country that it cannot be sustained. If you are resisting millions of people behind those embankments which you have built up, how long will it be before the surging sea from the other side will wash over and destroy the embankments which you have raised?[6]

And, although he was addressing the House of Commons, it was to those millions of Britons beyond these embankments that Bright looked, and not in vain, for the surging support that forced Parliament, and both parties in it, to open the dikes to the seemingly irreversible flood waters of democracy. And he, and they, were without question encouraged in this resolute course by the example of their counterparts beyond the Atlantic. As he had said at Rochdale in 1863:

> The existence of that free country and that free government has had a prodigious influence upon freedom in Europe and in England. If you could have before you a chart of the condition of Europe when the United States became a nation, and another chart of the condition of Europe now, you would see the difference, the enormous stride which has been made in Europe; and you may rely upon it that not a little of it has been occasioned by the influence of the great example of that country free in its political institutions beyond all other countries.[7]

The impact of the Civil War and Reconstruction upon British life and liberalism cannot be seriously doubted, and the main weight of it was felt in the advancement of British democracy. Without it the later accord between Britain and America and their indispensable and vital joint defense of freedom and democracy would not have been possible. Without the victory of the North in the war, Woodrow Wilson fifty years later could never have spoken for both peoples when he declared, setting the tone for the twentieth century, that "The world must be made safe for democracy."[8]

---

[6] Ibid., Vol. 182, pp. 173–4 (Villiers); Vol. 182, p. 1901 (Bright).
[7] Quoted in Lillibridge: *Beacon of Freedom*, p. 121.
[8] James Brown Scott, ed.: *President Wilson's Foreign Policy: Messages, Addresses, Papers* (New York, 1918), p. 110.

France
and the Civil War

David H. Pinkney

*I*n *an attempt in 1872 to explain America's "republican super-stitions" to Frenchmen, the Unitarian minister Moncure D. Conway, a humanitarian reformer, insisted that the subject deserved as much attention in Paris as in London. He anticipated that the French defeat in the recent war against Prussia would make the former sensitive to America's Civil War experiences and earlier history.*[1]

Professor David Pinkney's more critical evaluation, which follows, argues the overblown characteristic of Conway's supposition, and of Motley's similar judgment of 1868 that "so close an electric chain unites America and Europe, so instantaneous are their action and retroaction, that the American civil war, at least in Western Europe, became as much an affair of passionate party feeling as if it were raging on that side of the Atlantic."[2] *His emphasis is rather upon the significant economic consequences of the American Civil War for France.*

---

[1] Conway: *Republican Superstitions as Illustrated in the Political History of America* (London, 1872), p. 4.

[2] John L. Motley: *Historical Progress and American Democracy* (New York, 1869), pp. 35–6.

The American Civil War had no single impact on France, and it affected not France but Frenchmen, touching different parts of the population in different ways. To intellectuals the war was an episode in a universal ideological battle between liberal democracy and authoritarianism. Partisans of the imperial regime looked to it and to the breakup of the Union for vindication of Napoleon III's authoritarian regime, which had replaced the democratic republic a decade earlier. Their republican opponents sought in it means to confound predictions that republics were doomed to failure. For many Frenchmen the central issue was slavery and the war a part of the struggle for equality in which France herself had long been deeply involved, both emotionally and intellectually. A few army officers took interest in novel aspects of the military operations—citizen armies, the utilization of railroads, the services of supply—but to most of their kind this war on the frontier had no lessons for practitioners of the sophisticated warfare of the Continent.

The first historical studies of the effect of the Civil War on French opinion relied largely on newspapers, journals, a few diplomatic reports, and parliamentary debates. The last sources yielded little, for the Legislative Body and the Senate rarely discussed the war. Diplomatic dispatches reflected newspaper opinion or the views of the writer's necessarily limited personal contacts and his equally limited direct observations. A newspaper or a journal might do no more than provide a forum for the owner or editor, and at most it would express only the ideas of the political faction that supported the publication. The *Revue des deux mondes* presented opinions of the Orleanists; *Le Siècle*, a Parisian daily, those of the moderate republicans; *Le Pays*, another Parisian daily, those of authoritarian imperialists. All were subject to censorship by the state, which limited their freedom of expression, and some were susceptible to bribery or less questionable blandishments that agents of the North and of the South offered them. Studies of the press have, moreover, extended little beyond the limits of Paris. The capital is, indeed, the fount of French ideas, but the provinces may hold opinions different from those currently accepted there, and one cannot assume that Parisian reactions to the Civil War either determined or reflected those of the country at large.

Napoleon III was deeply concerned wtih the state of public opinion in France. He ruled the nation by no legal right of succession, having seized power by a *coup d'état* in December 1851; a year later the Senate, which he himself had created, declared him the Emperor of the French. His title and his authority rested only on force and on the sanction of popular endorsement by plebiscites. On these two foundations of the Empire he lavished much concern, assuring the loyalty of the army, building an efficient police, and watching carefully the reactions of public opinion to imperial policies, to political debates, and to economic conditions. For information on the state of public opinion the imperial government relied heavily on the prefects, who were the administrative officials of the Ministry of the Interior in the eighty-eight departments into which France was divided, and the *procureur-généraux*, representatives of the Ministry of Justice in each of the twenty-eight judicial districts of France, who were similar to the district attorneys in the United States. All made periodic reports to their ministers in Paris, but the prefects' reports for the period of the Civil War are missing from the archives, and for the succeeding years they are short and perfunctory. The procurators sent to Paris four times each year full and conscientious reports on the state of the economy, public order, political activity, and popular opinion in their districts. In preparing them they drew both on their own observations and on the observations of their subordinates, who were ordinarily in close personal contact with a cross section of the population. The procurators' reports offer the best available measure of the reactions of Frenchmen throughout the country to the Civil War in America.[1]

---

[1] Lynn M. Case, ed.: *French Opinion of the United States and Mexico, 1860–1867; Extracts from the Reports of the Procureurs-Généraux* (New York, [c. 1936]), pp. ix–xii, 241–3 (hereafter Case: *Opinion of the U.S.*); Case: *French Opinion on War and Diplomacy during the Second Empire* (Philadelphia, 1954), pp. 1–14; Frank Lawrence Owsley: *King Cotton Diplomacy; Foreign Relations of the Confederate States of America* (2nd edn.; Chicago, [c. 1959]), pp. 63, 197–202; Donaldson Jordan and Edwin J. Pratt: *Europe and the American Civil War* (Boston, 1931), pp. 202–43; W. Reed West: *Contemporary French Opinion of the American Civil War* (Baltimore, 1924).

These reports reveal little public interest in the war except in districts where it threatened or actually hurt the local economy. In his first dispatch after the war's outbreak the procurator in Nancy dismissed it lightly. "As for the internal quarrel of the United States," he wrote, "except for some manufacturers whom it interests because of raw materials coming from America, it is occurring too far from us to exercise any influence whatsoever on public opinion." The *avocat-général* in Besançon, a subordinate of the procurator, in October reported a similar reaction. People in the area recognized the war as an important event, but, he continued, the conflict "was taking place far from France's frontiers and involved directly neither its security nor its wealth, . . . public opinion would scarcely be affected by the crisis in the United States." Interest might develop, he conceded, if the issue of abolition should become clearly involved.[2]

Early in 1862 the *Trent* affair and the threat of a conflict between Britain and the United States into which France might be drawn did heighten interest. At that time public opinion, even in textile districts concerned over cotton shortages and in manufacturing areas hurt by the closing of Southern markets, was generally sympathetic to the United States, uniformly hostile to Britain, and especially anxious for French neutrality.[3] The procurator in Douai in the industrial district of northern France made a report typical of those sent up to Paris in the first weeks of 1862.

> Opinion on the Anglo-American conflict is almost unanimous. . . . It is desired that war not break out, and our industrialists foresee that, even in case the blockade of Southern ports should be ended, cotton would still run too many risks of capture for it to reach our markets under acceptable conditions. At no price would one want to make common cause with England to destroy a navy that could someday be her rival, for us an auxiliary.[4]

Lyons and Saint-Etienne, hurt by the loss of markets in the South and at first sympathetic to the Confederacy and not averse to seeing American pride humbled, now had second thoughts.

---

[2] July 6, Oct. 22, 1861, Case: *Opinion of the U.S.*, p. 245.
[3] Ibid., pp. 243–4.
[4] Jan. 10, 1862, ibid., pp. 251–2.

But reflection has come (wrote the procurator in Lyon at the end of December 1861), and the facts have spoken. The internal struggle in the United States paralyzes business. It halts the progress of a necessarily friendly navy. A final break-up [of the Union] would only create an agricultural state in the South which would then be exploited largely by England.

Also since the *Trent* incident there are only ardent wishes for peace. All the classes are united by the same thought.[5]

But even in these months of widespread anxiety, the war failed to stir universal interest. The procurator in Nîmes wrote on January 31, 1862, that to his dismay only material interests could arouse public concern. "The American war affects it only by the commercial interests that it compromises or affects." The Emperor in his address at the opening of parliament on January 27, 1862, dismissed the war in two brief sentences.[6]

Soon after this—in the spring of 1862 and in the next twelve to fifteen months—the harmful effects of the cotton shortage and the loss of markets stimulated much more widespread concern, accompanied by a shift of sympathy to the side of the South. The procurators' reports from April 1862 through April 1863 noted a growing popular sentiment in favor of French mediation to end the war and hope for Southern independence. From Rouen, center of that district of the cotton textile industry hardest hit by the loss of Southern cotton, came word of the most agitated public opinion. The procurator's dispatch of July 10, 1862, declared:

The American struggle continues; and, in proportion as the hope of a solution appears to recede, the industrial crisis of which the conflict is . . . the sole cause, is aggravated to the point that one can fear, within a short time, a general stoppage of business. The concerns that so delicate a situation arouses in an industrious country like Normandy, dominate all the other events of general politics. . . . The big industrialists and, after them, almost the entire mass of the population, would like to see us intervene in the Amer-

---

[5] Dec. 27, 1861, ibid., p. 252.
[6] Ibid., p. 255; *Le Moniteur universel* (Paris), Jan. 28, 1862, p. 115.

ican conflict; they share the thought, . . . perhaps justifiable, that the union is becoming more and more impossible. . . . At Le Havre as at Rouen, all the sympathies are for the cause of the South.[7]

In both cities opinion favored France's joining Britain in an offer of mediation to the belligerents.

From another textile district, Alsace, came a similar report.

The events that tear apart the United States are followed by everyone with an anxious curiosity. This is to be expected in Alsace, whose industrial fate is so strongly involved in the conflict. . . . The cause of the Confederation of the South gains ground every day. Opinion is more and more in favor of that young, ardent, intrepid nationality that has given so many proofs of its virility and its energy. Any collective intervention of the European powers to put an end to that fratricidal struggle . . . would be viewed with satisfaction.[8]

Among the dispatches dealing with the third quarter of 1862 only two reported no sentiment in favor of French intervention in the war. One of these came from an exclusively agricultural area, scarely touched by the industrial and commercial consequences of the war. The other was from Paris, and the *avocat* who wrote it thought the desire for neutrality that still prevailed there a strange attitude in a district adversely affected by the war. Accurate measurement of public opinion in so large and diverse a city was virtually impossible, and the reporting officer had in his soundings perhaps encountered members of the liberal opposition, who were particularly strong in Paris and who hoped for a Northern victory as a vindication of free government.[9]

Possibly influenced by evidence of popular support for intervention in the war, the French government in November 1863 proposed to Britain and Russia that the three governments inter-

---

[7] Case: *Opinion of the U.S.*, pp. 257–8, 281. The quotation is on pp. 262–3.

[8] Oct. 12, 1862, ibid., p. 265.

[9] *Avocat-général* (hereafter A.g.), Agen, Oct. 6, 1862, Paris, Nov. 14, 1862, ibid., pp. 264–5, 266.

cede to impose a six-month truce on the American combatants. Neither London nor St. Petersburg would join in the *démarche*, and in January the French foreign ministry acted alone in offering to Secretary of State Seward the good offices of the imperial government to mediate the dispute between the United States and the Confederate States. Seward declined—politely but, nonetheless, making clear that the dissolution of the Union was not negotiable. French opinion, revealed in the procurators' reports for January and April 1863, almost unanimously approved the government's action. Resentment at its failure turned more against Britain for her refusal to cooperate than against the United States, an odd diversion in view of earlier anti-Northern sentiment. One procurator referred to "new fuel for the antipathy for the British people and their government"; another to "the ill-will of England"; and yet a third to "a new ill-will against England, adding itself to old resentments."[1]

Although some evidence suggested French concern with the issue of slavery at the beginning of the war and anxiety to see the institution ended in the United States, the news of President Lincoln's plans for emancipation and the Emancipation Proclamation itself stirred little interest. In Paris the liberal *Journal des débats*, which had long regarded slavery as the central issue of the war, devoted several columns to praise of Lincoln's policy, but it found few echoes in the country. Indeed, the procurator in Colmar in Alsace, where the cotton shortage had turned opinion against the United States, reported popular indignation at the hypocrisy of Lincoln's preliminary emancipation proclamation of September 1862, which ended slavery in the rebellious states but left it untouched in the North. From Dijon came reports of the press heaping crude abuse on local abolitionists.[2]

Beginning in the spring of 1863, French concern with the war declined. The nadir of the cotton crisis passed that summer as raw cotton began to arrive in France from other sources, prices stabilized, and unemployment diminished. News of the war itself excited little interest. Military operations dragged on

---

1 Ibid., pp. 257–8, on Nov. 1863. On Dijon, Jan. 8, 1863; Paris, Feb. 3, 1863; Douai, Apr. 1, 1863, see ibid., pp. 272–3, 275, 277.

2 Jordan and Pratt: *Europe and Civil War*, pp. 38–9; Colmar, Jan. 24, 1863, Dijon, Jan. 8, 1863, Case: *Opinion of the U.S.*, pp. 271–2.

through 1863 and into 1864, each side alternating between successes and reverses, neither able to win a decisive victory. Even so ardent a democrat and abolitionist as Louis-Auguste Blanqui, a pioneer socialist, admitted in October 1863 that he was bored with the war in America, bored with the pointless military operations, and tired of the "speeches of Father Lincoln, all steeped in Protestant hypocrisy." But for the Mexican problem he "would gladly let Biblical brutes exterminate themselves."[3] The official prose of the procurators was not so colorful, but it made clear the altered state of opinion. From centers of the textile industry came reiteration of hopes for peace, but even here interest waned. The procurator in Douai noted in July 1863, "The American conflict is too old for the necessities of that war to the death much to concern public opinion." In the district of Lyons the Polish revolt attracted more attention than the endless war across the Atlantic. Even the Rouennais, recently so agitated by the war, grew bored. "The affairs of the United States," declared the procurator on October 15, 1863, "no longer have the power to impassion anyone." Like most Frenchmen at this time they despaired of its early termination either by the victory of one combatant or by mediation from the outside. The presidential election of 1864 revived a modest French interest in the war, chiefly because a Democratic victory, many Frenchmen believed, might lead to a negotiated peace. Lincoln's re-election ended both the hopes and the interest. Sympathy for the South continued, but a desire for an end to the war came to prevail over the increasingly forlorn wish for a Southern victory.[4]

Word of the fall of Richmond reached Paris on April 15, 1865, and that afternoon an opposition deputy, Eugene Pelletan, exultingly broke the news to the Legislative Body. From the floor of the house came a cry of *"Tant pis!"* ("So much the worse!"). At the moment the deputies were discussing their reply to the annual address from the throne, and a group of liberals had just introduced an amendment hailing the imminent Northern victory.

---

[3] Maurice Dommanget: *Blanqui et l'opposition révolutionnaire à la fin du Second Empire* (Paris, 1960), p. 16.

[4] July 3, 1863, Case: *Opinion of the U.S.*, p. 282; Oct. 10, 1863, ibid., p. 284, on Lyons; Oct. 15, 1863, ibid., p. 285; and, on 1864, ibid., p. 281.

We have proclaimed from the beginning our sympathy for the northern states of America.

Thanks to heroic efforts, slavery is abolished. We shall be happy to see the powerful Republic of the United States, the natural ally of France, reestablished, and we shall hail with joy a triumph that will cost nothing to the cause of liberty.

The amendment won just twenty-four ayes; 195 deputies cast their votes against it. The final text of the reply presented to the Emperor the next day carried not even an allusion to the war in America.[5] The shout of *"Tant pis"* probably represented parliamentary and public opinion more accurately than the peroration of the handful of liberal deputies.

The sentiment in favor of the South drew sustenance from concern over the fate of the French expedition in Mexico should the North win the war. In 1862 France, Britain, and Spain had joined in the occupation of certain areas of Mexico to assure the protection of their citizens in that war-torn state and also to enforce the payments of indemnities promised to their nationals who had suffered losses of property in Mexico. From the outset the expedition was unpopular in France, and after the British and the Spaniards withdrew and French troops became involved in bloody fighting with the Mexicans in the spring of 1863, public opinion, as reported by the procurators, became almost unanimous in favoring the withdrawal of the expedition. While it remained in Mexico, the threat of French conflict with American troops worried Frenchmen. In the succeeding year, as the attitude of the United States government grew increasingly hostile, this worry nourished further resentment against the North.

Another source of French sympathy for the South, especially strong among imperialists, was hostility to liberal democracy.[6] Lucien Prévost-Paradol, a liberal journalist favorable to

---

[5] *Moniteur,* Apr. 16 and 17, 1865, pp. 461, 463.
[6] Case: *Opinion of the U.S.*, pp. 281, 310–11, 349; Jordan and Pratt: *Europe and Civil War*, pp. 219–20; West: *French Opinion*, pp. 30–1.

the North, analyzed it in an article in the *Courrier du dimanche* for May 10, 1865:

> A large number of Frenchmen have contracted in the midst of four sterile revolutions and after so many deceptions, a sort of general aversion to democracy, and for them the probable fall of the Republic was not without comfort. Still others, friends of democracy, but of democracy disciplined, conducted by a single master, or rather incarnate in a chief, saw with no less joy the appoach of a dissolution which would give proof to their theories and show once more that democracy cannot exist in this earth except in resigning itself not to be free.

These people were obviously not so much friends of the South as enemies of the United States. Their ideological aversion was akin to an unsophisticated resentment, noted by some of the procurators, against the United States for having progressed too rapidly and for crudely assuming its own superiority.[7]

> For a long time the presumptiousness of the great republic of the United States [wrote the procurator in Agen early in January 1862], its pretensions to the exclusive domination of half of that great continent, its disdain for old Europe and its institutions had aroused natural irritation, and if that claimed superiority finds itself contradicted by events, people are more interested in the just punishment of that juvenile and brutish boasting than in ideas of civilization and humanity.

This hostility to the United States drew some support, too, from the much more deep-seated feeling against Britain. Opinion in Alsace, persistently favorable to the Confederacy, in late January 1862 "saw in the covetous and ferocious obstinacy of the North, the English genius that it abhors." Popular association of leadership in the antislavery movement with Britain offered another

---

[7] West: *French Opinion*, p. 150, for *Courrier* quotation. Other data in Pierre Guiral: *Prévost-Paradol (1829–1870); pensée et action d'un libéral sous le Second Empire* (Paris, 1955), p. 296; Case: *Opinion of the U.S.*, pp. 246, 266.

curious channel for diversion of anti-British feeling against the North.[8]

Sympathy with nationalist aspirations—a currently fashionable view in France, sanctioned in word and deed by the Emperor himself, won the South many positive supporters among both imperialists and legitimists. They saw the war in America as a struggle for Southern independence, and the Southerners, they thought, had no less right to national self-determination than the Italians or the Poles, and the North had no more justification to oppose it than Austria or Russia.[9]

Some Frenchmen felt a sentimental attachment to the Southern "Cavaliers," whom they somehow transformed into Latins, in their struggle against the Anglo-Saxon "Roundheads" of the North. For some the attachment was a form of snobbism. "Slavery is well-patronized," wrote Cuvillier-Fleury to his former student, the Duc d'Aumale, in October 1861. "The planters have whiter hands than the men of the North. The Yankees are under the ban of the salons of Paris."[1] One might expect this in Parisian society, where Southern gentlemen and their ladies, frequent visitors and even residents before the war, were well-known, but it flourished, too, in the provinces, which had few if any personal connections with the South. In Alsace this particular form of admiration increased as the South managed to sustain the conflict month after month despite the overwhelming material superiority of the North.[2]

Both the Union and the Confederacy attempted to create and nurture favorable public opinion in France, using methods suggestive of the activities of twentieth-century public information offices. Immediately after the outbreak of hostilities the American minister in Paris, William L. Drayton, urged Secretary of State Seward to send to Paris an experienced journalist or a

---

[8] Jan. 6, 1862, ibid., p. 246; *Procureur-général* (hereafter P.g.), Colmar, Jan. 24, 1863, ibid., pp. 271–2; West: *French Opinion*, p. 150.

[9] P.g., Colmar, July 14, 1862, Jan. 24, 1863, Case: *Opinion of the U.S.*, pp. 260–2, 269.

[1] Guiral: *Prévost-Paradol*, pp. 296–7.

[2] Owsley: *King Cotton Diplomacy*, p. 63; Jordan and Pratt: *Europe and Civil War*, pp. 219–20; P.g., Colmar, Oct. 12, 1862, Oct. 16, 1863, Case: *Opinion of the U.S.*, pp. 265, 283.

literary man to work with the French press. Seward found the man in John Bigelow of New York, who had recently sold his interest in the *Evening Post* after twelve years as its co-editor and publisher. He already had business connections with a number of French journalists, and during several weeks of residence in Paris in 1860 he had become acquainted with French liberals and with Americans living in the city. In August 1861 Seward named Bigelow United States consul in Paris with the understanding that routine duties of the office would be handled by clerks and that he would devote himself to cultivating opinion favorable to the United States.[3]

Once in Paris, where he arrived in September 1861, Bigelow learned that he must start his task at the very beginning. Drayton, a courtly and dignified gentleman who spoke no French and had no contacts outside the foreign ministry, had done nothing to influence opinion. Most of the imperialist press was hostile, and even the liberal journals, though sympathetic to the Northern cause, then saw little hope for preservation of the Union. Within a few days of his arrival Bigelow launched a propaganda effort that before the war's end utilized almost every conceivable means—exploitations of personal friendships, official handouts, planted articles, and veiled and not so veiled bribery. Early in October 1861 the *Journal des débats* and *La Presse* published articles favorable to the North—the first by Edouard de Laboulaye, professor of comparative law in the Collège de France and author of a history of the United States, the second by a lawyer who for several years had practiced in New York. Bigelow wrote to both of them expressing his appreciation and his hope that he might meet them. Both did come to see him, and with Bigelow's encouragement both continued to write articles in defense of the Union. Some of Laboulaye's pieces Bigelow reprinted as pamphlets, which he distributed to intellectuals, journalists, and diplomats. Laboulaye in return accepted gifts of American books

---

[3] Margaret Clapp: *Forgotten First Citizen: John Bigelow* (Boston, 1947), pp. 122–6, 140–1, 146–56, 170–3, 189, 217–18; John Bigelow: *Retrospections of an Active Life* (New York, 1909), I, 533–6, 539, 540; Slidell to J. P. Benjamin, Apr. 7, 1864, in U.S.: *Official Records of the Union and Confederate Navies in the War of the Rebellion* (Washington, 1894–1927), Ser. II, Vol. III, p. 1078 (hereafter U.S.: *O.R.N.*).

from Bigelow, but his support of the North sprang from conviction, not from financial reward. Editors and writers of Orleanist papers came to Bigelow for suggestions on how to deal with controversial issues in French-American relations. He encouraged other writers and editors by buying large quantities of papers carrying their favorable articles. When he learned that an editor of *La Presse* was in financial difficulties, Bigelow quietly gave him a thousand francs from secret funds. He paid the gambling debts of a high official of the government's censorship office, as the Confederate agent Slidell believed, and Slidell reported home that this official was banning articles favorable to the South. The offer of the editor of *La Nation* to give Bigelow control of his paper's editorial policy on America in return for either a loan of fifty thousand dollars or purchase of half-interest in the paper Bigelow declined.

Bigelow himself did much writing in defense of the Union. When the *Trent* affair turned all shades of opinion against the North, he wrote an explanation of the United States' position, induced Winfield Scott, who happened to be in Paris on an unofficial mission, to sign it, and sent it to all the Parisian papers. They published the letter, and so, too, did *The Times* of London and many other British and Continental papers. He compiled a statistical reference book on the United States, released in 1863 by the Parisian publishing house of Hachette under the title *Les Etats-Unis d'Amérique en 1863*. The book had a favorable reception from reviewers, and it sold well. Bigelow helped the editor of *La Revue contemporaine* write a pamphlet on French-American relations during the war, emphasizing the French government's unneutral partiality toward the South, and he himself bought 1,650 copies and distributed them to influential persons.[4]

The Confederate government also attempted to shape French opinion in its favor, but because material interest predisposed most Frenchmen to sympathy with the South, Confederate efforts probably had even less impact than those of the North. In the first six months of the war the Southern government was so confident of support from the French élite and so sure that the shortage of cotton would soon force France as well as Britain to

---

4 Clapp: *Bigelow*, pp. 156–8; 184–7, 215–16; Bigelow: *Retrospections*, I, 386–90, 580.

intervene in the war that it sent no information officer to Paris. Soon after Slidell arrived in the city in February 1862, however, he became concerned about Bigelow's activities, and he urged that his government supply him with funds for similar operations. Richmond responded by dispatching to Paris Edwin De Leon, a former American consul in Alexandria, with $25,000 to be used, as De Leon put it, for "the manufacture and improvement of public opinion through the press." Even before he reached French shores, he had compromised his usefulness. Aboard ship crossing the Atlantic he opened and read the dispatches entrusted to him for delivery to Confederate representatives abroad. Slidell, outraged at his presumption, never forgave him and refused to introduce him to his influential French friends or even to give him information. De Leon in less than two years spent the original $25,000 and $5,000 more on the French press, and he claimed that he won to the Southern side several papers in provincial cities. Slidell charged that all the money had been wasted.

De Leon's influence on the French press is at best dubious, but clearly his experiences in France influenced him, notably in his opinion of French journalists. He found them a "mercenary race" lacking in any ethics, and late in 1863 he made the mistake of writing out this opinion in a dispatch to the Confederate foreign minister and in a letter to President Davis. Intercepted by the North and published in the *New York Daily Tribune* they ended his usefulness in France. In February 1864 the Confederate government recalled him.[5]

More successful, even in France, was Henry Hotze, the South's propaganda officer in London. Although only twenty-eight years old when the secretary of state sent him to Britain in 1862, he had had experience both in the foreign service and in journalism, having been secretary of the American legation in Brussels in 1858–9 and from 1859 to 1861 associate editor of the *Mobile* (Alabama) *Register*. In London he established a newspaper, *The Index*, and paid popular writers of the daily London press to contribute to it with the expectation that they would reflect pro-Southern views in their writings for their own papers. He distributed *The Index* to a few editors in France hop-

---

[5] Clapp: *Bigelow*, pp. 163–9; Owsley: *King Cotton Diplomacy*, pp. 163–8; J. Franklin Jameson: "The London Expenditures of the Confederate Secret Service," *American Historical Review*, XXXV (July 1930), 815 *n.*

ing to mold their views, but his attempt to enlist French journalists as writers had no success, possibly because his financial offers fell short of the going price, possibly because all the able journalists susceptible to such temptation were already in the pay of Bigelow. He did, however, influence the French press more effectively in another way. Early in 1864 he began to supply the Havas news agency with news stories on the South and on the war, and Havas, apparently convinced that they excelled any available from the North or other sources, distributed them, at no expense to Hotze, in Britain and on the Continent. French newspapers depended heavily on Havas for foreign news, and through it Hotze succeeded in placing the Southern version of events in America before thousands of French readers. Perhaps the Havas-Hotze news had some part in the growth of French sympathy for the South in the final years of the war, but economic concerns and fear for the French army in Mexico, should the North win the war, were surely more influential.[6]

Although the cause of the North won no widespread popular support, it did have many articulate defenders among intellectuals and among the liberal opponents of the Empire. Indeed, the Union cause in France became closely identified with political opposition to Napoleon III. Most important in this opposition were the Orleanists, generally well-to-do, educated supporters of the constitutional monarchy that had fallen in the Revolution of 1848, and Republicans, out of power since Napoleon's ending of the Second Republic in 1851. As forums for their opinions the Orleanists had the Parisian daily, *Le Journal des débats*, the fortnightly *Revue des deux mondes* (probably the most widely-read French journal of the time), and the meetings of the Académie française, an Orleanist stronghold throughout the Second Empire. The Republicans spoke through *Le Siècle*, which led all other French dailies in circulation, and *Le Temps*, another Parisian daily.

---

[6] Jameson: "London Expenditures," pp. 812, 822–3; Owsley: *King Cotton Diplomacy*, pp. 169–71; Clapp: *Bigelow*, pp. 183–4; Hotze to Benjamin, May 7, June 3, 1864, in U.S.: *O.R.N.*, Ser. II, Vol. III, pp. 1115–16, 1142–4.

The Union's individual supporters included a formidable array of intellectuals. Among them were Alexis de Tocqueville; Victor Hugo; Edouard de Laboulaye; Alphonse Guizot, distinguished as historian, Protestant leader, and first minister of King Louis-Philippe; the historian Henri Martin; Montalembert and Lacordaire, leaders of the Liberal Catholic movement; Augustin Cochin, editor of the Catholic journal, *Le Correspondant;* and Agénor de Gasparin, former deputy of the July Monarchy and a leading Protestant layman. They spoke publicly in support of the North—Lacordaire's inaugural address on the occasion of his reception into the Académie française included a defense of the United States and its institutions, and Laboulaye gave a series of lectures on the American Constitution at the Collège de France in 1862 and 1863.[7] They wrote articles and published books explaining the North's position in the war and France's relation to the conflict and defending the cause of the United States. From Cochin's pen came a two-volume work, *L'Abolition de l'esclavage,* published in Paris in 1862, a fourth of it devoted to slavery in the United States, which he saw as the source of all that country's troubles. Gasparin contributed two substantial volumes. The first, *Un grand peuple qui se relève; les Etats-unis en 1861* (Paris, 1861), was a veritable manifesto hailing the North as the defender of liberty; he predicted a Northern victory because, he held, injustice can never prevail over justice. A second edition appeared in 1862, and in that year Gasparin published a second book, *L'Amérique devant l'Europe; principes et intérêts,* equally sympathetic to the North and equally confident of its victory. Most widely read of the books by the intellectual friends of the Union was Laboulaye's *Paris en Amérique,* a collection of chatty essays and stories first published in 1863; the thirteenth edition appeared in 1865, the thirtieth in 1875. Witty and satirical, appreciative of the best of American life, it was particularly influential in combating prejudices against Yankees in fashionable circles in France.[8]

---

[7] Jordan and Pratt: *Europe and Civil War,* pp. 229–30, 240–1; Guiral: *Prévost-Paradol,* p. 296; John Bigelow: *Some Recollections of the Late Edouard Laboulaye* (New York [1888]), 8–9, 14.

[8] Théodore Borel: *Le Comte Agénor de Gasparin* (6th edn.; Paris, 1879), pp. 54–6; Bigelow: *Laboulaye,* p. 7.

The motives of the liberals' support of the North were mixed, but primary among them stood hostility to slavery. To these men slavery was the great issue of the war; the South fought to preserve it, the North to limit and, later in the war, to abolish it, and in these circumstances liberals could see no alternative to the Union. When word reached France of the ratification of the Thirteenth Amendment to the United States Constitution, Augustin Cochin urged the archbishop of Paris to celebrate a *Te Deum* after the solemn high mass in the cathedral of Paris on January 14, 1866. "These two sacred lines," he wrote, referring to the text of the amendment, "which end a crime expiated by war, merit thanks to God."[9] The liberals were anxious, too, that the American democracy should survive and grow strong as a model for free governments everywhere. They agreed with Lincoln, even before Gettysburg, that on the outcome of this war hung not only the fate of democratic government in America but the fate of any government "so conceived and so dedicated." In 1865 Prévost-Paradol writing in the *Journal des débats* hailed the re-election of Lincoln as a "solemn pronouncement upon the main point of the struggle, declaring to the entire world that the Union would not perish . . ." The *Revue des deux mondes* rejoiced that the popular endorsement of Lincoln and his policies would "console, reassure and encourage in Europe the friends of liberty."[1] The Liberal Catholics, Montalembert and Lacordaire among them, found their own special reason for defending the North—the American example of a free church in a free state, which they advocated for France.[2]

Nationalist hostility and suspicion of Britain added to the liberals' sympathy with the North. A strong United States provided a healthy balance to the maritime power of Britain—

---

[9] Owsley: *King Cotton Diplomacy*, p. 199; West: *French Opinion*, p. 152; Jordan and Pratt: *Europe and Civil War*, pp. 235, 239; and Henry Cochin: *Augustin Cochin, 1823–1872; ses lettres et sa vie* (Paris, 1926), I, 90–1.

[1] West: *French Opinion*, p. 143, on Lincoln's re-election; *Revue des deux mondes* (hereafter *R.D.M.*), Ser. II, Vol. XXXIV (Dec. 1, 1864), p. 760.

[2] Jordan and Pratt: *Europe and Civil War*, pp. 240–1; Charles de Montalembert: *The Victory of the North in the United States* (Boston, [1866]), pp. 3, 23).

France's "one enemy in the world," according to one optimistic liberal paper. Only the Americans could maintain the freedom of the seas against the pretensions of the English.[3]

Liberal spokesmen were not uncritically pro-Northern. Forcade, editor of the *Revue des deux mondes,* for a time doubted that the Union could ever be reforged once hostilities began, and like the *Journal des débats* he thought that Europe would eventually have to intervene to end the war and oversee the establishment of two republics. By early 1863 both the *Revue* and the *Journal* had decided that slavery was the great issue of the war, and they had become frank partisans of a Northern victory and opposed to foreign intervention.[4] In June 1861 Forcade had set down the guidelines of his publication's policy and at the same time expressed the basic position of the liberals and the intellectuals.

> Without doubt the cause represented by the northern states is the most in conformity to the principles and to the interests of France. French policy is incompatible with the pretensions of the Southern states, pushing their pro-slavery theories to the most barbarous consequences; French policy which . . . has found in the power of the American republic such a useful element of maritime equilibrium cannot watch without regret the rupture of the union. . . . From the double point of view of humanity and French interest we ought to hope that the policy of the north prevails and that the union be maintained.[5]

Defense of the United States served a partisan political purpose for the opponents of the Empire, permitting them to advocate ideas and institutions in America that censorship forbade their openly espousing for France. Laboulaye lectured not only on the virtues of the American Constitution but also, by implication, on the defects of the French political system. When Prévost-

---

[3] Owsley: *King Cotton Diplomacy,* p. 202; *R.D.M.,* Ser. II, Vol. XXXI (Dec. 15, 1861), pp. 1016–17; Guiral: *Prévost-Paradol,* p. 295.

[4] Jordan and Pratt: *Europe and Civil War,* pp. 237–9; *R.D.M.,* XXXI (June 15, 1861), 1002; Owsley: *King Cotton Diplomacy,* pp. 198–9; Louis M. Sears: "A Neglected Critic of Our Civil War," *Mississippi Valley Historical Review,* I (Mar. 1915), 534–5, 541.

[5] *R.D.M.,* XXXI (June 15, 1861), 1001–2.

Paradol praised the North for continuing in wartime to tolerate free assembly even of its enemies and the publication of a hostile press, his readers understood that he was thinking not only of the United States. To defend Seward's opposition to a foreign state in Mexico was a way to attack the Emperor's Mexican venture, and the liberals' generous eulogies of Lincoln in 1865 had double meanings.[6]

Largely an intellectual exercise of a handful of Frenchmen, the debate over the war scarcely ever reached the level of practical politics. Only rarely did the war come to the floor of the Legislative Body. In 1862 the proposed reply to the Emperor's annual address contained an innocuous paragraph deploring the war and its effects on French commerce and industry. The five republican deputies in the house proposed a clearly partisan amendment.

> France should not interfere in the civil war that devastates the republic of the United States of America; but it declares strongly that its sympathies are attached to the states of the North, defenders of right and humanity. It hopes that their victory will lead to the abolition of slavery, and that, thus, once more, it will be proved that the most grave crisis cannot be disastrous to a people who do not separate democracy and liberty.

The final clause slapped unmistakably at the imperial regime. "The Five," presumably wanting only to put their sentiments on record, shortly withdrew their amendment in favor of another expressing merely the hope that the war might bring about the abolition of slavery. The government's spokesmen opposed even this mild commitment, holding that to mix in the fundamental issue separating the North and the South would be inappropriate for a neutral state anxious for reconciliation of the combatants, and the majority rejected the amendment.[7] A year later a discussion of the reply to the Emperor's address produced a plea

---

6 West: *French Opinion*, pp. 14–15; Jordan and Pratt: *Europe and Civil War*, pp. 221, 242–4; Guiral: *Prévost-Paradol*, pp. 219, 379.

7 *Moniteur*, Mar. 14, 1862, p. 368.

from an imperialist deputy that the European powers hasten the end of the war by making clear to the Confederacy that they would never recognize its separate existence. This advice found no serious support in the chamber and no echo in the formal reply. Neither the Emperor's address nor the reply in 1865 made any reference to the Civil War, and the effort of a group of opposition deputies to write into the reply an expression of satisfaction with the Northern victory met overwhelming defeat.

The triumph of the United States had no discernible influence on the evolution of the Liberal Empire in France. In 1860 Napoleon III had begun to relax the authoritarian regime established a decade earlier; in that year he opened parliamentary sessions to the public, permitted debate on a reply to the annual address from the throne, and created ministers without portfolio to defend governmental projects in the legislative assemblies. He continued both to extend personal liberties and to increase the powers of parliament until by 1870 parties and press enjoyed a broad measure of freedom, and the Empire had become virtually a parliamentary monarchy with a responsible ministry. The initiative for these changes came from the Emperor himself. On only one occasion during the evolution of his new Liberal Empire did he refer to the example of the United States, and, paradoxically, his purpose then was to justify his resistance to demands for further reforms. In his address to the opening session of the Legislative Body in 1866, when the prestige of American democracy stood at a high point, he referred to the victory of "the great American Republic," chided those who complained of the absence of ministerial responsibility in France, and declared, "Our constitutional forms, which have a certain analogy with those of the United States, are not defective because they differ from those of England."[8] Nevertheless, when, three years later, Napoleon undertook the substantial modifications of the constitution that consummated the evolution of the Liberal Empire, he followed not the example of the United States' presidential system but the example of British parliamentary government. The institutions across the Atlantic apparently inspired neither

---

[8] Ibid., Feb. 10, 1863, p. 202; Feb. 16, Apr. 17, 1865, pp. 147, 463; Jan. 22, 1866, p. 660.

him nor Emile Ollivier, a leader of the opposition and later the Emperor's collaborator in the liberal reforms of 1869 and 1870.[9]

Frenchmen generally welcomed the end of the war in America, although many deplored the Northern victory. Some of the imperialist press appeared reluctant to concede that hostilities had indeed ended, predicting that the Southerners would continue to resist, even through guerrilla warfare. Nonetheless, the procurators were almost unanimous in reporting public satisfaction over the end of hostilities. "The end of the American war," wrote one official in the commercial city of Bordeaux, on July 13, "has been welcomed with the most lively satisfaction." From the textile district of Alsace the *avocat* in Colmar noted "the joy" with which the cessation of hostilities had been welcomed. Sympathy for the South had vanished, he added; "In Alsace one thinks only of congratulating oneself on the return of cotton."[1] Liberals were apprehensive lest the victors undermine the newly forged Union and tarnish the image of triumphant democracy by enforcing a vindictive peace, a concern widely felt in the country. Indeed, in one district public opinion favored official representations to Washington in support of moderation. Prévost-Paradol, despite his partisanship, expressed a concern that others must have felt over the greatly increased power that the United States would now exercise in the world. Its strength in North America would be irresistible, he wrote in 1865, and it would pluck Canada "like a ripe fruit." A year later he opined the passing of Europe's hegemony in the world and the beginning at an age of Anglo-Saxon predominance.[2]

The assassination of President Lincoln shocked all France. Universally deplored by men of every shade of political opinion, it brought forth an amazing outpouring of sympathy for the

---

[9] Emile Ollivier: *Journal, 1846–1869* (Paris, [c. 1961]), II, *passim;* Theodore Zeldin: *Emile Ollivier and the Liberal Empire of Napoleon III* (Oxford, 1963), *passim;* Guiral: *Prévost-Paradol*, p. 452.

[1] Case: *Opinion of the U.S.,* pp. 297, 300–4; West: *French Opinion,* pp. 145–56.

[2] West: *French Opinion,* pp. 147–8; Case: *Opinion of the U.S.,* pp. 297–8; Guiral: *Prévost-Paradol,* pp. 381, 504.

United States. The procurators wrote of "horror" and "indignation" inspired by the "execrable" and "odious" attack. "A universal movement of stupefaction," declared Forcade in the *Revue des deux mondes,* "of indignation, and of affliction was the reaction to that crime." Added to it was the dismay at the loss of the man on whom the French pinned their hopes for a speedy reconciliation of the warring states.[3]

The day after the news of the assassination reached Paris the American minister, Bigelow, spent most of the afternoon receiving delegations that came to express their condolences. The police, fearing street disturbances and possibly antigovernment demonstrations, restricted access to the streets leading to the legation. From his window that afternoon Bigelow counted sixteen policemen patrolling the streets. Bigelow himself decided against a public memorial service because in the "profound excitement" produced in France by the assassination he feared that it might set off a demonstration. Throughout May and into the following month the mail brought to the legation a stream of letters of condolence for Mrs. Lincoln and for the American government and people. Collected and published they occupy some fifty pages in a volume of diplomatic correspondence.[4]

The imperial government presented its formal condolences, and both legislative houses through their presidents associated themselves with the government's statement, but the great outburst of feeling had clearly partisan overtones. Praise of Lincoln often veiled an attack on the Emperor, and the government knew it. A group of opposition deputies asked the vice president of the Legislative Body to call a special meeting to express the assembly's sentiments on Lincoln, and when this move failed, seventy-four of them signed an address of sympathy and of their admiration for the United States and sent it to Bigelow. No representatives of the government appeared at the memorial service held in the American Episcopal chapel, but six opposition deputies

---

[3] West: *French Opinion,* pp. 148–9; Case: *Opinion of the U.S.,* pp. 297–304; Bigelow: *Retrospections,* III, 522–4, 549, 579; *R.D.M.,* XXXV (May 1, 1865), 242.

[4] Bigelow to Seward, Apr. 28, May 10, 1865, in U.S., Department of State: *Diplomatic Correspondence of 1865,* Part 4, "The Assassination of Abraham Lincoln," pp. 66–8.

were there. Liberals and republicans considered opening a public subscription to erect a monument to Lincoln. A republican newspaper in Nantes did start a campaign to collect hundreds of two-centime contributions for a commemorative medal; the police stopped it, but not before more than ten thousand persons had contributed. Twenty eminent opponents of the Empire, including Victor Hugo, Jules Michelet, and Louis Blanc, sent to the President's widow a gold medal inscribed to "Lincoln, an honest man, abolished slavery, saved the Republic"; the reverse bore the revolutionary motto, "Liberty, Equality, Fraternity."[5]

Some of the letters and addresses sent to Bigelow openly expressed hostility to the Empire, the signers apparently feeling confident that to an American they could safely speak their minds. A group identifying themselves as "republicans of Lyons" declared, "Let them [the citizens of the United States] know that they have brothers who . . . like them love liberty and understand the power of institutions that resist assassinations and oppose conspiracy." Accompanying an address signed by more than two hundred "democrats of Tours" was a letter stating that the hands of the workers who signed the address "will break in this country all the bonds and fetters that are put upon liberty under the specious pretext of measuring and regulating its government." From a retired merchant in Caen came the poetic but subversive prayer that the United States "may send back to France with the winds of the ocean—with its tempests if need be—those powerful blasts of liberty which France sent to them a century ago at its first awakening."[6]

II

The American war's most widely and deeply felt impact on France was economic. The war upset the established pattern of commercial relations between France and the United States. More

---

[5] *Moniteur*, May 2, 1865, pp. 523, 525; Bigelow to W. C. Bryant, May 16, 1865, Bigelow to Seward, June 2, 1865, Dec. 7, 1866, in Bigelow: *Retrospections*, II, 558, 596–7, III, 53–4; U.S.: *Diplomatic Correspondence 1865*, Part 4, pp. 50–4, 111, 133.

[6] U.S.: *Diplomatic Correspondence 1865*, Part 4, pp. 57, 61, 108–9.

important, it almost completely cut off the flow of American cotton to the French textile industry, and the prolonged shortage of raw cotton caused massive unemployment and serious distress in the principal cotton textile districts, stimulated a search for new sources of supply, and opened new markets for rival textiles. It disrupted the flow of French goods westward across the Atlantic, depriving many French industries of important markets and bringing unemployment and hardship to yet other areas of France. On the other hand, the upset of established commercial relations was not without beneficiaries in France: speculators in raw cotton (some of whom were themselves textile manufacturers); importers of Egyptian and Indian cottons; cotton producers in French Algeria; manufacturers of woolen and linen textiles; and one small, esoteric group that the peculiar circumstances of war brought briefly into the pages of history—the producers of resin.

In the trade between France and the United States the Southern states had a part both as exporters and as importers that was out of proportion to their population and area. Until the 1850's they supplied 80 to 90 per cent of France's imports from the United States, chiefly cotton and tobacco. The opening of the Middle West in the fifties gave greater prominence to agricultural products of that area, but in 1860 products of the South—largely cotton and tobacco—still constituted 60 per cent of French purchases in the United States. French exports to the United States were mainly luxury goods that found a large part of their consumers in the South. French silk, of which the United States was the second largest foreign consumer, constituted nearly a third of all French sales to the United States. Silk cloth from Lyons and ribbons from Saint-Etienne were fashionable and in demand. So, too, were fine woolen fabrics and quality printed cottons from Alsace. Two thirds of the American imports of wines and brandies came from France, and they ranked second after textiles among France's exports to the United States. America's other purchases included industrial products, most of them small and highly finished, such as watches and clocks, cutlery, leather goods, porcelain, glassware, perfume, and brushes. Most of this trade moved through Northern ports—Boston, Philadelphia, and especially New York. In 1860 only one port in the Southern states—New Orleans—had any substantial trade directly with Europe, and the volume of its freight amounted to only a third of that of New York.[7]

A few days after the attack on Fort Sumter in April 1861 President Lincoln ordered a blockade of the entire Southern coast from the Chesapeake Bay to the Mexican frontier. This alone would have sufficed to end most Southern shipments to Europe, since few European shipowners would assume the risks of defying the blockade, and the South had few ships of its own. Whatever gaps may have existed for the passage of the Southern product most prized in Europe—raw cotton—the Southerners themselves closed by embargoing the shipment of cotton. By withholding the raw material of a vital British and French industry, the Confederate government hoped to force Britain and France to intervene in the war to the advantage of the Confederacy, but President Davis's government had underestimated the adaptability of the cotton industry to new sources of supply and overestimated the pressure likely to come from unemployed textile workers. In 1863 he lifted the embargo, but the hoped-for revival of the cotton and tobacco trade did not develop. Blockade runners carried small quantities of these products to the Bahamas, Bermuda, and Cuba for reshipment to Europe, and some were sold across the Rio Grande to French and English dealers who had established themselves in Mexico when the port of New Orleans was closed, but the Union's blockade remained an effective barrier. Little of this cotton reached France. In 1863 the French imported only 254 metric tons of cotton from America, in 1864 900 tons; four years earlier they had taken 109,000 tons. They did continue to receive American tobacco, not through New Orleans but through New York, which during the war years became the center for export of Kentucky and Middle Western tobacco, which moved to the eastern seaboard by rail.[8]

The blockade raised no obstacle to French exports to Amer-

---

[7] Claude Fohlen: "La Guerre de Sécession et le commerce franco-américain," *Revue d'histoire moderne et contemporaine*, VIII (Oct.–Dec. 1961), 260–3; Arthur L. Dunham: *The Anglo-French Treaty of Commerce of 1860 and the Progress of the Industrial Revolution in France* (Ann Arbor, Mich., 1930), p. 271; Case: *Opinion of the U.S.*, p. 7.

[8] Fohlen: "Guerre de Sécession," pp. 264–7; Fohlen: *L'Industrie textile au temps du Second Empire* (Paris, [c. 1956]), pp. 284–5.

ica, for they entered almost exclusively through Northern ports, but since no commerce moved between North and South, France lost her Southern markets. More formidable as a barrier to French trade than the blockade were the Morrill tariff of 1861 and the tariff and revenue acts passed by Congress in the succeeding four years to pay the heavy costs of the war. The internal revenue acts levied a wide range of excise taxes, gross receipts taxes, license taxes, manufacturers' taxes, and an income tax, which siphoned off a part of the purchasing power that sustained the American market for luxury goods, to which the French particularly catered. The Morrill tariff, approved by the House in May 1860, was not a wartime measure, but in February 1861 the absence of senators from six seceded Southern states facilitated its passage through the Senate. The war with its ever mounting pressure for revenues did inspire and ensure approval of the subsequent increases in tariffs that came out of every session of Congress from 1861 to 1865, although some of the duties were admittedly protectionist.[9]

The Morrill tariff raised duties on most imports from 24 per cent to 30 per cent, but it hit the principal imports from France even harder. The rate on high-grade silk went from 19 to 30 per cent, on wines from 30 to 40 per cent, and the duty on brandies was changed from 30 per cent *ad valorem* to a specific duty of one dollar per gallon, which more than doubled the rate on the most commonly imported French brandies. In 1862 Congress added another twenty-five cents per gallon on brandies and in 1864 yet another, bringing the rate to $1.50 on the gallon. Just before the war's end it raised the levy to $2.00. The tariff of 1864 lifted the rate on quality silks to 60 per cent and imposed a combined specific and *ad valorem* duty on wines that could amount to as much as 125 per cent of value.[1]

The combined effect of the war and the tariff quickly made itself felt in scores of French communities from the English

---

[9] Frank W. Taussig: *The Tariff History of the United States* (8th edn.; New York, [c. 1931]), pp. 160–7; Edward Stanwood: *American Tariff Controversies in the Nineteenth Century* (Boston, 1903), II, 121–30.

[1] 11 *United States Statutes at Large* (1855–9), pp. 192–5 (hereafter *U.S. Stat. at L.*); 12 *U.S. Stat. at L.* (1859–63), pp. 178–98, 543–61; 13 *U.S. Stat. at L.* (1863–5), pp. 203–18, 492; *Congressional Globe*, 26th Cong., 1st sess. (1860), pp. 1977–8.

Channel to the Mediterranean, from the Bay of Biscay to the Rhine. The town of Saint-Nicholas d'Abermont near Dieppe saw its major industry—clocks and watches—wither for want of orders from its principal market, the United States. Before the end of 1861 employers there had cut back production by one third, and local officials were anxiously seeking stopgap jobs for the unemployed. Far to the south the perfume makers of Grasse and the hat makers in Aix-en-Provence complained of declining business owing to the loss of American customers.[2] Nearby, in Marseilles, sugar refineries that sold to the American market were hit by the dislocation of the war, and more particularly by the increase of the United States tariff from two cents a pound in 1861 to five cents in 1864, and by the rise of a native sugar industry in the United States. In 1864 several hundred workers were laid off, and the next year one refinery closed its doors permanently.[3] Pencil manufacturers in Lorraine lost their source of cedar, which they had imported from America, and basket makers in the same area and glass manufacturers both there and in the north found fewer American buyers and were obliged to reduce production. For the already ailing embroidery industry that occupied thousands of women in the rural areas of the departments of the Meuse, the Meurthe, and the Vosges, the loss of American markets was possibly a death blow; the industry did not survive the war.[4] In another eastern department, the Haute-Marne, four thousand persons were engaged in the manufacture of gloves, chiefly for American consumers. The war had scarcely started before American orders were cancelled, shipments refused, and the principal plant in the town of Chaumont had released a third of its workers. Not until late in 1862 did orders from Britain and Germany begin to pull the industry out of depression. Limoges, center of the production of porcelain popular in the United States, faced a bleak prospect in 1861. As

---

[2] P.g., Rouen, July 8, 1861, Jan. 9, 1862, A.g., Aix, Oct. 6, 1862, P.g., Aix, Jan. 9, 1863, Case: *Opinion of the U.S.*, pp. 17, 43, 84, 101.

[3] Fohlen: "Guerre de Sécession," p. 267; 12 *U.S. Stat. at L.* (1859–63), pp. 543–61; 13 *U.S. Stat at L.* (1863–5), pp. 203–18.

[4] P.g., Metz, Oct. 9, 1861, Jan. 8, July 8, 1862, Jan. 10, Apr. 9, July 9, 1863, Jan. 12, 1866, P.g., Douai, Apr. 17, 1862, Jan. 5, 1863, P.g., Nancy, Oct. 10, 1862, A.g., Nancy, Oct. 15, 1864, P.g., Nancy, July 18, 1865, Case: *Opinion of the U.S.*, pp. 22, 32, 51, 76, 108, 111, 128, 139, 192, 224, 235; Fohlen: "Guerre de Sécession," p. 267.

demand fell off that autumn, employers, anxious to hold skilled workers, tried to keep them at work, but some had cut the work-day by one half, and the procurator feared serious distress in the city before the winter passed. Within the year, however, new markets had been found, especially in England, and sales to the United States resumed. Both production and employment slowly recovered to approximate the prewar levels.[5]

The war and the tariff deprived the silk industry of four fifths of its American market, a blow that struck immediately at both wages and employment and in the long run contributed to the transformation of the industry from a craft to a factory industry. The prewar industry, especially in Lyons, had been oriented to a luxury market for high-cost, figured silks. The war virtually eliminated the large American part of that market and quickly idled about a third of the silk looms of Lyons and threw an equal proportion of silk weavers out of work.[6] Sales to England rose during the war years, but the increase proved to be but a fraction of the loss across the Atlantic, and the new English demand, like that which survived behind the 40 per cent tariff in the United States, was for low-cost fabrics. The sale of French figured silks abroad fell in value from 69,000,000 francs in 1859 to 26,000,000 in 1861 and after the war plummeted to 7,000,000 in 1868. This altered demand could be most economically served by power looms concentrated in factories, and during the war and after production shifted increasingly to them at the expense of the hand weavers of Lyons. In nearby Saint-Etienne, the center of the manufacture of silk ribbons, a similar combination of loss of American markets and changing demand—here owing to declining fashion of ribbons—threw the local silk industry into deep depression in the early sixties.[7]

---

[5] P.g., Dijon, Apr. 6, 1861, A.g., Dijon, Jan. 8, Oct. 11, 1862, P.g., Dijon, Jan. 8, 1863, A.g., Limoges, Oct. 5, 1861, Oct. 7, 1862, Oct. 18, 1863, P.g., Limoges, Apr. 3, July 27, 1862, Jan. 15, Apr. 16, 1864, Case: *Opinion of the U.S.*, pp. 20, 29, 53, 75, 89–91, 107, 146, 158, 176, 192.

[6] A.g., Lyons, Oct. 8, 1861, P.g., Lyons, Nov. 9, 1861, ibid., pp. 20–1; Monique Coulesque: "La Guerre américaine et la crise de la soierie lyonnaise, 1860–1864," *Cahiers d'histoire*, IX (1964), 261–9.

[7] Ibid., pp. 266–78; A.g., Lyons, Oct. 7, 1862, P.g., Lyons, Apr. 1, 1862; A.g., Lyons, Oct. 7, 1862, P.g., Lyons, Dec. 29, 1862, P.g., Lyons, Dec. 29, 1862, Apr. 2, 1863, Mar. 26, 1864, Mar. 29, 1865, Case: *Opinion of the U.S.*, pp. 53–4, 91–2, 110–11, 127–8, 176–7, 212–13.

The war and tariffs hurt French wine producers and exporters, especially in Champagne and in the Bordeaux district, whose clarets, Sauternes, and brandies had a considerable market in the United States. American imports of French wines fell off by a fifth between 1860 and 1863, and brandy imports dropped by three fourths in the same period. Beginning in the autumn of 1861 the government heard frequent complaints from Bordeaux and from Agen, in the same area, about the stagnation of business and the specter of bankruptcy facing exporting firms owing to the decline in American demand for wine and brandies.[8] In November it learned of similar troubles in Champagne, and here exporters reported difficulties in collecting on deliveries already made to the United States. In both districts officials and wine men themselves attributed their troubles to the war, apparently unaware of the new, higher tariffs, but all conceded that the poor quality of recent vintages contributed to the slackening demands at home and abroad. Indeed, the loss of American markets had no disastrous effect on the French wine industry, because the treaty of commerce with England drastically reduced British duties on French wines. The new rates, which were graduated according to alcoholic content, especially favored the light wines of Bordeaux, and the annual volume of wine exports from the Gironde district to England quickly doubled, and it continued to grow with only minor fluctuations throughout the 1860's.[9] No more complaints came from Bordeaux or from Champagne after January 1863. By that time, one may assume, houses that dealt chiefly with America had been able to replace their American customers with English buyers. Brandy producers, less favored by the peculiarities of the British tariff, continued to complain throughout the war.[1]

One remote corner of France prospered on the dislocation

---

[8] Fohlen: "Guerre de Sécession," p. 267; A.g., Bordeaux, Oct. 12, 1861, Oct. 6, 1862, P.g., Bordeaux, Apr. 15, 1862, July 11, 1862, P.g., Agen, Jan. 6, 1862, Jan. 7, 1863, Case: *Opinion of the U.S.*, pp. 18–19, 26, 46, 70, 86, 100–1.

[9] P.g., Paris, Nov. 26, 1861, A.g., Bordeaux, Oct. 12, 1861, P.g., Paris, Nov. 26, 1861, Feb. 3, 1863, ibid., pp. 19, 37, 115; Dunham: *Anglo-French Treaty*, pp. 283–6.

[1] P.g., Poitiers, Oct. 15, 1863, June 14, 1864, Feb. 10, 1865, P.g., Agen, Apr. 3, 1865, Case: *Opinion of the U.S.*, pp. 150, 185, 205, 209.

of French-American commerce. Hostilities cut off the supply of resin from the United States. In France the price more than tripled, and the Landes, the poverty-stricken pine forest area between the Garonne River and the Pyrenees, quickly found an unprecedented prosperity. It continued through the war years, but with the coming of peace the price of resin fell rapidly, and the Landes faced a difficult period of readjustment to its earlier situation.

French exporters and government officials placed the blame for loss of American markets on the war, and they assumed that once hostilities ended demand would rise at least to prewar levels. In fact, France never recovered her prewar position. German and Swiss manufacturers had captured much of the altered market for silks, and the American textile industry, expanded during the war and continuing to develop behind the high tariff wall that remained after 1865, supplied most of the demand for other textiles formerly purchased from France. By 1865 the duties on wines and brandies had reached almost prohibitive levels, and local substitutes, strongly entrenched during the war, continued to hold most of the market. The impoverishment of the South hampered recovery of the French position in that area. In the movement of trade westward from the United States to France cotton did not again achieve its prewar volume until the 1870's, and even then it shared the French market with other cotton-producing countries. Gold and silver replaced cotton as France's principal import from the United States, and petroleum occupied an increasingly important place among French purchases.[2]

All of these lasting changes in the pattern of French-American trade would probably have occurred eventually even had there been no Civil War. The United States was becoming increasingly industrialized—capable of supplying her own needs, and protectionist—determined to encourage home industries. The war at most simply accelerated this process. The building of the railroads into the Middle West and West made possible the movement of their products quickly and cheaply to Atlantic ports, and these products—precious metals, grain, cattle, petroleum—were

---

[2] P.g., Bordeaux, July 11, 1862, Jan. 13, Apr. 24, 1866, P.g., Pau, Oct. 4, 1862, July 13, 1865, ibid., pp. 70, 96, 102, 224, 237; Fohlen: "Guerre de Sécession," pp. 268–9; Dunham: *Anglo-French Treaty*, p. 252.

certain, war or no war, to occupy a larger place among American exports to France and to other European countries.

The war's most devastating impact on France fell upon the cotton industry. In the immediate prewar years the industry drew 90 per cent of its raw cotton from the United States. The blockade and the embargo drastically reduced this flow of raw cotton across the Atlantic. They never produced a cotton famine, since cotton was always available at a price—but the price was two or three times the prewar level. This soaring increase hit the industry in a period of difficult readjustment to English competition resulting from the signing of the treaty of commerce with Britain in 1860. For more than sixty years French cotton textile manufacturers had sheltered behind prohibitions on the importation of English cotton cloth, and in 1860 the industry was technically far behind its new competitor across the channel. Only in Alsace and in parts of Normandy had power looms commonly replaced hand looms. Spinning was generally mechanized, but inefficient machinery kept the price of thread high. The treaty gave French industrialists eighteen months of grace—prohibitions remained in force until October 1, 1861, and in those months many manufacturers, with financial assistance from the government, invested in new equipment and reorganized their mills to meet the impending competition. The rise of the price of raw cotton to unprecedented heights confronted manufacturers with pressing demands for increased working capital at the very time that they had made heavy capital commitments in new machinery.

These pressures were not immediately felt, however, for in the spring of 1861 France had very large stocks of cotton on hand. In 1859 and 1860 importers, benefiting from two bumper cotton crops in the United States, had increased their purchases by some 50 per cent over the levels of the preceding years. Indeed, the war, by reversing the decline of prices consequent upon abundant harvests, probably saved some importers and speculators from bankruptcy and forestalled the development of a crisis of overproduction in the industry. During the early months of hostilities France's surplus of raw cotton quickly dwindled. Le Havre's stocks dropped from 644,000 bales in mid-April to 187,-

ooo in October. For a time cotton moved westward across the Atlantic from Liverpool and Le Havre to Boston, New York, and Philadelphia, as the Union bought for its own needs. Some cotton even came back to Le Havre from manufacturers in the interior for re-export.

In the next four years almost no American cotton came to replace France's vanishing supplies. In 1862 a mere 295 metric tons got through the blockade to French ports, the next year even less, and in 1864, 900 tons. Some additional American cotton came from Liverpool, which continued to obtain reduced but still considerable supplies from blockade runners.[3]

In the first full year of the war France's total imports of raw cotton from all sources fell to forty thousand metric tons, a serious shortage but not a famine, and in the succeeding years the quantity gradually recovered from that low. Prices advanced only slowly in 1861, but in May 1862 the Union's capture of New Orleans destroyed the belief, widely held in France, that large stocks of cotton were available in America, and set off a feverish speculation. This, combined with disappointment of the expectations of arrivals of Indian cotton in quantity, forced the price index of high-grade American cotton at Le Havre (based on the average price for January–June 1860) from 150 in February 1862 to 215 in August and to 335 in September. Once again some manufacturers found it more profitable to sell their stocks than to retain them, and raw cotton again returned from the interior to Le Havre for sale. In the autumn prices declined, probably owing to Napoleon III's efforts to mediate the war, but moved upward again when these efforts failed. Northern victories at Gettysburg and Vicksburg again raised hopes of a quick end to the war and produced another decline in the summer of 1863, but the disappointment of these hopes led to a rise back above three hundred in October 1863. The combined effects of increased arrivals of Indian and Egyptian cotton, which ended fears of a cotton famine, and the increase in the bank discount rate in both France and Britain, which curbed speculation, kept prices relatively stable throughout the next year. When the end of the war

---

[3] Fohlen: *Industrie textile*, pp. 128, 284–7, 303, 502; Dunham: *Anglo-French Treaty*, pp. 186–93; P.g., Rouen, Oct. 12, 1861, Case: *Opinion of the U.S.*, pp. 24–5.

came into sight in the autumn of 1864, the price index dropped within three months almost to the prewar level.

For the individual manufacturer the critical problem was not to find cotton to buy but to find capital with which to buy it at inflated prices, and to finance technical adaptations to short-fibered Indian cotton. At the same time he had to cope with sharply fluctuating prices that threatened at any moment, in rising, to diminish the purchasing power of funds allocated for raw materials or, in falling, to leave the manufacturer with a stock of high-cost raw materials on hand.

The first troubles in the industry attributable to the war in America appeared in the autumn of 1861. In all four of the principal cotton districts—Alsace, Normandy, Picardy, and Flanders—production declined, in the latter two areas owing to loss of American markets, in Alsace and Normandy to the shortage of raw cotton. A number of small plants closed, others reduced hours of labor or released some of their workers. The procurator in Rouen reported in October that at the current price of raw cotton only the most efficient spinning plants could operate at a profit. Three months later profit margins had narrowed even more, and the undercapitalized and unmechanized producers faced serious difficulties.[4]

The rapid rise in cotton prices after the North's capture of New Orleans in May 1862 threw the Norman industry into deep depression. The district produced heavy cloth in which raw material was a larger element in the cost of production than in the finer percales of Alsace or the tulles of Flanders, and consequently the industry of the area was especially sensitive to fluctuations in cost of raw materials. The demand for its product was relatively inelastic, its market being composed of low-income consumers who lacked the reserves to absorb higher prices. The Norman weavers usually bought their supplies of thread in July, and in July 1862 they found prices 25 to 30 per cent above their levels six months earlier. Many of them lacked the capital to buy

---

[4] Fohlen: *Industrie textile*, pp. 256–7, 285, 294–9, 514; P.g., Rouen, Oct. 12, 1861, Jan. 9, 1862, Case: *Opinion of the U.S.*, pp. 23, 38–41.

at these prices, and others who had the means feared, in such an unpredictable market, to tie up unprecedentedly large sums in stocks. At the beginning of 1863 three fifths of the looms of Normandy lay idle, and in districts dominated by hand looms the level of idleness rose even higher. The declining demand for cotton thread at the currently inflated prices forced spinners to cut back their production. In some centers half or more of the spinning machines were closed down in 1863. Among thirty spinning establishments in one area of Normandy twelve had gone out of business by 1864. Larger establishments that could afford to adapt their machinery to Indian cotton were less hard hit, but they were few in number.[5]

In Picardy the industry, dominated as in Normandy by many small operators, was similarly affected. Alsace and the north, having more large establishments, weathered the cotton crisis somewhat better. In March 1863 one fifth of the spindles and one third of the looms lay idle in the Department of the Haut-Rhin, the heart of the Alsatian district. Many plants operated on reduced schedules, but few closed their doors, and those that did were commonly small, undercapitalized enterprises. In the Department of the Nord the presence of many large operators and the diversity of the textile industry—wool and linen as well as cotton held an important place—cushioned the impact of the cotton crisis. In Lille both the high prices of raw cotton and dwindling markets for certain specialties of the district forced a number of closings, but the woolen and linen industries absorbed many of the cotton workers, and in 1864 cotton manufacturers exerted themselves to hold skilled workers against the lure of competing textiles. In Roubaix small spinning businesses found themselves in difficulties, and six closed for lack of cotton, but the large establishments, which operated more than 80 per cent of the spindles, always managed to have a supply of cotton, and one of them even added to its capacity during the war.[6]

The cotton crisis brought grave personal distress to thou-

---

[5] P.g., Rouen, Jan. 9, 1862, July 10, Oct. 12, 1862, Case: *Opinion of the U.S.*, pp. 40, 83–4, 96; Fohlen: *Industrie textile*, pp. 257–60.

[6] Fohlen: *Industrie textile*, pp. 260–5, 267; A.g., Douai, Oct. 4, 1862, Oct. 2, 1863, P.g., Douai, Jan. 5, Apr. 1, 1863, Jan. 1, 1864, P.g., Colmar, Jan. 24, July 10, 1863, Feb. 2, 1864, Case: *Opinion of the U.S.*, pp. 88–89, 103–5, 108, 126, 138, 145, 156–8.

sands of Frenchmen thrown out of work or forced to subsist on the sharply reduced income of partial employment. Incomplete records, records that make no distinction between full and partial unemployment or between full-time textile workers and part-time workers with supplementary occupations, make impossible any accurate measurement of unemployment in the industry. Partial figures, can, nonetheless, vividly suggest the seriousness of the dislocation in many areas during the winter of 1862–3 and the succeeding spring, when unemployment reached its peak. A somber report from the procurator in Rouen dated January 10, 1863, declared that among 31,000 persons usually employed in the textile industry in the city 7,700 were completely unemployed, and another 5,400 worked reduced hours insufficient to support themselves and their dependents. The load on the city's public relief offices had risen from a usual ten thousand or eleven thousand cases to nineteen thousand. Among the total population of the Department of the Seine-Inférieure (which included Rouen) —790,000 in 1861—more than 82,000 textile workers were totally or partially unemployed at the end of December 1862, and diminished activity in related businesses—shipping in the ports of Le Havre and Rouen, for example—added to the total. The Comité national de Bienfaisance placed the number of unemployed textile workers in the Department of the Haut-Rhin in April 1863 just under fourteen thousand, in the Nord at ten thousand, and for the entire country at nearly a quarter of a million.[7]

These statistics reflect but dully the deep poverty and dire suffering into which unemployment threw textile workers and their families. The burden of relief exceeded the resources of charitable institutions, and supplementary aid had to be sought from both private and public sources. Normandy, hardest hit by the crisis, led the way. Late in 1861 the municipal government of Rouen raised a public subscription of 250,000 francs for relief, and the Conseil général of the department appropriated 1,500,000 francs, which the prefect matched from state funds, for work on roads in the department to provide emergency em-

---

[7] Case: *Opinion of the U.S.*, p. 43 *n.*; P.g., Rouen, Jan. 10, 1863, ibid., pp. 119–20; Fohlen: *Industrie textile*, pp. 266–7; Dunham: *Anglo-French Treaty*, pp. 197–8.

ployment. A year later a group of Norman industrialists led by Pouyer-Quertier, a member of the Legislative Body, alarmed by soaring unemployment, organized the Comité central de Bienfaisance au Profit des Ouvriers sans Travail de la Seine-Inférieure. The committee immediately opened a drive for contributions, a drive that extended beyond the limits of the department to Paris and to the Department of the Nord. Within six weeks it had raised two million francs, from which it made modest relief payments to jobless textile workers of the Seine-Inférieure. Similar committees appeared in Alsace and other textile centers, and in February 1863 they joined the Norman committee, now transformed into the Comité national de Bienfaisance au Profit des Ouvriers sans Travail de l'Industrie cotonnière. The new committee distributed its resources among all affected departments.[8]

The forthcoming private resources failed to match the demands for relief, and the state had to provide large sums both for direct relief and for public works. In March 1862 the parliament granted the Ministry of the Interior a special appropriation of 2,000,000 francs for these purposes, and in January 1863 it approved a project, vigorously supported by Pouyer-Quertier, appropriating 5,000,000 francs for public works in departments affected by the cotton crisis. In May it added another 1,200,000 francs to this sum. The government also sponsored in the winter and spring of 1863 a nationwide public subscription, which raised more than 2,500,000 francs. From this fund the minister of the interior distributed 600,000 francs among twenty departments in April and another 500,000 in December 1863. The crisis began to ease in the latter half of that year, but the shortage of cotton and the instability of prices prevented recovery of the industry to prewar levels of employment until the end of the war. The minister of the interior continued to make relief payments throughout 1864 and into 1865, the last distribution being in February 1865.

The efficacy of these relief measures is debatable. Louis Blanc, the radical republican leader of 1848, living in exile in England, condemned them as pitifully inadequate, a drop in the huge bucket of misery, and he contrasted the 2,000,000 francs

---

[8] Fohlen: *Industrie textile*, pp. 269–72; *Moniteur*, Jan. 1, 3, Feb. 1, 1863, pp. 5, 14, 148.

raised by Pouyer-Quertier's committee with the 13,500,000 francs that the first appeals alone brought forth in Lancashire. Loss of population in some textile districts suggest that there relief fell short of needs. On the other hand, nowhere during the crisis years did workers resort to violent protests against their lot, although this may reflect the efficacy of the police more than the adequacy of provision for the unemployed.

The easing of the cotton shortage in 1863 stemmed in large part from the arrival of raw cotton from new sources of supply, especially from India. Indian cotton had enjoyed little favor in the industry before the war; it had a short fiber that broke easily, and it was costly to work. In 1859, when France imported 114,000 metric tons of American cotton, it took fewer than 1,000 from India. The severance of the American supply, however, induced manufacturers with sufficient capital to adapt their machinery to Indian cotton, and in 1863 imports rose to 9,300 tons, in 1865 to 11,000.[9]

One obstacle to the rapid establishment of a flow of Indian cotton to France was the absence of commercial organizations prepared to handle the necessary transactions, for France had little trade with India. The gap was in part filled by the firm Maison Siegfried Frères, founded in 1862 by two Alsatians, Jules and Jacques Siegfried. Encouraged by several Alsatian industrialists they opened an office in Bombay, and it quickly prospered, selling in the season 1863–4 200,000 bales of Indian cotton at a profit of 1,250,000 francs. After the war they organized a branch in New Orleans, and the volume of its business soon surpassed that of the original office in Bombay.[1]

France also turned to Egypt as a substitute source of cotton. There French capital joined with British and German to finance a fourfold expansion of production between 1861 and 1865, and

---

[9] Fohlen: *Industrie textile*, pp. 272–81 (and pp. 275–6 n.), 359–60, 362; Dunham: *Anglo-French Treaty*, pp. 198–9.

[1] Fohlen: *Industrie textile*, pp. 361–2; André Siegfried: *Mes souvenirs de la Traisième République* (Paris, 1945), pp. 19–23. Through this stimulus to the rise of the house of Siegfried the Civil War exerted a delayed but important influence on French understanding of the United States, for in the next generation of the family, Jules' son, André, wrote one of the most perceptive of French books on the United States in the 1920's, *Les Etat-Unis d'aujourd'hui*, translated as *America Comes of Age*, and it owed something to the family's long connection with America.

French imports of Egyptian cotton rose from 3,300 metric tons or less in the immediately prewar years to 7,900 tons in 1863 and to 12,000 in 1864. Used almost exclusively for certain products manufactured in Alsace and in the Nord, it tempered the impact of the cotton shortage there.[2]

In the decade before the war the French government and some industrialists had been interested in developing French sources of raw cotton in Algeria. Stimulated by government subsidies colonists had planted in 1859 some 3,600 acres in cotton, but the product scarcely exceeded one hundred tons. The war-born cotton shortage revived interest, particularly among Alsatian industrialists. A number of companies were formed, including one in England, to acquire large areas of land in Algeria and to plant it in cotton, but technical difficulties—especially the problem of irrigation, the reluctance of the government to concede strategically important lands or land belonging to Arabs, and the uncertainty of future demand prevented the realization of any of the large-scale projects. Individual producers did respond to the stimulus of higher prices and increased their output of cotton or undertook to raise it for the first time. Production rose steadily from 119 metric tons in 1861 to a high of 1,022 in 1866.[3]

Although the substitute sources of supply never approached meeting the deficit created by the Civil War, one lasting effect of the conflict was the breaking of the American near monopoly of the French market for raw cotton. Demand for Algerian cotton scarcely survived the end of hostilities, but French manufacturers continued to buy both Egyptian and Indian cotton in large quantities. In 1850, 78 per cent of France's cotton imports came from the United States and in 1860, 93 per cent. By 1869, the fourth year of peace, the United States had recovered less than half the French market, and India's and Egypt's combined share in the

---

[2] Fohlen: *Industrie textile*, pp. 128, 356–9, 514; for the consequences of the cotton boom for Egypt and for one French banking house see David Landes: *Bankers and Pashas: International Finance and Economic Imperialism in Egypt* (London, [1958]).

[3] Fohlen: *Industrie textile*, pp. 346–55; W. O. Henderson: "The Cotton Famine on the Continent (1861–65)," *Economic History Review*, IV (1933), 204–5; Marie-Joseph Bopp: "Les Alsaciens et la culture du coton en Algérie pendant le Second Empire," *Actes du 79ᵉ Congrès national des Sociétés savantes* (Algiers, 1954), pp. 273–81.

market, which had been less than 5 per cent, now exceeded 35 per cent.[4]

The American war, so unfortunate for the cotton textile industry, proved a blessing for the linen and woolen industries. As the rising cost of raw cotton priced cotton fabrics out of the market, linens and woolens recovered much of the demand that they had lost to this young competitor in preceding decades. On the eve of the war the French linen industry suffered from high costs of raw materials that precluded effective competition with cotton goods, and an increase of imports after the conclusion of the treaty of commerce with England raised doubts of the industry's ability to survive English competition. The war brought new demands and higher consumer prices, which quickly moved the industry from threatening crisis to high prosperity. In the Department of the Nord, which benefited especially, the number of spindles devoted to spinning linen thread rose from 416,000 in 1863 to 513,000 two years later. Manufacturers in Lille hired spinners and weavers away from the cotton industry and recruited men from Belgium and Ireland. The linen workers themselves benefited from both steady employment and higher wages.

The woolen industry achieved an unprecedented prosperity in the mid-sixties attributable in part to technical advances in the industry initiated in the 1850's, to access to new sources of raw wool in Australia and the Argentine, and to the elimination of tariffs on wool in 1860, but also in part to the eclipse of its cotton rivals. In the principal centers—Roubaix, Tourcoing, Armentières, Reims—enterprising owners and managers reinvested rising profits in new machinery and new mills. Reims, which in 1860 had but a few hundred mechanical looms, by 1866 had five thousand, and in the same six years the number of hand looms dropped from twenty-two thousand to six thousand. Roubaix in 1860 had about a thousand power looms, seven thousand in 1866, and ten thousand in 1870. The number of spindles approximately doubled in the sixties, machine combing replaced hand combing, and production increasingly deserted the countryside to concentrate in urban factories. By the latter sixties the Department of the Nord, which included Roubaix, Tourcoing, and Armentières, with a million spindles and

---

[4] Fohlen: *Industrie textile*, pp. 128, 359, 362, 442, 514.

most of the country's power looms, had become the leading center of the woolen textile industry in France, an eminence that it owed in part to the Civil War's dislocation of the cotton industry.[5]

III

The economic impact of the Civil War operated impersonally and inexorably through dwindling supplies of raw materials and disrupted markets. The war's military impact reached France indirectly, usually filtered through the minds of professional officers, most of them with little sympathy for the particular problems of the American conflict, and it was much less strongly felt.

A popular American legend once gave currency to the belief that the battle between the *Merrimac* and the *Monitor* in Hampton Roads inspired European navies to adopt ironclad warships. In fact, European powers were then far ahead of America, either North or South, in the construction of ironclads. The introduction of naval shell guns in the 1820's and 1830's and of rifled guns in the 1850's made armored ships essential, and developments in the technology of iron production and in shipbuilding made them technically possible. The French led the world in drawing practical conclusions from these changes. In the Crimean War they had a number of armored floating batteries before Sebastopol, and these vessels sustained scarcely any damage from Russian shell fire, which wrecked conventional wooden ships. With the backing of Emperor Napoleon III, Dupuy de Lome, directeur du matériel of the Ministry of Marine,[6] drew plans for an ironclad fleet, and in 1858 and 1859 the government authorized construction of eight ironclad frigates and four armored floating batteries. The first of them went down the ways before the end of 1859. In September 1860 Dupuy de Lome, noting that in the past five years France had not built a single wooden warship, recommended expansion of the new fleet by

---

[5] Ibid., pp. 315–44, 461–5; Dunham: *Anglo-French Treaty*, pp. 224–35, 244.

[6] The *directeur du matériel* was the equivalent of the chief of the Bureau of Construction and Repair in the United States Navy.

the addition of ten seagoing ironclads and nine coastal defense ironclads, and the government shortly approved construction of ten high-seas vessels. When the war began in America the French navy had twenty-five ironclads afloat or under construction. The first engagement between ironclad warships—the encounter of the *Merrimac* and the *Monitor* in March 1862—came as no revelation to the French. It simply confirmed their own views of the future of naval warfare. At that time their construction program was already well established, and the American experience had no discernible influence on it. After 1862 they laid down only two additional ironclads before 1865.[7]

One innovation revealed at Hampton Roads—the revolving turret on the victorious *Monitor*—did attract the interest of French naval officers. Only a few months after the battle the Conseil des Travaux of the Ministry of Marine recommended initiation of studies of naval turrets. This task, too, fell to Dupuy de Lome, and over the next several years he worked out the practical design, subsequently adopted by all navies, of a turret mounted atop a circular, armored redoubt or barbette that revolved with the turret itself and reduced the danger of a hit on the turret reaching the powder magazine. The *Revue maritime et coloniale* in the 1860's published three articles on American turreted vessels, but in the same period it devoted more attention to the same type of ships in the British fleet.

The French navy sent only one senior officer to America as an observer of naval operations in the Civil War, and aside from mechanical means that the Americans had devised to work their artillery he found little of interest. The fullest official report on the wartime navy of the United States came from the pen of a very junior officer, a man twenty-six years old at the time the report appeared in 1866, which suggests the minimal interest of the French naval command in the conflict across the Atlantic.[8] The combined sea and land operations mounted by the North in Georgia, at Mobile Bay, and at New Orleans attracted the in-

---

7 James Phinney Baxter III: *The Introduction of the Ironclad Warship* (Cambridge, Mass., 1933), pp. 3–4, 99–101, 103, 111–13, 115, 302, 311; Bernard Brodie: *Sea Power in the Machine Age* (Princeton, [c. 1941]), pp. 171–8.

8 Baxter: *Ironclad Warship*, pp. 323–4, 330; "Table des matières," 1861–78, *Revue maritime et coloniale* (Paris).

terest of some officers. They saw these operations as confirmation of the French experience in the Crimea that naval attacks on land fortifications bring no advantage unless land forces are at hand to occupy them when they have been reduced or forced to surrender. In the later 1860's the French naval command worked on plans for a combined operation on the German coast, probably in part inspired by the American example, but when the war with Prussia broke out, the plans were still incomplete, and the navy lacked the means to carry them out.[9]

The minister of war in September 1861 announced that he would grant no requests for leave to visit America and that any officer who did go would lose his rank. A few officers eventually crossed the Atlantic to observe the war, and popular journals published reports on the military operations, the most well-known being that of the Orleanist prince, Joinville, son of the late King Louis-Philippe. It appeared under the pseudonym, A. Trognon, in the *Revue des deux mondes* and was later published as a book. Except for railroad operations, however, no aspect of the war attracted the attention of a single leading military figure in France before 1870, and none wrote about it.[1]

Important lessons were to be learned in America—lessons on the significance of increased firepower, on the need of entrenchments for protection, on the training of citizen soldiers and amateur officers. An occasional rare observer perceived them, but professional officers of the army of Vauban and Louvois, of

---

[9] V. de Mars: "La Marine en France et aux Etats-unis en 1865," *R.D.M.*, XXXV (Aug. 15, 1865), 777–819; Theodore Ropp: *The Development of a Modern Navy; French Naval Policy, 1871–1904* (unpubl. Ph.D. dissertation, Harvard University, 1937), pp. 25–38; J. Layrle: "Les Opérations maritimes dans la Baltique et dans la Mer du Nord," *R.D.M.*, XLII (July 15, 1872), 254; Edouard Chevalier: *La Marine française et la marine allemande pendant la guerre de 1870–1871* (Paris, 1873), pp. 9–14, 33, 108–9, 113, 139–77; Jay Luvaas: *The Military Legacy of the Civil War: the European Inheritance* (Chicago, [c. 1959]), pp. 89–90, 145.

[1] Luvaas: *Military Legacy*, pp. 80–6, 150; A. de Trognon: "Campagne de l'Armée du Potomac, Mars–Juillet 1862," *R.D.M.*, XXXII (Oct. 15, 1862), 798–867. On his return to Europe Joinville began a detailed history of the Civil War, which he left unfinished at his death in 1894. Its eight completed volumes were published in both France and the United States: *Histoire de la Guerre civile en Amérique* (8 vols.; Paris, 1874–83); *History of the Civil War in America* (4 vols.; Philadelphia, 1875–88; including the text of the eight French volumes).

Gribeauval and Carnot, and of the two Napoleons saw little to learn in a war fought in uncleared forests by masses of ill-trained civilians under improvised commands. The principal French military theorist of the 1860's, Colonel Ardant du Picq, insisted that the quality of soldiers was much more important than their quantity and that only long years of service in the ranks could produce the qualities of good soldiers—courage, moral force, discipline, military spirit.[2] Adolphe Thiers, influential politician of four French regimes, echoed this view in a speech before the Legislative Body in which he argued against a mass army for France. "Ask the experts," he advised, ". . . why the American Civil War cost more blood, more money, than any other war of our time and they will tell you that it is because soldiers who are not accustomed to war hesitate before positions instead of storming them." Had the war been fought by professionals, he claimed, it would have ended in a year and at one tenth the cost in casualties. By the war's end many French officers did recognize the American army, now forged by battle, as the equal of the best in Europe, but its experience had little relevance to France, they thought, because no European country could use two or three years after the outbreak of war to train an army and still survive.[3]

In 1867 Napoleon III and his minister of war, Marshal Niel, alarmed by the Prussian army's spectacular victory over Austria at Sadowa, undertook to improve the French army, but for guidance they looked not westward to America but eastward to Prussia. In the long debates on their army bill in 1867 and 1868 the American war was scarcely mentioned. The opposition deputy Jules Ferry praised the United States for disbanding its army after victory had been won in 1865. Ollivier noted that even in the crisis of war the American government had permitted drafted men to purchase replacements. A government partisan, contesting the opposition's advocacy of a volunteer army, observed that if the United States had possessed a per-

2 François Charles du Barail: *Mes souvenirs* (Paris, 1894–6), II, 288–290; Luvaas: *Military Legacy*, pp. 96, 227; Richard D. Challener: *The French Theory of the Nation in Arms, 1866–1939* (New York, 1955), pp. 15–16.
3 *Journal officiel de l'Empire français*, II (July 1, 1870), 1143; Luvaas: *Military Legacy*, pp. 227–8.

manent professional army in 1861 it could have ended the war in a few months and America would have been spared four years of bloody conflict.[4] Tactical lessons of the war had no better reception. The French army entered the war with Prussia in 1870 using infantry regulations essentially unchanged since 1833.

The transportation and supply services of the Union army were one aspect of the military operations in America that did interest French observers, as they did other Europeans, and indirectly they influenced the organization of a part of the French army. The first professional reports published in France on the Civil War came from the hand of a Swiss staff officer, the editor of the *Revue militaire suisse*, Major Ferdinand Lecomte, who was attached to McClellan's staff in the early years of the war. His *Guerre des Etats-Unis d'Amérique: Rapport du Département militaire suisse*, which appeared as a book in Paris in 1863, and his *Campagne de Virginie et Maryland*, a collection of documents published in the same year, emphasized the Union army's unprecedented and effective use of railroads and predicted that railroads would become increasingly important in all military operations. The French army's own military mission, finally dispatched to America in 1864, spent three months at the headquarters of the Army of the Potomac and also inspected hospitals, munitions plants, and supply installations. The mission's reports covered a wide range of subjects—causes of the war, resources of the two sides, analysis of field operations, supply and equipment—but the members of the mission, like Lecomte, were especially favorably impressed by the Union army's services of supply and transportation. The head of the mission, François de Chenal, a colonel of artillery, published in 1872 *L'Armée américaine pendant la Guerre de Sécession*, and in this book he again emphasized the importance of these services.[5]

The French in the 1860's had good reason to be interested in the American supply and transportation, for only a few years earlier the Crimean War and the Italian War had strikingly revealed the deficiencies in their own services. In both wars supply

---

[4] Emile Ollivier: *L'Empire libéral: études, récits, souvenirs* (Paris, 1895–1915), X, 293–349; *Moniteur*, Dec. 10, Dec. 24, 1867, pp. 1584, 1611; Jan. 11, 1868, p. 51.

[5] Luvaas: *Military Legacy*, pp. 86–7, 90–4, 149–50.

had been hastily improvised with results that combined the ludicrous and the tragic. The command had rushed troops to the Crimea in steamships but sent their supplies in sailing ships. The first French units across the Alps in 1859 arrived in Lombardy without tents or blankets, without fodder for horses or cooking equipment for men, and at the time of the principal battle of the war—at Solferino—desperately needed medical supplies lay on the docks at Genoa. Regulations drawn up in 1851 and 1855, when the French railway network was still under construction and far from complete, governed military rail transport in the 1860's.[6]

President Lincoln in 1862 had appointed a military director and superintendent of military railroads and granted him authority to seize any railroad equipment necessary to move men and supplies. This official had created a Transportation Department to operate military railroads and a Construction Corps trained and equipped to repair damage to railroads and to reconstruct lines captured from the enemy. In 1869 *Le Spectateur militaire*, a French professional military journal, published two articles on the American Construction Corps and pointed out that the Prussian army had copied it. Marshal Niel in that same year named a committee of army officers, railway officials, and representatives of the Ministry of Public Works to study reorganization of the military railway services. They prepared a plan, based closely on the newly organized services in Prussia and in Austria, which had been inspired in part at least by the American example. Unfortunately, the plan still lay on Niel's desk at the time of his death in August 1869, and his successor took no action on it. The weaknesses that in the Crimea and in Lombardy had been ludicrous and unfortunate were disastrous in war against Prussia. Only after this experience did the French army in 1875 reorganize its military railways, creating in that year—after the Prussian model—field railway sections and railway troops to build and operate railways and to destroy those of the enemy.

Except for the concern with transportation and supply the French military's modest interest in the Civil War scarcely sur-

---

6 Michael Howard: *The Franco-Prussian War: the German Invasion of France* (New York, [c. 1961]), p. 17; Edwin A. Pratt: *The Rise of Rail-power in War and Conquest, 1833–1914* (London, 1915), p. 138.

vived the end of hostilities in America. The Swiss Lecomte wrote a three-volume political and military history of the war that was published in Paris in 1866–7. A professor of military administration in the Staff School, Vigo Roussillon, at the request of the minister of war, prepared a thorough study of the American army. In addition to reiterating the usual praise of the supply services he emphasized the superior performance of the signal corps and the demonstrated value of cavalry as a weapon against railroads. His specific recommendations, however, were petty— that the French army adopt the American camp latrine, the quartermaster's wagon, and the McClellan saddle, and they probably reflected the French professional's fundamental disdain for this remote and amateur war of improvised armies.[7]

When in the autumn of 1870 France herself had to improvise an army, it was to the United States that her leaders looked for instruction. With the French professional army prisoners in Germany or besieged in Metz, the new Government of National Defense, which had replaced the fallen Empire in September 1870, acted in the French revolutionary tradition of the *levée en masse,* drafting into military service all Frenchmen between the ages of twenty-one and forty. Officers had to be found for this huge force. An official of the Ministry of War, Charles de Freycinet, had studied the American Civil War, and he now proposed that the French follow Lincoln's example of granting commissions to civilians. Despite protests from professional officers his proposal was embodied in the Decree of October 14, 1870. It guaranteed a supply of officers, and it granted them the same ranks and pay as their professional counterparts. Being in operation for only four months instead of for several years as in the United States it produced no distinguished commanders. The regional training camps organized to concentrate and train the mobilized civilian soldiers may also have been modeled on similar American institutions, but Freycinet did not openly acknowledge an American inspiration for this innovation as he did for the commissioning of civilians.[8]

---

[7] Pratt: *Rail-power,* pp. 17, 20, 138–9, 149–50; Luvaas: *Military Legacy,* pp. 87, 143–6, 149.

[8] Charles de Freycinet: *Souvenirs, 1848–1878* (Paris, 1912), pp. 148–149, 151–2; J. P. T. Bury: *Gambetta and the National Defense* (London, 1936), pp. 136–7, 143, 303; Challener: *French Theory,* p. 28.

The disastrous defeat of 1870–1 shook the complacency of the French officer corps and stimulated a more urgent interest in professional study of warfare abroad as well as at home. The echo of the last shots had scarcely died away when the minister of war in 1871 established the Revue militaire de l'étranger. Later in the decade the Ecole militaire supérieure was organized. The studies there and in other schools focused especially on the War of 1870, but beginning in the eighties a prolonged debate over the role of cavalry in modern warfare drew attention once again to the American Civil War. Many articles on cavalry in that war appeared in the professional journals such as the *Revue militaire de l'étranger*, the *Revue de cavalrie*, the *Journal des sciences militaires*. It was the subject, too, of a number of books published at Paris and Saumur, the seat of the Cavalry School, between 1883 and 1903, and occasional lectures at the Ecole supérieure de Guerre. These writers and lecturers drew varying lessons from the American experience, and they had little influence on official doctrine. Some of them pointed out the advantages to be gained by the use of cavalry to achieve mobile fire power, but they failed to shake the army's commitment to traditional shock tactics. No more successful in altering accepted ideas was a captain of engineers, L. Anger, who in his book *La Guerre de Sécession*, published in 1895, maintained that the American Civil War had demonstrated that modern fire power had shifted the balance in war to the defensive. Lee, he noted, had by skillful use of entrenchments been able to repulse attacks by Grant's superior numbers, and Grant himself had made effective use of entrenchments at Petersburg. The French doctrine of the offensive and the charge with cold steel was, he declared, suited to an earlier age but not to the present. Soldiers should now be trained in the improvisation of entrenchments. Anger even predicted the nature of the next war—a war of attrition in which trenches would have a critical place. He was, however, out of step with his superiors. His reiteration of warnings from the experience of the American Civil War, which had been discerned by some contemporary observers thirty years earlier, went unheeded in France until the First World War spelled them out in the blood of a million Frenchmen.[9]

---

[9] Luvaas: *Military Legacy*, pp. 96, 151–3, 154–64, 166–8.

The Civil War
and Central Europe

John Hawgood

*I*t appears unremarkable that a pioneering atmosphere should
attend a scholarly examination of the reception of the American Civil War in tsarist Russia or Latin America. But it is remarkable that historians have not invested significant amounts
of time and energy on inquiries concerning the effects in Central Europe of that war and its aftermath.

Professor Hawgood's realistic analysis illustrates how and
why Central Europe's concerns about America's destiny were
less intense than was true farther east or west. The Habsburg
and Prussian societies accommodated themselves easily to the
New World's distresses. But if the economic and intellectual
effects of the Civil War were less direct and sharp in Central
Europe than in England, France, or Russia, there were effects.
They deserve attention and description.

Professor Hawgood is well prepared to provide the latter.
A scholar of unusual versatility, his publications have inquired
into the evolution of modern European constitutions, examined
T. O. Larkin's California consulship, and, in a recent prize-win-
ning volume, surveyed America's successive western frontiers.
An Englishman, on the history faculty of the University of Bir-

mingham, Professor Hawgood's wide-ranging interests and impressive competencies now afford insight into American and Central European reciprocation and interaction a century ago.

The impact of the American Civil War in the countries of Central Europe—the German states and the Habsburg monarchy—was not everywhere very profound, but varied widely both in degree and in kind. In the states of *Klein-deutschland* it was confused and blurred by the peoples' varying interests and their different levels of public education and information, and for a number of reasons was most positive in Bismarck's Prussia. In many parts of the Austrian and Hungarian realms it must all have seemed like a dream, for this was before the mass emigration to America had really commenced from those areas; America was a remote and little understood continent.

Here many remnants of feudalism still survived, and a great gulf still separated the governing class, with its client intelligentsia (of all national groups), from the handful of educated liberals and nationalists (many of whom, like Kossuth, had been driven into exile in 1849) and the relatively inert mass of provincial peasants and laborers. Some interest stirred, especially in and around the court at Vienna, with the startling news, in 1863, that an Austrian archduke was being made emperor of Mexico—an event that Americans, both Northern and Southern, seemed, most unreasonably, to object to with almost equal vehemence—but there were many things much nearer home than the Mexican adventure or the War Between the States to worry about—crop failures, taxation, the persecution of minorities for both ethnic and religious reasons, the risk of further losses of territory and prestige in Italy, the Schleswig-Holstein question, the increasingly overbearing attitude of Prussia, the continuing problems of relations with Russia and with the Sublime Porte, even the latest Strauss waltz or the forthcoming Opera Ball—all of which seemed at the time more important to the subjects of the Habsburgs.

Both groups of states, or provinces—overlapping within the moth-eaten fabric of the *Bund* which was still lingering on at Frankfurt am Main as an Austrian status symbol more than anything else—had for generations been faced with problems of federal union and particularism comparable in many ways to those the United States had appeared to solve by a happy compromise in 1787. This compromise had withstood the onslaught both of the Hartford conventionists and of the South Carolina nullifiers. The United States had provided an example and a stimulus to men in Switzerland, in the German states, and in the Habsburg crown lands who also desired "a more perfect union." This had been achieved in Switzerland in 1848, after the short and sharp "Sonderbund War." It had been drafted for Germany as a whole in the Frankfurt Constitution of 1849 and for the Austrian Empire in the Kremsier Constitution of the same year. These last two were both to be killed on the drawing board by the resurgent forces of reaction and autocracy, which were greatly aided by an even more deeply seated particularism than had existed either in the Catholic cantons of Switzerland or among the New England Federalists.

It was not realized in Central Europe, even in the late 1850's, that an irrepressible conflict of social ideals and economic interests existed in the apparently united American states and that the issue of slavery and its expansion or abolition had become such a burning question in that country. Even the well-informed Bismarck professed not to know what the Americans of the North and South were fighting each other about, two years after the war had broken out, and appealed (tongue in cheek, perhaps) to his old friend and fellow-student John Lothrop Motley, for further elucidation: "What are you fighting about? Do you know?" he asked. Motley told him, at considerable length. Three years later (1866) Motley was to write to him:

> You see that I did not mislead you with regard to the American War. That was the only politics about which I ever pretended to know anything and I believe you were one of the very few Europeans who ever cared to know my opinion (which was that of every loyal American) and who thought that an American could possibly know something about his country. . . . I have said much more of politics than I intended. I shall refrain from giving you any advice as to how to deal with Schleswig-Holstein.[1]

Although Bismarck was the third Prussian minister-president to hold office during the American Civil War, his views may

---

[1] G. W. Curtis, ed.: *The Correspondence of J. L. Motley* (2 vols.; New York, 1889), Vol. II.

be said to have predominated in determining Prussia's attitude toward the war. George Bancroft, in a famous and carefully considered appraisal of that attitude, which he sent to Secretary of State Seward on February 26, 1869, wrote:

> The conduct of the Prussian government towards us in the time of our civil disturbance has seemed to me an object worthy of the most exact and thorough inquiry. The political papers of those days are for the most part already removed from the Foreign Office to the Archives; and, as the policy of this Government since Count Bismarck has been the first minister has been frank and open beyond that of any government in Europe, I am able to make to you a report, which is the fruit of a thorough search of the documents and of other inquiries made with the best opportunities of obtaining trustworthy information.
>
> As there were two ministers of Foreign Affairs, viz: Count von Schleinitz and Count von Bernstorff, after the inauguration of Mr. Lincoln and before Count von Bismarck-Schönhausen in October 1862 took the seals of the Foreign Office and the presidency of the ministry, the opinions of the King are of the most importance as showing the policy that was scrupulously observed during the whole period of our long struggle. The King from the first took the ground, that the question involved in our war was a question of right and wrong, that there is but one right and but one wrong; that the right was with the established government of the United States which represented their union and that the wrong was with the seceding states which placed themselves in rebellion against their just government. The ministry did indeed lay down the principle of non-interference and neutrality; but on the part of Prussia there was no concession of belligerent rights to the South either on the Ocean or elsewhere. This government pays the closest attention to military movements everywhere, and it had observers in various parts of the United States to take notice of the wonderful improvement in the science of war which grew out of the application of American enterprise to that subject. But every request of officers for a leave of absence in order to serve in the Southern army was sternly refused. As the war was protracted, there grew up in the aristocratic squiralty a sympathy for the South; and those who piqued themselves on their religious orthodoxy and piety forgot the wrongs of slavery and sympathised with the South they described as the land of gentlemen.

Against this opinion the King steadfastly declared that it was not a question between landowners or so-called gentlemen and the industrial classes under the appellation of mechanics and shopkeepers; that the question was simply a question of right and wrong and that without a doubt the right was entirely on the side of the North. When some of this fraction of the Prussian landed aristocracy gave a dinner to two officers of the Southern Confederacy who happened to be in Berlin, the King expressed his extreme displeasure at the act. Baron Gerolt the Prussian Minister at Washington always in his despatches supported the right of our government and steadfastly held the belief that it would succeed in putting down the Rebellion. For this conduct the King honored him with his special approbation and, as a distinguished mark of it gave him at the end of our war an order of the kind which is most in request among the Prussian statesmen and generals. I may cite as one of my authorities in this matter the King himself who at my audience of reception said to me that Prussia from the first existence of our government had never failed on its part to cultivate the most friendly relations with the United States of America.

All the papers that issued from the Foreign Department from the inauguration of Lincoln to his death are marked by this spirit. It regulated the conduct of Counts von Schleinitz and von Bernstorff, who were both remarkably reserved and silent men; it came out more clearly during the ministry of Count Bismarck who maintained unreservedly the view that the North was right. If the sympathy of the squiralty of the kingdom manifested itself socially, or, as it once did, through the press, it served only to make the fixed and immovable attitude of the Minister more conspicuous. Especially when, on one occasion, one or perhaps two remarkable articles appeared in a very able Prussian newspaper strongly favoring the cause of the South, Count Bismarck regarded it as a sympton of incipient opposition to the government of which he was the head; and the knowledge of his displeasure and the earnestness of his remonstrances checked the further publication of such articles.

No formal overture was made by any European power to this government to recognise the independence of the Southern Confederacy. To hints, insinuations and rumors to do so this government gave no encouragement; but remained true to the simple principle that the government of the Union had the right on its side; that the Southern Confederacy was in the wrong, and that therefore the government of the North was entitled to the best wishes of all powers friendly to order and justice.[2]

The pro-Northern attitude of the King of Prussia and his chief ministers was widely supported in their country and the pro-Southern feelings among army officers and in the "squiralty" was that of a small minority. This pattern of opinion is attested to by the success of the Union's fund-raising activities in Prussia during the war. Well before its outcome was clear, Robert J. Walker, who had been President Polk's secretary of the treasury and a senator from Mississippi, but who was a Northerner by birth and a staunch Union supporter during the Civil War, went on a fund-raising mission to Europe for President Lincoln's government in 1863. He was subsequently to write:

> Satisfied that any call for a loan would be defeated by the machinations of France & England, I never announced my official capacity, nor asked for any American loan. I published my financial essays over my own name, merely as an American citizen, exhibiting the vast resources, the wonderful progress of our country, and the certainty of our success in crushing the rebellion. These essays were sent by thousands to all the principal bankers of Europe. In a few months I visited again nearly every city of Holland and Germany, giving me an opportunity to discuss the question personally with these bankers, and enforce the written arguments already made. The result was that in a brief period the people of Germany, emphatically the great masses of the people, took several hundred millions of our loan at the same rates as our own citizens.[3]

By March 1865 over $200,000,000 had been loaned by German citizens, twice as much as was raised up to that date in England.[4]

---

[2] Bancroft to Seward, Berlin, Feb. 29, 1869. Received Mar. 15, 1869. Quoted by Otto, Graf zu Stolberg-Wernigerode: *Germany and the United States During the Era of Bismarck* (Philadelphia, 1937).

[3] Robert J. Walker: *Our National Finances—An Open Letter to the American People*, dated Nov. 30, 1867 (Washington, D.C., 1867).

[4] E. P. Oberholzer: *Jay Cooke, Financier of the Civil War* (2 vols.; Philadelphia, 1907), I, 513.

Bismarck is believed to have encouraged the German bankers to participate in this loan, and, indeed, in his old age, boasted to an American visitor:

> It was reported to me that Lincoln could not keep the war going if he did not receive financial aid from Germany. His Commissioners stated that they had been rebuffed in London & Paris. We wished the Union to be restored. The North seemed to me to be morally right, but, quite apart from that, we desired a strong prosperous and united Nation on the other side of the Atlantic.[5]

Baron Raphael Erlanger, acting for the Confederates, was far less successful in raising money in Germany on the security of the Southern cotton crop than he was in France. On October 10, 1864, the Confederate government issued a circular[6] to its agents expressing alarm at the amount raised by the Union government in Germany and suggesting countermeasures.

> For some months past the United States have been able to uphold their sinking finances by the sale of large amounts of public stocks in the German market. . . . We deem it advisable to present an analysis of the financial condition of the United States drawn from their official reports for the information of European capitalists . . .

But it was too late for countermeasures, which might have succeeded in 1862 when the United States consul general in Frankfurt am Main, the financial capital of Germany, expressed the opinion that "another defeat and we shall have lost our credit in Europe for years to come."[7] But both the Frankfurt and the Paris Rothschilds were pro-Northern in sentiment, and the head of the Frankfurt branch of the family openly deplored the pro-Confederate activities of Baron Erlanger.[8] On February 18,

---

[5] R. Bartholdt: *From Steerage to Congress*, pp. 75, 142, according to Stolberg-Wernigerode: *Germany and the United States*, pp. 70–1. No copy of Bartholdt's book could be found for verification.

[6] Copy in the Pickett Papers, Manuscripts Division, Library of Congress.

[7] William Walton Murphy to the State Department, Sept. 15, 1862, National Archives.

[8] A. D. White: *Autobiography* (2 vols.; New York, 1905), I, 97.

1864, the American minister in Berlin had reported that at last public opinion there was accepting the view that the Southern rebellion would be crushed, although Charles Francis Adams, in London, did not discern a similar realization in England until February 1865.[9] The Prussian government maintained a strict, formal neutrality of attitude throughout the war, and neither recognized the Confederate states as a belligerent power nor associated itself with Napoleon III's efforts to mediate between North and South. But this neutrality was, according to Carl Schurz, "of a friendly and benevolent nature."[1]

There is no evidence that the other states of northern and southern Germany that were to be united by Bismarck in 1867 and 1871 were less inclined toward neutrality with a pro-Northern bias than was Prussia and her leaders. Northern Germany was not affected economically to any serious degree by the war, apart from disruption of the Atlantic shipping lanes and the reduction in emigration from ports such as Hamburg and Bremen, whose commercial ties were mainly with the American North. Germany's cotton imports from America up to 1861 had been far less than those of England and France, and her cotton textile industry was in its infancy. Bismarck was able to tell the Prussian *Landtag* on January 14, 1863, that Prussia's industry had only been to a minor—if irritating—extent adversely affected by the Civil War. South German industry, particularly in Bavaria and Saxony, was undoubtedly harder hit, especially in textile manufacturing areas, but the historian of German-American relations in the age of Bismarck has concluded that "the American war did not cut deeply into German economic life."[2] The industrial revolution, it must be remembered, had not come to Germany as early as to England and France and was still far from complete in the 1860's.

Another factor in stimulating pro-Northern attitudes in Germany and the hope that the Union would be fully and rapidly restored was that the bulk of the large German emigration of the 1840's and 1850's to the United States had gone to the North

---

[9] Stolberg-Wernigerode: *Germany and the United States*, p. 47.

[1] Carl Schurz: *Lebenserinnerungen* (3 vols.; Berlin, 1906–12; reprinted 1923–30), II, 205. (Eng. trans. 3 vols.; New York, 1907–8.)

[2] Stolberg-Wernigerode: *Germany and the United States*, p. 60.

and to border states like Missouri and Kansas. Many thousands of these emigrants joined the Union army and thousands more had flocked to the banners of the new Republican party. These emigrant families were the Union's best and most effective propagandists in their letters to relatives and friends in Germany, while many German-language newspapers published in the United States (some of them edited or contributed to by militant pro-Union and anti-slavery "Forty-Eighters"[3]) found their way to Germany too. Germans who were settled in the American South tended to be far less articulate on the subject of the war and slavery, quite apart from their smaller numbers, and although a considerable number of them fought for the Confederacy, there was also an exodus of Germans from the South to the North on the eve of or even during the war, among them the eminent political scientist and international lawyer Francis Lieber, who moved North in 1856.[4]

The Confederacy, as if it realized that its reputation there was irreparably unfavorable, did relatively little about improving its image in the states of Germany or even about collecting adequate information concerning opinion there with regard to the War Between the States. Its agents occasionally traveled to Germany during the war,[5] and it received help from Southern sympathizers resident in Germany,[6] who urged the appointment of special Confederate commissioners in Prussia and Austria.[7] But the Confederate government was short of trained diplomats

---

[3] See Adolf E. Zucker: *Forty-Eighters* (New York: Appleton; 1953) and Carl Wittke: *Refugees of Revolution: The German Forty-Eighters in America* (Philadelphia: Univ. of Pennsylvania Press; 1952).

[4] See Frank Freidel: *Francis Lieber* (New York, 1943). Lieber gave up a professorship at Columbia College (now the University of South Carolina) and migrated to New York, but in 1861 the whole student body of Columbia College—according to an inscription on a wall of the campus—enlisted, to a man, in the Confederate army.

[5] For instance, Henry Hotze, commercial agent of the Confederate States in London. See his report of Dec. 17, 1864, on the need to stir up unfriendly feeling toward the Union cause in Germany, where he was about to pay a visit. *Official Records of the Union and Confederate Navies in the War of the Rebellion* (30 vols.; Washington, D.C., 1894–1914), pp. 1209 ff.

[6] Like E. M. Hudson, a former legation secretary in Berlin. See Stolberg-Wernigerode: *Germany and the United States*, p. 46.

[7] J. D. Richardson: *Messages and Papers of the Confederacy* (2 vols.; Nashville, 1905), II, 455.

and it relied on the veteran and somewhat inactive Dudley Mann, resident in Brussels, to keep it *au fait* with German affairs. Mann, after his bitter and frustrating experiences as an American diplomatic representative in Germany during the 1848–9 revolutionary period,[8] was thoroughly pessimistic about that country. He reported to Richmond on August 28, 1863:

> The obstacles which defeated the hopes of the patriots in 1849 have lost none of their power in 1863; the same rivalry between Austria and Prussia, the same wild schemes of dreamy Professors, the same sectional jealousy and class interests are observable now as then . . .[9]

and he was not prepared to bestir himself even to the extent of visiting Germany again. He does not seem to have been aware of the phenomenon of Otto von Bismarck-Schönhausen and of his imminent transformation of Prussia and Germany.

No German state had an official representative at Richmond, although the Confederate capital was visited by the enterprising Rudolph Schleiden (resident minister of the Free City of Bremen in Washington, D.C., since 1853) in April 1861, in the course of a single-handed attempt, unauthorized by his government but with the knowledge and good will of Lincoln and Seward, to prevent the impending conflict. His three-hour interview with Alexander Stevens, vice president of the Confederacy, came to nothing, although it was duly reported back to Lincoln and Seward and to the Bremen and Prussian governments. His intervention came too late, and one man could by then hardly prevent the outbreak of a conflict that a whole generation of Americans had failed to avert.[1]

---

[8] See further, J. A. Hawgood: *Political and Diplomatic Relations between the United States and the German Provisional Central Government at Frankfurt am Main in 1848–1849* (Ph.D. dissertation, Heidelberg, 1928), *passim.*

[9] Pickett Papers, Manuscripts Division, Library of Congress.

[1] The complete story of the Schleiden mission to Richmond is given in his reports to the Bremen senate (photostat and microfilm copies in Manuscripts Division, Library of Congress) and is summarized by Ralph H. Lutz in "Rudolf Schleiden and the Visit to Richmond, April 25, 1861" (American Historical Association *Annual Report* for 1915, Washington, D.C., 1917) and also in his *Die Beziehungen zwischen Deutschland und den Vereinigten Staaten während des Sezessions Krieges* (Ph.D. dissertation, Heidelberg, 1911), pp. 38–9.

Schleiden, despite his attempt at mediation, was a Northern sympathizer and during the war he also acted as representative of Hamburg and Lübeck in Washington, as well as of Bremen, until April 1864, when he was recalled and succeeded by Dr. Rösing. Both of these men did their best to safeguard the trading interests of the cities they represented amid difficult war conditions and managed to preserve their good relations with the government of the United States. By 1864 emigration to America from Bremen and Hamburg had risen again to more than double the figure of 1862.

Baron von Gerolt, the Prussian minister in Washington throughout the war, was a veteran in the service of Prussia in the New World, having gone to Mexico in 1824 as a mining engineer and having subsequently served successively as Prussian consular secretary, *chargé d'affaires*, and minister plenipotentiary there. He was appointed Prussian minister to the United States in 1843 in succession to Friedrich von Roenne, and remained in that post for many years. He was on close terms with many American politicians and leaders and particularly with the family of Thomas Hart Benton. At times he appears to have identified himself with American life rather more closely than was wise for a foreign diplomat, as when he passed information to Benton concerning the situation in Mexico and when he engaged in private land speculation with the senator from Missouri, but his voluminous reports in the Prussian Secret State Archives testify to his value as an observer of the American scene, and this was recognized by George Bancroft, who had been given limited access to these archives.[2] Gerolt was a strong pro-Northern sympathizer and his reports therefore strengthened the already pro-Union attitude of the Prussian government. Throughout the war he never wavered in his opinion that the Confederacy would be defeated and the Union fully restored, stronger than before.

The United States was successively served by four ministers plenipotentiary in Berlin during the 1860's. By far the most eminent and influential of these in both his own country and in Prussia was George Bancroft, the historian, but he did not take the office until 1867, and the man who headed the Berlin lega-

---

[2] See above, p. 150.

tion throughout almost the whole Civil War was Dr. Norman Judd. He was a political appointee of the new Lincoln administration and a man of no particular influence or distinction, but his reports, though pedestrian compared with the brilliant if irrelevant essays of J. L. Motley from Vienna, presented to his government a useful picture of politics and opinions in Prussia and of that country's reaction to the Civil War.

By contrast with Motley and Bancroft, who had the sort of *entré* at Potsdam that Franklin and Jefferson had once enjoyed at Versailles, Judd and his *chargé d'affaires*, Kreismann, do not appear to have had any close social connections with the Prussian governing class or higher intelligentsia. They were occasionally received by the foreign minister and on formal occasions Judd had audiences with the King. His meetings with Bismarck were very few and he appeared not to be able to fathom the complex personality of that statesman. He never realized how pro-Northern Bismarck's sentiments really were and as late as July 1864 identified the views expressed in a pro-Confederate article in the *Norddeutsche Allgemeine Zeitung* with Bismarck's personal opinions, saying:

> Recent events at home have given occasion to Herr von Bismarck's official organ the *Norddeutsche Allgemeine Zeitung* to display great sympathy and partiality for the rebel cause, and in its zealous wishes for the downfall of republican government and the further establishment of Monarchical institutions on the American government, and it indulges in the grossest misrepresentations regarding our armies and finances . . .[3]

Judd proposed to make representations to the Prussian Ministry of Foreign Affairs against the "infamous and slanderous course" of the newspaper, but was instructed by Seward not to pursue the matter further.

In fact, Bismarck did not hold the *Norddeutsche Allgemeine Zeitung* on so tight a rein as to have justified Judd's assumption. Bancroft, as has been seen,[4] took the view that Bismarck actually used his influence to prevent "a very able Prussian newspaper

---

[3] Judd to Seward, July 30, 1864, National Archives.
[4] See above, p. 150.

strongly favouring the views of the South" from publishing further articles of a similar nature, although this is more likely to have referred to the *Kreuzzeitung* than to the *Norddeutsche Allgemeine*. Bismarck, in fact, never showed any hostility toward republican institutions in the United States. He is said to have answered Bartholdt's question in 1895 "So the monarchical feeling was no hindrance to giving succour to a republic?" with the words "Not in the least. . . . The main object of statesmanship is, or ought to be, to make people happy and prosperous, to give them peace and plenty. Let the different forms of government vie with one another to accomplish that great purpose."[5] Lest this be written off as a piece of window dressing for the benefit of an American visitor thirty years after the events referred to,[6] it can be matched by a remark made by Bismarck to Keudell on April 23, 1864, when a young officer who had visited the United States, Lieutenant Scheibert, denied the rumor that the Southern Confederate States were about to elect Prince Albert of England their king and said that Americans, both Northern and Southern, were firmly wedded to their republican form of government. Bismarck then commented, "You see my old doctrine: only that which has developed historically is conservative. The American republic is a conservative form of government. Napoleon's empire is a revolution."[7] This was a remark made in private conversation with fellow Prussians, and there is no reason to suspect that it was ingenuous. Bismarck wanted the North to win the war and the United States to be a strong nation because he considered it to be in the best interests of Prussia that this should happen, and he knew if it did so, that republican institutions on the other side of the Atlantic would be greatly strengthened.

---

[5] See above, p. 152.

[6] Yet he did butter up Henry Villard, another prominent German-American, outrageously, saying to him in a personal interview, *"Lebte Ich in Amerika, so würde Ich auch Republikaner sein* [If I lived in America, I, too, would be a republican]" (H. Villard [Hilgard] *Lebenserinnerungen,* pp. 492 ff. and 502). Perhaps he said this in an attempt to counteract Villard's unfavorable opinion of him expressed in articles in *The North American Review* (CXII, 165 ff., for example).

[7] Otto von Bismarck: *Gesammelte Werke,* VII, 86, as translated in Stolberg-Wernigerode: *Germany and the United States,* p. 91.

Judd had felt much more confident of Count Bernstorff's pro-Northern views when he noted from a conversation with the then Prussian foreign minister early in the war that

> . . . there is no doubt of the friendly feeling of the Prussian Government towards the Government of the United States, and its desire that the rebellion should be subdued, as, in every allusion to the pretended seceded States Count Bernstorff spoke of them as "rebels," "rebellious province" and "subduing the rebellion," in no instance designating them as a Government.[8]

But Bernstorff was not to remain Prussian foreign minister for long and Judd was to have some apprehensive moments when news of Northern reverses during the first two years of the war reached Berlin—often telegraphed in distorted form from London. He was correspondingly elated about the probable effects on Prussian opinion and policy when Northern successes were reported, writing, for instance, on April 8, 1862:

> I have the pleasure to say that those Europeans "of little faith" in the Government's ability are fully converted and now believe that rebellion in America is done for.
>
> The "Monitor" was a warning to Europe. It is the one absorbing topic in all circles. Your especial friends in the British Isles have ceased to sing, with any conviction in its truth, "Brittania [*sic*] rules the waves."[9]

Kreismann also reported with elation the favorable reception of the news that the United States government was to issue an Emancipation Proclamation, saying that this would "serve to reassure and strengthen the belief in our final success."[1] He went on rather optimistically (for August 1862) to say, ". . . all doubts and fears will soon be removed again and the speedy fall of Richmond will strike the rebellion a blow from which it will not recover." But nearly a year later Kreismann was again very worried, reporting that

---

[8] Judd to Seward, Dec. 14, 1861, National Archives.
[9] Judd to Seward, National Archives.
[1] Kreismann to Seward, Aug. 1, 1862, National Archives.

. . . the invasion of the loyal states by the rebel hords
[*sic*] it is to be hoped will be but of short duration . . . It
cannot be denied, however, that it has caused great surprise among the friends of our cause throughout Europe
that they should at all have been able to invade our soil.[2]

Three months later Kreismann was still worried about the military situation in the United States but took comfort from the
probable effects of speeches by Henry Ward Beecher and of a
letter of Francis Lieber's.

> The speeches of Henry Ward Beecher in England are
> exerting a remarkable influence here in Germany and
> greatly serve to enlighten the public as to the origin, char-
> acter, and interests involved in our struggle. A still stronger
> argument and testimony on behalf of our cause has been
> laid before the German people in the letter of Doctor Francis
> Lieber to the Union ratification meeting in New York. His
> letter has found its way into all the leading German papers
> and is carrying great weight with all classes of readers.

Kreismann, in this same report, considered that even the most
reactionary Prussian military circles (which, unlike Bancroft,
he credited with "controlling" the King himself) were at last
being shaken in their belief in the Southern cause.

> Court and military circles here have been quite decided
> heretofore in their leanings toward the rebels, and this has
> been particularly true of the king's brother Charles, and of
> Prince Frederick Charles, the son of that brother, the chiefs
> of the reactionary military camarilla which manages and
> controls the king. But our late remarkable artillery achieve-
> ments as well as our successes generally are reported to
> have impressed upon these military chieftains the fact that
> valor and achievements are not the exclusive property of
> the Southern rebels.[3]

But it was not until February 18, 1864, that Judd could feel
it safe to report that

---

2 *Ibid.*, July 7, 1863, National Archives.
3 *Ibid.*, Oct. 10, 1863, National Archives.

The belief in the final suppression of the rebellion and the reestablishment of the authority of our government over the entire territory of the Union is now almost universal throughout Germany. The leading reactionary papers in Berlin, which, during all of the struggle have omitted no opportunity to disparage our cause, now give utterance to the prevailing opinion as to the condition of affairs in the United States. This change of opinion is marked and radical . . .[4]

Yet as much as six months later the *Norddeutsche Allgemeine Zeitung* was still printing distinctly pro-Southern articles![5] Only on April 18, 1865, did Judd permit himself, for the first time, to relax and gloat:

On Saturday I hung out of the Legation our star-spangled banners and thus notified the people of Berlin that rebellion and slavery had met their doom. . . . The well-informed have expected the "collapse" . . . but, notwithstanding, the actual occurance produced impressions as enthusiastic as though the result had not been expected.

The number of "I told you so's" on the streets is rather remarkable. Still, the genuine reactionary and feudalist consoles himself with the vain belief that the nation, although successful in armed contest, is bankrupt, and that finance will bring down the [by him detested] Republic.[6]

Judd's amusement at this "divine right" ignorance and conceit very soon gave way to more serious concerns. By May 4, 1865, he had received the news of Lincoln's assassination. Judd reported to Washington that

. . . Whatever may have been done in the United States Mr Lincoln is being canonized in Europe. A like unanimity of eulogy by Sovereigns, Parliaments, corporate bodies, by the people and by all public journals was never before witnessed on the continent.[7]

---

[4] Judd to Seward, Feb. 18, 1864. National Archives.

[5] See above, p. 157.

[6] Judd to Seward, National Archives. The news of Lee's surrender, but not, of course, that of Lincoln's assassination, had been received in Berlin by the date this dispatch was written.

[7] Judd to Hunter, acting secretary of state, National Archives.

The American representative could not refrain from adding that "the most truthful and eloquent testimonials are now given by some of those that belied him most while living."

After April 1865 the assassination of President Lincoln overshadowed all expressions of opinion concerning the United States in Germany and indeed in all Europe, for months and in some cases for years. It was undoubtedly still exerting its influence when George Bancroft arrived to take over the United States legation in Berlin in 1867, and even when he drew up his famous report[8] in 1869. In addition, nothing succeeds like success, and the North had won the war. Nobody would admit to Bancroft, then, to having had Southern sympathies during the Civil War, and the documents from the Prussian archives referring to the war period that were made accessible to him may well have been a well-edited selection. While it may be that Judd and Kreismann were unduly worried about anti-Northern feeling in Prussia and Germany while the war was still being waged, and particularly concerning its influence on the King and on Bismarck, it is undoubtedly true that Bancroft (who, like Macaulay, tended to be "cocksure about everything") presented, *ex post facto*, somewhat too bland a picture. He also tended to believe everything that his friend Bismarck told him—always a very dangerous thing to do.

Prussia (and most of the rest of Germany) was too remote, both politically and economically, from the effects of the American Civil War for her to need to take up very positive attitudes or to pursue any very strong policy toward either the North or the South. Her government was content with a strict neutrality, but her public men were free to express their personal sympathies without fear of serious repercussions, which is perhaps one reason why Bismarck did so little to curb pro-Southern sentiments in the press or in court circles. The middle and working classes, to the extent that they were informed and articulate, undoubtedly favored the North, to which so many of their friends and relatives had emigrated, and the institution of slavery in the South was abhorred. While not yet ready for the democracy or interested particularly in the republicanism of the United

---

[8] See above, pp. 149–51.

States, these classes in Germany admired them both—but from afar. Everyone in Germany knew that Prussia would not go to war either to help preserve or to help disrupt the American Union and the man in the street was aware of pressing problems much nearer home, which he would be expected to play an active part in solving.

Therefore, compared with the impact of the American Civil War on France and Great Britain, either of which might have found itself engaged in a major war because of its attitude toward the Union and the Confederacy, and both of which were economically much more closely affected by the war, the impact on Prussia (and the other states of *Klein-Deutschland* that were to join together in the Bismarckian empire of 1871) was a "soft" one. The South attracted much sympathy in aristocratic and conservative quarters, but these relatively small circles were either unable or unwilling to lend it other than verbal assistance. The Northern cause was favored by most newspapers, and by the man in the street, but the latter did not in many instances yet have the vote and, in any case, the governments of Germany were, in the mid-1860's, still nearly all authoritarian or semi-authoritarian. Bismarck defied the Prussian Parliament with complete success over the reorganization of the army demanded by Roon—just at this time. He would not have listened to popular protests concerning his policy toward the American Civil War. As it happened there were none. Bismarck's Prussia was not the England of John Bright!

Bismarck was not uninfluenced by events in the United States between 1861 and 1865, as will be seen, or, indeed, by the development of political institutions there between 1776 and 1865, but he made up his own mind about them (as his good friend John Lothrop Motley well knew) even when he asked for other people's opinions—and, from 1862 on, Bismarck *was* Prussia.

Motley, who was American minister in Vienna throughout the Civil War until 1867, and in London from 1867 to 1870, was Bismarck's oldest and closest American friend. Temperamentally the two men stood poles apart: Motley was liberal-minded, frank, not excessively ambitious, and at times not a little naïve, yet he admired Bismarck tremendously and tended to give him the benefit of every doubt. He foretold Bismarck's rise to power and retained his faith in him through all his arbitrary actions and ruthless devices. He spoke publicly in 1868 of Bismarck's "courage, insight, breadth of vision, iron will and . . . warm and steadfast heart"[9] and also wrote privately, "He is a man of great talent and most undaunted courage. He is the most abused man by the English newspapers I believe just now going, and I like him all the better for that."[1] To his daughter on August 7, 1866, he even expressed the opinion that perhaps Prussia's military despotism would open the way more rapidly for freedom in Europe than all the Kossuths, Garibaldis, and Mazzinis could achieve in half a century. Motley was thus no more likely to question the motives of Bismarck than was Bancroft, but he did not believe (as Bancroft seems at times to have done, though in fact it was Bismarck using him) that he had any real influence on the minister-president and chancellor. During Bismarck's three-day visit to Vienna in August 1864 he and Motley had several long conversations and although no written record of these exists, it is clear from later correspondence between them[2] that they discussed the American Civil War and Europe's problems as well as indulging in boisterous reminiscences of their student days together at Göttingen and Berlin.[3] It is also known that some years later (in 1868–71), when the French government was endeavoring (with the connivance of the American minister in Paris, General John A. Dix) to get the excessively pro-Prussian George Bancroft removed as American minister in Berlin, Bismarck (who considered Bancroft to be "the ideal American Minister"[4] and wanted him to stay) enlisted the assistance of Motley, then American minister in London, saying in a private letter addressed to Motley on September 19, 1869:

---

[9] J. L. Motley: *Historical Progress and American Democracy*, An Address Delivered before the New York Historical Society on Dec. 16, 1868 (New York, 1869), p. 44.

[1] *J. L. Motley and his Family*. Further letters and records edited by his daughter and H. St. John Mildmay (London and New York, 1910), p. 178.

[2] For example, see above, p. 148.

[3] See further, L. L. Snyder: "Bismarck und Motley. Eine Studentenfreundschaft," in *Hochschule und Ausland*, Vol. III (Mar. 1930) and the same author's Frankfurt Ph.D. dissertation: *Die persönlichen und politischen Beziehungen Bismarcks zu Amerikanern* (Darmstadt, 1932), passim.

[4] H. von Poschinger: *Fürst Bismarck, Neue Tischgespräche und Interviews* (Stuttgart and Leipzig, 1895–8), II, 274.

> . . . Bancroft is one of the most popular personalities
> in Berlin, and if you still have your old liking for this city,
> which you watched from the windows of the Logierhouse,
> please do as much as you can to keep him here with us.[5]

This appeal to old school ties worked, and Motley passed on Bismarck's letter to President Grant's former private secretary, Badeau. Bancroft remained Prussian minister in Berlin until 1873.

Bancroft's reports from Berlin between 1867 and 1871 have considerable literary and historical value, despite the fact that they are so starry-eyed. He is even said to have characterized the Prussian military system as a "happy reproduction of the American";[6] he regarded German unification under Prussia as so much in accordance with the laws of nature that any attempt to frustrate it must be regarded as morally wrong,[7] and he wrote to the State Department on November 1, 1867,[8] that the interest of his stay in Berlin would be very greatly strengthened by his being a witness of the development of the most important events in Europe of the century. But the American Civil War had been over for two years and Bancroft had perforce little to say at first hand concerning its impact on Germany, although he did claim that the American Constitution of 1787 had some influence upon that of the North German Confederation of 1867.

Had Bancroft represented the United States in Berlin between 1861 and 1867 instead of between 1867 and 1873 he might have enjoyed himself less but his dispatches would have been of the utmost importance for assessing the impact of the Civil War on Germany. As it was, this task had been left to the less able and less sure hands of Judd and Kreismann. But between 1861 and 1867 the United States was represented in Vienna by a man no less brilliant, no less well-informed on the affairs of Central Europe, and no less able to participate in German literary, scholastic, and social life than was Bancroft himself (who had taught Motley to love German civilization and the German language at the Roundhill School in Massachusetts many years

---

[5] Bismarck: *Politische Briefe* . . . (2 vols.; Berlin, 1889–90), I, 373.
[6] Stolberg-Wernigerode: *Germany and the United States*, p. 119.
[7] Ibid., p. 118.
[8] National Archives.

before). Yet Motley's dispatches, though of great psychological interest, are extremely disappointing to the historian (as they must also have been to the State Department at the time). He was bored with his job, though he clung to it when it was suggested that he might find the Legation in Madrid more attractive. His heart and brain were so much involved with the life-and-death struggle then going on in his own country that he could only bring himself, at times, by a violent effort of the will, and even then with considerable distaste, to contemplate what he considered to be the petty problems and events of the Habsburg court and Empire. Unlike Bancroft, he considered himself utterly cut off from the world-shaking events of his day, all of which, in his opinion, were taking place on the other side of the Atlantic. He performed the routine duties of his post, took up the cause of American citizens who had appealed to him and his consular officers, made representations when necessary, attended court functions and sometimes legislative debates, reported audiences with the Emperor and interviews with his ministers and officials. But his heart was obviously not in all this. It was on the Potomac or in Tennessee or on the field at Gettysburg.

In his dispatch to the State Department dated June 18, 1864,[9] Motley said that he must "honestly confess" that "the breathless interest with which we have been following the Virginia campaign . . . has made it almost impossible for me to give to the comparatively less important affairs of Europe as much attention as it is my duty to do." He had on May 10, 1863, already apologized for "writing so little on the German-Danish War" (in which, of course, Austria was involved), and on April 5, 1863, in a communication marked "Confidential" even remarked, "There is nothing to be said about Schleswig-Holstein except what appears in all the public prints." On January 23 of the same year he made the defeatist remark (for a trained historian and head of Legation!): "It is of course impossible for me to communicate any news to you in regard to the current history of Europe."[1]

---

[9] Motley to Seward Dispatches (1864), National Archives.
[1] Ibid. (1863), National Archives.

On the other hand, Motley wrote voluminously about British opinions and attitudes concerning the American Civil War and he followed the British press and periodicals closely. These attitudes so infuriated him that at times he seems to have forgotten that it was the duty of Charles Francis Adams, in London, and not of himself, in Vienna, to comment on and quote from these, and that Adams was in a much better position to do so. When he did bring himself to report Austrian affairs he tended to be most perfunctory, saying for instance, on June 22, 1862, "There is absolutely no business before the Legation just now," and he padded out his dispatches with long translations of government speeches, statements of policy, and legislative debates, adding few or no interpretations or comments of his own. Occasionally he quoted excerpts from the Austrian newspapers, in particular from his favorite, *Die Presse*, which was liberal and "always genial toward our government," but, on the whole, he complained that "no great interest is felt in our affairs"[2] in Austria, and that "public opinion in Europe . . . is comparatively indifferent to us."[3] And this he found very annoying. His most interesting outburst was on July 26, 1864, when he wrote, after making this last comment:

> A century hence, if indeed an antiquary should amuse himself with collecting from German newspapers a complete series of semi-weekly telegrams, he would be amazed at the trivial and grotesque way in which the history of the great Anti-Slavery war was presented during its continuance to the most philosophical and thoughtful nation of Europe.

"An antiquary . . . a century hence" would also find himself amazed, though hardly amused, if he tried to reconstruct the not unimportant sequences of events in the Habsburg monarchy

---

[2] This quotation is also from Motley's Dispatches to Seward of June 22, 1862, which contained the excerpt from *Die Presse* of June 20, 1862. Marx and Engels had contributed bread and butter articles on "The Civil War in the U.S.A." to *Die Presse* in 1861 and 1862, although these were written in London and were, of necessity, concerned mainly with British attitudes toward the war.

[3] Motley to Seward, July 26, 1864, National Archives.

and in Germany out of the material provided by John Lothrop Motley's official dispatches and confidential letters to a long-suffering American secretary of state. Even when Motley did bring himself to comment on German affairs he tended to do so within an American framework, as when, in July 1863, he transmitted the Reform Plan for the German *Bund,* which was being submitted by Austria to the Confederation of Sovereigns in Frankfurt am Main, and somewhat superficially compared "thirty-four German states" endeavoring to bring themselves into closer union with "thirty-four States" of the U.S.A. "defending their Union." On another occasion he compared Hungary to "our seceded" states.[4]

Motley's personal relations with the Austrian government were satisfactory and, socially at least, even cordial. He approved of Count Rechberg's very correct neutrality and appreciated the Austrian foreign minister's approval of the way in which President Lincoln's government had handled the *Trent* affair.[5] On February 20, 1862, he reported that Rechberg had told him that he and the Austrian ministry were "sure of the result of the Civil War" though fearful of "the danger of our becoming a military power and no longer a peaceful Republic." This possible leg-pull on the part of the smooth Austrian diplomat produced from Motley the somewhat starchy retort that this would be "a very improbable result," for the United States was not so much a military power as "a Nation in Arms," which was "necessarily a passing phenomenon."

Motley was quite right in summing up the Habsburg monarchy's attitude toward the American Civil War as one of comparative indifference. Neither politically nor economically were the Austrian Empire or the Kingdom of Hungary vitally or even closely affected by it, as Motley ought to have realized better than he apparently did. Even the interest that existed in those parts of Germany which had sent large numbers of emigrants to America in the forties and fifties was absent in the Habsburg realm, from which large-scale emigration had not yet seriously commenced. To the Silesian or the Croatian or the Transylvanian peasant America was still over the horizon of his perception,

---

4 Ibid., June 22, 1862, National Archives.
5 Ibid., Jan. 30, 1862, National Archives.

and he had enough wars and rumors of wars at home to worry about, in the 1860's, to bother about other people's. His own state of semi-serfdom mattered much more to him than Negro slavery in America. He did not know what the American Civil War was about and he did not care.

Austrian governing class circles, apart from a certain amount of early social and sentimental sympathy for the Southern cause and a growing admiration later in the war for the military organization and skill of the North,[6] were also somewhat indifferent to the American Civil War. Motley realized that only the news of resounding Northern victories could create real enthusiasm for the cause of the Union among the easy-going and somewhat time-serving Austrians. "So long as we are under a cloud we shall be subjected to calumny, insult and wrong" he wrote in July 1864. The previous month he had begged for official United States telegraphic summaries and *maps* [his italics] for use by the legation in Vienna if he was to scotch false rumors, of which he gave examples.[7]

Only one issue during Motley's stay in Vienna brought Austrian and American affairs close together, and this was only obliquely concerned with the War Between the States. On February 20, 1862, Motley had reported, somewhat incredulously, that the Archduke Maximilian, the Austrian Emperor's brother, had been consulted by certain Mexican agents (Almonte, Estrada, and Guiterez were named) in Trieste as to whether he would accept the throne of Mexico. Motley did take the trouble to collect what information he could concerning this intrigue, despite the

---

[6] For instance, on January 16, 1864, Motley reported to Washington that Captain Gustav von Boleslanski, of the imperial and royal army, had returned full of enthusiasm from observing the Union armies in the field. The rebellion, he thought, could not last through the next summer. The Union leaders possessed remarkable capacities, and both Lincoln and Seward had received him. The Emperor Francis Joseph had now sent for him. Motley enclosed a letter he had himself received from Boleslanski dated January 14, 1864, praising the "brilliant inventions" introduced in the Union armies and saying that the Signal Corps was "unique of its kind." All this was music to Motley's ears, starved of news as he was concerning the detailed progress of the war, and always complaining of the isolation of his post: "Once again I appeal to you not to leave us thus hopelessly isolated" (to Seward, July 26, 1864, National Archives).

[7] Motley to Seward, June 18, 1864, National Archives.

polite stone-walling he encountered at the Hofburg and in the Ballhaus Platz. When it became clear in 1863 that the archduke was to become emperor of Mexico with the active support of Napoleon III, and that Francis Joseph was prepared to let him embark on this adventure, Motley's indignation knew no bounds. The Monroe Doctrine had been flouted (as all the chancelleries of Europe fully realized), yet the United States government was in no position to intervene, and Motley was not even asked by Seward to lodge an official protest with the Austrian foreign ministry. He did what he could to make his views on the matter clear to his Austrian friends (and in some Austrian liberal circles, including the friendly *Die Presse*, the Mexican adventure of the Archduke Maximilian was severely criticized), and when Maximilian met his fate in 1867 after his abandonment by Napoleon III, Motley could not restrain a certain amount of crowing. It is clear that the Habsburg Emperor could have created a large amount of good will for himself and his country in the United States (and perhaps also in the Confederate States) by forbidding his brother to accept the Mexican throne, but he was not very interested in the good will of the United (or rather, disunited) States, North or South, in 1863. In Berlin, of course, the whole adventure was followed with gleeful realization that it could only lead in the long run to difficulties and embarrassment for both France and Austria and simplify Bismarck's problems, as it did both in 1867 and in 1871.[8] It is virtually certain that the Mexican situation (with which, by that time, Motley's dispatches were brimming over) would have been discussed in the Bismarck–Motley conversations in Vienna in August 1863, although Bismarck was to play the Mexican affair very close to his chest and even in January 1866 sent an envoy to the court of the Emperor Maximilian while also retaining connections with the Juárez government.[9] Maximilian's regime, on its side, sent Santa Anna's

---

[8] Matías Romero, minister in Paris of the Mexican Republican (Juárez) government, reported on May 4, 1867, "Everybody now realises that the insane expedition to Mexico led to an enlargement of Prussia, whose Prime Minister, Bismarck, took advantage of the time when the feet of France were chained." M. Romero, in *Century Magazine*, IV, 1 (May 1897), 138 ff.

[9] See further, Frank G. Weber: "Bismarck's Man in Mexico, Anton Von Magnus," *Hispanic American Historical Review*, XLVI, 1 (Feb. 1966), 53–65.

old crony, General Almonte, who was already representing it in Paris, to be its minister in Berlin. The Habsburg monarchy had a minister (Baron Eduard Largo) in Mexico City by that time, so perhaps Bismarck—who may have realized that Maximilian was already doomed—wished to keep his ear closer to the ground.[1]

It is certain that the Mexican affair had a lot to do with determining the sympathies of the United States in the Franco–Prussian War, although that story is beyond the scope of this chapter. Napoleon III, already unpopular in the United States as a despot who had destroyed the democratic Second French Republic in 1852 and who in 1861 had recognized the Confederacy as a belligerent and sought to mediate between it and the Union government on the assumption that the United States could and should not be reunited, blotted his copy book still further by intervening in Mexico and restoring monarchical institutions there. Bismarck, by keeping his powder dry, helped to make the Prussian and German cause as popular in the United States in 1870–1 as the French was unpopular. His benevolent neutrality toward the Northern government then paid a rich dividend. Bismarck continued to have a good press in the United States and to cultivate it. He even won over that old revolutionary Carl Schurz by his honeyed words as well as by his bold deeds.[2] Only Friederich Hecker among the leading forty-eighters remained entirely unreconstructed on the subject of Bismarck.[3]

The extent of the influence of American federalism on the Frankfurt Constitution of 1849, on that of the North German Confederation and on the *Ausgleich* arrangement between the Austrian Empire and the Hungarian Kingdom of 1867, and finally on the German Imperial Constitution of 1871 (which was a revamping of the North German Constitution) has long been disputed. Much of this dispute and many of the arguments

---

[1] Copies of many of Magnus's papers are to be found in the *Magnus Nachlass* in the National Archives, under the classification T.291, according to Frank G. Weber: "Bismarck's Man in Mexico."

[2] Bismarck: *Gesammelte Werke*, VII, 240 ff. and Schurz: *Lebenserinnerungen* II, 488 ff. "I am proud of Carl Schurz," Bismarck told Andrew D. White, and Schurz undoubtedly came to be proud of Bismarck.

[3] Zucker: *The Forty-Eighters*, p. 320.

brought forward are irrelevant to a discussion of the impact of
the American Civil War in Central Europe, but the outbreak of
the war did administer a severe blow to the prestige of the American type of federal solution and put it under a cloud as well as
on the shelf for some four years.[4] America's institutional schiz-
ophrenia was obviously no cure for Germany's own split personality. In the *Fürstentag* at Frankfurt in 1863 references to
the American example were as conspicuous by their absence as
they had been by their profusion in the debates, the committees,
and the pamphleteering at Frankfurt in 1848–9.[5] In any case,
the *Fürstentag*'s proceedings were stultified because of Prussia's
boycott. The *Nationalverein* (founded in 1859) of those liberals
and near-liberals who were seeking a "lesser German" solution
to Germany's unification problem was also inhibited by the apparent "breakdown" of the American Constitution of 1787, and
the constitution of the Confederate States reminded them too
much of the old *Bund* of 1815 that they were seeking to improve upon to provide any sort of inspiration for them. The rival
Reformverein (founded in October 1862 as a "greater German"
counterattack on the ideas of the *Nationalverein*), despite the
prominent part played in it by Julius Froebel, an old liberal of
the 1848 revolution, also sought no comfort from a United
States locked in fratricidal war. (The turn of the tide at New
Orleans, Vicksburg, Gettysburg, and Antietam was not yet appreciated as such by Europe's liberals, who also regarded Lincoln's
Emancipation Proclamation, which had just been announced,
as woefully belated.) The arbitrary acts of the Northern government, necessitated by the emergencies and stresses of the war,
further served to sour European and German opinion concerning
the once greatly admired American Union. Friedrich von Roenne,
former Prussian and Frankfurt provisional government minister

---

[4] As was pointed out by the present writer in the revised *Cambridge
Modern History*, X, 208.

[5] See further, J. A. Hawgood: *Political and Economic Relations* . . .
(Ph.D. dissertation, Heidelberg, 1928), his unpublished London M.A.
thesis (typescript and microfilm copies in University of London library),
"The Influence of American Ideas at Frankfurt am Main in 1848–9"; and
A. Scholl: *Einfluss der nordamerikanischen Unions-Verfassung auf die
Verfassung des deutschen Reiches Vom 28 März, 1849* (Ph.D. dissertation,
Tübingen, 1913).

in Washington, and a devoted admirer of the United States (he died in 1865), was greatly distressed by "the wounds delivered on the American Constitution . . . which were disguised as *necessities of war*"[6] by President Lincoln's government.

Liberals like Friedrich von Roenne and Professor K. F. Neumann,[7] one of his disciples, were heartened by the Northern victories in 1864 and 1865, just as Prussian conservatives, including (as has been demonstrated) Bismarck himself, were impressed by them, and by 1867, when the constitution of the North German Confederation was being devised, the North American type of federalism was again being regarded with favor in Europe. Not only had the North American Union been strengthened by the reincorporation of the eleven seceding states and by new constitutional amendments, but the Dominion of Canada had been based on the principles of this stronger type of federalism, even to the extent of calling its units "provinces" instead of "states." Bismarck, therefore, had no compunction about borrowing American federal ideas, to the extent that they suited his book, just as the men of 1848 had borrowed them in framing the Frankfurt Constitution. He even employed another old Frankfurt liberal, Max Duncker—who had helped to draft the constitution of 1849—to prepare him a preliminary draft for the North German constitution.[8]

Bancroft sought to get the wily Bismarck to admit the debt

---

[6] Julius von Roenne, his son, in *Friedrich von Roenne . . . Hauptzüge aus seinem Leben* . . . (Berlin, 1867), quoting an obituary notice (1865) by Bierwirth, formerly Württemburg representative in New York. See further, Hawgood: *Political and Economic Relations* . . . , p. 75, and "Friedrich von Roenne: A German Tocqueville," *University of Birmingham Historical Journal*, III, 1 (1951).

[7] K. F. Neumann: *Die Geschichte der Vereinigten Staaten von Amerika* (3 vols.; Berlin, 1864). Neumann used Friedrich von Roenne's notes made for the latter's proposed *Constitutional History of the United States*, according to Julius von Roenne: *Friedrich von Roenne.*

[8] Max Duncker's "Vorentwurf zur Verfassung des Norddeutschen Bundesverfassung" was printed in full by H. Triepel in *Vorgeschichte der Norddeutschen Bundesverfassung* in the *Festschrift Otto Gierke zum Siebzigsten Geburtstag* (Weimar, 1911), pp. 630 ff., and Triepel's whole monograph is a valuable contribution to the subject. Triepel concluded that "Duncker's work built a useful bridge" between 1848–9 and 1866–7. The bridge between 1787 and 1848 already existed.

of Germany's 1867 federalism to the American federal principles of 1787 and 1865, and received a by no means negative, though characteristically equivocal, answer, Bismarck saying that he had used "a little of everything."[9] This delighted Bancroft, who had persuaded himself that the North German constitution "was based on the same principles that had guided the creators of the American constitution"[1] and, furthermore, "that the Constitution of the North German Confederation was liberal, or at least capable of development along democratic lines."[2] The historian Heinrich von Treitschke, who did not share such views, suggested that the constitution of the North German Confederation owed a debt to the Republic of the United Netherlands and that Bismarck had learned about this Dutch example from his friendship with John Lothrop Motley and from reading the latter's *Rise of the Dutch Republic* (first published in 1856) and *The United Netherlands* (1860–7).[3] However, it is far more credible that he acquired a working knowledge of the American Constitution through Motley and applied this knowledge to the needs of the North German States in 1867 and the German Empire in 1871. These constitutions certainly possess many points of similarity, though also differing from each other in a variety of ways. Nothing comparable to the reserved powers (*Reservatrechte*) granted to the South German States when they became part of the Empire in 1871, for instance, existed in the United States in 1787 or had become part of the American federal system by 1871.[4]

No comparable influence of the American federal Constitution is discernible in the various schemes devised for the better government of the ramshackle Habsburg Empire between 1860 and 1871. The Habsburg monarchy's one truly federal constitution, which had owed a number of its features to the Amer-

---

[9] Stolberg-Wernigerode: "Unbekannte Gespräche mit Bismarck," *Süddeutsche Monatshefte* (Feb. 1930), p. 304. Bismarck's phrase in German was "von jedem ein bisschen . . ."

[1] Stolberg-Wernigerode: *Germany and the United States*, p. 116.

[2] Bancroft to Hamilton Fish, Jan. 17, 1870, Dispatches, Prussia, No. 63, private, National Archives.

[3] H. von Treitschke: *Die Politik*, 3rd edn., II, 313.

[4] For parallels and differences, see further, J. A. Hawgood: *Modern Constitutions since 1787* (London, 1939), pp. 239–44.

ican example, had been the abortive Kremsier draft of 1849. This had not been intended to apply to the Kingdom of Hungary, which had secured through its "Ten Points" of 1847 and its "March Laws" of 1848 a wide degree of autonomy amounting to virtual independence, but a system of naked absolutism was reimposed on both Austria and Hungary between 1849 and 1851, and it persisted until 1860. Then came the October Diploma of 1860, relaxing the intense centralism of the fifties, but a rapid return was made under the February Patent of 1861 to bureaucratized centralization once again. The *Ausgleich* of 1867, following Austria's exclusion from Bismarck's newly united Germany, was not so much a constitution as a "deal" of the dynasty with the Magyar magnates and nationalists. It was as if Andrew Jackson had made a deal with the South Carolina nullifiers, giving them a privileged position in the Union that the other states did not share, or James Madison had accepted the terms of the Hartford Convention. Had the Confederate States either won the American Civil War or fought the Union government to a standstill, they might have been satisfied with something like Hungary's position under the *Ausgleich,* although it is more likely that they would have demanded full independence and a separate sovereignty. But this did not happen, and the restored American Union, still a federal state, but more centralized than before 1861, was not regarded in the Habsburg monarchy in 1867 as a relevant example, although in fact much could have been learned from it. Even Schaeffle's Fundamental Article of 1871,[5] which has been called "the only serious and broad-minded attempt between Kremsier and 1918 to solve the problem of the Habsburg Empire,"[6] was such a confused approach to a federal solution that no direct American or other outside influence upon it is apparent, and it was immediately set aside at the demand of the Magyars, who insisted that the corrupt bargain of the *Ausgleich* should continue, as it did until 1918.

To say that "the fine balance of the federative compromise was ended [by 1867], in America by the triumph of the unionists, in Germany by the triumph of the Prussian secessionists . . . [and

---

[5] See further, ibid., p. 261.
[6] O. Jászi: *Dissolution of the Habsburg Monarchy* (Chicago, 1929).

that] in the United States the triumph of the unionists preserved
federalism in North America; in Germany the triumph of the
secessionists sacrificed it in *Mitteleuropa*"[7] is perhaps too narrow
and pessimistic a judgment. Federalism was indeed preserved,
but also strengthened as a principle and an example, in North
America and in the world, by the outcome of the Civil War.
German federalism was not destroyed by the Prussian victory in
the Seven Weeks' War, because it did not yet exist; the old *Bund*
of 1814 had been a weak and ineffective confederation of sovereign states and the Frankfurt National Assembly of 1848–9
had aborted; yet Prussia's secessionists did produce a near-federal
solution in the North German constitution of 1867, leading the
way to a strong Hohenzollern Empire, which rapidly became a
great power, just as the United States also was a great power by
the end of the nineteenth century. Without the experiment of the
American Federal Union of 1787 and its successful emergence
from the ordeal by fire of 1861–5, neither of these great powers,
for better or for worse, might have come into existence.

---

[7] R. C. Binckley: *Realism and Nationalism, 1852–71* (New York, 1935;
paperbound reprint, 1963), p. 183.

Russia and the Civil War

Hans Rogger

*O*bvious implications for cold-war diplomacy underlie the recent upsurge in interest about Soviet understanding of American history.[1] A century ago, Russians found in America's Civil War and Reconstruction experience many significant implications for tsarist government and society. The Russian perception of America was ethnocentric, naturally enough. But unlike Britain or France, Russia had almost no economic interest in the United States. All she might be considered to have had in common with the divided Union was her own slave system, in the form of serfdom. Russia boasted a large and vigorous intelligentsia, whose sensitivity to American affairs was a factor in their hopes or fears regarding the adoption of Western ways in Russia.

In short, Russia was, as she is, different. And the following account by Hans Rogger, professor of history at the University of California at Los Angeles, of the impact within Russia of America's Civil War and Reconstruction reflects Russia's divergencies from the main currents of European life as well as her deep participation in them.

---

[1] A good example is Lawrence Burnette, Jr., and W. C. Haygood, eds.: *A Soviet View of the American Past* (Madison, Wis., 1960).

Alexander Lakier's *Travels in the North American States, Canada and the Island of Cuba* was one of the very few works published in nineteenth-century Russia whose author had first-hand knowledge of his subject. In a review of March 1859, the radical critic A. N. Dobroliubov welcomed its wealth of detail about American institutions and material achievements but complained that the author had neither understood nor conveyed the democratic and egalitarian quality of life in the transatlantic republic. Knowledgeable people, particularly those who knew French, would discover little that was new in the book; others would find it tedious. Unfortunately, there was little else for the ordinary reader to turn to, aside from translations of Friedrich Gerstäcker, the German writer on America, a few scattered articles, and, more recently, the novels of Harriet Beecher Stowe. As a result, Dobroliubov noted, most Russians held stereotyped and contradictory opinions about America and Americans—a country of merchants, material comfort, slavery, democracy, and individual liberty, which some compared to Russia and others described as anarchy. Here was a people whose women were happy in the enjoyment of their human rights but also, it was said, joyless, dry, and calculating creatures; a practical people who valued money above all else, were highly educated, yet shamefully ignorant of philosophy and the arts.[1]

It is far from certain that more and better books and articles would have removed the misconceptions that Russians shared with other Europeans, but the situation described by Dobroliubov existed. Before 1855, it could hardly have been otherwise. Only with the end of the stifling reign of Nicholas I, only with a more lenient censorship, could opinion, in any truly public sense of the word, be formed, expressed, and occupied with other than safe topics. Easier access to European news sources and travel abroad helped to widen horizons in the reign of Alexander II, as did the telegraph and the steamship. Still, the gaze of press and public remained turned inward to an extraordinary degree. Nor

---

I would like to gratefully acknowledge the support given me by the Institute of International Studies (University of California, Berkeley) and the Senate Research Committee (UCLA) for the preparation of this study.
[1] N. A. Dobroliubov: *Sobranie sochinenii* (Moscow-Leningrad, 1962), IV, 217–18.

was this surprising. Defeat in the Crimea had made it painfully clear that too many of Russia's problems had been neglected for too long, that administration and the courts, serfdom and local government, education and the military were crying out for attention and reform. And just as the government, preoccupied with reorganization and recovery at home, pursued a passive policy abroad, so the literate and articulate portion of Russian society gave most of its energies and attention to domestic affairs. Public opinion, noted a Bavarian diplomat in 1867—"no longer content to let itself be guided"—showed a concern with foreign affairs only on the Eastern Question, i.e., the Balkans and the Straits.[2]

Concern is not, of course, synonymous with interest, and interest in what went on outside of Russia was high; yet its expression was often but a pretext for the discussion of Russian issues by circumspection and indirection. Before the censorship at the end of 1857 permitted discussion of serfdom, articles dealing with Moroccan or American slavery were no certain indication of interest in America or Morocco. Even when the United States was the ostensible subject, writers' and readers' minds were focused on Russia. Russian scholarship ignored the United States to a degree unmatched in any of the major European countries, leaving to the journals of opinion the task of enlightening their countrymen about the United States, with results deplored by Dobroliubov.[3]

---

[2] Barbara Jelavich, ed.: *Russland, 1852–1871: Aus den Berichten der bayerischen Gesandtschaft in St. Petersburg* (Wiesbaden: Otto Harassowitz; 1963), p. 125; see also M. K. Lemke on the difficulties of discussing international affairs even after 1855 and the generally low level of interest and expertise in this area on the part of Russian journalists, in N. A. Dobroliubov: *Pervoe polnoe sobranie sochinenii* (St. Petersburg, 1911), IV, 823–826.

[3] P. G. Mizhuev: *Istoriia velikoi amerikanskoi demokratii* (St. Petersburg, 1906) lists only some twenty works on American history and institutions in the Russian language, thirteen or fourteen of them translations from English, German, and French. The remainder are by three Russian authors. N. A. Rubakin's bibliography, *Sredi Knig* (Moscow, 1913), II, 183–4, gives the names of forty authors of works on American history. Of these, fifteen are Russians, with perhaps two qualifying as serious students of the subject. B. Kamenetskii: "Materialy o russko-amerikanskikh otnosheniiakh XVIII–IX vv. v russkikh izdaniiakh," *Istoricheskii zhurnal*, No.

But, whatever the force or quality of its impact, the Civil War was Russia's discovery of America on a major scale, for never before or after it was there such a range of periodical literature and discussion on American history, politics, and institutions. Only when the threat and the dramatic reality of a major conflict attracted universal attention did literate Russians begin to take more than casual notice of the New World. Even for most of these, whether they viewed the United States with sympathy, indifference, or revulsion, the young giant across the sea remained terra incognita; the intensity of interest aroused by the crisis of sectional conflict and war did not long survive it. For the more summary or philosophical judgments that determined attitudes, Russians reverted to familiar or predictable positions. The war deepened and intensified certain views of the United States long held and confirmed prejudices, but it also modified and refined beliefs, either temporarily or, less often, permanently. Its impact cannot, however, be gauged apart from Russian perceptions of the character and nature of American society, and the shaping of these had begun long before the 1860's.

I

It is impossible to agree with an American assumption that before October 1917, and to a surprising degree after that date, Russians had "almost universally . . . [a] conception of the United States as a manmade paradise and of Americans as muscular, upright, free and happy demigods."[4]

3/4 (1943), pp. 72–4, lists not a single prerevolutionary Russian book on the Civil War and only three translations. The Soviet literature on American history in general and the Civil War in particular is much richer, especially for the period after World War II. See G. P. Kuropiatnik and I. A. Beliavskaia: *Sovetskaia istoricheskaia nauka ot XX k XXII s'ezdu KPPS: Istoriia zapadnoi Evropy i Ameriki* (Moscow, 1963), and Max Beloff: "Soviet Historians and American History," in John Keep, ed.: *Contemporary History in the Soviet Mirror* (London, 1964), pp. 306–14 and p. 252, *n. 2, below.*

[4] Robert Magidoff: "American Literature in Russia," *Saturday Review of Literature* (Nov. 2, 1946), p. 9.

The new nation, created to be a "haven for liberty banished from Europe by luxury and corruption," was not regarded uncritically even when it was most envied by high-minded subjects of Catherine the Great. Among these it was Alexander Radishchev, "admirer of the transatlantic republic" and "Russia's first radical," who was also the first to point out America's defects while praising her virtues. The shining example Russia was to follow, the home of free speech and worship where he wished his ashes to be buried, was also the land of cruel conquest and heartless exploitation. Indians and Negro slaves had no share in America's promise and were no better off than Russian serfs. Yet liberated America had taken a great step forward; she had set the course that Radishchev hoped all men would take.[5]

While Catherine and her son Paul reacted with fearful harshness to the French Revolution and Alexander I disappointed liberal hopes, America appeared as the one nation in the world that had given refuge to liberty and law. Demanding these for Russia, so that she might take her place in dignity among the nations, the conspirators of December 1825 were much impressed—not only by American inventiveness and energy, philanthropy and religious toleration, but also by a revolution that had avoided terror and despotism to erect a noble structure of constitutional federalism in which the rights of men were secure and their powers restrained. For republicans as well as monarchists among the Decembrists, the government founded by Washington and Franklin demonstrated that a state need not be harsh to be strong, that rulers need not be tyrants to be obeyed. The Decembrists' failure dimmed for succeeding generations this picture of America, yet its chief features survived: the republican

---

[5] Ibid., p. 9; A. Startsev: "Amerika i russkoe obshchestvo," *Internatsional'naia literatura*, IX/X (1941), 209–11; Max M. Laserson: *The American Impact on Russia—Diplomatic and Ideological, 1784–1917* (New York, 1950), pp. 53–71; D. M. Lang: "Radishchev and Catherine II," in John S. Curtiss, ed.: *Essays in Russian and Soviet History* (New York, 1963), pp. 22–3; A. N. Radishchev: *Puteshestvie iz Peterburga v Moskvu* (first publ. 1790; Moscow–Leningrad, 1964), pp. 123–4; *Izbrannye sochineniia* (Moscow, 1949), p. 280; N. M. Karamzin: *Izbrannye sochineniia* (Moscow–Leningrad, 1964), II, 116–17. See also N. N. Bolkhovitinov: *Stanovlenie russko-amerikanskikh otonoshenii, 1775–1815* (Moscow, 1966) for additional material on early Russian opinion of America and the American Revolution.

virtues of her founders, their political wisdom and the excellence of the institutions created by them. America's youth was always the period of her greatest attractiveness to Russians. But when, despairing of their own grim reality under Nicholas I, they launched upon a sea of speculation about the glorious future history had prepared for a fresh and youthful Russia, America came to appear less a new beginning than the extension of an old and declining Europe.[6]

The exponents of this historiosophy were the Slavophiles, a small but influential band of men whose nationalism was informed rather by love and pity for their people than hatred for others. Nor did their nationalism imply an unquestioning acceptance of the repressive rule of Nicholas I. The true Russia of their dreams lay beneath the cold façade of bureaucratic St. Petersburg, and it was this Russia—Christian, loving, and communal—that they contrasted with a selfish, rationalist, and materialist West that had corrupted America no less than St. Petersburg. When Ivan Kireevskii, one of the founders of Slavophilism, surveyed the state of Russian letters in 1829, he found only two nations free of the somnolence afflicting all mankind— Russia and the United States. Youthful, fresh, and full of hope, they alone flourished—or rather, one of them only, for the one-sided character of America's English culture and her remoteness from Europe reposed all hope in Russia. America was the crudest embodiment of Europe's faults, without Europe's virtues: a land without history, traditions, or a genuine nationality that proved the impossibility of building a living social organism with the tools and materials of pure reason. How brilliantly the experiment had begun, what a splendid future it had promised, now come to naught because the machinery of empty legalism, the hypocrisy of patriotic and humanitarian phrases, the greedy pursuit of personal advantage or comfort had dried up the sources of life and love and poetry.[7]

---

[6] Laserson: *The American Impact on Russia*, pp. 115–38; Anatole G. Mazour: *The First Russian Revolution, 1825* (Berkeley, 1937), pp. 78ff., Startsev: "Amerika i russkoe obshchestvo," pp. 211–12.

[7] Ivan Kireevskii: *Polnoe sobranie sochinenii* (Moscow, 1911), II, 39, and I, 153–4; Nicholas V. Riasanovsky: *Russia and the West in the Teaching of the Slavophiles* (Cambridge, Mass., 1952), pp. 112–13.

The bitterness with which Kireevskii and some later Slav-ophiles spoke of the United States had different sources than the contempt of men like Nicholas Pogodin, the Moscow professor and proponent of "official nationality" who saw America as tainted by her illegitimate birth. America is not a state, he wrote in 1837, but a trading company which had, to be sure, grown rich but would never produce anything great of national or universal significance.[8]

For the Slavophiles, less eager than Pogodin to exalt the tsarist state, the matter was not so simple. To them, America's worst sin was her denial of unique opportunities. According to Konstantin Aksakov, the "tribune of Slavophilism," a new nation, founded on new principles in a new world had become just an-other state, but one that turned liberalism into its opposite by making every citizen an official, a policeman of himself. "The lie inheres not in this or that form of state, but in the state itself as an idea," Aksakov wrote about America a few years before his death in 1860; "what has to be said is not which form is better or worse . . . but that the state *qua* state is a lie." Even the most democratic states were based on violence and could resolve their problems by violence alone. Only Russians were not a state-minded people. To preserve their inner freedom, they shunned power and politics, leaving these to the tsar as a divinely imposed duty. Americans had only the surrogate of freedom, a mutually limited license, because they trafficked with power and lacked the divine spirit.[9]

America's wealth and her surrender of ideals where these conflicted with interests (notably slavery) became common-places for others than romantic or conservative nationalists. Pushkin, that least dogmatic of men, also helped to perpetuate received opinions. In 1836 he observed that in spite of America's

---

[8] M. P. Pogodin: "Letter on Russian History," excerpted in Hans Kohn, ed.: *The Mind of Modern Russia* (Brunswick, N.J., 1955), pp. 60–8. On Pogodin see also Nicholas V. Riasanovsky: *Nicholas I and Official National-ity in Russia* (Berkeley, 1959).

[9] Riasanovsky: *Russia and the West*, p. 113; and Edward Chmielewski: *Tribune of the Slavophiles: Konstantin Aksakov* (Gainesville, Fla., 1961), pp. 53–4. For the views of other Slavophiles on the United States, see Laserson: *The American Impact on Russia*, pp. 146–9.

flourishing condition, respect for her people and government had been shaken by doubt and skepticism. Some of Europe's keenest minds had been repelled by the cynicism of American democracy, its savage prejudices and insufferable tyranny. They had seen grandeur, selflessness, and honor fall victim to egoism and the passion for comfort; an impudent majority leveling distinction; Negro slavery side by side with liberty and learning; on the part of electors, greed and envy; on the part of those governing, timidity and servility.[1]

Pushkin had read Tocqueville, as had Alexander Herzen, arriving at similarly pessimistic conclusions. "Tocqueville's 'America,'" Herzen wrote to a friend in 1838, "filled me with grief and sorrow. He says in his conclusion: 'Two countries carry the seeds of the future: America and Russia.' But where in America is the start of a future evolution to be found? It is a cold and calculating country. Russia's future, however, is without limit —oh, I believe in her progressiveness."[2]

It was a strange confession for one who was considered a radical Westernizer. Long before his disenchantment with a West that was bourgeois even where it pretended to be radical, long before his formulation of a specifically Russian socialism, this most influential of Russia's revolutionary intellectuals revealed an emotional attachment to his native land that remained constant. Even when America, like Russia, seemed to hold out prospects of human and social renovation that Europe had disappointed, his approbation had always something of reserve, a constant question whether "fresh, virgin soil" alone could liberate men from the fetters of the past. His youthful drama "William Penn" (1839) signaled a life-long doubt about the New World in the warning given to Penn by George Fox that in building a

---

[1] A. S. Pushkin: *Polnoe sobranie sochinenii v desiati tomakh* (Moscow–Leningrad, 1949), VII, 449–50. The occasion for Pushkin's strictures was a commentary to accompany a translation of excerpts from *A Narrative of the Captivity and Adventures of John Tanner . . . during 30 years' residence among the Indians . . .* (New York, 1830), published in a Russian magazine in 1836. See also J. T. Shaw, "Pushkin on America: His 'John Tanner,' " in *Orbis Scriptus: Dmitrij Tschizewskij zum 70. Geburtstag* (Munich, 1966), pp. 739–56.

[2] A. I. Gertsen: *Sobranie sochinenii v tridtsati tomakh* (Moscow, 1954–1964) XXI, 386 (hereafter Herzen: *Works*).

Christian community the moral purity of its founders was more important than the character of the building site.[3]

Herzen wavered between seeing America as the "last tidy edition of the same feudal-Christian text, in a crude English translation at that" and as "more than a revised edition of Old Europe."[4] But however often he quoted Goethe's *"Amerika, du hast es besser,"* told free men who would not bow before reaction to make for Kansas or Wisconsin, or praised American freedoms, decentralization, and the good sense of her citizens, he always doubted whether the American experience had relevance for the old continent. He was put off by all that was *juste milieu,* bourgeois, and money grubbing about the United States and most attracted to the sense of breadth and daring that the country's geography and enterprise and the spirit of its people and institutions conveyed. It was this that led him to prophesy that America and Russia, forging ahead of tired Europe, would meet on the shores of the Pacific, the Mediterranean of the future, to become traveling companions in years to come. When the Civil War freed America of what Herzen had called her greatest crime, black slavery, it confirmed his belief in her vigor and strength. But it brought no lasting change in his conviction that she could not go beyond the realization of the republican and libertarian ideals she had inherited from the eighteenth century. She had reached the shores of the Pacific with ease; the promised land of socialism she was not likely to see.[5]

---

[3] Ibid., I, 247–8; Martin Malia: *Alexander Herzen and the Birth of Russian Socialism* (Cambridge, Mass., 1961), p. 196.

[4] Herzen: *Works,* VI, 28, 68, 111; X, 73; XVIII, 627, and p. 220, *n.* 6, below.

[5] There are numerous references to and comments on the United States scattered throughout the vast body of Herzen's work. Besides Laserson (*The American Impact on Russia,* pp. 205–36) two other scholars have tried to extract from it his judgment of America and her people—David Hecht, in *Russian Radicals look to America, 1825–1894* (Cambridge, Mass., 1947), pp. 16–40, and Alexander Kucherov, in "Alexander Herzen's Parallel between the United States and Russia," in Curtiss: *Essays in Russian and Soviet History,* pp. 34–47. While I am grateful to these colleagues for simplifying my labors, I cannot, as I read Herzen, agree with their interpretations. Herzen did not admire America intensely (Laserson) or look to her, nor "did he come to know America well" or "formulate well-rounded attitudes and shrewd observations" about her (Hecht). Mr. Kucherov comes

Just before and after the emancipation of the serfs, slavery was the American problem that most absorbed Russians; it was also the reason for the popularity of *Uncle Tom's Cabin*. Though proscribed by the censor and not translated until 1858 (when the subscribers to *The Contemporary* received it as a free supplement), the book was known and read in Russia not long after its appearance in the United States. Herzen, in December 1852, berated Russian serf owners, those "slaveholders of the North" who toured Europe in the guise of civilized men, for reading "the great work," shuddering with horror at the sale of black flesh and returning home (with the book in their luggage?) to rob and torture their white slaves as before. By whatever means Uncle Tom reached Russia, he became a familiar figure in many homes. Tolstoy read the novel in 1854 and forty years later still talked of writing a Russian Uncle Tom. In 1852, Ivan Golovin, a political emigré, had done just that, but his French manuscript, sold to an Edinburgh publisher, never appeared in print.[6]

The leading Slavophile, Aleksei Khomiakov, on reading the book in 1855, found much in it that was familiar. But he insisted that the similarities with serfdom were only apparent, that the "impartial study of the domestic problem" he had made showed how different were the moral basis and consequences of slavery. Baron Nicholas Wrangel recalled in his memoirs that sometime late in the 1850's *Uncle Tom's Cabin*—"a book which was then in fashion"—was read to him and his sisters, to the accompaniment of tears and childish questions about the difference between slavery and serfdom. The governess explained:

---

closer to Herzen's real feelings—an ambivalence that is not, however, so much a reflection of the changing fortunes of European progressivism as a reflection of the curious and unstable mixture of ignorance, antipathy, and respect that made up Herzen's image of America. For some of its components, see particularly, *Works*, V, 21, 173, 183–5; VI, 151, 183–8; VII, 341, 349–50; IX, 399–401; X, 120–63; XI, 150, 161–5, 209, 226, 422; XIII, 95, 398–403; XIV, 9–20, 32, 180–1; XIX, 139–40; XXV, 24, 158, 418.

[6] N. M. Sikorskii: *Zhurnal "Sovremennik" i krest'ianskaia reforma 1861 g.* (Moscow, 1957), p. 75; *Bol'shaia Sovetskaia Entsiklopediia*, V (1950), 267; Magidoff: "American Literature in Russia," p. 10; Ernest J. Simmons: *Leo Tolstoy* (Boston, 1946), pp. 105, 539; Herzen: *Works*, XII, 7, 33; XXV, 371; Laserson: *The American Impact on Russia*, p. 156.

Slaves, my dear children, are poor Negroes torn from their native country and from their families, and so you can understand that they are naturally very wretched. Serfs are people of the same religion and race as their masters, living in their own country and among their own people, only they are attached to the soil.[7]

It was not mainly callousness or naïveté that obscured the similarity of servile status in dissimilar societies. The dimension of race exacerbated the problem in the United States, while its absence in Russia made easier the stilling of consciences and more difficult the reduction of serfs to chattel. Although Russia's abolitionists (like the former Decembrist Nicholas Turgenev) made much of the debilitating effect both slavery and serfdom had on masters and victims alike, Russian serfs shared with their owners a community of religion, race, language, and customs, which, though it might be ignored, was never forgotten by either lord or peasant, instilling in the former a sense of guilt and sustaining in the latter a trust in ultimate justice. The gulf between the classes was deep, but it was not one of caste, race, or nationality.[8]

Russians were amazed and shocked at the lengths to which Americans carried the segregation of the races, incredulous at a prejudice that barred Negroes from worshipping with whites even in the North. Emancipation could not have proceeded as smoothly as it did if the serf had been as debased as the Southern slave. That he was not diminished the impact of American anti-slavery literature. Ivan Turgenev's quietly ironic, almost nostalgic *Sportsman's Sketches*, stressing the peasant's innate humanity rather than his suffering, were more effective and better attuned

---

[7] Peter K. Christoff: *An Introduction to Nineteenth-Century Russian Slavophilism; A Study in Ideas*, Vol. I: *A. S. Xomjakov* ('S-Gravenhage: Mouton and Co.; 1961), p. 113; *From Serfdom to Bolshevism: The Memoirs of Baron N. Wrangel*, trans. by Brian and Beatrix Lunn (London, 1927), pp. 40–1; and Roger Dow: *"Seichas:* A Comparison of Pre-Reform Russia and the Ante-Bellum South," *Russian Review*, VII, 1 (Autumn 1947), 3–15.

[8] On Turgenev, Laserson: *The American Impact on Russia*, pp. 149–154; V. M. Tarasova: "Dekabrist N. Turgenev i bor'ba protiv rabstva v SShA," *Voprosy istorii*, No. 10, (1963), pp. 209–12; cf. also W. R. Dodge: "Abolitionist Sentiment in Russia, 1855–1861" (unpubl. Ph.D. dissertation, University of Wisconsin, 1951).

to Russian conditions. It was said that they had contributed to the Emperor's determination to free the serfs.[9]

Herzen was right when he predicted in 1852 that ending serfdom would happily be easier than its imposition had been. Only the most retrograde portion of the nobility would offer resistance, which could easily be overcome, because "all civilized nobles, all those in Russia who can be called an 'Opposition' are bound to support the government in this." Events bore him out. Except for a rear-guard action fought in governmental commissions by a few "planters," the freeing of the serfs was accepted as morally and socially necessary and economically desirable by government and public alike. There was no intellectual support for serfdom; it was not defended with the "fierce tenacity" of American slavery advocates. Herzen and others, consciously or not, took pride and comfort in this.[1]

The American case was distinguished also by its political aspects. In Russian eyes, the cohesion achieved by a diverse people with the help of a loose federal structure extending over a territory almost as vast as their own had been most impressive

---

[9] *Moskvitianin*, No. 17 (1850), pp. 11–13; "Sovremennaia letopis'," *Russkii vestnik*, Book 1 (Nov. 1860), p. 11; "Inostrannaia literatura," *Russkoe Slovo*, No. 9 (1860), p. 78; for the reception given Turgenev's sketches of peasant life see Adolf Stender-Petersen: *Geschichte der russischen Literatur* (Munich, 1957), II, 237–9. In spite of what Nicholas Turgenev and other Russians regarded as a real "difference between the Russian serf and the black slave of America," abolitionists in both countries saw certain parallels in their situation, deriving comfort and arguments from them. "I am thoroughly persuaded," Turgenev wrote to Maria Weston Chapman in a letter of September 29, 1855, subsequently published in the *Liberty Bell*, "that all success obtained in America in the cause of the coloured race will be eminently serviceable to my poor countrymen in Russia." When Andrew Dixon White, future president of Cornell University, who had been secretary of the American legation in St. Petersburg, lectured in 1857 on the "Development and Overthrow of the Russian Serf System," he and his American audience knew that he was delivering an "indictment against our own system of slavery" (Laserson: *The American Impact on Russia*, pp. 154, 81). And Ivan Golovin noted in his *Stars and Stripes; or American Impressions* (London–New York, 1856), p. 98: "It is not allowed to write about serfdom in Russia; it is not advisable to speak much against slavery in the southern American states." See also *The Liberator*, July 2, 1858, pp. 105–6, and July 23, p. 116, brought to my attention by Professor Sidney Kaplan of the University of Massachusetts.

[1] Herzen: *Works*, XII, 14.

and enviable. To see this unity dissolve was a dramatic illustration of the excessive regard democracy paid to property rights, whereas autocracy, as Herzen anticipated, could demand from the holders of privilege that they abide by the doctrine of obedience to authority which they so loudly preached. Ivan Golovin, recording his impressions of America in *Stars and Stripes* (1856), wondered whether that government which governed least was truly the best. "Witnessing the disorder resulting from the care of individual security being left to the exertion of the people, one must confess, there is some good even in despotism interfering sometimes to put down abuses or those who commit them." The American states, far from serving as a model to resolve the questions of the age, would fall apart because unlimited competition and love of material interests had made them lose sight of the principles that presided at their formation. Disunion was their manifest destiny. "I do not give eight years to the Union to last; all compromise is at an end and the abscess must burst." He was not distressed by that eventuality and thought the South's separation a greater good than the preservation of unity with slavery.[2]

That was one choice Rusisans did not have to make, and the more violently they condemned slavery, the more ready were they to contemplate America's purification by the secession or expulsion of the Southern states. Nicholas Turgenev in September 1855 praised Garrison for the clear, firm, and moral logic that let him prefer such a course to the maintenance of the hated institution. That same logic also permitted most Russian commentators, and more especially the radicals and democrats among them, to be impatient at what they regarded as temporizing on the issue of slavery during the war. Moderates and conservatives, on the other hand, were more likely to be gratified by the ease and decisiveness with which the Emperor, by a stroke of his pen, had on February 19, 1861, solved that burning question without such a vast upheaval as America was suffering. But as long as that day was still in the future and serf emancipation and its modalities were still being discussed, mainly behind closed doors, slavery, and the way Americans were or were not dealing with

---

2 Golovin: *Stars and Stripes*, pp. vii, 98–100, 117, 274–5.

it, continued to be of absorbing interest to Russians, opening the way to the most sustained discussion of American life and politics they were ever to conduct.[3]

The question raised most insistently was how such a seemingly free and happy people, a prosperous and harmonious society, could now be racked by bitter discord and on the point of dissolution. There had been bloodshed in Kansas and near-civil war; it was doubtful if passions would subside. The battles of parties, once merely loud and lusty, had taken on a threatening character. The lesser commercial and financial quarrels that normally divided them were overshadowed by the vital dispute over slavery, in which all others were involved—the admission of new states, the building of railroads, the size of the army. Such a striking change in the temper of public life demanded an explanation.

How had the struggle against slavery come to be such a bone of contention? How had America, so well favored by being spared the burdens of the past, so far advanced in reconciling individual freedom and the public welfare, fallen so far behind the other civilized nations? Reading the "thick" journals of the years after 1857 (the radical-democratic *Contemporary*, the more eclectically progressive *Russian Word*, the liberal *Fatherland Notes*, the as yet moderately conservative *Russian Messenger*, and Dostoevsky's Russophile *Time*), one often gets the sense that the America emerging from their pages had become fairer by contrast with the disfiguring blot of slavery. All her faults but one were momentarily forgotten in the recital of her virtues— political freedom, civil liberty and equality, the rights of women, the absence of a permanent proletariat, the high level of popular education, and the availability of land. "In all respects but one America forges ahead with giant steps. . . . Only one stain is visible on her star-spangled banner: slavery; that is the canker of her present and the menace to her future. . . . Her fate depends on the resolution of this question."[4]

---

[3] Tarasova: "Dekabrist N. Turgenev," p. 210, *n.* 9.

[4] "Zagranichnye izvestiia; zhurnalistika v Soedinennykh Shtatakh," *Sovremennik*, LXIV (June/July 1857), 119–27; "Istoricheskii ocherk konstitutsii Soedinennykh Shtatov," *Russkoe slovo* (Mar. 1860), pp. 151–84;

Opinion in the United States had always been against slavery, wrote the author of a survey of American affairs in *The Contemporary* (Apr. 1857); but restrictions on freedom of expression in the South, fears for national unity, respect for the Constitution, and confidence that this form of human bondage would in time disappear advised caution and restraint. Only in recent years had the religious and moral feelings of the masses and of prominent men alike been aroused: by the shock of the Mexican War, into which a peace-loving republic had been pushed by an expansionist South; by the attacks of planters on Texas and Kansas, by their inhuman treatment of slaves, by slave risings and slave codes. Antislavery sentiment had finally taken organized form in the abolitionist movement, which twenty years before represented an insignificant and unpopular minority. Compromise and reconciliation appeared less likely as moral revulsion grew in the North and as the South moved ever more boldly to safeguard its peculiar institution and its inordinate political weight. The North had finally realized that slavery would not abolish itself and that it was a growing threat to free labor.

"Smes'," ibid. (July 1860), pp. 1–22, and (Sept. 1860), pp. 197–236; P. Sokal'skii: "Vpechatleniia russkago v Amerike," ibid. (Nov. 1860); "Sovremennaia letopis'," *Russkii vestnik*, Book 1 (Oct. 1860), p. 232. I must apologize for an inconsistent system of citations to Russian journals, caused by confusing methods employed by publishers and binderies and often compounded by microfilm and microfiche firms. Since most Russian journals and reviews used were monthlies, the number of the issue (i.e. No. 1–No. 12) usually indicates the month of publication. Where this is clearly the case, I have adhered to that style of citation. In cases of doubt or of divergence from that pattern, I have included as much information in the reference as seemed necessary to make location and dating possible. A note is also in order about circulation figures. The highest circulation attained by *Fatherland Notes* was 8,000, by *The Contemporary*—6,500, by *Russian Word*—5,000, and by *The Cause*—5,700. The conservative *Russian Messenger* and *Time* reached 5,700 and about 4,000 subscribers respectively. Among newspapers, Katkov's *Moscow News* led with a circulation of 12,000. With illiteracy at 76 per cent as late as 1897, and above 90 per cent in most regions during the 1860's, these are impressive figures, the more so since the number of readers was bound to be larger than the number of subscribers. The impression that "Russia was obviously a land where public opinion, apart from Government circles, could scarcely be said to exist" needs therefore to be revised. (Donaldson Jordan and Edwin J. Pratt: *Europe and the American Civil War* [Boston, 1931], p. 199.)

White Southerners who owned no plantations were also being debased to poverty-stricken proletarians by the competition of black hands and the leisure class of the planters. If the newly elected President became the tool of the South, as his past conduct suggested, the North would do everything to assure its candidate—probably Frémont—of success in 1860. His victory would bring the hour of decision for the Union. The "contemporary chronicler" for the *Russian Messenger* also thought a lasting, peaceful settlement of the crisis unlikely; the make-up of Buchanan's cabinet alone made it improbable.[5]

The same journal's review of Olmsted's *A Journey in the Seaboard Slave States* dwelt on the harmful effects of slavery that Southerners were unable or unwilling to recognize. Deeply ingrained habits and traditions, a numbing conservatism of thought, prevented the ascendancy of an economic rationality that should, if Olmsted were right, have driven out the inefficient labor of slaves by that of free men. Instead, sluggishness, stagnation, and decline were the South's fate, the planter's revenge. No Russian could miss the point, although censorship still made its open statement impossible. *The Bell,* published by Herzen in London but widely read in Russia, was under no such constraint and his friend Nicholas Ogarev made it explicit in February 1858. In the North, a people free in its initiative and energy had made a wide application of science to agriculture, while the South stood still. Although the inertia of the planters, their reluctance to break with custom, and their ignorance of modern agriculture contributed to the stagnation of their states, the critical difference was that between free and slave labor. "Does not this remind you of the Russian landlords?" asked Ogarev, and although he and Russian radicals in general held no brief for the "cheap economic liberalism" of similar arguments, its implications were widely accepted. The South, argued a writer for *Russian Word* (who blamed the North equally for the evil of slavery), had not a fraction of the social, commercial, and intellectual energy of the more populous and prosperous free states. The difference between them was that between England and Naples (or papal

---

[5] "Vzgliad na vnutrennye otnosheniia Soedinennykh Shtatov," *Sovremennik,* Vol. LXII, No. 4 (1857), Section II, pp. 65–104; "Sovremennaia letopis'," *Russkii vestnik,* No. 9/10 (May/Aug. 1857), p. 47.

Rome), where also the inhibition of free thought and speech contributed to the general backwardness.[6]

In these comparisons, Russia played South to America's or Europe's North, and her defeat by Europe in the Crimean War made the lesson all the more clear. As a result, Russians were better prepared than most Europeans to interpret the news from American battlefields, for they had learned one of the lessons of backwardness by bitter experience—that courage and a martial spirit are of no avail against superior organization, equipment, and technique. In this respect, the impact of the Civil War was felt long before its outbreak and reinforced the universal clamor for the reform and modernization of Russia. It also predisposed Russians of every shade of opinion in favor of the Union; they were too conscious of its penalties and indignities to side with backwardness, even where class interests and prejudices might incline them to sympathy for the South. There is no record of any Russians fighting for the Confederacy, although Cassius Clay, the American minister at St. Petersburg, observed that "Russians of the higher classes are more like Southerners than the Southerners are like the Northerners." Affinity did not turn into active sympathy, as Clay realized when in the fall of 1861 he wrote to Secretary of State Seward on behalf of "a good many" young Russian officers who wanted to enlist in the union cause. The only Russians known to have fought in the Civil War did so on the Northern side; with the exception of some sailors who jumped ship and enlisted in the Union forces, they were men who probably left Russia for reasons not connected with the Civil War and in one case had come to America long before its outbreak: John Basil Turchin, a brigadier general who had served Nicholas I as Colonel Ivan Vasilievich Turchaninov; a Colonel Charles De Arnaud, who was invalided out of the federal army in February 1862; and Prince Alexander Eristov, member of a prominent family of Georgian nobles.[7]

---

6 Ibid., IX (1857), 70–3; Laserson: *The American Impact on Russia*, p. 225; V. Khankin: "Vopros ob emantsipatsii v Soedinennykh Shtatakh; teoriia Fits-Guga . . . ," *Russkoe slovo*, No. 9 (1860), pp. 77–102; "Vnutrennye novosti," *Vremia*, II (1861), 12. For an earlier expression of views on America by Herzen's friend Nicholas Ogarev see *Literaturnoe nasledstvo*, Vol. 61 (Moscow, 1953), pp. 708–9.

7 Albert Parry: "Cassius Clay's Glimpse into the Future," *Russian Review*, II, 2 (Spring 1943), 64; ibid., "John B. Turchin, Russian General

Herzen also equated the South and the Kingdom of Naples, but mainly to show how much like them the North had grown. The planters had made a religious dogma of slavery and persecuted any challenge to it with the vile methods of the Bourbons and Habsburgs; now even the free men of the North accepted it as the cornerstone of union and democracy. Discussing Robert Owen's mistaken belief that his teaching would take root in the New World, Herzen was led to ask at the end of 1860 "not whether Owen was right or wrong . . . but whether a critical attitude and moral independence are compatible with the existence of the state." Such doubts brought him closer to the Slavophiles, for if even in America, the most successful of experiments in limiting the state, the people carried out the functions of tsar, gendarme, and hangman, apprehended fugitive slaves and condemned John Brown, what hope was there for less favored nations? Never had there been such a happy combination of circumstances for a free and rational development as in North America. The teachings of the eighteenth-century philosophers and revolutionaries, the English common law—all of Europe's dreams had here come together in a republican, federal, democratic, self-governing union, only to issue in a society in which the majority performed the role of dictator and policeman.[8]

Herzen's reading of American events was a measure of his hopes for Russia. These had been buoyed by the promise of serf liberation that the Emperor had given in 1857. "Thou hast conquered, O Galilean!" Herzen said on that occasion, and the prospect of extensive reforms from above for a time moderated the tone of *The Bell*. It also increased his anger at the lengths to which a supposedly advanced people could be carried in de-

---

in the Civil War," I, 2 (Apr. 1942), 44–5; "I. V. Turchaninov i ego zhena—Gertsenu," *Literaturnoe nasledstvo*, Vol. 62 (Moscow, 1955), pp. 591–603; James Robertson: *A Kentuckian at the Court of the Tsars* (Berea, Ky., 1931), p. 178. Ella Lonn: *Foreigners in the Union Army and Navy* (Baton Rouge, La., 1951) mentions not a single Russian subject of the tsar besides Turchin, but considerable numbers of Poles. See pp. 212, 284, 602; and Sh. A. Bogina: *Immigratsiia v SShA nakanune i v period grazhdanskoi voiny, 1850–1865* (Moscow, 1965), p. 203. There is no mention of Eristov or De Arnaud in any of the standard Russian reference works. The latter was the author of *The Union and its Ally Russia* (Washington, 1890) and *The New Era in Russia* (New York, 1891).

[8] Herzen: *Works*, XI, 205, 209, 226–7; XIV, 44, 180–1.

fense of its comforts and quiet. Yet there remained, as in much Russian censure of America's betrayal of her legacy, respect for that legacy and its part in shaping what Herzen called the Jeffersonian Republic. Was there not also the unspoken assumption that if only America could purge herself of the corruption of her heritage she would fulfill her early promise? For Americans such an outcome was a conviction. "Strike out slavery, that Russian institution," said Lewis Henry Morgan, "and our country is paradise regained!" Not all Russians shared that conviction, certainly not Herzen, but when, like him, they drew parallels between the two youthful, vigorous countries, did they not also voice a hope that breaking the fetters of serfdom and slavery would reveal the full potential of both people? Emancipation and its aftermath, Civil War and Reconstruction, would soon put such hopes and expectations to the test.[9]

One man who had neither Herzen's trust in the progressive role of the autocrat nor his revulsion at democracy's self-betrayal was the former seminary student, social philosopher, revolutionary democrat, and populist socialist Nicholas Chernyshevskii. Contributor and editor of *The Contemporary*, radical critic of art, literature, and society, martyr of the revolutionary movement after his arrest and exile in 1862, Chernyshevskii became symbol and spokesman for the nihilist generation of sons who challenged inherited truths even if held by fathers who sided with them in the battle against autocracy. His generation was more cramped in its outlook than Herzen's, less generous to its foes, less tolerant of dissent, narrower in its revolutionary ardor and the tests of social utility it applied to the values of its precursors. It preferred prose to poetry, economics to aesthetics, and if its world (to speak with Turgenev's Bazarov) was a workshop rather than a temple, it can come as no surprise that Dobroliubov's and Chernyshevskii's views of America differed from those of Herzen. Chernyshevskii had no doubts that nearly all America's difficulties and shortcomings could be traced to one source, and that freed of the affliction of slavery, the country would recover its true identity and resume its place in the advance guard of progress. The corruption of legislators and the fraud-

---

9 Carl Resek: *Lewis Henry Morgan* (Chicago, 1960), p. 52.

ulence of politics, the use of force and the denial of liberties would all disappear once the political power of the planters was broken.[1]

Where Herzen was disheartened by the violence visited on those who disturbed tranquillity and property by open defiance of the laws protecting slavery, Chernyshevskii saw it as the beginning of a revolutionary struggle in which the abolitionists had wrested the offensive from the hands of their persecutors. That John Brown and his men were defeated at Harper's Ferry and that the survivors of his band would surely die was of no great importance to the larger issues at stake. What mattered was not John Brown's failure—all first attempts were bound to fail—nor his death—the abolitionists would in time avenge their martyrs —but that the effort had been made at all and that it would make abolitionism more militant. With its help, the people of North and West would realize the shame of silence and inaction; the boundaries of slavery, after having advanced for so long, would begin to shrink. Chernyshevskii's apotheosis of John Brown was followed by excerpts from his "Constitution," "interesting for the acquaintance it affords with the ideas of the people who make up the extreme abolitionist party."[2]

This was not the sole reason for reproducing the document.

---

[1] *Sovremennik*, No. 1 (1861), in *Polnoe sobranie sochinenii N. G. Chernyshevskago v 10 tomakh* (St. Petersburg, 1906), VIII, 23–33 (hereafter Chernyshevskii: *Works*). There is a more recent and more complete edition of Chernyshevskii's works (Moscow, 1939–51), but although I was able to consult it for purposes of comparison, it was not available to me at time of writing. References therefore are to the older edition.

[2] Chernyshevskii: *Works*, V, 440–6. For similar views of the abolitionist movement and Brown, see E. K.-di, "Razvitie rabstva v Amerike," *Russkoe slovo*, No. 12 (1865), pp. 1–30. Cf. I. P. Dement'ev: "N. G. Chernyshevskii i konstitutsiia Dzhona Brauna," *Voprosy istorii*, No. 12 (1959), pp. 137–44; I. Ia. Razumnikova: N. G. Chernyshevskii o grazhdanskoi voine v SShA," *Trudy Voronezhskogo universiteta*, XLVII (1957), 34–55, and I. I. Liagushchenko: *N. G. Chernyshevskii o grazhdanskoi voine v SShA* (abstract of dissertation for the degree of candidate of historical sciences, Saransk, 1952). According to a letter from Professor Dement'ev of Moscow University, another Russian scholar, N. Ia. Levitas, defended a dissertation in Spring 1964 on "Russian Society and the American Civil War." I have not been able to obtain or consult it, except for a portion dealing with reactions to the *Trent* affair: "Delo 'Trenta' i russkaia obshchestvennaia mysl'," *Uchenye zapiski Gor'kovskogo gosudarstvennogo universiteta*, issue 51 (1959), pp. 81–96.

There was muted talk in Russia of constitutions and the safe-guarding of citizens' rights, but what most attracted Chernyshev-skii to the abolitionists was their radicalism, which aimed, he believed, at a total reconstruction of society. The removal of slavery was but the first step; John Brown's "Constitution" and his deeds foreshadowed what was to follow and would complete what had gone before. In Chernyshevskii's eyes they were a resumption of a revolutionary tradition going back to Shay's Rebellion, of a demand for social justice taken up by Jefferson and met in the utopian communities on American soil; they reaffirmed all that had already been gained: federalism and local self-government; freedom of press and religion; public education, equality of the sexes, and publicly held reserves of land. De-termination, Chernyshevskii seemed to believe, would be as effective in clearing away obstacles to social progress as it had been in clearing forests, and he did not shrink from the cost. He looked forward to the war with equanimity and feared it less than the prospect of reconciliation. That is also why he was fascinated with the abolitionists. Here at last were Americans whom Rus-sian radicals could recognize as their own. History did not move without convulsions. Its road, he said in January 1861 (comment-ing on American affairs), is not at all like the Nevski Prospect in St. Petersburg. "It runs across fields of dust or dirt, through swamps or over debris. He who is afraid to be covered with dust and soil his shoes should not take part in the work of social renovation."[3]

---

[3] Chernyshevskii: *Works*, VI, 183–4; VIII, 37, from *Sovremennik*, No. 4/5 (1860) and No. 1 (1861); Laserson: *The American Impact on Rus-sia*, pp. 247–8, 282; Hecht: *Russian Radicals*, 121–2, 123, 126–7, 133–4, 137. The bond that linked Russian radicals to the abolitionists constituted for them a claim on American aid and understanding. When in 1881 an emissary of the revolutionary "People's Will" organization was sent to the United States, the New York newspapers published his appeal, which read, in part: "The abolitionists were your dearest and best sons. . . . We are the Russian abolitionists. . . . Your sympathy, like that of other nations, is dear to us." The author of the appeal predicted in an interview the success of the "nihilist" movement, which he represented: "Has not one of your noblest and best citizens, has not Wendell Phillips publicly expressed his respect and sympathy for the nihilists? Has he not spoken the noble words: 'If liberty cannot be gained by any other means but the dagger, then welcome the dagger!'?" (from Avrahm Yarmolinsky: *Road to Revo-*

Russia and the Civil War

As *The Contemporary*'s foreign-affairs commentator, Chernyshevskii followed American events with close attention. He greeted Lincoln's election as a turning point in the political evolution of the "great North American people," the beginning of a new epoch in its history. Heretofore, American politics had been dominated by descendants of an aristocracy who had received their lands and privileges from Stuart kings and were organized in a party that called itself democratic but was a screen for oligarchy. Some few thousand planters, keeping the mass of whites no less than Negroes poor and ignorant, had made the South a base of uncontested power which, by force and guile, they had extended over the nation. A small class of men, by virtue of inherited economic and political power had (as in Russia?) imposed its will on the majority. Chernyshevskii was consistent in applying a class analysis that derived from European experience.

> In general, the difference between Naples and Switzerland is not as great as that between the southern and northern halves of the United States. The northern (free) states have only recently begun to realize that it is the aristocrats of the southern (slave) states who have so far ruled the Union, and the basic meaning of the present struggle between abolitionists and planters is the determination of the democracy which prevails in the North to wrest power from the hands of the planter-aristocrats.[4]

---

lution: *A Century of Russian Radicalism* [New York, 1959], p. 297). John Brown in particular is still a much admired figure, the subject of biographies—two translations (Michael Gold's [Moscow, 1937] and John Ehrlich's [Moscow, 1940] and an original study by N. Kal'ma [Moscow, 1940 and 1957])—as well as of a recent article that takes to task all but a few "progressive" American historians for their less than worshipful attitude toward Brown—M. N. Zakharova: "Vosstanie Dzhona Brauna i amerikanskaia burzhuaznai istoriografiia," *Novaia i noveishaia istoriia*, No. 5 (1960), pp. 112–25. See also A. K. Savurenok: "Uolt Uitmen i abolitsionistskoe dvizhenie 1840–1850k godov," *Uchenye zapiski leningradskogo gosudarstvennogo universiteta; seriia filologicheskikh nauk*, issue 37, No. 234 (1957), pp. 159–72, and the articles by Dement'ev and R. F. Ivanov in A. V. Efimov and L. I. Zubok, eds.: *K stoletiiu grazhdanskoi voiny v SShA* (Moscow, 1961), pp. 74–109.

[4] Chernyshevskii: *Works*, VI, 184.

The rising of a majority that had become aware of its strength—this was how Chernyshevskii saw the Civil War, confident of its outcome in America—and Russia, should it ever come. Unperturbed by the changing fortunes of the two sides, by the skillful defense waged by a desperate South or by faintheartedness in the North, he was sure that victory would go to the most numerous and virtuous class, the farmers of the North and West who worked the land with their own hands. On November 6, 1860, they had shed a yoke borne for many decades. No matter what setbacks might be in store for them, they would reach their goal—recovery of the heights that America had not attained since Jefferson's day. Joined by the poor whites of the South, they would restore America's good name. "And the good name of the North-American people is important for all nations."[5]

Throughout late 1860 and early 1861, Chernyshevskii cited facts and figures to support his contention that history had decreed the triumph of the North and the end of slavery. Southerners knew this; their threats of secession spelled fear that time was against them, that antislavery sentiment and the Republican party were growing stronger and that each passing day would harden resistance in the North. The disintegration of the state in which Southerners had held excessive power would only hasten the disappearance of slavery and bring moderates who wished to save the Union closer to abolitionism. Yet secession was no guarantee that a union of slave states could survive in close proximity and competition with a politically and economically superior nation. The future was with the people of smallholders, workers, and traders (who had come from the land and would in a generation or two return to it), a people that for all its commercial and industrial success had escaped the concentration of wealth and the dominance of cities. The South could never adjust to a way of life demanding calculation, commerce, and capital.[6]

North and South were not simply regions of one country; nor, in case of separation, would they be merely two coun-

---

[5] Ibid., VI, 731.
[6] Ibid., VI, 755–7; VIII, 367–88; 389–403.

tries, though as different as Turkey from England or China from France. They represented distinct kinds of societies, distinct stages of history. Common political necessities had held them together, and when these disappeared their separate identities reasserted themselves. But the "general course of civilization," the "general character of progress in all civilized countries," made it predictable that the Northern pattern would prevail throughout, as it had already begun to do in the border states. And in that case the American example would speed up the processes of social change in Europe. The crisis would have a very strong influence on the fate of the civilized world. Conservatives and progressives awaited its outcome for confirmation of hopes and fears. What happened across the Atlantic would be reflected in a general disposition of European thought to follow the old or to forge ahead, to fear the future or to welcome it.

> In a year or two . . . a change must take place in the history of Western Europe as a consequence of the resolution of the present crisis in North America. But for decades the North American Union will influence the direction of that history, as it did by its very foundation—but with this difference; the example is set not by a small state, weak in comparison with the countries of Western Europe, but by a mighty nation which has already taken its place in the first rank of powers.[7]

Chernyshevskii had less of the sense of mission—Christian, Slavic, or social—than was common among the Russian intelligentsia. The dream that the last would be first and add a unique voice to the chorus of humanity held little attraction for this materialist, even if he thought that backwardness might make it easier for Russia to bypass the horrors of capitalism on her way to the socialist future. Russia for him was part of Europe, subject, therefore, to the influence of America. He would wish Russian peasants and revolutionaries to follow the example set by American farmers and abolitionists, or at least be inspired by it in their own struggle for equality and justice.

---

[7] Ibid., VII, 389–90.

II

When the Tsar decreed the end of serfdom on February 19, 1861, and Russia took her first step towards these goals, it fell far short of what Chernyshevskii expected America to achieve out of her crisis. It was not, of course, fair to measure Russian reality by American promise—Chernyshevskii did not anticipate that the freed slave would receive even less land than the former serf—but the comparison magnified dissatisfaction with the Emancipation Manifesto. Amid the almost universal jubilation that greeted its publication on March 5, Chernyshevskii and *The Contemporary* remained silent. Instead, the March issue carried a translation of Longfellow's "Poems on Slavery" and an extended review of John S. C. Abbott's *South and North*. Even if these were not protests against the inadequacies of peasant reform (since they were probably prepared before its specifics became known), they indicate a lasting concern with legal or economic bondage. Longfellow's "Warning"—"There is a poor blind Samson in this land/Shorn of his strength, and bound in bonds of steel/ Who may in some grim revel raise his hand/And shake the pillars of this Commonweal"—could indeed be read as a warning after an emancipation that left its beneficiaries disgruntled, while Abbott's praises of the free labor of free citizens kept their pertinence as long as the peasantry still suffered special civil and economic disabilities.[8]

Chernyshevskii was not alone in his dissatisfaction with the "sham" emancipation from above, but even among his comrades of *The Contemporary* and in the loosely defined camp of populist radicals, his optimism about the power and purpose of the American example was exceptional. The poet M. L. Mikhailov, translator of Longfellow, was also co-author of an appeal, "To the Young Generation," which in the winter of 1861, besides calling

---

[8] "Pesni o negrakh," *Sovremennik*. No. 3 (1861), pp. 267–78; V. Obruchev: "Nevol'nichestvo v Severnoi Amerike," ibid., p. 297–308; N. M. Sikorskii: *Zhurnal "Sovremennik" i krest'ianskaia reforma 1861 g.* (Moscow, 1957), pp. 146–9; V. A. Alekseev: *Istoriia russkoi zhurnalistiki: 1860–1880 gody* (Leningrad, 1963), p. 33; D. B. Petrov: *Avraam Linkol'n* (Moscow, 1960), p. 49, *n.* 1.

for a true, a revolutionary emancipation, proclaimed a special road for Russia. "We have already been apes of the French and the Germans; are we now to be apes of the English . . . ? Why cannot Russia arrive at some new order unknown even to America? We not only can, we must . . ."[9]

America, however unique, was to be no model for the Russia of the future. "We do not bow before the principles of American society; for us they constitute no ideal," wrote the reviewer of Abbott, though absolving America's political institutions of blame for her sins. "In the present condition of Russia, no work can be of greater interest than one describing the relative advantages of forced and free labor." That was the great lesson America taught, and ignored, concerning not only slaves but also those poor Chinese coolies, who were free only in law. "It is not enough to be free; men must also be strong, secure and guaranteed the preservation of their freedom. Otherwise, freedom will be worse than slavery." Insofar as America had given such guarantees, a self-reliant and literate citizenry had made even the cold and barren parts of the country flourish, while sections more favored by nature languished in ignorance and beggary. A Russian reader was forced to conclude that it was political and civil liberty after all that had created the conditions for America's progress, not accidental peculiarities of race or territory, as some of her detractors suggested. And was not the point of such a conclusion that Russia's unfriendly latitudes were no more hostile to the seeds of liberty than the plains of the New World?[1]

Russian populism, that conglomerate creed of pre- or non-Marxian revolutionaries who were at one in looking to the peasant commune and the craft cooperative as the building blocks of a socialist Russia, was a house of many mansions. As much a product of moral indignation and youthful ardor as of philo-

---

[9] "N. V. Shelgunov," *Bol'shaia sovetskaia entsiklopediia*, Vol. XLVII (1957), and James H. Billington: *Mikhailovsky and Russian Populism* (London and New York, 1958), p. 47.

[1] Obruchev: "Nevol'nichestvo v Severnoi Amerike," pp. 279–91; Sikorskii: *Zhurnal "Sovremennik,"* pp. 147–8; "Istoriia nevol'nichestva v Soedinennykh Shtatakh," *Otechestvyennye Zapiski*, No. 1 (1861), pp. 249–50.

sophical reflection or economic theory, its views of the United
States were not uniform, But even those populists who discounted
the benefits of reform or a liberal political order after the American pattern recognized the tactical advantages it would confer
in the battle against autocracy. Whatever populism's final aspirations for Russia might be, and they were certainly not fashioned
in the image of America, the freedoms Americans enjoyed were
still worth striving for, although they might be put to different,
and better, use than Americans had made of them. That was the
essence of the populists' perception of the United States, and
for most of them its limit.[2]

Chernyshevskii was alone when he went beyond this and
saw in the radicalism of the abolitionists and the utopian communities of the New World the pledge or at least the prospect
of America's advance to an egalitarian socialism. Kept by the
censor from speaking plainly, he possibly embellished his vision
of America to heighten its effectiveness as a criticism of Russia,
but there must also have been an element of self-deception, of
unconscious distortion. When he reviewed a Russian translation
of *Democracy in America* in June 1861, he denied Tocqueville's
stature as a thinker as well as his evidence showing democracy's
tendency to centralization. For Chernyshevskii these were mutually exclusive categories. To see liberty and equality leading to a
strengthened governmental authority seemed to him perverse,
and intolerable. If Tocqueville were writing now his mistake
might be understandable, for war would increase the scope of
federal power. But such a conclusion was not justified thirty
years ago. The present growth of governmental functions had
nothing in common with centralization, for the issue of the war,
the spirit that animated the North, was self-government. Guided
by the popular assemblies of the localities, dependent on them

---

[2] To justify its use of terror, the "People's Will," which had succeeded
in March 1881 in the assassination of Alexander II, condemned the killing of President Garfield that same year because political freedom made
terror unnecessary. "In a country where personal freedom makes honorable
ideological struggle possible, where the free will of the people determines
not only the laws, but the personality of the governors—in such a country
political murder as a means of struggle is an example of the very same
spirit of despotism that we are seeking to destroy in Russia." (Billington:
Mikhailovsky and Russian populism, p. 109.)

for the means of making war, the Union government, after using its enlarged powers to assist in the reformation of the South, would again resign these into the hands of the people, and the principle of decentralized self-government would have a new and more splendid birth.[3]

There were not many who saw American events in this light, and the fact that disagreement came from all points of the political compass indicates that the argument was as much about Russian possibilities and probabilities as about American realities. Chernyshevskii could not admit that an increase in freedom might also give rise to the growth of a power that could threaten it. If that were the case, history made little sense. The thought that progress could lead back to something reminiscent of Russian bureaucratic absolutism was obviously too horrible to be borne.[4]

Herzen, in one of his few comments on the war made during its course, saw it in just those terms: the Democrats of the South fought for the slavery of the blacks and the Republicans of the North for the slavery whose name is indivisible state power. The war had not yet made him think the better of America for finally confronting the issue of slavery. That it could happen at all was a revelation of her true nature, of the cynicism and shamelessness that were hers alone and that stood fully revealed only now. This was not his last word on America, yet for all his intemperateness, Herzen showed an awareness of one of the central issues of the war—the integrity of national power and authority—to which Russian conservatives proved as a rule more sensitive than their liberal compatriots.[5]

People with more sanguine or loyal views of the motives and meaning of serf emancipation than those of Chernyshevskii were even less disposed than the majority of radicals to look to America for guidance and instruction. To Pogodin, the son of a serf, whose dynastic patriotism harbored visions of a broadly based union of tsar and people, the "miracle" of February 19

---

[3] Chernyshevskii: *Works*, VIII, 189–206.
[4] Laserson: *The American Impact on Russia*, p. 267; N. Al'bertini: "Politicheskie idei Tokvilia i otzyv o v nem 'Sovremennike,'" *Otechestvennye zopiski*, No. 8 (1861), pp. 92–6.
[5] Herzen: *Works*, XVI, 162, 9.

seemed all at once to have placed Russia in the vanguard of mankind. It was now the turn of the Europe of Wilberforce and Bentham to pay her tribute, for she had transformed 23,000,000 victims of their betters' whims into full-fledged human beings. The time had come when Russia would do away with rigid distinctions of class, when yesterday's serf could be tomorrow's minister of state and the whole peasant estate had become landed proprietors, some settled in ready-made phalansteries that would be the envy of Fourier, Saint-Simon, and Owen. What an indulgent minister of the interior called Pogodin's extravagant foolishness was as rare on the Right as was Chernyshevskii's immoderate American bias on the Left, yet the feeling that the Tsar's glorious deed marked a turning point for Russia was not uncommon. "Russia begins a new period of her history," exclaimed a writer in the Dostoevsky brothers' *Time*, words reminiscent of those Chernyshevskii had used for the election of Lincoln. All the conditions had now been created for the nation's return to the native sources of its being, for that free development of its material and spiritual resources that could alone prevent surrender to Europe's soulless rationalism.[6]

It was not likely that a Pogodin or Dostoevsky, or anyone near them in outlook, would seek inspiration in the Yankee republic, or anywhere outside of Russia. Still, it would be wrong to assume a simple equation between domestic positions and attitudes toward America and the Civil War. It is not true, as a Soviet historian has said, that conservative and liberal circles sympathized with the slaveowners and that Russia's "revolutionary democrats" alone were consistent advocates of the Negro's cause. Neither men nor situations are as uncomplicated as that, and there was a wider latitude of opinion among the staff and contributors of most publications than would appear possible to Russians a century later.[7]

V. A. Zaitsev, a radical writer for the pro-Northern *Russian Word*, for example, could invoke the authority of Darwin to

---

[6] P. A. Valuev: *Dnevnik* (Moscow, 1961), I, 94; "Vnutrenniia novosti," *Vremia*, No. 2 (1861), pp. 12–14. Similarly ecstatic reactions to the emancipation from liberal and conservative publications are described by Sikorskii: *Zhurnal "Sovremennik,"* pp. 142–4.

[7] Levitas: "Delo 'Trenta,'" pp. 82, 95.

maintain that the natural inferiority of the blacks made slavery an appropriate and beneficial state. It was the best a colored person could wish for on coming into contact with the white race, for the alternative was slow extinction. "The sentimental opponents of slavery can do no better than to quote texts and sing psalms, but they can cite no single fact to show that education and freedom can make the mind of a Negro into that of a white." Zaitsev's literal-minded scientism applied to race was as exceptional on the Left as his approval of the South's wish for a "free federation of states," and he was condemned for both. But the Left had no monopoly on the "correct" attitude toward Negroes and the American war. At other points of the political spectrum, humanitarianism, Christian principles, or a clear-headed appreciation of Russian national interest could without great difficulty lead conservatives and moderates of all shadings to sympathy and identification with the North and the cause for which, in most Russian eyes, it was fighting.[8]

That is why *Time,* which greeted February 19 with joy, no less than *The Contemporary,* which kept a demonstrative silence on that occasion, could publish one of Longfellow's "Poems on Slavery"—not, to be sure "The Warning," which appeared in the apolitical *Readers' Library* as well as in *The Contemporary*— but "The Slave's Dream." That is also why the review founded by the religious, antiliberal, and mystical nationalist Dostoevsky could publish what was perhaps the most passionate indictment of American slavery in the same issue that hailed the Emperor's great deed. And there is no reason to see a revolutionary intent in the specter of a vast and ferocious rising which the author of that indictment conjured up as the likely result of the despair to which the slaves were driven by the inhuman cruelty of their treatment. Anyone who wished could, of course, read even this article as a protest against the exploitation and debasement of Russian peasants, although it was made clear that the degradation of the latter had never reached American proportions.

The burden of the charge was rather that all Americans had

---

[8] Alekseev: *Istoriia russkoi zhurnalistiki,* pp. 54–5; Charles A. Moser: *Antinihilism in the Russian Novel* (The Hague, 1964), pp. 54–55; James A. Rogers: "Darwinism, Scientism, and Nihilism," *Russian Review,* XIX, 1 (1960), 18–21.

turned their backs on those moral and legal imperatives by which, supposedly, their country was governed. Southern legislators who provided unusually severe punishment for the crimes of black men, public servants who infringed the liberties of freedmen or the civil rights of the Negro's champions—these could hardly claim to represent the conscience of the nation. Things were not much better in the North. If it were truly the home of freedom, it would meet fugitive slaves with open arms rather than with hunger, poverty, and hostility; its churches would speak out against bondage in the South and discrimination at home, and the profitably illegal slave trade would soon be stopped. The prime motive of abolitionism was not the wish to extend the rights of citizenship to all, to create a great, republican community or bring about the brotherhood of man. It was fear of competition from unfree labor that caused the North's implacable hostility for the slave states and the likelihood of conflict.[9]

Such a conclusion reflected the intellectual nativism of the men who published and wrote for *Time*. It was a rejection of Western materialism and hypocrisy, a warning to Russia against relying on the formal safeguards of laws or institutions for the protection of human dignity and the performance of Christian duty. The warning was repeated in a discussion of "The Dissolution of the United States." Nowhere in America had the end of legal bondage diminished economic envy or racial prejudice. The all-powerful court of public opinion negated even the best of laws and denied black men a share in the rights, joys, and sorrows of their fellow citizens. Indeed, the planter's treatment of his slave was in some ways more humane than the impersonal coldness that Northerners erected as a barrier against the recognition of the Negro's needs and humanity. Admittedly, it was difficult for two races to live together in equality, but it was more difficult in the United States than elsewhere. An individual can overcome the prejudices of his race and country, and if he achieves great power he can bring about great changes. But to expect this of a whole people, to ask that it rise above itself, is

---

[9] "Son Negra-Nevol'nika," *Vremia*, I (1861), 417–18; "Chernye liudi v Soedinennykh Shtatakh," ibid., No. 2 (1861), pp. 493–519; "Predostorezhenie," *Biblioteka dlia chteniia*, No. 8 (1963), p. 28.

impossible. "A mighty ruler could, perhaps, force the Americans to join with their former slaves, but as long as America has a democratic form of government, this cannot be." And as long as profit took precedence over neighborly love, as long as governments had to abide by the lowest common denominator of majority rule, things would not change. That is why the coming conflict, begun over tariffs and property rights, would end by giving to the United States a strong government which could command obedience to charity and justice. The country had gained by the departure of the South; freed of the constraint of states' rights, the government could act. And whether monarchy or republic, a great state had need of a strong central authority. America would at last be truly united and strong; now there would be a real nation, not thirty-four states.[1]

When the war began, *Time* called it one of the most absurd and hideous ever fought; the habit of past association alone made the North try to keep the South from departing in peace. Chernyshevskii agreed that a peaceful dissolution of the bonds of union would be better than an indecisive accommodation. He preferred the judgment of battle in this conflict of patricians and plebeians provoked by upper-class hatred for the republican order. The response of the Northern masses to the news of Fort Sumter, the stiffening determination of all classes, as shown by the outpouring of volunteers, were hopeful signs. So was the Negro's awakening, which a writer for the *Russian Word* pointedly described as inevitable among the oppressed and exploited, slaves or starving proletarians, everywhere. Influenced by the teachings of the "foremost phalanx of the abolitionists," the slaves might soon begin their own liberation. Unfortunately, this elite of determined men was too small, while the majority, too much governed by interest or fugitive emotion, lacked firmness and conviction. These qualities, for a Russian radical of the 1860's, were the only sure guides to action; without them, the North might compromise. In any case, there would not be a bold and speedy resolution of the conflict. And if the planters should win, theirs would be a state like Rome or Austria—centralized, bureaucratic, with a secret police and an inquisition.

---

[1] "Raspadenie Soedinennykh Shtatov," ibid., II (1861), 1–22.

"May God preserve all peoples, black or white, from such an affliction." It was hardly possible to be more outspoken.[2]

The question posed by all Russians who followed the fortunes of the two combatants was really the same: How would the North acquit itself? The doom of slavery was but a question of time, whatever the outcome of the war. What mattered was its conduct, how and how quickly it would end the bondage of the Negro. War would reveal the character and qualities of a people that had never yet been put to such a test as old Europe knew only too well, and simple patriotism was not enough to meet it. Would America, in her trial, revert to more stringent patterns of rule and social organization; would she be able to preserve the great measure of public and private liberties she had enjoyed and resume, in peace, her unconstrained and prosperous life, as well as her role in world affairs? How would men so little used to the needs of collective discipline respond to the call to arms?

Much of the answer depended on the questioner, somewhat less on news from the battlefields, still less on promptings of commercial benefit or envy. There was a depression in the textile industry and the drop in production and employment was related to the dwindling cotton supply. But the 76,000 workers and 683 enterprises affected had no such weight, either numerical or political, as did the mill hands and owners in Manchester or Rouen. Russia competed with the United States neither in trade nor in international politics, and even those of her statesmen and citizens who had no love for democracy or representative government recognized (as did her minister to Washington) that the preservation of the Union was in their own best interest. As a result, Russians generally took a principled stand on the issues surrounding the Civil War. Having accomplished the legal emancipation of their peasants, untroubled by the danger of national disunity until the outbreak of the Polish rebellion in January 1863, they judged the United States by the highest standards of moral and political conduct and, particularly in the early period of the war, found it wanting. Not that there was

---

2 "Politicheskoe obozrenie," ibid., IV (1861), 84–87; Chernyshevskii: *Works*, VIII, 435–6, 439–40, 452; V. Toporov: "Nevol'nichestvo v iuzhnykh amerikanskikh shtatakh," *Russkoe slovo*, No. 3 (?), pp. 1–28. The journal bears a publication date of March, but the article is signed "17 April."

an easily traceable consistency in all Russian views. While the war lasted, and in response to changing news, positions changed rapidly and unexpectedly. This was a sign of impatience, disappointment, or inadequate knowledge, not of whim, and although more reflective evaluations had to wait, there was an underlying continuity of outlook.[3]

This inconsistency in detail and constancy of larger views was particularly noticeable in the case of *Time*, making its moral absolutism resemble *The Contemporary*'s unyielding radicalism. During most of 1861, *Time* regarded America's agony with little understanding and less sympathy for the North. Its belligerent enthusiasm, especially among noncombatants, was thought surprising and quite unnecessary, like the war itself. When the conflict brought increased taxes, tariffs, emissions of paper money, and the silencing of those who had remained aloof and critical in the midst of collective intoxication, this was regarded as the first step down the road of coercion. Energy and money,

---

[3] James Mavor: *An Economic History of Russia* (London, Toronto, and New York, 1914), II, 370–1; Michael T. Florinsky: *Russia: A History and an Interpretation* (New York, 1960), II, 930–1; Albert A. Woldman: *Lincoln and the Russians* (2nd edn.; New York: Collier Books; 1961), p. 44. For figures on cotton imports see N. A. Khalfin: *Politika Rossii v Srednei Azii* (Moscow, 1960), pp. 156–7. I have not dealt at all in these pages with the diplomatic or political relations between the two governments. There is a large literature on this, summarized on the Russian side by M. M. Malkin: *Grazhdanskaia voina v SShA i tsarskaia Rossiia* (Moscow-Leningrad, 1939) and his more recent "Russko-amerikanskie otnosheniia v period grazhdanskoi voiny," in Efimov and Zubok: *K Stoletiiu grazhdanskoi voiny v SShA* pp. 417–51; on the American side by Woldman. Both writers characterize the directors of Russian policy as blindly hostile to American republicanism and democracy. While this may be true of Edouard de Stoeckl, the Russian minister in Washington, his immediate superior Prince Gorchakov, as well as other members of the government, were not unthinking reactionaries and were able to make more discriminating judgments than either author thinks them capable of. This is not to say that Russia's American policy was formed by tolerance or liking of representative and republican government. But Stoeckl's narrow and inflexible conservatism was not, in 1861, an accurate reflection of the diversity of opinion to be found even in his own government and the Russian upper classes. It is not altogether impossible that Stoeckl, who had lived in the United States for twenty years and was married to an American woman, expressed as much the doubts of American as of Russian conservatives about the prospects and attractions of democracy.

which the Union had in such profusion, could undoubtedly ensure victory, but would the spirit of its leaders and soldiers prove equal to the task? After two major defeats, the volunteers who had rallied to the colors quickly lost heart and clamored to go home. Were superior resources and numbers enough to overcome the advantages of military and social discipline?

While *Time* praised the Lincoln administration's restraint in the *Trent* affair, it also accused it of temporizing, of hoping that the Union could be restored without "the great upheaval that would be the consequence of ending slavery." Victory demanded a wholehearted dedication to that cause, without prevarication about the priority of national unity. "Let Congress now declare boldly and openly that the Civil War in America is being fought not for the abstract principle of unity, which no one in Europe needs or cares for, but specifically for the elimination of slavery; there would arise in all Europe such sympathy for the North that it would force even the cotton manufacturers into silent acquiescence." Europe would gladly wait for the flow of cotton to resume if only Lincoln promised it together with freedom. Without hope of recognition and aid from Britain and France, the South would have to yield.[4]

As 1862 wore on and the federal armies recovered from their defeats, there were signs that the North had made an unqualified commitment to abolition, that the war had taken on a new character and that its issues had at last been clearly defined. By spring *Time* already saw victory inclining to the side of freedom and defeat for the separatists. Most important, military successes had made possible congressional action to end slavery in the District of Columbia, although the legislators' vote (ninety-three to thirty-six) showed the "unforgivable slowness" of their conversion to "new and sounder concepts." Until that conversion was complete and Congress abandoned its unthinking respect for the rights of ownership over human property, the war would drag on; neither ingenuity, ironclads, nor material preponderance could ensure an early victory. It was time to recognize that tariffs, free trade, even unity, were but side issues, time

---

4 "Politicheskoe obozrenie," *Vremia*, V (1861), 43; VI (1861), 25–8; VII (1862), 6–18.

to declare that slavery would forever be abolished in all occupied territories or end the bloodshed. "But because of mistaken ideas or prejudices concerning property and the war, the Washington Congress does not dare to speak out boldly or to take firm and logical measures."[5]

In June, whoever wrote the "Political Survey" for *Time* spoke of America's war as unprecedented in its scope and ferocity. This time he had no doubt that the North fought to end, and the South ignobly to preserve, slavery. The volunteers who had a few months earlier seemed little better than deserters were now pouring in by the thousands and hundreds of thousands; now, citizen soldiers were preferable to a burdensome standing army and more than a match for the South, which had neither military genius nor talent to lead it. The sons of the North, rising as one under the banner of freedom, would surely prevail over coercion and backwardness. Even cautious, republican Lincoln assumed heroic, almost imperial proportions because he understood that a government is strongest when its actions are in harmony with the public spirit. Armed with that knowledge, he governed well, gaining the confidence even of capital, which is never ruled by sentiment.[6]

But by August, with the North having failed to take the step that would end hostilities, Lincoln was once again an ordinary mortal, and if he embodied the spirit of his countrymen, it was that of narrow materialism. This was no war of principle, but of tariffs and trade, and Lincoln himself unwittingly admitted the secondary importance of slavery when he advised a Negro deputation to settle in Panama or Liberia because the gulf between them and white Americans was unbridgeable. He had, in effect, conceded that there was no remedy for the resentment and economic envy caused by black men and that the fight was not for their liberty. How could Lincoln ever have been considered an abolitionist, and what did the word mean in America? It was hatred, not love, that motivated the opponents of slavery.

---

[5] Ibid., VIII (1862), 47; IX (1862), 29; X (1862), 31–6.

[6] Ibid., XI (1862), 30–5. In 1862, three issues of the review—designated on the microfiche cards as vols. XI–XIII, Nos. 6–8—carried a special supplement with a translation of Richard Hildreth's *Archie Moore, the White Slave*.

As 1862 drew to its close and as the war grew more costly
in treasure and blood, it came to look less noble and more use-
less. The volunteers of spring turned into mercenaries enlist-
ing for pay and bonuses; their commanders were men without
skills or gifts who ordered troops into shameful, bloody attacks
against impregnable positions; the government was castigated
for rejecting European offers of mediation and the President's
year-end message to Congress was said to have destroyed the last
pretense that this was a war against slavery. His scheme for
compensated emancipation, to be completed by the year 1900,
appeared reprehensibly modest and slow to men who saw serfdom ended boldly from one day to the next but who forgot that
even Russian autocrats had hesitated and wavered for more than
fifty years. If that was all Mr. Lincoln expected of the twentieth
century, the carnage and the unspeakable horror of war were
hardly justified.[7]

> It is difficult to find a more spineless document than the
> President's message. Standing at the head of a great nation,
> he should have spoken out. He is the responsible leader of
> an undertaking which will decide the political life or death
> of his people. The solemn moment arrived when he had the
> opportunity to render an account, before the Old World and
> the New, of what has been done and of what he still hopes
> to do. But he expressed not a single thought which was out
> of the ordinary or rose above current commonplaces; he
> advanced not a single fundamental proposal and did no
> more than with evasive wordiness to suggest the redemp-
> tion of the slaves in the 20th century—and only if their
> masters consent.

In the first four months of 1863 *Time* turned its attention
to other parts of the world, particularly to Poland, perhaps because they were closer, perhaps because the marches and coun-
termarches of armies on a distant continent obscured the larger
issues of right and justice without which history and politics
were meaningless and cruel games. It was the insertion of such
sentiments into a perfectly loyal discussion of the Polish re-

---

[7] Ibid., No. 8 (1862), pp. 25–7; No. 9 (1862), p. 115; No. 12 (1862),
pp. 131–4.

bellion that may have caused the censor to order the journal's closing in April. It did not resume publication until 1864, when the Dostoevsky brothers gave it a new start and a new title, *Epoch,* only to fail finally, this time for financial reasons, within a year.

Before and after its own, rather more predictable eight months' suspension for "harmful tendencies" in June 1862, *The Contemporary,* while impatient, remained sanguine about the course and outcome of the war. Where *Time* was appalled by the spectacle of a vast bloodletting unredeemed by an overriding moral purpose, Chernyshevskii, Dobroliubov, and their successors were heartened by the fact that the battle had been joined. As they watched events across the Atlantic, they too hoped that these represented larger goals, of which abolition, though the most immediate, was but one. If the men of *Time* looked for a pledge of America's moral regeneration in her speedy and decisive solution of the slavery problem, Chernyshevskii and his comrades wished that the conflict might be transformed into a popular crusade for social justice. The very manner in which they described it, their willingness to countenance its widening and deepening, their optimism in the face of defeat, betray a readiness to accept violence and bloodshed as necessary to change. Even if the war ended in a compromise peace, leaving basic issues unsettled, it would not be entirely fruitless. A cause that had once engaged so many men so deeply would not be denied forever. Change was in the air at home: student riots, peasant unrest, liberal demands for a representative assembly, and revolutionary appeals for "land and freedom" showed that emancipation had been only a beginning. If this was the effect of reforms from above, there was reason to expect that civil war in America would set in motion processes as vast and lasting in their consequences as in their causes. After the long night of repression that followed 1848, after the airless, hopeless years of Nicholas I, both worlds were on the move again and for a brief moment their rhythms and aspirations seemed to coincide.[8]

That is why the columns of *The Contemporary* reflected no alarm over Union reverses in the summer of 1861 and Bull Run

---

[8] See the "Politika" columns of *Sovremennik* for April, May, and June, 1861, in Chernyshevskii: *Works,* VIII, 435–6, 437–56, 467.

was dismissed as only a skirmish. When the full scope of the disaster became known, there was no fear for the successful prosecution of the war. Defeat would only spur the North to greater effort. There was proof of this in the unexpected support that New York's financiers were giving to the war effort, in the unanimity with which Congress was voting more men and money than the government asked, in the energy with which it imposed taxes and tariffs, and in the ending of partisan strife. If the country's economic and political leaders displayed such confidence, the masses were even more ready to sacrifice for victory. The Confiscation Act of August 1861—providing for the freeing of the few slaves employed in arms or labor against the Republic—rather than being considered the half-hearted measure for which *Time* would have taken it, was greeted as a decisive step toward emancipation, a sign that the war had entered a new phase. As for suspensions of *habeas corpus*, passport requirements, prohibitions on intercourse with citizens of rebel states, measures against dissident newspapers—Dobroliubov made light of fears expressed on that score. These were not the result of abolitionist policies but legitimate measures of defense for which the South alone, the instigator of subversion and sedition, must bear the blame. "Events in America have justified our prediction that the war . . . cannot end in compromise—now less than ever."[9]

Its very prolongation, Chernyshevskii wrote in September, would serve to radicalize it. On this the abolitionists based their hopes, as did Chernyshevskii when he likened the American to the English Civil War. The latter too had at first been marked by vacillating leaders, moderates who were afraid of extreme measures. But gradually, more determined men had come to the fore, taken control of the army and defeated the royalists with ease. When applied to America this anatomy of revolution made Lincoln, Seward, and Scott the moderates who rejected any idea of freeing the Negroes and showed themselves insensitive to the meaning of the struggle. As the armies enlisted and trained new men to replace professionals whose sympathies were often with

---

[9] *Ibid.*, VIII, 478–81 (for the July "Politics" commentary), and Dobroliubov: *Sobranie Sochinenii*, VIII, 205–18 (for that of August, previously attributed to Chernyshevskii).

the South, as the people of the free states tired of their command-ers' lack of resolution, they began to listen to the abolitionists and to see that there could be no end of sectional conflict with-out an end to slavery. This mood was also penetrating Con-gress, which had forced the first Confiscation Act upon a reluc-tant President. There were already calls to go further. Frémont's actions in Missouri were another portent of the future, and their partial reversal by Lincoln did not make Chernyshevskii doubt that unless the war ended quite soon, a radical emancipation would be its inevitable conclusion. During the last months of 1861 he compared the strength of the two armies, disputed the opinion of "some military writers of the old school" about the superiority of regulars over militia and volunteers, and warned of the fate awaiting the South if the North was forced to call upon the Negroes to revolt. In all this he had constantly in mind the example of a revolutionary *levée en masse* that would sweep all hesitation, all timidity, all the advices of caution and narrow legalism from its path.[1]

Such a prospect distressed the political commentator of the liberal *Fatherland Notes*. "The character of the present American revolution," he wrote in early 1861, "has nothing in common with European revolutions" that liberals, radicals, or conservatives fought over political institutions and principles. There were no such parties and contests in the United States, where both sides accepted the Constitution, which had artfully reconciled freedom and power, stability and progress. The slave-owners had risen not for political forms or ideas, but to defend selfish interests, and in doing so they had laid a hand on the best realization of Europe's thoughts and hopes. Such reasoning was meant to reassure believers in a representative federal sys-tem that its eclipse in North America was but a passing illness. Even after the secession, there would be a powerful federation of twenty million people to fulfill in even nobler and purer form Europe's aspirations. The South must be let go in peace, for con-straint was alien to America and a compact entered into freely should be dissolved peacefully. Therefore, Lincoln's moderation and hesitation were praiseworthy, designed to avoid a senseless war such as Europe would long since have precipitated. With

---

[1] Chernyshevskii: *Works*, VIII, 507–9, 517–18, 528–30.

war, there came ill omens that even in the North law was bowing to force. In August it still seemed possible that the spirit and the habit of freedom would survive; by October, the American democracy seemed doomed. The country was moving to dictatorship and dissolution. There were illegal arrests, repression of dissent, mob justice against independent minds. "The fort which bears the glorious name of Lafayette is now the Bastille of democratic America." Separatism would not end with the South. The West would develop similar strivings and there would soon be three states instead of one, each fearful of its neighbor, with standing armies and regimented societies.[2]

To Chernyshevskii the new year brought fresh evidence that the men in charge of the federalists' fortunes, far from despots, were still lagging behind the country's resolve. In Congress, which better reflected the popular mood than the President and his Cabinet, abolitionist sentiment was growing. Some first steps had been taken to carry out the abolitionist program; the rest was being debated with growing chances of passage as the war continued and the army too came to be dominated by the extreme party. There was also good news from the fronts, with the capture of Fort Donelson, the Shiloh campaign, and the taking of New Orleans, which, Chernyshevskii recalled, the South's European partisans had thought impossible. The war, he felt in the spring, had finally taken a serious turn after the North had learned from its experience with McClellan that one should not entrust a cause to men who are not fully committed to it. But before McClellan's star was dimmed by failure and suspicions of incompetence or worse, Chernyshevskii had assured his countrymen, especially the liberals among them, that there was not the slightest risk of Bonapartism in the dissension between the commander in chief and the dominant party in Congress. Even if McClellan were to achieve Napoleonic victories, they would be credited not to one man but to the people themselves, to the masses of army and nation. Americans, it was true, were impressionable, excitable people, easily given to noisy celebrations of success. But they had a sound sense of their own worth, never

---

[2] "Politicheskoe obozrenie," *Otechestvennye zapiski*, No. 3 (1861), pp. 87–92; No. 4 (1861), pp. 90–3; No. 7 (1861), pp. 39–40; No. 8 (1861), pp. 71–2; No. 10 (1861), pp. 55–6.

forgetting that the hero of the hour was their own creation. If he should think his importance due to his own merits, they would throw him over and return him to obscurity. There was no chance of a military dictatorship in the United States.[3]

In Russia, the radicals' disenchantment with Alexander II, their propaganda, and the formation in early 1862 of "Land and Freedom," a secret society of radical revolutionaries, did not convert an era of reforms into one of civil war or revolution. Neither the government's will nor its ability to defend itself were affected by the scattered activities of "nihilists" or by peasant and student unrest. When a series of fires broke out in St. Petersburg, the authorities, blaming subversive elements, struck back with the approval of the majority of citizens. Here there were neither political parties nor a Congress that the radicals could hope to dominate, only a few journals and sympathizers. In June, *Russian Word* and *The Contemporary* were suspended for eight months; Dobroliubov had died in 1861; Chernyshevskii and many others were arrested. He never again contributed to the review on which he had placed the stamp of his personality and convictions, and although he continued to write in prison and exile until his death in 1899, he no longer played an active role in radical journalism or the revolutionary movement. He became its martyr and inspiration, was read and revered, but he was far from the center of events. How remote is shown by one of his last comments on American matters, an optimistic prediction—based on the great progress that he thought had been made in the two decades since the Civil War—that as the memory and the traces of slavery receded into the past, so would the prejudices to which it had given birth, allowing Negroes to become fully integrated in American political and social life.[4]

Chernyshevskii's most popular work was the novel *What Is to Be Done?*, subtitled "Tales About New People." One of these, a naturalized American who now called himself Charles Beaumont, appears to stand for the energy, the practicality, and the opportunities of his adoptive country. Yet when his Russian fiancée suggested emigrating to America—"There I will do some-

---

[3] Chernyshevskii: *Works*, IX, 197–8, 221–4, 227–8, 243–6.
[4] Ibid., X, Part 2, p. 92; and Laserson: *The American Impact on Russia*, pp. 249–50.

thing. Ah! How happy I should be!"—Beaumont demurred, revealing the native radical under the American disguise. "One may find an occupation in St. Petersburg also." There was too much to be done at home in the fight against ignorance and oppression.[5]

Russian radicals admired America's part in that fight, but thought that its main battles would be lost or won in Europe. Not one of them enlisted in Union ranks, and even Michael Bakunin, the anarchist who was constitutionally incapable of staying away from riot or rebellion and who found himself in America for two months in late 1861, rushed back to Europe. A Bostonian abolitionist who met him attributed his impatient departure to the wish to be reunited with his wife, otherwise "he would have cast his fortune with the Americans and heartily joined in the events of the war." In reality, Bakunin's love for this lady was no greater than his attachment to the United States. Although the North had all his sympathy and America promised to emerge purified and "better poised in her social life" from her trial, he told Herzen and Ogarev how little he cared for the "banality of material welfare" in this country without a heart, where an "infantile national vanity" reigned. America and Russia had, alas, arrived at the same result, one by way of democracy, the other by despotism. Bakunin could expect to find understanding from his friends. Had not Herzen agreed with Garibaldi that America was the land for forgetting home and had he not compared emigration to flight?[6]

For those Russians who did not know it at first hand, the world of bourgeois liberalism and republican democracy that Herzen and Bakunin found so dispiriting was still enviable in many respects. America was part of it, perhaps the best part, and the drama being played out on her soil continued to be of interest and importance, especially while its outcome was in

---

[5] N. G. Chernyshevskii: *What Is to Be Done?*, trans. by Benjamin R. Tucker (New York: Vintage Books; 1961), p. 336; Hecht: *Russian Radicals*, pp. 94–5, 132.

[6] Ibid., pp. 62, 69, 29; Oscar Handlin: "A Russian Anarchist Visits Boston," *The New England Quarterly*, XV (Mar. 1942), 104–9; Edward H. Carr: *Michael Bakunin* (New York: Vintage Russian Library; 1961), p. 247; Herzen: *Works*, X, 73, 163; XVIII, 627 (*n.* to p. 343).

doubt. When *The Contemporary* resumed publication in early 1863, it devoted nearly twenty pages of its first "Politics" survey to a discussion of American affairs. The man in charge of that department, a minor writer by the name of Ernest Vatson, was no Chernyshevskii in character or convictions. Both before and after his association with the leading radical review, he wrote for liberal and even moderately conservative publications. But the tone of his lengthy summaries of the politics and progress of the Civil War was so much in keeping with that set by the journal's guiding spirit that Vatson's columns have been taken for those of his more illustrious predecessor.

As Chernyshevskii had done, Vatson proclaimed his indifference to the question whether America broke into two or three states, whether Lincoln, McClellan, Seward, or even Jefferson Davis would be President, whether the Union would be restored or how its borders would be drawn. What mattered, and what it had now become clear the war was all about, was the extinction of slavery. That is why, in spite of little change in the military situation, it was possible to say now, in early 1863, that things had moved forward, that Lincoln was ready to act more boldly. When the President's plan for compensated emancipation (submitted to Congress December 1, 1862) met the fate common to measures that try to please everyone and end up by satisfying no one, he had had to realize that restraint would bring neither emancipation nor reunion. Excessive concern for the rights of enemies had served, however (perhaps by design), to demonstrate their recalcitrance and had laid the basis for the proclamations of September 22, 1862, and January 1, 1863. The former was met by much protest in a North far from unified in its abhorrence of slavery. But Britain and France were wrong to see the election of a few Democrats in New York, Ohio, and Illinois as evidence of war weariness or justification for their attempted mediation. The hungry Manchester workers had shown a better understanding of the spirit of the American people and the intentions of its leader. These were made manifest on January 1, 1863.

Vatson found merit only in two objections made to the Emancipation Proclamation, which he quoted in its entirety— that it exempted certain states and localities from its action and qualified the right of taking up arms. "Such things there must not be in such an important deed." He dismissed the argument that it violated the Constitution by saying that it was not a petrified idol, that different circumstances and needs must make constitutional changes possible. And to minimize the significance of the Proclamation by calling it a mere tactic of war was to question Lincoln's sincerity without reason. Even if this were so, even if he wished to withdraw the Proclamation on the South's willingness to submit, he could no longer do so. Events had moved beyond him and to their inexorable denouement—emancipation.[7]

Convinced that history would prove him right, Vatson was still afraid in July 1863 that America's leaders were not doing enough to help history along. He was not much impressed by the strength of antiwar sentiment expressed at protest meetings in the North. One should not look at America with European eyes and conclude that people were exhausted and yearning for peace. Where citizens met freely and often for all sorts of reasons, where to complain about one's government was a national pastime, and where there were five or ten meetings calling for an energetic prosecution of the war for every one of protest, there was no basis for seeing serious opposition or disgruntlement. Ordinary citizens were ready to give life, property, and liberty to restore the Union and defeat the South and that meant, *nolens volens*, to work for the end of slavery. Vatson was not alarmed by conscription and the suspension of *habeas corpus*, as were *Time* and the *Fatherland Notes*, but by the government's failure to act even more firmly. Recoiling from every extreme measure with horror, Lincoln and his Cabinet did more harm to their own just cause than Southern armies. Why had General Butler, who understood that the time was past for coddling planters at the expense of artisans, workers, and slaves, been recalled from New Orleans? Why such delay in forming Negro regiments, in arming the black masses who would not, it was hoped, remain silent witnesses to the fight that so directly concerned them? Racial antagonism in the North, the wish to keep the sheep whole while satisfying the wolves, the policy of good sense and the golden mean kept Americans from seizing

---

7 "Politika," *Sovremennik*, Nos. 1/2 (1863), pp. 331–49.

what was now within their grasp. A people less practical and of greater moral manliness would rush forth to complete the operation that those who began it might not have the strength or ability to conclude.[8]

If there was an implication here that the welfare and freedom of the masses were safer in their own hands than in those of their too-prudent rulers, it was not further spelled out. This would, in any case, have been difficult, since in early 1864 *The Contemporary* recorded Northern advances, the stiffening determination of the government, and draft riots among the lower classes. A populist bias put these too in proper perspective and excused the outrages against Negroes and abolitionists as the just, though misguided anger of men who carried an undue share of the war's burdens. But the military successes and the political victories were so clearly the result of planning and organization that it was hard to remain contemptuous of that Yankee common sense which was also blamed for a lack of fervor and moral courage. When Lincoln rejected retreat from the goal of emancipation as dishonorable and ill-advised because it would mean divesting the North of a useful weapon, it was the pragmatic part of his argument that found the most emphatic echo. His words were said to be more important than hundreds of speeches by French, Prussian, Italian, and other orators who prattled much of liberty but did little of practical value to bring it about. There were further tributes to principle (to it, not to their generals, the armies owed their victories) and to the common people (only Europe's workers had never let material considerations determine their loyalties in the Civil War), but these grew more perfunctory, as did *The Contemporary*'s coverage of the war once its outcome was no longer in doubt.[9]

Epoch, too, decided in December 1864 that it was time for Russians to turn to their own affairs. The South had lost the war for slavery and its privileged political position in the Union. Even as an independent state it could not maintain its separate,

---

[8] Ibid., No. 7 (1863), pp. 63–81.
[9] Ibid., No. 2 (1864); "Soedinennye Shtaty Severnoi Ameriki," ibid., No. 5 (1864), pp. 205–33, and No. 8 (1864), pp. 291–312; "Statistika Severo-Amerikanskikh Shtatov," ibid., pp. 171–9.

agrarian, aristocratic identity against the Northern democracy in an age of trade and industry. Most of the Left had long taken this view of the struggle and its result. According to *Russian Word* in May 1863, the North was entitled to victory and assured of it as soon as it inscribed "Liberty! An End to Slavery!" on its banners. Europe's workers had always understood this to be the meaning of the conflict. It had saved America from the curse of slavery and removed a threat to the rights and liberties of her free citizens, the democratic journalist N. V. Shelgunov wrote later that year in the same journal. The safeguarding of these was the main goal of American institutions, so that individual abilities might develop without harm to the whole and liberty not be sacrificed to the needs of the state. America had already gone far in rejecting her European inheritance (of which slavery was part), in demonstrating the benefits of freedom and tolerance; the war would advance that process. "In many ways," Shelgunov concluded, "America's experience foreshadows Europe's future." It was a daring prophecy to make in Russia, especially if read together with the Gettysburg Address, which could be found on another page of the magazine.[1]

That the Civil War marked or foreshadowed profound changes, if not in Europe then in the United States, was accepted even where the outlook of *The Contemporary* and *Russian Word* was not. *The Reader's Library* predicted long before emancipation that abolitionism's task would not end with that triumph, that the uprooting of age-old prejudices, which everywhere barred the Negro from a full and normal life, would be more difficult. Even the readers of the *Stock Exchange News* were told on New Year's Day 1863 that "in its significance and consequences the Civil War is the most important event of our time," but they were left to decide for themselves what these might be.[2]

The newspaper of the capital's business community was generally favorable to the North, opposed to slavery and rebellion,

---

1 "Politicheskoe Obozrenie," *Epokha*, No. 12 (1864), pp. 24–6; No. 12 (1864), pp. 4–5; "Politika," *Russkoe Slovo*, No. 5 (1863); No. 11/12 (1863), p. 33; N. V. Shelgunov: "Staryi svet i novyi svet," ibid., pp. 34–50.

2 G. Simonenko: *Abolitsionizm* (St. Petersburg, 1862), pp. 190–4, reprinted from *Biblioteka dlia chteniia*, No. 11 (1861); *Birzhevye vedomosti*, Jan. 1, 1863.

and not entirely convinced of the necessity of the war. Beyond that it was not guided by any broader principles in the reporting of events. It was sparing of comments on the news that it took for the most part, and with little discrimination, from the European press. It agreed with *The Contemporary* in 1862 that Lincoln should dismiss McClellan and purge his government of Southern sympathizers, expatiated like *Time* on the cost and horror of war and reproached General Butler for his inhumanity. It saw the Emancipation Proclamation weakened by the signature of Seward, a compromiser, and two months later described him as the candidate of abolitionist fanatics who were pushing the President into actions that, taken by a European monarch, would be decried as tyrannical. "There are rulers who respect constitutions only so long as they find it expedient, and President Lincoln does just that." Three weeks later the paper dismissed fears of a military dictatorship as a phantom born in Europe, ascribed the dissolution of the country not to an excessive but to an incomplete application of the representative principle, and insisted that neither the rights nor the prosperity of Americans had suffered any diminution. Saved by the love of the people for the Union, the American political and economic system had successfully passed the test of war.

> The instinct of a youthful, powerful nation achieved what neither the wisdom of statesmen nor a dedication to principle could have brought about. The nation did not want to perish and in order to preserve its integrity, one by one threw overboard prejudices, interests, indeed, its past. Today, Washington's birthday is celebrated with an almost universal clamor for a constitutional provision that would end slavery throughout the Union, whereas only a short while ago curses rained down on those who dared to utter the true watchword of a great revolution.[3]

The most unexpected reactions came from the most unexpected quarters, as a Soviet student of Russo-American Civil War diplomacy noted with some surprise in commenting on the editorial reception given the Emancipation Proclamation by the

---

[3] *Ibid.*, Sept. 1 and 23, Oct. 17 and 26, Nov. 2, 1862; Jan. 24, Mar. 28, Apr. 20, 1863; Mar. 11, 1864.

government-owned *St. Petersburg News,* which was at this time in the hands of a liberal concessionaire. The newspaper defended Lincoln against the accusations of the London *Times*—that his proclamation had been called forth by calculation and necessity rather than principle or conviction; that it came late in the day, when all hope of the South's peaceful return to the Union was gone, and that it abolished slavery only where the writ of his government did not run. The writer of the editorial professed little interest in the President's character or beliefs. The act itself was the only important thing. The Magna Carta too would have to be condemned if judged by the man who granted it. True, Lincoln had never been an abolitionist or for immediate emancipation, but the action of January 1 was not the product of insincerity. Its restraint bespoke a due regard for the constitutional rights of states that had not broken the constitutional compact, while the delay in taking it reflected the changing naure of a war that only time and circumstance had made an antislavery crusade. Before that happened, "the emancipationists were yet too weak, the desire to preserve the Union and the prejudice against the Negro too strong."[4]

The idea of the progressive radicalization of the war was no monopoly of the Left. "Little by little," wrote a Washington correspondent for the *St. Petersburg News* in September 1862, "a purely military conflict is becoming a revolutionary situation," a domestic contest between moderates and extremists and the social interests they represent. The moderates—President, Cabinet, and generals—wanted to put down the rebellion without touching slavery; the radicals wished to go beyond that to confiscate lands and property of the rebels and free and arm the slaves. The revolutionary tendency had evidently not been arrested by the Proclamation, for the fight between the Jacobins (led by Sumner and Stevens, the "American Robespierre") and the Girondists (led by Seward) attracted the paper's attention into March, when it compared the heated congressional debates between them to meetings of the Jacobin Club.[5]

---

[4] Malkin: *Grazhdanskaia voina v SShA i tsarskaia Rossiia,* pp. 196, 200, n. 2, and Belle B. Sideman and Lillian Friedman, eds.: *Europe looks at the Civil War* (New York, 1960), pp. 203–6.

[5] Malkin: *Grazhdanskaia voina v SShA i tsarskaia Rossiia,* p. 187.

When made outside of the radical camp (where they were never so explicit), such comparisons must be taken as dramatic exaggerations rather than products of a theory of history or of revolutionary sympathies. Yet they recurred time and again to lend credibility to fears that extremism in a society at war enhanced the possibility of Caesarism. The antiradical *Russian Messenger*, which became in the years after 1863 the organ of archconservatism, also spoke (in a review of Trollope's *North America*) of the abolitionist radicals, those Marats of the North, as wanting to "Robespierrize, to preach terror in a country without a hungry rabble." It wasn't loud talk and excesses that would finish slavery and sedition but the political influence and antislavery sentiment of the West, whose farmers knew the evil institution at first hand and lived what they believed. As Trollope had shown, Americans were not an unruly people prone to demagogy; seeing the need of a firm hand in time of crisis they submitted quietly, even passively, to the dictatorship of Lincoln and Seward. Indeed, they were beginning to ask for a still stricter rule and looked to McClellan to play the role of Cromwell, which he refused.

What explained this yearning among a free people, asked the reviewer? Trollope and others had observed that the Americans, like the French, valued equality more than liberty, and taking the latter for granted rarely elected their best people to the Presidency or Congress. Their political leaders were not up to the demands of a heroic epoch. Trollope had not noted, however, that Southern victories were wrongly credited to an energetic, centralized dictatorship that many in the North now wished to copy. While such a system would unify the military command, end peculation, and improve the organization of men and materials, it would not ensure success and would create more ills than it cured. A dictatorship would never be accepted by the liberty-loving, self-reliant men of the West but lead to new and more horrible secessions and discords.[6]

It was a preference for orderly and stable government rather than an attachment to constitutional democracy that lay

---

[6] A. Druzhinin: "Angliiskii nabliudatel' v Severnoi Amerike," and "Rasskazy noveishikh turistov o iuge Soedinennykh Shtatov," *Russkii vestnik*, XLIV (1863), 253–96, 851–88, 185–206.

behind such warnings. Liberal by Russian standards in their advocacy of free trade and a freer press, of greater autonomy for
local government and the courts, the *Russian Messenger* and its
editor, M. N. Katkov, were far from being doctrinaire supporters
of representative government. Katkov's liberalism, even before
he and his journal acquired the unsavory reputation of being
kept by the government, was always of an aristocratic, Anglo-
phile kind; and if he wished to reduce the state's intervention
in the life of society, it was to check the "radicalism" of an arbitrary bureaucracy by the conservatism of property and the
traditionalism of the landed classes.

It was the Polish rebellion of January 1863, brought on,
Katkov and many Russians felt, by a loosening of the strict
bonds of authority in St. Petersburg, that caused his retreat
from his own, most temperate endorsement of reform and made
his name a byword for reaction. The waves radiating from the
shock of the Polish rising (a shock deepened by the frightful
results of rebellion in America), bore Katkov, who became editor
of the daily *Moscow News* in 1863, to a height of influence and
popularity never attained by any other private figure or journalist in Russia. Although he changed views with what his enemies
regarded as opportunistic frequency and ease—from qualified
liberalism to rigid conservatism; from free trade to protection;
from opposition to advocacy of alliance with republican France
—he held always to one point: the preservation and heightening
of state power at home and abroad. That is also the perspective
from which he saw the Civil War and commented on it in his
editorials.

Like many of his countrymen, Katkov was not at first loath
to see a parting of the ways between North and South. He deplored the harm done Europe's prosperity almost as much as the
destruction and loss of life in the no-longer United States; was
uncertain of the outcome of the war, except that the federalists
would be unable to restore the Union; and believed that sooner
or later the exhaustion of the combatants would lead to successful European mediation. Perhaps the only hopeful note he struck
in early 1863 was that the probable liberation of most slaves
would be some compensation for all the sufferings of the war.
He characterized proposals for recognition of the South as realistic and a basis for eventual reunion, but warned European cabi-

nets against pressing such a course upon the North for fear of offending feelings of pride and sovereignty. The two sides would more easily get together without outside help. Katkov trusted the good sense of Americans.[7]

With the flames of rebellion, fanned by European sympathy and diplomatic intervention, spreading at Russia's own doorstep, Katkov no longer watched the breakup of the United States, temporary though it might be, with equanimity. In September, he began to see striking similarities between sedition in Poland and secession in America. In both cases, the weaker side had taken up arms against the stronger; in both, the issue was separation and the danger it posed to national unity and power if allowed to go unchecked; on both sides of the Atlantic there was a clash of different ways of life, with the federal and tsarist governments representing progress, whatever Russia's short-sighted enemies might say. But there similarities ended. The South had organized a genuine government and state; fighting openly and successfully, it controlled extensive territories and regular armies on the basis of law and established procedures. The Confederacy had all the attributes of statehood and did not need to have that fact confirmed by French and British recognition. But even if Europe accorded belligerent status to the Poles, they would never be more than mutineers, their stealthy murders directed only by some obscure committee that ruled no territory and disposed of no forces greater than a few armed bands who could not stand up to Russian detachments in open battle.[8]

For Katkov the essential difference lay in Europe's differing reactions to what he regarded as comparable instances of

---

[7] *Moskovskie vedomosti*, Jan. 10, 12, 14, 17; Feb. 16, 1863, in M. N. Katkov: *Sobranie peredovykh statei Moskovskikh vedomostei* (Moscow, 1897), I, 28, 32, 34, 40, 80–2 (hereafter Katkov: *Editorials*) and Malkin: *Grazhdanskaia voina v SShA i tsarskaia Rossiia*, p. 219–20.

[8] *Moskovskie vedomosti*, Sept. 27, 1863, in Katkov: *Editorials*, I, 565–8. The Slavophile ethnographer A. Helferding (Gil'ferding) also compared rebellious Poland and the American South, as did Pogodin when he remarked in 1863 that although confederations and unions of the Swiss type might in the distant future become the general European form of political organization, at the present moment most developed European states were demanding the absolute fusion of their component parts. (From Frank Fadner: *Seventy Years of Pan-Slavism in Russia* [Washington, D.C.: Georgetown Univ. Press; 1962], pp. 215, 236.)

civil strife. The Polish rising, which need have been of no concern to any other state (with the possible exception of Prussia and Austria), had united Europe's opinion and chancelleries against Russia, whereas the vast and bloody Civil War, affecting the entire world, led only to timid attempts at mediation. Russia was judged by standards not applied to others, although there were more compelling moral and material reasons for intervention in America than in Poland. The cause of Europe's restraint was the confident strength of the Washington government and the damage it could and would inflict on any power threatening its vital interests. If only Russia's statesmen, Katkov implied, were less concerned over the good opinion of Europe and put their country's interests first, they would be respected and feared as the Americans were.[9]

Russian fears of war with France and England over Poland may have been the expression of an uneasy conscience, as well as of military weakness and diplomatic isolation. These fears were, in any case, strong enough to cause the dispatch of two naval squadrons into American waters, a precautionary measure that Katkov likened to the winning of a major battle. There, in the harbors of the United States, the fleet's three hundred guns would render great service to Russia and be of no little weight in improving her position vis-à-vis her Western antagonists. Inevitably, America was drawn into the balance of powers that was no longer purely European; in case of war, she would be a natural, true, and active ally. Katkov made no bones about Russian

---

[9] Katkov was slow to make the link between Poland and the South, for it could be turned against republican America and tsarist Russia alike. A French newspaper, *La Patrie*, on January 12, 1864, employed the parallel to argue the independence of Poland and the Confederacy, asking whether it was right that fifty million Muscovites should inflict their detested rule on ten to twelve million Poles or twenty million Germans and Irishmen impose on eight million Southerners an association they spurned. There was little to choose between the massacres and pillage carried out in the name of Alexander II or that of Lincoln, between Butler in New Orleans and Muraviev in Poland (Robertson: *A Kentuckian at the Court of the Tsars*, p. 146). Even Herzen, not without sarcasm, spoke of Carl Schurz, who owed him an accounting for some American investments, as carrying out in the South "the functions of a republican Muraviev." "Hangman Muraviev" was the pacifier of Poland (Herzen: *Works*, XXVIII, 148).

motives—"We have come neither to seek conquests nor to confer benefits"—but even the most frankly avowed necessity seeks to clothe its nakedness in the garment of some principle. It became easier to do this as Northern successes made the end of disunion and slavery only a matter of time.[1]

In January 1864, Katkov represented Russo-American friendship as having deeper roots than mutual convenience, and he found additional reasons for liking this "young and enterprising people." Fate, as if by design, had lately fortified their solidarity by identical afflictions and achievements—the Polish rising and the abolition of serfdom; the Southern secession and the emancipation of the slaves. Whatever the newspapers of England and France might say, however slightingly they spoke of Lincoln's Proclamation as an unconvincing tactic of war, events now spoke for themselves. Slavery and rebellion were doomed; aware of this, the people of the South (as was already happening in Louisiana) were deciding to end the institution that for so long had been inviolate and to return to the bosom of the national family. They were helped to do so because Washington was quickly restoring areas under martial law to the orderly government of the citizens. Katkov no longer doubted that unity would be recovered and the Negroes freed. Intrigue, whether in Poland or America, and however powerfully abetted by men in high places, could never prevail against the needs of national survival and the superior attractions of the more just society.

That was one lesson of the Civil War. The other was condemnation of the federal structure whose weaknesses the war had made manifest and whose future was at stake in the elections of 1864. In these, only the Republicans stood for an indivisible nation at any price, but to secure it for all time they would have to renounce that federalism which harbored the seeds of new discords and divisions. The alternatives were clear: political cohesion and the abandonment of the federal system or disintegration into petty Latin American republics, endless squabbles, and an end to national greatness. Since the Republicans too had made a fetish of federalism, Katkov predicted that they would make the wrong choice, losing power and prosperity forever. "Let our own misguided and muddle-headed federalists

---

[1] Katkov: *Editorials*, I, pp. 579–80 (Oct. 4, 1863).

reflect on this example." They wanted to join Poland to Russia by a bond that had proved too weak even in America, where there had been common institutions, common laws, and, above all, a common nationality to preserve unity and prevent rebellion. The war had shown that a great nation shuns no sacrifice to mend the broken unity of its state; the re-election of Lincoln testified that the will to achieve it had not been sapped. Were Russians, Katkov was asking, capable of less? Would they prove their greatness in like ways?[2]

I I I

With the war over, or nearly so, Russian interest turned from its ephemeral happenings to examinations of its meaning and probable consequences. In the process, the Russian picture of America recovered a certain simplicity. The political strife and confusion attendant upon rebuilding a battered nation that had lost its leader and the gigantic task of integrating the Negro into a hostile society continued to provoke comment and discussion, but in decreasing measure. The victory of the North and the conclusive settlement of the slavery question by the Thirteenth Amendment allowed a return to broader perspectives, to speculation and generalization about America's character, fate, and future.

Epoch in January 1865 had only praise for the Union's leaders and people. Grant, unlike his predecessors, had understood the significance of the grim contest, declaring it a farce if it did not lead to abolition. Lincoln's stature too was enhanced by success, and what had once appeared to be weakness and trimming was now the shrewd practicality of a man who knows that an idea must ripen to be accepted. That time had come, and *Epoch*, no longer disturbed by setbacks and delays, attached great value to the fact that a universal emancipation was being carried out quietly and constitutionally. There would be no retreat from that goal, for in re-electing Lincoln the people had embraced it along with unity. It was a unity, moreover, that re-

---

2 Ibid., II, 69 (Feb. 21, 1864); 116–17 (May 18, 1864); 593–6 (Sept. 28, 1864); 723–6 (Nov. 16, 1864).

spected the rights of states whose independence would have been lost in case of a radical victory. How greatly a nation made whole again, and the South in particular, would benefit from the addition of four million pairs of hands capable of hard, sustained work; how little those who preached the Negro's need of a stick and master knew of his real nature. Had not the same arguments been heard about the Russian serf and been disproved?

When *Epoch* reported congressional passage of the Thirteenth Amendment, only Russia's emancipation was deemed worthy of comparison. But would the Negro attain full citizenship or would he be denied the right to vote for and serve in local and national assemblies? If so, the measure was a betrayal of the Constitution it was designed to perfect, whereas the Negro's unqualified participation in politics would best dispel prejudices about his incapacity for the "so-called higher spheres of human activity." This was a plea not for the Negro alone. The writers gathered around *Epoch*, the "men of the native soil" (*pochvenniki*), championed simple men as the purest source of the humble, Christian, Russian virtues of humility, loyalty and honest toil upon which the privileged classes, infatuated with Western luxury, liberalism, or radicalism, had turned their backs. Selfishness and pride, social or intellectual, were the grave sins of Russian society. Cleansed of sin by suffering, the peasant had best preserved those national and human values that his betters had forgotten. To exclude peasants (or Negroes) from the national community would be to cast out its healthiest part. "To our mind's eye the future of the United States appears in the most cheerful light. Aside from the enormous increase which 4 million Negroes will bring to its material wealth, they may, perhaps, be destined to carry into the life of the North American federation that element of idealism and poetry which the businesslike Yankee has so often been accused of lacking." It was comforting to think that the very depth of their degradation had prepared ex-serfs and ex-slaves to rise to new heights of compassion and nobility and that through them their tormentors too would be redeemed. For Dostoevsky, this became in time suffering Russia's mission to the world, when America had long ceased to be exempt from the condemnation visited upon a materialistic, irreligious West.

Fresh from her military, political, and moral triumphs,

America still had a claim to uniqueness that Russians quickly and generously recognized. What went on in Western Europe, observed *Epoch's* commentator, paled before her accomplishments. The Union, the lodestar of Europe's progressives, had justified their hope and refuted predictions of its impermanence; the idea of federation was spreading to Latin America and Canada. In the Old World, freedom's every step had to be wrested from bureaucrats and feudal parties in bitter combat; in America the reconciliation of liberty and authority had advanced so far that with the Negro's enfranchisement her last blemish would be wiped out. Without a standing army, centralization, or feudal and clerical reaction, the United States had gone as far as possible in facilitating the individual's development of his gifts. The excellence of the Constitution that had aided such progress lay in the fact that it had been fashioned by experience, not theory; that it was not a copy of an alien example but a response to popular and national need. It was *Epoch's* last comment on America, a tribute to her people and an admonition to Russians to seek their own road, to shun the hand-me-down garments of Western doctrine, even the best of them.[3]

In Katkov's tributes to an America that impressed him most by her might and energetic pursuit of unity, there was also admiration for the respect power was paying to law, for the successful avoidance of despotism and anarchy, despite the tragic loss of Lincoln. The speed and ease with which huge armies were demobilized and brilliant officers returned to the humble pursuits of peace were as remarkable as the genius of improvisation that had called them into the field. Martial law was already being lifted in the South, Katkov reported in October 1865, and there was no enslavement of that region, as Europe, judging from its own experience, had feared. True, grave problems remained and Johnson had to steer a cautious course between radicals and Democrats

---

3 "Politicheskoe Obozrenie," *Epokha*, No. 1 (1865), pp. 1–18; No. 2 (1865), pp. 1–4. Cf. D. Zavalishin: "Negry v Soedinennykh Shtatakh," *Russkii Vestnik*, LVII (1865), 682–703, for somewhat similar views. Dostoevsky's feelings about the United States in later years become apparent in *The Devils* (*The Possessed*, Penguin Classics, 1957), pp. 147–8, first published in 1871, and in *The Brothers Karamazov* (New York: Signet Classics; 1957), p. 690. See also Valentin Kiparsky: "The American Westerner in Russian Fiction," *Russian Review*, XX, 1 (Jan. 1961), 37.

on the issue of the Negro and the readmission of rebel states. But America was a unique state, united in language and national feeling, and would overcome political and social differences. Southerners were not Poles, not a separate people with troublesome memories of their own distant past, but citizens of one, indivisible nation who accepted defeat with little more resentment than a lost election.[4]

Nor did Herzen withhold his admiration now. But the America he celebrated was a country of the mind, emblem and product of philosophical abstractions, political principles, or historical tendencies. He needed this symbol of vitality as a stick to belabor old Europe immobilized by reaction and mediocrity and to sustain his faith in Russia, which, like America, was destined to leave its European parent behind. He was much impressed, as Russians generally were, by the alacrity with which simple soldiers and laurel-covered generals returned to their prosaic homes, businesses, and farms, refuting the argument for standing armies. But that was as specific as he would ever be about the postwar evolution of the United States. The Civil War proved that a democratic, federal republic, governed by the "rabble," was not appropriate only for "small cantons and large dissertations," but could sustain a long war over a huge territory more successfully than any kingdom or empire. Another conclusion to be drawn from the élan and vigor of Americans at war was that this old world in new quarters was, after all, the only one in which survived what was left of energy and life—Cromwell and 1789, the Puritans and the Encyclopedists, stern revolutionaries and severe Calvinists. Muscular, classless America and peasant Russia moving toward classlessness had always been for him, Herzen said, the countries of the immediate future. "Notwithstanding the agronomists, history is introducing the three-field system, and while Europe, exhausted by rich harvests, lies fallow, history is plowing and harrowing the other two fields." These yielded different fruit, different yet complementary solutions to what Europe considered impossible, absurd, or ruinous tasks. "That is why everything that is being accomplished in America and Russia is vastly more interesting to me than what happens in Europe from

---

[4] *Moskovskie vedomosti*, Feb. 27, 1865; Apr. 20, 1865; May 18, 1865; October 19, 1865, in Katkov: *Editorials*, III, 121–2, 235–6, 300–1, 657–9.

Stockholm to Lisbon." As far as America was concerned, Herzen exaggerated.[5]

One is tempted to say that he respected America almost as an intellectual duty; but he loved Russia. His abiding loyalty, however, was to an ideal—socialism. When Herzen predicted that where America had left off—fulfilling the eighteenth century's legacy of popular government, the rights of man and the citizen— Russia would begin, bringing social justice to her people, he did so not because what was visibly happening there was truly more significant than what happened anywhere else, but because in Russia his love and his loyalty merged. His evidence was of things not seen, a faith that the last would be first, that it was precisely on "our lowly fields" that the seed of the future would fall. And if socialism, discarded even by France, no longer existed? "Even if it were, in fact, dead and buried in Europe, that would carry little weight with us. It passed its heritage on to us while still alive." In the third article of a series in which he envisioned the United States and Russia supporting each other in their joint progress to political liberty and social justice, America was left behind, not to be mentioned again in the remaining three. All questions of politics were becoming questions of the people's welfare, and for these America had no answer. "That is what the American Brisbane, whose words I have quoted more than once, wanted to say to the workers of Paris in 1848, 'that the American republic has reached the limits of its achievement, that a political structure established under the most favorable circumstances, but on old foundations, did all that it could, but that it could not, did not and will not solve the questions preoccupying the workers . . .' " "Russia is full of hope," Herzen concluded in September 1865, "and Europe is in an impasse."[6]

In 1866, however, when politicians, pundits, and the press saw in the enthusiastic reception of an American mission to Russia the portent of lasting collaboration between two peoples who so recently shared similar afflictions and triumphs, Herzen could not resist pointing out that he had long foretold their meeting and becoming traveling companions for the future. Again he stressed their affinities, their freedom from ancient prejudices,

---

[5] Herzen: *Works*, XVIII, 94, 343–51.
[6] Ibid., XVIII, 357–61, 379.

only to ask whether the "most fateful antinomy" of Western history was not now expressed in the atomization of American society on one hand and the collectivism of the Russian village commune on the other. "*America fara dà se*," he told Polish comrades in 1867. Strong, crude, powerful, persistent, and energetic, unencumbered by the ruins of the past, she would realize republican ideals. But to see life breathed into the ideals of socialism, men would have to turn to Russia, where these ideals were in ferment. "Let us leave the venerable ancients to their old age, the strong to their strength and let us Slavs consecrate our efforts and our labors to the seed in our soil."[7]

The visit that Assistant Secretary of the Navy Gustavus Fox and units of the American fleet paid to Russia in the summer of 1866 to congratulate her people and Emperor on his escape from an assassin's bullet was the high point of the diplomatic and emotional rapprochement between two nations, who, if they were alike in nothing else, were matched in the intensity of their feelings. The delight that Russians and Americans took in each other on that occasion can only be described as an infatuation, and American sailors became as much the rage in St. Petersburg as Russian seamen had been in San Francisco and New York. A Countess Apraksin, visiting the monitor *Miantonomoh* (hailed as a symbol of America's technical genius), wore a costume whose bodice was of a blue material spangled with stars, a skirt of alternate stripes of red and white, and a sailor hat bearing the name of the American vessel. America's institutions became almost as much a fashion as her colors; there was many a toast drunk to them by ministers, merchants, and municipal councilors who drew parallels, as inevitable as they were superficial, with their own reformed organs of local government and justice, with the sacrifices they too had made for freedom and equality, with their own near-loss of a beloved leader. Pogodin's old-Muscovite chauvinism and contempt for the huckster state were quite forgotten as he told the guests at a banquet honoring Fox:

> I will add that this sympathy is increased by the resemblance of our institutions, by our connections with Europe and by history generally. I do not speak of the likeness as

---

[7] Ibid., XIX, 139–40; XX, 87.

regards the extent of our territory, our power and means; nor of the abundance of our natural productions. As regards institutions, the United States is a republic and Russia an absolute monarchy; but here, as well as on the map, extremes meet. In the Russian absolute monarchy there is a democratic stream that flows uninterruptedly throughout its history. As regards the forms, all of them have lost much of their original meaning, and our honorable guests have justly remarked . . . that under our form one may progress; and they now hear . . . that the Russians, thanks to our gracious Emperor . . . may express their ideas and reason as freely as people do in New York.[8]

The guest of honor had indeed received such impressions as Pogodin described, and he reported them to Senator Sumner, chairman of the Foreign Relations Committee. If these impressions were not altogether inaccurate—Russia had done much to reform her internal life since 1861—they were uncritical to the point of blindness, inspired by euphoria rather than knowledge. There was also a measure of self-congratulation in all this, as in the presentation, by Fox, to a Russian mayor ("elected by *universal suffrage*") of an American flag that represented, that worthy was told, the ideas his Emperor was promulgating. "This Emperor is evidently impregnated with the democratic ideals of the age and instead of waiting to be driven he is leading these ideas, amongst a people that look up to him, almost with adoration." Like many of his countrymen, the secretary took a temporary community of interest for a permanent community of

---

[8] Joseph Florimond Loubat: *Narrative of the mission to Russia in 1866 of the Hon. Gustavus Fox . . .* , ed. by John D. Champlin, Jr. (New York, 1873), pp. 250–2 for Pogodin's speech; Woldman: *Lincoln and the Russians*, pp. 241–50; Florinsky: *Russia*, II, 973–4, and Laserson: *The American Impact on Russia*, pp. 186–95, who points out that Pogodin did not use the word "democratic" (*demokraticheskaia*) in his speech but *zemskaia*, which Laserson translates as "local self-governing." A more accurate rendering would be "popular" with implications of at least consultative representation as in the old Assembly of the Land (*zemskii sobor*) of Muscovy. For other descriptions of the visit see Kiparsky: *English and American Characters in Russian Fiction* (Berlin, 1964), p. 117; S. Iakovlev: *Chrezvychainoe amerikanskoe posol'stvo v Rossii* (Moscow, 1866); P. V. Shermetevskii: *Amerikantsy, dorogie gosti russkoi zemli* (Moscow, 1866); *Amerikantsy v Peterburge . . .* (Peterhof, 1866); *Amerikantsy v Rossii i russkie v Amerike* (Moscow, 1866).

belief, yet he should not be blamed for his ignorance of Alexander's stated motives and convictions, which were anything but democratic. For Congress itself had sent him in the belief that the Tsar's life had been attempted by a reactionary opponent of emancipation. Alexander was no Lincoln and Karakozov no Booth, but a revolutionary who was hanged, Herzen acidly remarked, to the strains of Yankee Doodle played for the departing Americans. Nor did Herzen take seriously, as had Fox, Pogodin's boast of speech as free in Moscow as in New York, and he used it as the ironic motto of an article telling of a secret trial for *lèse majesté*.[9]

There were not many on either side of this love feast who kept their sobriety or their skepticism. One of them was Minister of the Interior Valuev, a normally tolerant man, who noted in his diary that most of the orators at the official banquet were drunk and that a General Menshikov, on concluding his speech, had kissed the hand of Mr. Fox. "Mordvinians and Cheremiss behave like that, not Europeans. What standards, and what a future they promise." In the United States, it was Franz Sigel who said of the enthusiasm with which Russian sailors were there embraced that it almost made him doubt the common sense of the American people. They had gone mad over the Muscovites, a writer in the *Continental Monthly* complained, "forgetting the woes of Poland while they kissed the hands of the knout-bearers of the Czar and agitated for alliance between what they called the sister empires of the future." Katkov was not carried away, and although he rhapsodized about the arrival of the *Miantonomoh* and the brilliant prospects awaiting the two peoples, his ardor was reserved for the benefits that Russian diplomacy would derive from their association. "An alliance between the United States and Russia . . . can be based only on mutual interest, and contains therefore neither self-delusion nor deceit." Two years later he was already disturbed over dangerous American competition in the grain trade and warned that relations would suffer rather than gain from the sale of Alaska and geographical proximity. "Concessions have never yet served to

---

[9] Fox to Charles Sumner, Jan. 4, 1867 (Sumner Papers, Houghton Library, Harvard University, No. 26, Vol. 80); Herzen: *Works*, XIX, 138, 141. The Fox letter was supplied to me by Professor Hyman.

strengthen international friendships." The staunchly liberal newspaper *Voice* insisted, however, that the warm reception tendered the Americans was animated by the common ideals of humanity and progress that both nations had so recently affirmed.[1]

It was these very ideals, or any ideals for that matter, that the Slavophile Ivan Aksakov, following his brother Konstantin, denied to the Americans and their futile war. Only time would reveal the magnitude of the brute energy expended to keep the South in forcible union with the North; for him the monstrous immorality of their fight was apparent before it was quite finished. He did not require new evidence to confirm old prejudices. Fratricide committed by free men armed with all the weapons of despotism proved anew the fragility of a nation bound only by contract and an addition of individual wills. And what was the fight about? The North demanded the extinction of slavery; the South its retention, and the classic land of liberty and democracy fell apart. What did freedom mean if its most basic principle was debatable? Federalism too, its very essence voluntary agreement, had been trampled upon in a war that had given birth to the demands and instincts of a great power and nourished violence and coercion. This was the legacy of a conflict that in the dimensions of horror was truly worthy of America—a kind of madness, an orgy of killing employing all the refinements of civilization, as if its goal were the invention of the most convenient means for the extinction of mankind. The Emancipation Proclamation, rather than justifying the war for Aksakov, made it unnecessary, emphasized its ultimate senselessness and the cruelty that had entered the soul of every participant. This was of the nature of the state and of war, but the Americans, as in so much else, excelled in carrying both to perfection and absurdity. Without a deep and shared religious faith, without a true nationality, therefore without art and philosophy,

---

[1] Valuev: *Dnevnik*, II, 146. The Sigel and *Continental Monthly* quotes are from James M. Callahan: *Russo-American Relations during the American Civil War* (Morgantown: West Virginia University Studies in American History; 1908, Series I, Diplomatic History, No. 1), pp. 11, 216–20; Katkov: *Editorials*, IV, 17–19, 339–41, 369–70, 424 and VII, 9, 714 from *Moskovskie vedomosti*, Jan. 8, July 29, Aug. 11, Sept. 12, 1866, and Jan. 3 and Nov. 3, 1869; A. A. Kraevskii, ed.: *Piatiletie gazety "Golos"* (St. Petersburg, 1878), p. xxii.

America had contributed little to the treasury of mankind except machines and their products. For the moment, they still lived off the spiritual capital accumulated by their European ancestors.

> When these traditions disappear, a truly American nation will be formed, a state without faith, without ethical foundations and ideals; either it will perish from the unbridled passion of selfishness and the unbelief of the individual or it will become a terrible despotism of the New World. . . . But who knows what history and human nature still have in store for us![2]

One of history's surprises was Aksakov's conversion to power politics, when, as the leading spokesman of Pan-Slavism, he urged upon a reluctant government military intervention on behalf of the Balkan Slavs. He did so in the name of Orthodoxy and Slavic solidarity, never admitting or realizing how far his abandonment of the gentler Slavophile precepts had gone, how close he had moved to the great power chauvinism of Katkov, which he condemned in Germans and Americans.

The deed of Karakozov, the immediate cause for the dispatch of Fox, also induced the tsarist government to take stern measures against the revolutionary conspiracy that was believed to have inspired it. *The Contemporary* and *Russian Word*, repeatedly warned or suspended, were suppressed in June 1866. Pogodin's words were thus belied and the two reviews prevented from joining in the chorus of welcome for the transatlantic visitors. It is in any case doubtful that they would have done so wholeheartedly, for with the South's defeat a certainty or a fact, their columns reflected a more critical attitude toward America.

A series of unsigned articles published by *The Contemporary* from May to August 1864 turned from the events of the war

---

[2] Ivan S. Aksakov: "Ob otsutstvii dukhovnogo soderzhaniia v amerikanskoi narodnosti," *Den'*, Jan. 30, 1865, in *Sochineniia I. S. Aksakova* (Moscow, 1887), VII, 52–65; cf. ibid., II, 47. By 1868, however, Aksakov was prepared to see the United States take an active interest in the Mediterranean, because "the intervention of the American people into the affairs of Turkey can bring only benevolent results for its Christian subjects." (Cited by Fadner: *Seventy Years of Pan-Slavism*, p. 236.)

to inquire into its underlying causes and significance for the "general life of mankind." The achievement of American statehood after the War of Independence had been a compromise between centralist and federalist, republican and monarchical, aristocratic and democratic elements and factions, an accommodation that was bound to break down. Unity and the Constitution were not products of an organic, historical growth, of experience or the needs of the whole country; they were dictated by fears of a common enemy, by the wish of the propertied classes for a strong authority to deal with social disorders, and perhaps by dreams of a great and mighty state. While the North's victory was a victory for the country's progressive forces and spelled the end of the Southern oligarchy, it also marked the emergence of a new ruling class of financiers and manufacturers. "Its influence on the political and administrative order is already clear, as is the distrust of the masses for the rising industrial giants." As yet, the Northern democracy's enmity for the planters far exceeded its distrust of the North's economic aristocracy, but it might in time become great enough to lead capital and landed wealth into a defensive alliance.

The Civil War, in short, had left untouched social and economic grievances first manifested in the local rebellions of the post-Independence decade, grievances which the Jeffersonian revolution had dealt with superficially and demagogically and which America's special circumstances and opportunities kept from growing into a conscious and solid movement of social protest. "We are far from pessimistic about the entire situation of the United States," a survey of Andrew Johnson's first months in office concluded bravely; "it may all turn out for the best." But the confidence of the war years was clearly lacking. At the end of 1865, *Russian Word* also drew up a balance sheet of "the results of that great drama which was so long in preparation, was played out so triumphantly and ended so miserably." With the assassination of Lincoln through a reactionary plot—which conferred upon him in Russian eyes a martyr's crown—the main actors had all left the stage, to be replaced by small men without talent or vision, who had done little to make emancipation more than a legal fact. The Negroes themselves would have to fight to give substance to their rights. Johnson, a short-sighted bureaucrat, tried to brake a genuine emancipation and his reconstruc-

tion of the South was but a carrying out of empty juridical for-
mulas.[3]

For the Russian Left a period of history had ended. What
had given that period its identity and to its events a certain sym-
metry—the Great Reforms and Russia's stirring to life; the Civil
War and the Polish rebellion—was now destroyed by reaction in
the Old World, by a relapse into the politics of cautious compromise in the New, and by a preoccupation with international
power politics on the part of governments and large sectors of
opinion. "Emphatically," a contemporary recalled, "1866 finished
off what is known as the sixties, if we define it not in its strict
chronological sense, but in its basic meaning of a period of hope,
of reform and social renovation."[4]

The radicals' deteriorating situation, their isolation from a
public that had rallied to the government over the Polish question
and still believed in the efficacy of gradual reforms from above,
made them, too, see America in a less cheerful light. True, there
was still in the United States a significant party that aimed at a
radical reformation of the Union; there was reason to believe
that it had the sympathy of the majority of the people and sufficient strength in Congress to stop the comeback of the South's
adroit and pliant politicians and carry out its program—punishment of rebel leaders, full civil, political, and economic liberty
for the Negroes, confiscation of Southern property to pay off the
federal war debt. But although Congress understood much better
than the President the real aspirations of the people, there was
far less certainty of its winning that confrontation than there
had been of the North's victory in the war.

> Thus, the conflict between the President who is convinced
> that his way is right and a Congress which is assured of the
> support of the nation has obviously not ended and in view
> of the obstinacy of both sides may become still broader in
> scope. America will then present to us the curious spectacle
> of one of those constitutional clashes between the executive

---

[3] "Soedinennye Shtaty Severnoi Ameriki," *Sovremennik*, No. 5 (1864),
pp. 205–33; No. 8 (1864), pp. 291–312; "Politika," *Russkoe slovo*, No.
12 (1865), pp. 1–8.

[4] N. F. Annenskii: *Na slavnom postu* (St. Petersburg, 1906), p. 433,
quoted by Billington: *Mikhailovsky and Russian Populism*, p. 25.

and legislative powers which are so familiar in Europe. Whether this clash will have a similar character and what its end result will be is now, because of its very novelty, difficult to foresee.[5]

If it was hard for Chernyshevskii's followers to think or say any longer, as he had done, that the history of Europe would be changed by the outcome of the American crisis, more modest expectations, more modestly expressed, could still be nurtured by American successes in solving certain concrete and specific problems. In this more limited sense, America was for about a decade after the Civil War a frequent model for the journals that tried to carry on the work of social criticism and political debate: the resurrected *Messenger of Europe*, whose very title was a statement of liberal Westernism; the reorganized *Fatherland Notes*, which, moving further to the left, inherited some of *The Contemporary*'s writers and many of its readers; and a new review, *The Cause*, which attempted to carry on more discreetly the tradition of the defunct *Russian Word*. The more comprehensive and revolutionary goals that America had betrayed or failed to reach had now to be expressed abroad or in the underground. But America's failure also made her a safer topic for the legal press than the radical republic of radical dreams could have been.

The Messenger of Europe took issue with the view that the results of the war were not equal to the sacrifices exacted and expressed confidence that the people's representatives would win their duel with the executive—"which in America cannot dispose arbitrarily of the fate of an entire nation"—and carry out the will of the majority. This might have to await the election of a new President, but sooner or later the real emancipation of the Negro would be achieved, with land to make him independent of his former master and a federal presence in the South to safeguard his civil rights. Johnson's impeachment and trial, reported with a wealth of detail on constitutional procedure, was called the "crowning of the building of liberty and popular government." "Crowning the building" was the phrase Russian liberals used to

---

5 "Politika," *Sovremennik*, No. 1 (1866), pp. 94–137; quotation from p. 131.

demand that the limited degree of local self-government granted in 1864 be broadened into a national parliament.[6]

The other two opposition journals also stressed the role the Constitution had played before and during the war in saving America from anarchy and despotism. It had kept intact the balance of order and freedom, national strength and individual liberty that testified to the political intelligence of her people. But constitutions and political freedoms were never panaceas, not ends in themselves for Russian leftists. They were desirable mainly because they facilitated the struggle for the just society of abundance, equality, and humanity. All the more impressive, therefore, what had been done by a bourgeois republic to give social content and economic meaning to political democracy.[7]

"The Woman Question," so important to Russian progressives as a test of dedication to their values, was not the only one that America, with women taking a hand in their own emancipation, was expected to solve more fully and more quickly than Europe. On her soil there would also take place a fusion of all races and nationalities, religions and philosophies, a fusion from which there would emerge a new people, better and greater than its component parts.[8]

This people, which had already gone far in supplying an

---

[6] "Inostrannoe obozrenie," *Vestnik Evropy*, I (Mar. 1866), 38–66; "Ezhemesiachnaia khronika," ibid., No. 4 (1868), pp. 865–6; No. 5 (1868), pp. 405–7; No. 3 (1868), pp. 117–22.

[7] N. V. Shelgunov: "Amerikanskie patrioty proshlago stoletiia," *Delo*, Nos. 1 and 2 (1861), in *Sochineniia N. V. Shelgunova* (2nd edn., St. Petersburg, 1895), I, 575–624. Cf. ibid., I, 507–75, and A. S. Slabkii: *Mirrovozzrenie N. V. Shelgunova* (Khar'kov, 1960), pp. 57–8; "Sovremennaia khronika: Inostrannaia literatura," *Otechestvennye zapiski*, No. 9 (1867), pp. 63–75.

[8] E. L.: "Zhenskoe dvizhenie u nas i zagranitsei," ibid., No. 4 (1870), p. 237, and "Zhenskii vopros," ibid., No. 5 (1870), pp. 314–42; S. S. Shashkova: "Zhenskoe delo v Amerike," *Delo*, No. 1 (1872), pp. 34–59, and No. 2 (1872), pp. 152–84; "Politicheskaia i obshchestvennaia khronika," ibid., No. 7 (1872), pp. 40–2. For observations on the racial situation: "Politicheskaia khronika," ibid., No. 8 (1868), pp. 78–80; "Osnovanie novykh shtatov v Amerike," *Otechestvennye zapiski*, No. 12 (1871), p. 402. Even Katkov believed at one time in the possibility of a social transformation that would give Negroes full citizenship. See Katkov: *Editorials*, IX, 847, and XII, 588, for contrasting views of December 20, 1871, and September 16, 1874.

answer to the most thorny problem of the age—the conflict of nationalities—owed much of its happiness and harmony to a system of popular education that was in keeping with the character of the society it served and made no distinctions of race or sex, nationality or class. "If America had adopted our dual kind of education—one for people of substance and another for the poor—democratic principles would never have struck such deep roots and there could be neither brotherhood nor solidarity . . ."[9]

Basic to all these advantages was the availability of land at moderate cost to those who would work it with their own hands. And it was not the least of America's attractions that together with an escape from the prison of poverty and dependence she offered Europe's immigrants the dignity of free citizens.[1]

The portrait was not without its shadows: the Ku Klux Klan, the moral cowardice of liberal bourgeois and politicians, grasping capitalists, corruption and exploitation, hypocritical and cruel treatment of Indians and Mormons in the name of progress and civilization. But for the moment, as a contributor to *The Cause* put it, "We are firmly convinced that the sum of advantages and achievements far outweighs the shortcomings, and that it is easier to battle against these inadequacies in America than anywhere in Western Europe," and, needless to say, in Russia. This attitude was reinforced by a spate of books about America that appeared in the 1870's, all but a handful translations. There was regret only, said one reviewer, that the friendship remained platonic and that no more came of it in Russia than literary exercises.[2]

---

[9] "Novye knigi," *Delo*, No. 5 (1872), pp. 23–7; A. Mikhailov: "Pervonachal'noe obrazovanie v Severo-Amerikanskikh Shtatakh," ibid., No. 9 (1873), pp. 1–36, and No. 10 (1873), pp. 36–84. See especially pp. 55 and 84 of the latter.

[1] B. Ongirskii: "Emigratsiia v Severo-Amerikanskie Soedinennye Shtaty," ibid., No. 11 (1871), pp. 60–83; "Osnovanie novykh shtatov v Amerike," *Otechestvennye zapiski*, No. 12 (1871), pp. 369–402.

[2] "Politicheskaia khronika," *Delo*, No. 10 (1871), pp. 64–70; ibid., No. 5 (1872), pp. 52–5; ibid., No. 7 (1872), pp. 35–75; "Novye knigi," ibid., No. 6 (1873), pp. 27–35; Mikhailov: "Pervonachal'noe obrazovanie . . . ," ibid., No. 9 (1873), pp. 4–6; Nikolai Slavinskii: *Pis'ma ob Amerike i russkikh pereselentsakh* (St. Petersburg, 1873), especially pp. 301–3; M. D. Butin: *Pis'ma iz Ameriki* (St. Petersburg, 1872); A. Trachevskii: "Ocherki istoricheskogo razvitiia Ameriki," *Beseda*, Nos. 11 and 12 (1872), pp. 124–184, 192–252; Stepan Fortunatov: *Politicheskiia ucheniia v Soedinennikh Shtatakh* (Moscow, 1879). On Fortunatov, see Laserson: *The American Impact on Russia*, pp. 375–7.

The American vogue had one practical, if minor and temporary, result. Postwar America appeared a possible laboratory for social experimentation. She offered opportunities for putting into practice ideals of communal labor and living that did not exist in police-ridden Russia. Among the small number of Russians who went to the United States before the great wave of Jewish emigration that began in the 1880's, there was a score or so of Russian populists, some of them members of an "American Circle" in Kiev, who either wanted to establish or to join utopian communities in the United States. For the members of the Kiev circle, only three of whom actually reached their goal, the aim was from the start to return home and use their American passports and experience for the benefit of their own people, but nearly all these ideological exiles found the real America a disappointment and soon made their way back to Russia or Western Europe. Americans, as one radical writer described them on his return to Russia, though basically decent, just, well-meaning, if crude, knew nothing of philosophy and politics and less of social reality than a Parisian worker.[3]

It is difficult to explain why in the middle 1870's a negative image of America began to prevail and to last for most of thirty years. A rising curve of revolutionary optimism and liberal hopes in Russia and a revival of public debate and political interest connected with the Balkan War may serve as partial explanations. But the major reason for the change was probably America herself. The deterioration in the quality of her public life and morals was too striking to escape notice and adverse comment, was too far-reaching to be dismissed as a temporary aberration.

In 1876, the *Fatherland Notes* commemorated the centennial of America's birth by recalling the heroic portion of her past that had led to independence and made the present seem all the more sordid. It was easy to wonder whether the Civil War was a

---

[3] Yarmolinsky: *Road to Revolution*, 178–9, 190, 257; Kiparsky: "The American Westerner in Russian Fiction," pp. 38–40; Franco Venturi: *Roots of Revolution*, trans. by Francis Haskell (London, 1960), p. 473. See also Dostoevsky: *The Devils* (p. 234, *n.* 3; above), pp. 147–8, where he writes of three men who go to the United States to find out for themselves "what the life of the American worker was like and in this way to check by *personal* experience the state of a man living under the worst possible social conditions," and Hecht: *Russian Radicals*, pp. 174–5, 196–216.

sign of vitality or decline. "America is obviously entering a new stage of development," an article called "The Struggle of the Races in America" began; "The end of her formation is near." Her lands were being filled up, her natural resources were no longer inexhaustible, immigration was ebbing, and her greatness of spirit, like her limitless horizons, was shrinking. Increasingly, denial of the most ordinary human rights to Negroes was justified by trumpeting the inherent superiority of whites, whereas the real question was not one of race, but of civil rights, of education and, most important, of decent working conditions and wages. This was the central concern of Russian social critics, whether they believed that Russia could escape the horrors of capitalism or thought that she was condemned, like the United States, to live through them on the way to the common socialist future.[4]

The degeneration of public life in America reduced the value and the magnitude of her accomplishments. Her government was a plutocracy; the success of her educational system appeared questionable, as did the gains her women had made. Her republican institutions and values were threatened and without a radical reconstruction of the economic system would fall victim to financial oligarchy. The most fateful decision she faced was how to order the relations between labor and capital, whether to follow the worn-out paths trodden by Europe or carry further the experiments in profit-sharing and mutual help that had been made on her soil by a few religious communities and cooperative enterprises.[5]

---

[4] N.P.—ii, "Bor'ba ras v Amerike," *Otechestvennye zapiski*, Nos. 1 and 2 (1876), pp. 69–93, 212–28. It is interesting to note that *The Gilded Age*, Mark Twain's collaborative effort with Charles D. Warner, was translated into Russian in 1874, a year after its publication in the United States.

[5] "Trud i obrazovanie v Amerike," *Otechestvennye zapiski*, No. 5 (1876), pp. 97–119; F.: "Prezidentskaia kampaniia v Amerike," ibid., No. 2 (1877), pp. 415–53; Ia. P-r: "Amerikanskaia plutokratiia," *Delo*, No. 11 (1876), pp. 145–73. "Amerikanki razlichnykh sloev," *Ustoi*, No. 1 (Dec. 1881), pp. 1–37; Ivan Kamenev: "Studencheskaia molodezh' v Amerike," *Russkoe Bogatstvo*, No. 5 (1897), pp. 209–35; Z. S.: "Amerikanskie negry," *Vestnik vsemirnoi istorii*, No. 7 (1901), pp. 208–13; V. F.: "Politicheskiia partii v Amerike nakanune izbraniia novogo prezidenta," *Russkaia mysl'*, Book III (Mar. 1881), pp. 98–121; Kiparsky: "The American Westerner in Russian Fiction," p. 40.

The prognosis was not helpful, for the period of American exceptionalism was over. During and after the Civil War she had become mighty and rich, but she was no longer in the advance guard of humanity. Russia too was being prodded by her rulers and a growing middle class into a modernity that spelled power for the state, profit for its beneficiaries, destitution and a faceless anonymity for the masses. This was perhaps the most basic reason for the changing view of America: the fear that she was enacting, without the pretense that older civilizations still found necessary, the tragedy that would befall all nations which in the race for wealth and power ignored the rights, welfare, and humanity of their people. For Russian socialists after Chernyshevskii this was a matter of moral and intellectual conviction; for the Marxists among them it was a scientific certainty. But even anarchists and populists who rejected Marx sustained the influence of his teachings and of the European environment that had shaped them. They were not much tempted, therefore, to see in the bourgeois republic across the seas a perfected version of the bourgeois monarchies of Europe.

What these men had to say about the Civil War and the society it produced had much to do with the change in Russian attitudes. "The great and salutary principle of *Federalism*," which Bakunin so warmly recommended to European socialists in 1868 because of its recent vindication in America, had not, he also noted, prevented the war. Unable to deal with slavery, federalism would hardly solve the question now confronting the United States—the rise of an industrial proletariat in the factories of the North, whose growth had been stimulated by the defeat of the agrarian South. Before long, these workers would be no better off than their European brothers, governed by a class that paid lip service to a fictitious democracy. In all states, Bakunin wrote in 1871, "even in the United States"—where there had once been the chance of escaping concentrations of power and poverty— "everything is under the . . . control of a special, altogether bourgeois class . . . of so-called politicians or business people in politics, whereas the great mass of toilers live under conditions which are just as wretched and frightful as those which prevail in the monarchic states." Dedicated, principled, sincere as they might be, the Republicans would not make government by the people a reality. That would require a more thoroughgoing revolution than any that had yet shaken the Old World or the New.[6]

Peter Lavrov, one of the theorists of populism, agreed. The best of Republican parties or republican principles and constitutions, no matter how great their contribution to the victory over slavery and the attainment of political liberty, could not answer the needs of contemporary man. What had happened after the Civil War showed up the inherent limitations of the American system. Before it, the Democratic, or slaveholders', party had dominated Congress and the Republican minority had proclaimed liberty for the enslaved, sending Brown to rouse the Negroes, producing Lincoln, and fighting for a noble program and progressive ideals. It had then seemed to be playing a decisive role in the history of man and succeeded in crushing its enemies and the enemies of American unity. But what transpired when the Confederacy fell?

> Those who had fought in the name of an idea showed themselves to be the most ordinary political traders and . . . exploiters. Venality, robbery, indifference to the general welfare, speculation . . . and political hypocrisy . . . were more clearly manifested in the "model republic" than in the senile states of Europe. The victory of the party of liberty . . . ended in moral decline and proved that the foremost party of the freest state in the world is without a progressive political program and without political conceptions whatever. No sincere political idealist can now point to the United States as a political model. The triumph of unity has toppled America from her place of eminence in history.

The classical land of political liberty had turned into "The Republic of Humbug," the home of a soulless industrial civilization that liberated slaves and women only to convert them into lackeys or proletarians.[7]

The end of American exceptionalism deepened doubts about

[6] M. A. Bakunin: *Polnoe sobranie sochinenii* (Moscow, [1903?]), I, 56–60, 154–5; II, 52, 64; G. P. Maximoff, ed.: *The Political Philosophy of Bakunin* (New York, 1953), pp. 212, 223, 276; Hecht: *Russian Radicals*, pp. 58–77.

[7] P. L. Lavrov: *Izbrannye sochineniia* (Moscow, 1934), IV, 31–8. Cf. Hecht: *Russian Radicals*, pp. 158–62. For the views of another populist thinker, see Billington: *Mikhailovsky and Russian Populism*, p. 113, and Hecht: "Mikhjlovskij and the United States," in Hugh McLean et al., eds.: *Russian Thought and Politics* (Harvard Slavic Studies, IV, 1957), pp. 263–280.

a special, a Russian, road to socialism. It also strengthened the Marxist argument that no country would be spared the convulsions that everywhere attended the growth of capitalism and the working class. Georgii Plekhanov, the father of Russian Marxism, used the example of America to convince his former populist comrades that the laws of history had universal validity and that democracy conferred no immunity from class struggle. Democracy had not saved America from civil war. If that was the price which had had to be paid for ending slavery, what assurance was there "that the American proletariat will not be forced to clear the road for its economic liberation?"[8]

Marxists looked upon violence as the inevitable or probable accompaniment of change, the midwife of a better world; Tolstoy, in his old age the preacher of nonresistance to evil, condemned it, regardless of its ultimate benefits. Domination and coercion of one's fellowmen, by slaveowners or abolitionists, was wrong. No good had come of the use of force, only a war of brothers, a purely external solution of the slavery question and the introduction into American life of the immorality that is the byproduct of every war.

> The essence of the question remains unresolved, and the same problem, only in a new form, now stands before the people of the United States. Then the question was how to free Negroes from the violence of their owners; now it is how to free Negroes from the violence of all the whites and whites from the violence of all the blacks. The solution of this problem in a new form will certainly not be accomplished by lynching Negroes or by any skillful or liberal measures of American politicians, but only by the application to life of that same principle [i.e., nonresistance] which was proclaimed by Garrison half a century ago.[9]

Tolstoy's moral law was as sweeping as Plekhanov's historical law; neither could encompass the recalcitrant reality that

---

[8] G. V. Plekhanov: *Selected Philosophical Works*, trans. by A. Rothstein, A. Fineberg, R. Dixon (Moscow, n.d.), I, 85; David Hecht: "Plekhanov and American Socialism," *Russian Review*, IX, 2 (Apr. 1950), 112–13.

[9] Leo Tolstoy: Introduction to Vladimir Tchertkoff and Florence Holah, *A Short Biography of William Lloyd Garrison* (London, 1904), pp. viii–ix, original in L. N. Tolstoy: *Polnoe sobranie sochinenii* (Moscow–Leningrad, 1936), XXXVI, 95–9.

was America or avoid interpreting an unfamiliar historical experience in familiar categories. The less doctrinaire approach of a few liberals, constitutionalists, and scholars was better able to account for the contradictions of American life without falling into extremes of condemnation or praise, grand theorizing or journalistic impressionism. Yet they were a small minority that gained a wider and more sympathetic hearing only in the few years after 1905 when Russia had a brief taste of a very limited kind of representative government and civil liberty. These beginnings for a deeper understanding of America were swept away by the holocaust of a revolution and civil war that in the eyes of the men who unleashed it would be justified by history and progress, as revolution and civil war in America had been earlier.[1]

Lenin, following Marx, ascribed to the war's second or post-constitutional phase (1863–5) "great, world-historic, progressive and revolutionary significance," and thus defined the terms of subsequent discussion. This allowed Russian Communists to sustain belief in the existence of a revolutionary tradition in America and to remind their critics that Bolsheviks were not the only people who had recourse to violence. "The Second American Revolution," the struggle between the forces of modern capital and feudalism, was not a proletarian revolution; but like all great social cataclysms it had cleared away the obstacles in America's path to progress and ushered in the continuing conflict between the masses and the capitalists. The war had been revolutionary also in its scope, and when Lenin in a "Letter to American Workers" (1918) stressed that the overthrow of slavery and slaveholders was worth the price of war, destruction, and terror, he was not so much describing America's revolution as pleading for his own.[2]

---

[1] For indications of a more serious and intensive, though now more often favorably biased, study of America, see Laserson: *The American Impact on Russia*, pp. 372–96; Aleksei Babin: *Istoriia Severo-Amerikanskikh Soedinennykh Shtatov* (2 vols.; St. Petersburg, 1912); Pavel G. Mizhuev: *Istoriia velikoi amerikanskoi demokratii* (St. Petersburg, 1906); N. A. Borodin: *Severo-Amerikanskie Soedinennye Shtaty i Rossiia* (Petrograd, 1915); Evgraf Kovalevskii: *Narodnoe obrazovanie v Soedinennykh Shtatakh Severnoi Ameriki* (St. Petersburg, 1895), and p. 180, *n.* 3, above.

[2] V. I. Lenin: *Polnoe sobranie sochinenii* (5th edn.; Moscow, 1963), XXXVII, 58. American history in general and that of the Civil War and

Trotsky asked also that the Revolution which had cast him out be not misjudged because of that or condemned for the ruthlessness which he, like Lincoln, had been forced to employ. "History has different yardsticks for the cruelty of the Northerners and that of the Southerners. A slaveowner who uses cunning and violence to shackle the slave, and a slave who uses cunning and violence to break the chains—only contemptible eunuchs will tell us that they are equal before the court of morality!" The perspective of time, he told an American radio audience in 1932, would let them see the October Revolution, like their Civil War, as laying the basis for a new society.[3]

Whatever elaboration or detail would be carried into subsequent Soviet studies of the Civil War, the basic definition of its character by Marx and Engels as a struggle between two socioeconomic systems was retained and its justification before the court of history assured. And such a treatment required no funda-

---

Reconstruction in particular has been given much more emphasis by Soviet historians than by their prerevolutionary predecessors, especially in the years since 1955. A convenient introduction to Soviet Civil War literature is Joseph A. Logsdon: "The Civil War—Russian Version (II): The Soviet Historians," *Civil War History*, Vol. VIII, No. IV (Dec. 1962), pp. 365–71, where some striking continuities in Russian assessments of certain aspects of the war become visible. A Soviet critique of the article and the issue of *Civil War History* in which it appeared is D. B. Petrov: " 'Russkaia versiia' grazhdanskoi voiny v SShA," *Voprosy Istorii*, No. 1 (1963), pp. 194–5. The view of the Civil War as the Second American Revolution is set forth in a book by that title—G. P. Kuropiatnik: *Vtoraia amerikanskaia revoliutsiia* (Moscow, 1961). For other Soviet treatments of the Civil War and related issues, see: A. I. Blinov: *Period revoliutsionnoi diktatury radikal'nykh respublikantsev vo vremia rekonstruktsii SShA; 1866–1868* (Krasnoiarsk, 1960), and the same author's *Kriticheskii period istorii Soedinennykh Shtatov. Rekonstruktsiia shtatov . . . posle okonchaniia grazhdanskoi voiny; 1865–1877* (Krasnoiarsk, 1957); I. I. Cherkasov: "Iz istorii rasprostraneniia marksizma v SShA, 1848–1865," *Novaia i noveishaia istoriia*, No. 3 (1958), pp. 24–42; I. P. Dement'ev: *Amerikanskaia istoriografiia grazhdanskoi voiny v SShA, 1861–1865* (Moscow, 1963); R. F. Ivanov: *Avraam Linkol'n i grazhdanskaia voina v SShA* (Moscow, 1964); Ivanov: *Bor'ba negrov za zemliu i svobodu na iuge SShA, 1865–1877gg.* (Moscow, 1958); V. Lan [V. I. Kaplan]: *Klassy i partii v SShA* (2nd edn.; Moscow, 1937), pp. 75–81, 90–7.

[3] From Isaac Deutscher: *The Prophet Outcast* (New York and London, 1963), pp. 185, 440.

mental revision of what had been the prevailing Russian opinion at the time of the war: that it demonstrated the inevitability of progress and the universality of the standards of civilization that history was forcing the American South and Russia to accept. There was agreement also that the ending of human bondage, too long delayed by both societies, was the major test of their obedience to the commands of history and morality and the necessary condition for their further advance. But beyond that, there was a divergence of views as to where the advance should or would lead, whether it was right or possible for Russia to choose the road America had taken, and whether America's experience had any bearing on Russia's perplexing situation.

The way Russians interpreted the American Civil War, which was, for all the interest they took in it, an event of peripheral importance to them, did not determine or deeply influence the answers they made to these questions. The war and its results supplied corroboration for a variety of positions and prescriptions. For Katkov it confirmed the dangers of federalism and the preeminent necessity of national unity and strength; for Chernyshevskii, the need of radical measures and radical men to overcome indifference and reaction and involve the masses in the work of social regeneration; for Bakunin, the conviction that "struggle is life, life is power," and civil war a welcome disturbance of the people's sheepish submission to the authority of princes and politicians.[4]

To Herzen the war proved little, and too much: that republics could fight wars as well, if not better than monarchies, a point Katkov was willing to concede; and that since one young giant was on the move, the other was too and certain to reach the desired goal. As for Ivan Aksakov—the war might never have happened. It was only the occasion for an elaborate reiteration of the anathemas that earlier Slavophiles had hurled against America, although it probably helped to impress him with the utility of force. There were those like the constitutional monarchist and legal philosopher Boris Chicherin who saw the Union's agony as vindication of their preference for a power sufficiently strong and independent of party, privilege, and passion to carry

---

[4] Maximoff: *The Political Philosophy of Bakunin*, pp. 407–8.

out needed reforms. And there were many who believed with him and the skeptical liberal Moisey Ostrogorsky that the Civil War had introduced, or brought to the fore, the least attractive sides of the American character, that wisdom, balance, and respect for the law, represented by the Constitution, were being overwhelmed by democracy, party, plutocracy, and centralization.[5]

Military men studied the war, but evidently not with such care or profit as their German colleagues. One of them, General Fadeev, "speaking *en passant*" in 1870, called the United States Russia's only possible ally who was not inimical to her historic tasks, a counterpoise to the Western maritime powers, but incapable of helping Russia on land.[6]

"*En passant*" is how the vast majority of Russians who thought about such things at all approached the United States. Those who were favorably disposed toward its institutions and values saw these as a useful counterpoise or instructive contrast to their own, but neither before nor after the war did they think that their own most difficult problems were susceptible of American solutions. America was the dreamland of romantic boys, land-hungry peasants, and persecuted Jews, the political ideal of a few professorial liberals. But neither Russia's upper classes nor her intelligentsia ever developed for the United States the deep emotional attachment that tied them to France or the intellectual fascination that drew them to Germany. The Civil War did not change this pattern. While it was in progress it aroused interest, respect, and feelings of solidarity for the Union. What it left was

---

[5] For Chicherin and Ostrogorsky, see Laserson: *The American Impact on Russia*, pp. 377–81 and 387–96; and Boris Chicherin: *Kurs gosudarstvennoi nauki* (Moscow, 1894–8), III, 287, 370; *O narodnom predstavitel'stve* (2nd edn.; Moscow, 1899), pp. 76–7, 98, 107, 116; Moisey Ostrogorsky: *Democracy and the Party System in the United States* (2nd edn.; New York, 1921), pp. 49–60.

[6] I. Gausman [Haussmann]: *Voina v Soedinennykh Shtatakh Ameriki, 1861–1865* (2 vols.; St. Petersburg, 1877–8). Haussmann was a professor at the General Staff Academy in St. Petersburg; see Kamenetskii: "*Materialy o russko-amerikanskikh otnosheniiakh*," p. 74. The Russian minister to Washington and Chernyshevskii were aware of the military importance of the *Monitor–Merrimac* encounter, the former regretting that no Russian naval officer was present to study it. The Fadeev quotation is from Michael B. Petrovich: *The Emergence of Russian Panslavism, 1856–1870* (New York, 1956), p. 267.

a memory of these and a somewhat detached liking that could coexist with more critical attitudes. When common interests or dangers required it, the memory and the liking could be fanned into manifestations of love and cited as evidence of shared traditions and ideals. But memory, like sympathy, is a process of selection and so, for people who are not its direct participants, is the impact of a distant historical event.

Canada and the Civil War

John A. Williams

*T*he *nearest neighbors to the United States, yet as different from that war-torn country as they were from each other, Canada and Latin America were more sensitive to Civil War events than other nations. This sense of intimacy and involvement took many forms, as the following essays by Professor John A. Williams, on Canada, and Professor Harry Bernstein, on Latin America, make clear.*

Canadians' concerns centered on border security, economic upsets, and, finally, governmental institutions, constitutionalism, and federalism. Because of the point that Canadians had reached a hundred years ago in their own history, their stake in the American war was almost as great as the Americans'.[1]

This complex story warrants the kind of detailed description that Professor Williams, of the University of Washington, offers in the following pages.

---

[1] Historians who debate whether Union victory in 1865 made possible or inevitable Britain's 1867 Reform Act accept W. L. Morton's judgment that "as the Confederacy sank in the South, then, the [Canadian] Confederation arose in the North." Morton: "Canada and Reconstruction, 1863–1879," in Hyman, ed.: *New Frontiers of the American Reconstruction* (Urbana, Ill., 1966), p. 124.

From 1841 to 1867 British North America progressed from a dependent colonial status to a quasi-national status. At the beginning of this period the old colonial system stood nearly intact if not unchallenged. The first step in reorganization, the uniting of the two St. Lawrence colonies—Upper Canada and Lower Canada—into one colony had just been made. Neither this union, with its sectional division between the French East and the English West, nor the Maritime colonies of New Brunswick, Nova Scotia, and Prince Edward Island, yet enjoyed responsible ministerial government over even their internal affairs. Lord John Russell, the colonial secretary, had recently denied that such responsible government was compatible with the imperial connection.[1] The trade of these colonies was tied to Great Britain by the preferential timber duties and the Corn Laws. Indeed, the advantage these staple products enjoyed in the British market was the basis of British North American prosperity, and a vigorous canal-building program had been launched to keep the trade flowing through the St. Lawrence rather than to New York.

These preferences for colonial products amounted to a subsidy paid to the colonies by British consumers. Under the strong impact of laissez-faire thinking in the 1840's, neither Whig nor Tory governments could justify their continuance. Between 1843 and 1851 the Corn Laws, Navigation Acts, and timber duties were repealed. Henceforth the Montreal grain and timber merchants and the Maritime shipbuilders would have to reach the British market on competitive terms or find other outlets. The repeal of the preferences might imply, in fact, even greater changes. The old merchant group, their markets lost, might give way to new men exploiting new products for new markets. Such possibilities implied social and political as well as economic changes.

Some of the political changes were immediate. With the coming of free trade, no tangible imperial interest could be served by the continuing political subordination of the colonies, no interest harmed by the severing of the ties. This may overstate the case, but a growing number of people in Britain were saying that

---

[1] J. H. Stewart Reid, Kenneth McNaught, and Harry S. Crowe: *A Source-book of Canadian History* (rev. ed.; Toronto, 1964), p. 117.

colonial independence was inevitable, some that it was desirable. The third Earl Grey, colonial secretary in Lord John Russell's Whig administration, believed rather that a free grant of colonial self-government would establish new sentimental bonds of Empire, as strong and more permanent than those existing under the old system of subordination. First in Nova Scotia and then in Canada, ministries responsible to a majority in the house were formed, even though this meant turning out the old Tory establishment in favor of the reformers. Grey's calculation was correct. The reformers who had been pressing for responsible government were loyal and stable in office. It was the loyalist Tories, their economic and political privileges gone, who rioted, burned, and pillaged in Montreal in 1849. Some of them even called for annexation to the United States. These events discredited the old Tory oligarchy, enabling the Reformers to strengthen their hold on power. During the 1850's the Reformers gave way to more moderate Conservatives.

On the eve of the Civil War the British North American colonies had been self-governing for more than a decade. During this time the Canadas had grown markedly. Canada West reached nearly 1,400,000 in 1861, pulling ahead of Canada East with its 1,100,000, because of rapid immigration. The Maritime colonies, growing much more slowly, had a combined population of only 862,000.[2] Even combined, this population was minute next to the United States population of 31,513,000, and the provinces were not combined. Canada and the Maritimes were isolated from one another, and the three Maritime colonies were wrapped up in petty local controversies.

There was, indeed, an increasing doubt whether the British North American colonies were viable political units, capable of solving their problems of political stability, the parochial narrowness of political life (especially in the Maritimes), the future of the great British North American west, economic prosperity, and defense. None of these problems had reached crisis proportions in the 1850's. They were simply deferred. The American Civil War would make them urgent, and it would also make their solution a political possibility.

---

[2] M. C. Urquhart and K. A. H. Buckley, eds.: *Historical Statistics of Canada* (Cambridge and Toronto, 1965), p. 14; *Historical Statistics of the United States; Colonial Times to 1957* (Washington, D.C., 1957), p. 7.

As the sectional crisis mounted in the American South, the Canadas were having sectional problems of their own. Year by year party divisions were coming more and more to approximate the division between East and West, French and English, and this trend was making stable government impossible.

The leader of the government party from about 1856 on was John A. Macdonald of Kingston, who represented a new conservatism purged of the old oligarchical mentality and the excesses of the Montreal riots of 1849. Macdonald saw the best future for Canada in the political cooperation of French and English. Disraeli-like in the shrewdness of his maneuverings, he strove to preserve a party based on conservative principles to represent both the Protestant West and Catholic East.[3]

Macdonald's longtime partner in the party was George E. Cartier, a practical and effective politician and railroad lawyer, who held the phalanx of Bleu party supporters in solid conservative alliance with the English. Though perhaps more inclined to French-Canadian nationalism, the opposition Rouge party could not challenge Cartier's hegemony, for they were socially too radical and too anticlerical to attract wide support. Rouge accusations that Cartier was subservient to the English were therefore ineffective.

Sectional dissatisfaction centered on English Canada. The two sections of the province were equally represented in the legislature, and Canada West had been underrepresented on a population basis since 1851. Macdonald's Conservatives, placing a high value on the French alliance and inclined to deny the democratic premise that members of Parliament were constituency delegates, chose to ignore this. The opposition in Canada West—the Reformers, Liberals, or Clear Grits—could therefore effectively raise the cry of "representation by population."

The leader in this campaign was George Brown, proprietor of the Toronto *Globe*, and Macdonald's archopponent in politics. Brown was Gladstonian in his adherence to liberal principles and his moral view of politics, but narrowly sectional in his attacks on French domination and sometimes bigoted in his anti-Catholicism. Above all, he hated Macdonald, who had attempted to link Brown's name to corruption in the penitentiary

---

[3] Donald Creighton: *John A. Macdonald, the Young Politician* (Toronto, 1956), pp. 149–50, 217–18, 226–7.

system, and who tricked him out of office by political sharp practice in the infamous "double shuffle" of 1858. With his deepest moral convictions he opposed Macdonald's political methods, and the Conservatives he labeled as the "corruptionist" party. Briefly in 1859 Brown came to wonder whether such corruption might be inherent in the ministerial system. More sweeping reform might be necessary, but "representation by population" was the slogan that had the greatest appeal. The depth of Brown's dislike for Macdonald, the difficulty of cooperation between them, was the measure of Canada's sectional crisis and the seeming hopelessness of solution.[4]

From 1857 Macdonald's government had only a minority in English Canada West. In 1858 they were defeated when French supporters deserted them on the question of placing the new capital in Ottawa—but no other government could stay in office either. Macdonald reconstructed his ministry but did not find stability. In the election of 1861, he made "representation by population" an open question, and many of the new western Conservative members were pledged to electoral reform. In this way Macdonald maintained a majority on all questions except the issue that mattered most.

In 1859 and 1860, then, the Canadian union too seemed to be breaking up. Rule of one section by a majority in the other was intolerable on any of the many sensitive questions. Some politicians believed that a majority in both sections should be required; but a government bound by this rule would be impotent. The Reformers and Brown came dangerously close to calling for more drastic reform—elected executives and a written constitution—but finally they reasserted their faith in the parliamentary system. Denied democratic representation within the Canadian union, the Reform convention of 1859 debated whether to dissolve the union or to federate it. In the end they resolved for dissolution, proposing only "some joint authority" to join the two sections loosely together.[5]

---

4 Paul G. Cornell: *The Alignment of Political Groups in Canada, 1841–1867* (Toronto, 1962), *passim*, J. M. S. Careless: *Brown of the Globe*. Vol. I, *The Voice of Upper Canada, 1818–1859* (Toronto, 1959), pp. 288–9, 299–304.

5 G. W. Brown: "The Grit Party and the Great Reform Convention of 1859," *Canadian Historical Review*, XVI (Sept. 1935), pp. 245–65.

The Macdonald government's proposal to end the political stalemate was not this disintegration of territories but rather the integration of the existing Canada's union into a broader British North American nationality. This idea of a federation of all British North America had been widely discussed, but was usually considered premature or impractical. The governor, Sir Edmund Head, was its ardent supporter, and the man who gave it temporary political life was Alexander T. Galt, a railway financier and former Rouge, who joined Macdonald's government in 1858.

Confederation was the term already being used for the federal union of British North America. As Galt used it, the term implied not a weaker but a stronger central government than that of the United States. Already he said that the basis of confederation should differ from that of the United States. Its authority would be derived from Parliament rather than the people, and the local legislatures would be barred from "the exercise of the same sovereign powers which have frequently been the cause of difference between the American states and their general government." Galt expanded on the merits of confederation —the growth of a common national sentiment, the prosperity to be gained from a large domestic market, and the chance for a continental state stretching from sea to sea.[6] In broad essentials, these were the ideas that bore fruit in 1867. In 1858, however, they made little progress. They were condemned as a partisan maneuver not seriously put forward. The British government insisted that the initiative must be imperial; the Maritimes were uninterested or hostile; the opposition agitated for less grandiose reforms. The government party itself lacked the conviction to persist. It would take the American Civil War to clear these obstacles away and give clear direction to Canadian statesmanship.

The problem of the British North American west was also becoming acute just before the Civil War. The question was whether this great area should remain British or become American like Oregon. The first challenge had been overcome with surprising ease before the beginning of the war. When thousands

---

[6] W. L. Morton: *The Critical Years; the Union of British North America, 1857–1873* (Toronto, 1964), p. 68; O. D. Skelton: *The Life and Times of Alexander Tilloch Galt* (Toronto, 1920), pp. 239–44; Chester Martin: *Foundations of Canadian Nationhood* (Toronto, 1955), pp. 258–70.

of Americans had moved into the Fraser River area to seek gold, James Douglas, the governor of Vancouver Island, had extended his authority over the gold camps. This unauthorized action was accepted by the miners and sanctioned by the creation of British Columbia as a separate colony in 1858. A minor but potentially dangerous disagreement remained in the area—a boundary dispute in the San Juan Islands.

British statesmen were less confident about the position in the vast and sparsely populated territory of Rupert's Land, ruled by the Hudson's Bay Company. Several factors were combining to weaken the company's authority in the 1850's, most of the trouble centering on the slowly growing Red River settlement, present-day Winnipeg. Since 1849 Red River traders had openly and effectively defied the company's monopoly of trade. A small community of settlers from Canada were agitating against the authority of the court and council of Assiniboia, the company's government for the settlement. They were calling for the annexation of the settlement to Canada, a cry that found answering echoes in Canada West. The agitation there, beginning about 1856, was the special project of George Brown and his Toronto *Globe*.[7]

The presence of a contingent of British troops at Red River from 1857 to 1861, ostensibly to deter American aggression, was really to maintain internal order. The force did enable the company to keep a minimum of authority. This support did not mean, however, that the British government wanted the weak company rule to continue. The British felt that trading monopolies were anomalous in the era of free trade. The company's trading license was allowed to lapse in 1859. The Colonial Office was also trying to arrange a court test of the company's charter, but neither the company itself nor Canada was willing to bring the case. These British activities further undermined the company's authority by making it obvious that a new regime would soon take over.

Many hoped and many feared that the new regime would be American. The booming settlement of Minnesota during the 1850's seemed destined to expand north along the Red River into British territory. The traders around Fort Garry already

---

7 John S. Galbraith: *The Hudson's Bay Company as an Imperial Factor, 1821–1869* (Berkeley and Los Angeles, 1957), pp. 329–32, 334–5.

looked mainly to St. Paul. In 1859, for mail or goods, contacts with the outside were more frequent than by the bay, quicker and more reliable than by the river and lake route directly to Canada. The Northwest Transportation Navigation and Railway Company, founded in 1859 to carry mail by this direct route (and for more grandiose purposes), was unable to compete with the service to Pembina and through the United States.[8]

If the northwest was to remain British in these circumstances, strong political action was needed to overcome the economic disadvantages. One possibility was to establish interior crown colonies under the Colonial Office. The colonial secretary, the Duke of Newcastle, toyed with this idea, but plainly Parliament would be opposed to the necessary expenditure. Canada might annex the territory, but here too lay political danger. In the existing situation, the annexation of the northwest would probably mean an extension of Protestant Canada West, further overbalancing the French Catholic East. Finally, either of these projects demanded a direct transportation system that would require large public subsidies to build. A number of promoters were already seeking guarantees and concessions from the British and Canadian governments to support their projects.

The system of private railway enterprise seeking public guarantee, subsidy, and support was already well established in Canada. In looking to the northwest for further railway expansion, the promoters were in fact looking for a way to make their unprofitable lines pay. The Canadian Treasury, too, was already deeply involved in these once private ventures. Transportation was one of Canada's main problems, and this problem was about to become linked with the problem of the northwest.

Canadian transportation development had occurred later than in the United States. Disunity, political unrest, and a lack of domestic capital had delayed canal building, and the system of St. Lawrence canals was not completed until 1848. By that time the United States had turned to railroad development, and Canada again found herself behind. Canada's new railroads, like the canals designed to draw the products of Canada West and the American prairies through the St. Lawrence route, were thus faced from the beginning with American competition. Most of Canada's railroads, therefore, were almost at once in financial

[8] Ibid., pp. 359–64.

difficulties, and they dragged the Canadian government in with them.

At the center of Canada's railroad problem was the Grand Trunk Railway. Serious miscalculations of the construction costs put the railway in trouble before it opened, and light and hasty construction resulted in continuing high maintenance costs. Completed in 1860 from Sarnia on the Detroit River through Montreal to Portland, Maine, the Grand Trunk was supposed to tap the bulk staple exports of the American middle west. But these goods could move more cheaply on the St. Lawrence canal system. Between 1855 and 1867, therefore, the Grand Trunk had to receive $26,000,000 of loans—virtually grants—from the Canadian government.[9]

Another project that was to be a center of controversy was the Halifax to Quebec route, or Intercolonial. Disagreement over the route delayed the building of the line for fifteen years. New Brunswick wanted the line to pass through the populated St. John Valley, and therefore close to the Maine border. The British government, looking to strategic factors, wanted the line to follow a longer route along the south shore of the lower St. Lawrence and through northeastern New Brunswick. The Intercolonial proposal was also controversial in Canada. George Brown and the Reformers opposed it as an expensive distraction from the more vital expansion to the northwest and as a needless concession to the Tory financiers of Canada East. Railroads were suspect to the Clear Grits as a source of corruption and patronage in government.[1]

Railroad development in the 1850's had been directed toward shoring up the St. Lawrence commercial system, disrupted by the depression of the late 1840's and the repeal of the imperial tariff preferences. Another aim of Canadian commercial policy in these years was to replace the European market with the new metropolitan centers of the United States. The idea of reciprocal reduction or abolition of duties by Canada and the United States was popular in Canada; the obstacle was American indifference or hostility.

---

9 W. T. Easterbrook and H. G. J. Aitken: *Canadian Economic History* (Toronto, 1956), pp. 307–14.
1 J. M. S. Careless: *Brown of the Globe*. Vol. II, *Statesman of Confederation, 1860–1880* (Toronto, 1963), p. 59.

American acceptance of an agreement was complicated by the growing sectional crisis. The South, a staple-producing region like Canada, was traditionally free trade in sentiment, but Southern senators feared that reciprocity in trade might be a prelude to annexation and the admission of several free states. The governor-general Lord Elgin's job was to convince these senators that reciprocity would prevent annexation by giving Canada enough prosperity to continue her separate existence. In addition, the British gave the Americans something to gain by agreement: they began enforcing the exclusion of New England fishermen from the Maritime inshore fisheries, as provided in the Convention of 1818. The resulting treaty, signed and ratified in 1854, granted American access to these fisheries in return for free trade in national products—grain, flour, fish, meat, livestock, coal, and timber. The duration of the treaty was ten years, to the end of 1864, after which it could be renounced by either party on a year's notice.[2]

How beneficial the treaty was to Canada is difficult to measure. Increasing Canadian prosperity, beginning before 1854, stemmed not only from the treaty but also from general increases in world trade and a continued market for Canadian grain in England. Locally, the railway building and increased trade between the colonies stimulated the economy. But reciprocity received great credit, perhaps more than it deserved. The treaty therefore enjoyed increasing popularity in British North America, but opposition was soon heard in the United States.

American doubts about reciprocity began with the Canadian tariff changes of 1858 and 1859. The slump of 1857 had caused Canadian revenues to drop off just as the government was called upon to back up the shaky finances of the Grand Trunk and other railroads. The tariffs provided moderate increases in manufactured products, particularly iron, machinery, and textiles. The main purpose of the increases was revenue, and protection was incidental. Nevertheless, these tariffs were a first concession to the growing urban manufacturing sector in Ontario. Canada's economy was differentiating, and staple exports were beginning to lose their dominance. These tariffs were also important because they offered A. T. Galt a chance to assert Canada's fiscal

---

[2] Donald C. Masters: *The Reciprocity Treaty of 1854* (Toronto, 1963), Chap. iii, pp. 140–4.

autonomy. Finally, they turned some Americans actively against reciprocity. The tariffs did not break the treaty, but they deprived the United States of one of its expected benefits by blocking the entry of some American manufacturers. Thus the campaign against reciprocity predated the Civil War, which was merely to provide the opponents of the treaty with their opportunity to denounce it.[3]

The Colonial Office should have welcomed Galt's insistence on fiscal autonomy. Galt was helping to define the exact extent of Canada's autonomy, and it needed defining. The parliaments of Canada and the Maritime colonies were responsible for the full range of internal affairs. Additional powers, such as the Post Office and Indian Affairs, had been transferred to colonial legislature in the 1850's. On the other hand, the governors retained a certain amount of independent communication with the Colonial Office. All diplomatic actions, including the Reciprocity Treaty, were handled by the British Foreign Office. During the Civil War, American diplomatic agents were warned that it was improper to approach Canadian officials directly. Any reorganization of British North America, such as that proposed by Galt in 1858, would require imperial sanction. These matters were fairly clear. The ambiguous question, the controversial question, was the division of responsibility for British North American defense.

Since 1851 it had been British policy to reduce her military expenditures in the self-governing colonies, and to call upon the colonies to bear the responsibilities as they enjoyed the privileges of self-government. By 1855 only about three thousand troops remained in all British North America, concentrated at important posts such as Halifax, Kingston, and Montreal. After the Crimean War a few were restored, so that by 1861 there were some four thousand, equally divided between Canada and the Maritimes. These troops were reinforced as soon as the war began.

Canada did not take up her new defense responsibilities until 1855. There seemed little need. The Crimean War finally prodded a reluctant province into action. The Militia Act of 1855 added to the old sedentary militia a new active militia of paid

---

[3] Ibid., pp. 64–8.

volunteers who were to be uniformed and drilled, ready for service in emergency. But many Clear Grits believed, with George Brown, that "the whole thing was unnecessary." In 1858 and 1859 the pay, drill periods, morale, and effectiveness of the volunteers were cut back because of the financial pinch and this attack of the opposition. But the force was retained, and when the Civil War began there were about five thousand partially trained militia in Canada, another five thousand in the Maritimes.[4]

II BRITISH NORTH AMERICA DURING THE CIVIL WAR

The long border, the intimate economic connections, the similar social outlook all seemed to determine that Canada would sympathize with the North in the Civil War. The Northern public expected such support. Abolitionist sentiment had been influential in Canada before the war, George Brown himself being a leader of the movement.[5] There was a large community of free Negroes, many of them escaped slaves. The Canadian public had applauded British resistance to any criminal extradition treaty leading to the return of slaves accused of crimes committed in the act of escaping from slavery.[6]

Anti-Northern sentiment grew rapidly, however, from the early months of the war, for several reasons. The Union standard was raised not to abolish slavery but to save the Union; to some Canadians this made the war a struggle for power rather than justice. Furthermore, the course of the new Republican administration in foreign affairs was not at once clear. Would Secretary of State Seward try to unite the quarreling states by launching a foreign adventure? Lord Lyons, the British ambassador in Washington, feared such a maneuver, and with some justice.

---

[4] C. P. Stacey: *Canada and the British Army, 1846–1871; a Study in the Practice of Responsible Government* (rev. ed.; Toronto, 1963), pp. 89–91, 93–4, 102, 118.

[5] F. Landon: "The American Civil War and Canadian Confederation," Royal Society of Canada, *Transactions*, 3rd Series, Vol. XXI, section 2 (1927), p. 56.

[6] F. Landon: *Western Ontario and the American Frontier* (Toronto, 1941), pp. 204–15; Alexander L. Murray: "The Extradition of Fugitive Slaves from Canada: a Re-evaluation," *Canadian Historical Review*, XLIII (Dec. 1962), 309–10, 314.

Before the outbreak of war, Seward and others were considering using the disputed boundary in the San Juan Islands as a pretext for a British war, so that the United States would be reunited, but nothing came of the idea. British and Canadian officials remained suspicious and uneasy.

On May 13, 1861, the Queen proclaimed British neutrality and recognized Southern belligerency. This wise decision ended any prospect that Britain would seek to intervene in America's troubles. But the decision meant that the North could not even buy arms in British North America. To the press of the North, especially the New York *Herald,* the neutrality proclamation seemed like a stab in the back. From that time on, British Americans ready to oppose the North found ample evidence of Northern enmity in the hysterical attacks of the *Herald.* On the battlefield, the fiasco of the Union Army at Bull Run emboldened this swelling British American feeling to become confident and vocal. As the war progressed, the activities of "crimps" who kidnapped Canadians into the Northern army and the presence of many "skedaddlers," escaping Northern conscription, further soured Canadian opinion, especially in border communities. The tension between England and America, often directly centered on Canada, lasted through the four years of war, reaching its deepest point in 1864.[7]

Canadian hostility to the United States was not, of course, new. Memories of 1812 and the border incidents of 1837 had not died out. And it was natural for the Canadians to assert their identity by emphasizing their differences from the United States. The descendants of upper Canadian and New Brunswick loyalists, in particular, saw their provinces as monarchical, parliamentary, and conservative—in contrast to republican, democratic, and radical America. Thus Canadians, especially Conservatives, mistrusted American policy because in its formation the intolerant zeal of the democracy seemed to have no checks restraining it. Lincoln was assumed to be a demagogue or a tool of demagogues. In the American political system, John A. Macdonald assumed, the rights and property of individuals were not safe, and freedom was sacrificed in the quest for equality.[8]

---

[7] Robin W. Winks: *Canada and the United States; the Civil War Years* (Baltimore, 1960), p. 178, for a discussion of crimps and skedaddlers.

[8] T. W. L. MacDermott: "The Political Ideas of John A. Macdonald," *Canadian Historical Review,* XIV (Sept. 1933), pp. 251–5.

Not all Canadians, of course, agreed with this assessment of the United States. The sharp contrast that Conservatives such as Macdonald saw between monarchical Canada and republican America was that separating a political ideal from a social reality. Admiration for the United States, though not necessarily a desire to imitate her political practices, informed a large segment of liberal Canadian opinion. For example, the Irish-Canadian D'Arcy McGee proclaimed that "all that is most liberal, most intelligent, and most magnanimous in Canada and the Empire are for continental peace, for constitutional arbitration, for universal, if gradual emancipation, for free intercourse, for justice, mercy, civilization, and the North."[9] George Brown, too, with his intimate family and business connections in the United States and his staunch abolitionism, consistently favored the North and deplored loose talk of Anglo-American conflict.[1]

There was some correlation, then, between the Conservative and Liberal positions in Canadian politics and the anti-Northern and anti-Southern attitudes toward the Civil War. This correlation was to be expected. The Macdonald Conservatives claimed to be in the loyalist tradition; the upper Canadian Reformers worked for a Canadian version of democracy that would be partly American, partly English, in inspiration. The former blamed the Civil War on the faults of the federal and republican system, the latter on the evils of slavery. The two groups were to have differing opinions about the value of American precedents in the Canadian nation building that was about to begin.

Canadians of all persuasions soon came to see the war as a turning point in Canadian as well as American affairs. However the war ended, North America would never be the same. If the South became independent there might be a kind of balance in North America, and Canada might hope to avoid domination. The danger, on the other hand, was that the humiliated North might seek to take Canada by way of compensation. Others saw an equal danger from a victorious North, dominant on the continent and eager to seek vengeance against Britain for her alleged wartime hostility.[2] As the war progressed the probability

---

[9] Quoted in Winks: *Canada*, p. 241.
[1] Ibid., p. 68.
[2] For an analysis of these contingencies, see W. L. Morton: "British North America and a Continent in Dissolution, 1861–1871," *History*, XLVII (1962), 139–56.

of invasion or filibustering raids across the border into Canada was increasingly feared. Canadian politicians regarded the first weeks and months following the end of the war as critical. At first they expected a brief civil war followed by an Anglo-American crisis, but the length and bitterness of the war merely confirmed their apprehension. Just at the end of the war Macdonald wrote to Brown, "Either the United States, flushed with success, with their armies full of fight and their fleet in prime condition, will at once put the pistol to England's breast . . . or, we may look for peace for a series of years. Should the first contingency arise, it will be sudden and speedy." The first weeks, the first two years at the most, were thought to be the most dangerous period.[3]

Prophecies of the outcome of the war tended to coincide with the wish of the prophet. The Northern fiasco at Bull Run had emboldened the anti-Northern press in Canada and had convinced many Canadians of ultimate Southern victory. Nor was Northern military success easily to unconvince them. Even with Sherman marching through Georgia, Southern supporters in Canada still doubted that the North would win. George Brown, on the other hand, remained steadily convinced that the North would win victory, even though by a long and bitter struggle.[4] This opinion was the concensus of the generally pro-Northern Reformers.

The division between pro-Southern and pro-Northern groups in British North America reflected existing political divisions and did not create new ones. Whether taken on grounds of philosophical conviction or expediency, a Canadian's views about the war did not commit him to any fundamental Canadian struggle. The great issues of the war were not directly Canadian issues. There was no question of Canadians killing Canadians. Conservatives and Reformers were agreed on the need to avoid an Anglo-American conflict and to defend Canada if one came. They were disagreed only on the likelihood of such a conflict and the measure of preparedness needed. But as the war progressed, several potentially dangerous incidents, any one of

---

[3] Quoted in Donald Creighton: *The Road to Confederation; the Emergence of Canada, 1863–1867* (Toronto, 1964), p. 275.

[4] Winks: *Canada*, pp. 68, 242; Creighton: *Road*, p. 244.

which could have led to conflict on the border, made the danger and the need for full preparedness clear to all. These incidents brought Canadians closer together and deepened the gulf between Canada and the United States.

The restive, uncertain Canadian attitude toward the North suddenly hardened into hostility with the *Trent* affair. On November 8, 1861, an American naval vessel seized two Confederate commissioners who were traveling to England aboard the British mailship *Trent*. The possibility of war between Britain and the United States was suddenly posed, for Britain demanded release of the prisoners, seized in violation of neutral rights. She supported her stand by sending fourteen thousand troops to Canada, many of whom had to cross New Brunswick by sleigh because of the closing of the St. Lawrence. The tension mounted all through December, but the fact was that neither side wanted war. The deftness of British diplomacy and Lincoln's patience in riding out the excitement of the press finally brought a settlement with the release of the commissioners. But the effect in British North America was more enduring. The sudden and intense outburst of patriotism and the more sober realization that defense must be taken in hand were significant results of the *Trent* affair in that they hardened Canadian opinion and established greater support in Canada and Britain for British North American unity.[5]

The years 1862 and 1863 saw a slow relaxation of tension, with no incidents directly threatening to involve Canada in the war. Canada was probing toward a solution of her defense problems; war had nearly broken out and might do so again. From July 1863, with its climactic turning point at Gettysburg and Vicksburg, Canadians began to look to the problems of postwar relations with a re-established Union, dominant in North America. Canadians gave increasing attention during this midwar period to the old question of the British-American west, remote from the war but still influenced by it. On the Pacific, the colonies of Vancouver Island and mainland British Columbia provided stable government, and despite ominous rumors, the war had

---

[5] A detailed and comprehensive account of the incidents involving British North America during the Civil War is furnished by Robin W. Winks's book, cited above. The following account leans heavily on this work. For the *Trent* affair, see Winks: *Canada*, Chap. vi.

little direct impact. The San Juan Islands boundary dispute had to await a general Anglo-American settlement, for Britain did not want to open this potentially dangerous issue during the war. Farther east, in the Red River settlement, there was less certainty. Oriented as it was toward St. Paul, the settlement was strongly pro-Northern, and there seemed a good prospect that the inhabitants would call for annexation to the United States. Britain and Canada seemed indifferent.

By the end of the war, however, the situation had changed. The Civil War had slowed the pace of American trade and settlement in the region. The protracted Sioux uprising of 1862 and 1863 had cut the settlement off from St. Paul, and the withdrawal of American troops from the region late in the war decreased its dependence on the United States.[6] The settlers now looked more to Britain and Canada; British and Canadians responded with a renewed interest in the territory. When the International Financial Society purchased the Hudson's Bay Company in 1863, the problem of providing stable government for the company's territories came perceptibly nearer solution. The Society was controlled by Grand Trunk Railway interests, which were planning to recoup their finances by expansion to the Pacific. The sale of the company was therefore to simplify the problem of transferring the west to Canada and to increase the chances of preserving British sovereignty from sea to sea.[7]

At the end of 1863, the war reached a new and dangerous phase for Canada. The Confederacy, its fortunes shaken and reeling, now hoped to ease the pressure by provoking an incident to bring the United States into conflict with Britain. The method chosen was to violate the neutrality of British North America. The agents of this policy were Jacob Thompson of Mississippi and Clement C. Clay of Alabama, both former senators. Early in 1864 they ran the blockade to Bermuda, proceeded to Canada, and established headquarters in Toronto, where they began a loosely coordinated and inefficient effort to aid the Confederate cause.[8]

---

6 Winks: *Canada*, pp. 174, 176; Alvin C. Gluek: *Minnesota and the Manifest Destiny of the Canadian Northwest* (Toronto, 1965), Chap. vi, esp. pp. 159–62, 172–80.
7 Galbraith: *Imperial Factor*, p. 390.
8 Winks: *Canada*, pp. 272–4.

In December 1863 fourteen Confederates seized a Northern coasting vessel, the *Chesapeake*, and took her to Nova Scotia. Low on fuel and cornered by the U.S.S. *Dacotah*, these buccaneers were unable to carry out their plan of raiding Union shipping, but they were nearly successful in causing an Anglo-American war. Nova Scotian and American authorities came into conflict over two points: the *Dacotah*'s violation of British waters and the question of extradition of the Confederates as pirates. Hard feelings were increased when a pro-Confederate mob freed one of the prisoners, a British subject, as he was coming ashore to be turned over to the local authorities. The job of rounding up the conspirators and prosecuting them was slow, and some of them tried to concoct new plots. The incident was dangerous but did not raise the explosive tempers of the *Trent* crisis, and the passage of time calmed opinion on both sides.[9]

During the summer of 1864, dozens of rumors foretold other attempts to launch a Confederate coup from Canadian soil. Some of the rumors were well founded, but most of the schemes fell through because of increasingly strict Canadian surveillance. In the end, little was accomplished for the Confederacy by these schemes. Indeed, the main result was probably to harm the Confederate reputation in Canada, for although Anglo-American relations were also poisoned by the threat of Confederate border raids launched from Canada, at least the Confederacy failed to gain the support of many Canadians or to goad the United States into a British war.

One scheme was to free the Confederate prisoners on Johnson's Island near Sandusky. It would be necessary, first, to neutralize the armed S.S. *Michigan*. The plan of Confederate agent Jacob Thompson was to organize a boarding party, who could take the ship while a spy distracted the crew with a wine party. On September 18 and 19, 1864, a band of Confederate adventurers steered the small ship *Philo Parsons* toward the *Michigan*. But the plan leaked to federal authorities and the crew of the *Michigan* was alerted rather than distracted. Deprived of the advantage of surprise, the Confederates had no chance of success. They withdrew, hoping to renew their attempt. Canada was quickly to increase her vigilance against breaches of

---

[9] Ibid., Chap. xii.

neutrality, and Confederates henceforth found it impossible to run even small armed vessels on Lake Erie.[1]

Yet in spite of Canadian precautions, just a month later came the Confederate raid on St. Albans, Vermont. On October 19, 1864, twenty-six men robbed the St. Albans bank of $200,000, setting several fires and wounding two men in their flight back into Canada. Canadian authorities arrested thirteen of the raiders. The government determined this time to avoid criticism over the handling of the prisoners. But the disposal presented a dilemma. Were they belligerents whose principal crime was breaking Canada's neutrality laws; or were they criminals to be extradited and tried before an American court? Before these questions could be settled, a Montreal magistrate, C. J. Coursol, released the prisoners on a technicality on December 14. Even the stolen money was refunded to them. This act and not the raid itself was critical in outraging Northern opinion. Although the Canadian government disapproved of Coursol's action, the Americans saw only that once again Canada had failed either to maintain neutrality or to provide just redress by punishing the offenders.[2]

The defense of the provinces had been a prominent question since 1851. The *Trent* affair and the series of border incidents of 1864 were to make it almost dominant. To the question of responsibility for Canadian defense, Canadian statesmen had a ready answer. For internal disorders or small raids the volunteer force would be adequate. The only other likely source of trouble was war between the United States and Britain. "Any such conflict," the governor, Sir Edmund Head, had written in 1857, "would originate in matters not concerning us. Under any circumstances, we should have to bear a heavy loss in destruction of property and trade. Is it unfair that we should expect Great Britain, who conducts negociations committing us, to furnish troops to protect us against foreign aggression?[3] This view remained the starting premise of Canadian thought on defense throughout the war.

The British admitted a moral obligation to defend all areas of her Empire, but a lack of a sense of self-interest made Britain

---

[1] Ibid., pp. 287–94.
[2] Ibid., Chap. xiv.
[3] Quoted in Stacey: *Canada and the British Army,* p. 103.

hold back. Any large commitment had to overcome the criticism of the economy-minded radicals in Parliament. Having reinforced the Canadian garrison after Fort Sumter and during the *Trent* crisis, the British government expected Canada to make a full contribution on its own. The British press and political circles were therefore furious when the Canadian Parliament defeated a militia bill early in 1862. *The Times* believed the only explanation was that "Canada has learnt to trust to others for the performance of services for which weaker and less wealthy populations are wont to rely exclusively on themselves." Members of Parliament called upon Britain to act in her own self-interest just as Canada had done.[4]

It did not matter that the Macdonald-Cartier government had in a sense courted defeat on the bill to escape from its weak position in the nearly deadlocked Canadian house. The bill, with its proposed expenditure of $500,000 in a year, seemed extravagant and far ahead of Canadian public opinion. The misguided Canadian attitude was well summarized by George Brown's *Globe*: "We are not afraid of the Americans provoking a war; we are not afraid of them if they do provoke it."[5] The next three years were to provide a serious education for the Canadian public. The education was started with a scaled-down and more realistic militia bill, which passed in 1863.

This modest effort was dwarfed by the enormous growth of the Northern military machine. Still dissatisfied with the Canadian contribution, British military experts began to doubt whether Canada was fully defensible against such a force. Colonel W. F. D. Jervois of the Royal Engineers had toured British North America and reported that Canada West was indefensible without an unattainable supremacy on Lakes Huron and Erie. He recommended concentrating British forces in Canada East around Montreal and Quebec. This proposal became the War Office policy temporarily, but Canadian objections against leaving the wealthiest and most populous section undefended forced a reconsideration. In 1864, at the time of the St. Albans raid, with British North American statesmen meeting in conference at Quebec, Colonel Jervois issued a second report in which he

---

[4] Quoted in ibid., p. 137.

[5] Quoted in ibid., p. 135; see also James A. Gibson: "The Duke of Newcastle and British North American Affairs, 1859–1864," *Canadian Historical Review*, XLIV (June 1963), 149.

assured the ministers of the Canadian government that Canada was defensible if $1,750,000 were spent on fortifications for Quebec, Montreal, and Kingston.[6]

By 1864 Canadians no longer scorned the Union army as they had after Bull Run. Their respect for American military might was increased by the critical situation on the border and the knowledge that war was possible, some thought even likely. The measure of their respect was the creation of several military colleges and the vote of one million dollars in 1864, double the amount rejected two years earlier. Particularly striking was the change in George Brown's attitude. He still denied being tainted by war fever, but he now saw the Americans as a warlike people. "The carnage of war," said Brown, "has to them been stript of its horrors. . . . Unless we are willing to live at the mercy of our neighbors, we, too, must put our country in a state of efficient preparation . . ."[7]

With Brown's conversion, Canadian politicians were united on the defense question. They agreed that defense was urgent and Canada's responsibility great. They also agreed that Britain should still share the burden.

Mutual suspicion still hurt Anglo-Canadian relations: there were fears, on the one hand, that Britain would desert Canada, and, on the other hand, that imperial troops would be sacrificed because of Canada's lack of preparedness. The British had not forgotten Canada's rejection of the militia bill of 1862, and she was determined more than ever to complete the prewar policy of calling home her garrisons. In spite of Colonel Jervois's recommendations, therefore, Britain voted only fifty thousand pounds for Canadian defense. Now the Canadians were outraged. Macdonald found the appropriation so inadequate that he said a zero may have been omitted by mistake.[8]

In April 1865 a high-level delegation composed of Brown, Macdonald, Galt, and Cartier sailed to England to consider these questions. Their prime purpose was to press for a more generous British contribution to defense. On this question they stood

---

6 Stacey: *Canada and the British Army*, pp. 165–6.
7 Quoted in Martin: *Foundations*, p. 306.
8 *Parliamentary Debates on the Subject of the Confederation of the British North American Provinces* (hereafter *Confederation Debates*) (Quebec, 1865; Ottawa, 1951), p. 703.

against an economy-minded chancellor of the exchecquer, W. E. Gladstone, and behind him an unrepentant Parliament. Although the British cabinet agreed to defend Canada in time of war, they refused to make further contributions immediately, resolving to wait until the confederation of the provinces had been completed.

It was the month of Appomattox. Although the assassination of Lincoln had brought forth a strong current of pro-Northern feeling, Canadians still feared the immediate postwar period, when the great Northern army might turn north. American actions to safeguard the border were variously held to be provocative preparations or merely expedient safeguards against raids from neutral territory. At times they seemed to be efforts to avoid conflict, or at others primitive measures to punish Canada for her neglect or enmity. These American responses to the border troubles of 1864 were the threat to cancel the Rush-Bagot convention of 1817 limiting naval armaments on the lakes; the order requiring passports of persons wishing to enter the United States; the order providing for pursuit of future raiders into Canadian soil; and the mounting attack on the Reciprocity Treaty of 1854.

Secretary of State Seward had first required passports just a few months after the war started. His purpose was to prevent Confederates from leaving Canada via American ports. But the system had proved ineffective. The regulations were partial and inconsistent, and only very slowly could a staff be created to carry them out. At first there was almost no way of acquiring a passport in Canada. On December 17, 1864, just a few days after the release of the St. Albans prisoners, President Lincoln issued a new and more sweeping passport order. It suffered from the same disadvantages as the first. It was no check to hostile incursions. Insofar as it was enforced, it caused hardship on both sides of the border. Its real intent was to bring pressure on the governments of Canada and the Maritimes to strengthen and enforce their neutrality laws. When the American government became satisfied of Canadian actions, the order was withdrawn, although the system was enforced somewhat longer in the Maritime colonies.[9]

More menacing was the Union threat to end the long-stand-

---

[9] Winks: *Canada*, pp. 135–6, 326–31.

ing agreement to limit naval armaments on the lakes to four lightly armed vessels of one hundred tons each. The British and Canadian apprehension was the greater because British access to the lakes depended on the season. Also, because of the long years of relative security, Canadian shore defenses had been abandoned or converted to other uses. The abrogation of the Rush-Bagot convention would therefore underline the defenseless position of Canada West, especially in the Niagara area. With the 685-ton *Michigan* on Lake Erie, the United States was already technically in violation of the agreement, but it remained officially in force. At the time of the attempted raid on Johnson's Island, the government formally suspended the convention and proceeded with work on armed revenue cutters for the lakes. In November 1864, shortly after the St. Albans raid, Secretary of State Seward gave six months' notice for the termination of the agreement, with the proviso that he would judge the need for such drastic action at the end of that period. Although congressional leaders assumed that the step was irretrievable, Seward apparently did not want the Rush-Bagot convention ended. As with the passport order, the American purpose was to push Canada into more effective action. When Canada took effective steps to safeguard the border, the notice to end the Rush-Bagot convention was withdrawn in March 1865.[1]

The most serious threat of American retaliation came as a direct result of the St. Albans raid. As soon as he heard of the raid, General John A. Dix, commander of the military district in the East, ordered that such raiders should be pursued into Canadian territory if necessary. This order stood throughout the autumn of 1864, and when Judge Coursol released the raiders, General Dix confirmed the order, adding that raiders captured in Canada should not be surrendered to Canadian authorities. This pursuit order posed the threat of war more directly than any of the other actions to safeguard the border. The desperate Confederacy was hoping for an Anglo-American war, and American invasion of Canada under the order would be very likely to start one. The order, therefore, made raids perhaps even more likely. Furthermore, although the Canadian public had reacted strongly against the South after the raid, feeling against the Northern order was also strong. Yet it stood for two months,

---

[1] Ibid., pp. 55–6, 303–4, 330.

not because the government wanted to carry it out, but because Seward wanted to press hard for the extradition of the raiders and for a stronger Canadian initiative in patrolling the border. Finally, on December 19, 1864, Lincoln revoked the order, preferring to rely on the more moderate pressure of the passport system.[2]

The stimulus afforded the Canadian economy by the Civil War made the threat to terminate the Reciprocity Treaty all the more serious. After a period of dislocation early in the war, the American demand for horses, grain, other foodstuffs, and timber mounted steadily, continuing to increase even after the end of the war. The volume of this trade had begun to rise before the war and before the treaty but was now accelerated, enabling Canada to diversify its output and move into new activities, not only agricultural but also industrial.[3] The motion that notice be given to terminate the Reciprocity Treaty passed the United States House of Representatives in December 1864 and the Senate in January 1865—that is, immediately after the release of the St. Albans prisoners. Just half a year earlier, a motion to renegotiate the treaty had been more popular than the cancellation motion. By December opinion had changed, and the prominent expression of hostility toward Britain and the British provinces, especially in the House, indicate that the St. Albans raid might have caused the change. It is tempting to assert that the Reciprocity Treaty was a victim of the Civil War.

Such a conclusion would be too simple. As we have seen, by 1860 the treaty was already under attack in the United States. The high-tariff Republicans won the election of that year, and the Morrill tariff of 1860 already indicated the coming change in American trade policy. Justin H. Morrill of Vermont had questioned the treaty as early as 1859, and it was his motion that finally passed in 1864. Before that date the opponents of the treaty had not been able to gather the votes to challenge it.

---

[2] Ibid., pp. 303–4, 319.

[3] Ibid., p. 342; D. G. Creighton: "Economic Nationalism and Confederation," Canadian Historical Association, *Annual Report* (1942), p. 49; D. G. Creighton: *British North America at Confederation; a Study prepared for the Royal Commission on Dominion-Provincial Relations, 1939* (Ottawa, 1963), p. 18; Donald F. Warner: *The Idea of Continental Union; Agitation for the Annexation of Canada to the United States, 1849–1893* (Lexington, 1960), p. 34; Morton: *The Critical Years*, p. 138.

They were strengthened by several factors. Secession had, of course, removed the large bloc of Southern senators who had voted for the original treaty. By 1864 the need for revenue had become urgent and was the leading argument against the treaty. The items included in the agreement, it was argued, were receiving special exemption from taxation, causing a needless sacrifice of revenue. Finally, advocates of revision of the treaty were told that abrogation was the best means of bringing pressure for more favorable terms. By the end of 1864 they too were ready to vote against renewal. Only when these factors are noted can the element of anti-British sentiment be seen in the correct proportion. Economic objections to the treaty were more important. The political argument—hostility to Britain—was important in making congressional action against the treaty prompt and decisive. It was unfortunate for British North America that the depth of anti-British feeling following the St. Albans raid coincided so closely with the end of the original ten years that the treaty was to run.[4]

The Canadian response to American demands for stricter border control was prompt and energetic. Rewards were set for the apprehension of the released St. Albans raiders, and several of them were recaptured. In addition, Macdonald set two thousand volunteer militiamen to guard the border. At the same time he set up a detective force to patrol the border and gather information about planned violations of Canadian neutrality. This force, under the command of Gilbert McMicken, not only controlled Confederate activities but also watched for retaliatory raids from the United States and illegal Northern recruiting activity. As soon as the Canadian Parliament met in January 1865, it considered and quickly passed a new Alien Act. This act provided for the deportation of aliens involved in hostile acts against a friendly foreign state. It also set a three thousand dollar fine against aliens for such activities and provided for the seizure of armaments intended for their use.[5] This act, along with the other safeguards, did a great deal to reassure the American government and calm some of the more excited expressions of public hostility. But for Canada these measures were mere stop-

---

4 Masters: *Reciprocity*, pp. 82–7.

5 Creighton: *Macdonald, the Young Politician*, p. 393; Winks: *Canada*, p. 329.

gaps. The dangers of the Civil War and the threat of a United States transformed by its pressures could be met only by a broad reorganization of British North American affairs, a reorganization that would involve defense, external relations, and the internal political and economic affairs of half a continent. This broader response receives examination in the final section of this chapter.

III BRITISH NORTH AMERICAN RESPONSE TO THE CIVIL WAR

"What is to become of Canada and her sister provinces in the new arrangement of these times?" asked D'Arcy McGee, the eloquent prophet of British North American nationality. Things would not be the same. As McGee summarized it in 1867, the Civil War had taught Canadians "that the days of the colonial comedy of Government were over and gone, and that politics had become stern, and almost tragic for the New World." "Canadian vigilance," he added at another time, "must sleep no more except upon its arms."[6] Adjustment to these new circumstances was the challenge of the immediate postwar years.

The sense of jeopardy expressed by McGee remained alive in Canada for at least six years after the end of the war. After the Treaty of Washington of 1871, American pressure on Canada receded rapidly. But during these years the unpredictable course of American politics, the presence of contentious issues between Britain and the United States, and the possibility of direct American moves to annex British territory in North America were all constant factors in Canadian affairs. These conditions, rising as the aftermath of the Civil War, make these years as critical as the years of the war itself. In this period of postwar readjustment, the most important aspect of British American affairs was the successful drafting and implementing of a plan for confederation of the provinces. In conceiving and dedicating this new nation the lessons British American statesmen discerned in the Civil War were of basic importance.

---

[6] Quoted in Martin: *Foundations*, pp. 308, 326; P. B. Waite: *The Life and Times of Confederation, 1864–1867; Politics, Newspapers, and the Union of British North America* (Toronto, 1962), p. 29.

The end of the Civil War was followed in just over two years by the confederation of all British North America. Contemporaries did not doubt the connection between the two events. Why should British North America unite? D'Arcy McGee again supplied a stirring answer: "Look around you and you will see the reasons. . . . Look around you to the valley of Virginia, look around you to the mountains of Georgia, and you will find reasons as thick as blackberries."[7] But the connection is difficult to define. D. G. Creighton has described the relationship between the Civil War and confederation as important, complex, imprecise, and ambiguous.[8] The confederation idea, as we have seen, had already been raised in 1858. The problems were also more or less clear before the war: the Canadian political deadlock; the lack of an adequate base for expansion into the British American West; the weakness of the economy and lack of sufficient economic strength to build both the Intercolonial and Pacific railways.

The Civil War did not, then, sweep British North America into entirely new channels, but rather provided the opportunity and stimulus for projects already conceived. The Civil War made solution of British North America's problems at once both urgent and feasible. It led British and Canadian leaders to concentrate on confederation as the solution to these problems. National feeling increased in Canada, and the British became determined to withdraw militarily from North America, transferring its responsibility to a newly united British North America. A strong drive toward union in Canada was now matched by an initiative just as strong from Britain: for this fact the military threat caused by the war and its aftermath was overwhelmingly responsible. Confederation itself was not the simple result of the Civil War. The impact was more ambiguous and imprecise than this. It can be traced in the nature of the union, in the status of the union, in the allegiance that the new confederation would receive from its citizens, and in the orientation of its economy.

It would be out of place here to trace the dismal and petty narrative of Canadian party politics in great detail. Sandfield

---

[7] Edward Whelan: *The Union of the British Provinces* (Charlottetown, 1865), p. 123.
[8] D. G. Creighton: "The United States and Canadian Confederation," *Canadian Historical Review*, XXXIX (Sept. 1958), 209.

Macdonald's government of moderates hung on for nearly two years after the fall of John A. Macdonald in 1862. With Sandfield's fall and the failure of the old Macdonald-Cartier regime to re-establish itself, Canada's sectional deadlock became intolerable. All the obvious political combinations had been exhausted. Canada West would no longer accept the existing system of representation; Canada East would accept no change. To federate these sections within a broader British North American union now seemed the only solution.

The key figure in Canada's new drive for union was George Brown. Brown had matured during the war years and overcome some of his sectional narrowness. He had reaffirmed his faith in British parliamentary democracy since the bitter personal defeat of 1858. He could now see that the various problems of British America might be brought together, especially in view of American hostility. He therefore muffled his opposition to the intercolonial project, while insisting that it be combined with northwest expansion; he saw that the existing union need not be dissolved but could be broadened. In moving for a committee to investigate Canada's constitutional problems, Brown based his motion on the Galt dispatch of 1858. When John A. Macdonald's short-lived ministry fell in 1864, Brown went further. Swallowing his personal hatred for Macdonald, he offered to join a coalition government for the purpose of establishing a general federation of British North America. The coalition cabinet had been agreed upon by June 22, 1864. It included Macdonald and Cartier, A. T. Galt and D'Arcy McGee (former Rouges), Brown and William McDougall, one of the original Clear Grit group. To Brown, the aim of redressing Canada's sectional grievances was still perhaps uppermost. There was a deadline on Brown's cooperation; federation must be achieved quickly, for it would be difficult in the passing months to stifle party differences within the coalition. If a formula could not be found to embrace all the provinces, Brown insisted, then let the existing Canadian union be broken into a federation by itself. Brown's commitment was limited; but the danger of political paralysis amid the turmoil and danger of the Civil War had brought him a great distance.[9]

---

[9] On the formation of the coalition government, it is revealing to place side by side the accounts of Careless: *Brown*, II, 120–46, and Creighton: *Macdonald, the Young Politician*, pp. 354–8.

The new coalition did move quickly. Taking office only in June, they were presenting their proposals to delegates of the Maritime colonies in Charlottetown by September, and had convened a general conference at Quebec by October 10 to draft a constitution. In the method of drafting and ratifying this constitution, and in the content of the constitution, the Canadian and Maritime politicians and statesmen were conscious of their differences from the American precedent—the more conscious of this because of the breakdown of the Republic in the Civil War.

The Quebec conference laid the foundation for a new nation, but a nation unlike the United States. The very principle of authority, the theory of sovereignty, would be different. As the Quebec delegates saw it, the Philadelphia convention had been a meeting of the representatives of the people from a number of independent states, each of which gave over some of its sovereignty to the general government by a contract subject to popular ratification. The Quebec conference was not a constitutional convention in this sense. The governments represented did not possess sovereignty, their powers being derived from the imperial authority. The representatives of the various colonial parliaments drafted the seventy-two Quebec Resolutions, but they did not seek popular ratification. The Queen, not the people, was sovereign. Therefore, the constitution would go into effect only when it was passed as an act by the imperial Parliament in Westminster.[1] The British government was interested, for practical rather than constitutional reasons, that no colonial government should be forced into the new constitution. Each colonial parliament had to pass on the Quebec Resolutions. In the province of Canada, they were debated and passed in 1865, all moves for popular ratification being defeated. In Nova Scotia, this was impossible; a mere resolution in favor of union but not of the Quebec Resolutions was finally passed, and this proved sufficient to bind the province. The delay of two years in carrying confederation was caused by New Brunswick, the one essential province, lying between Nova Scotia and Canada East. There, the fall of S. L.

---

[1] W. L. Morton: "The Conservative Principle in Confederation, "*Queen's Quarterly*, LXXI (Winter 1965), 535–6; Creighton: *Road*, 137–38, 141–3; F. R. Scott: "Political Nationalism and Confederation," *Canadian Journal of Economics and Political Science*, VIII (Aug. 1942), 406–7.

Tilley's proconfederation government forced elections in 1865, which took on some of the character of a plebiscite. The confederation cause was at first defeated. Within a year, however, the Fenian scare, the lack of capital for independent railway development, and the abrogation of reciprocity brought about the break-up of the anticonfederation government.

Steady pressure from the British government also helped revive confederation. Desiring to be quit of the anxiety and expense of North American defense, the British hoped that confederation would enable Canada to defend herself. The Colonial Office ordered Governor Gordon of New Brunswick to use his full influence for confederation. Britain then underlined her concern by guaranteeing the loan interest for the Intercolonial Railway, considered vital as a strategic line to link Canada with an ice-free British port. These circumstances, and a generous disposal of election funds, were effective. Tilley was successful in the elections of 1866, and the movement toward confederation could proceed.[2] The British North America Act, closely based on the Quebec Resolutions, finally came into force on July 1, 1867. The new structure proved strong enough, within four years, to expand by incorporating the western provinces of Manitoba and British Columbia, thereby forestalling the seemingly inevitable expansion of the United States. With the building of the Pacific and Intercolonial railways, both original commitments of the confederation, the gristle of the union, in Macdonald's words, would harden into bone.

British North America would differ from the United States not only in its source and derivation, but also in its constitutional structure. John A. Macdonald, whose copy of the federal convention debates was annotated to show passages favoring a strong central authority, wanted a unitary state with no federal features. However great the American experiment had been, it had failed because of the great weakness of states' rights. A large body of opinion agreed with Macdonald. One paper predicted that a war of succession "must flow from copying the errors in statesmanship of our republican neighbours." Another paper asked, "Must we steer our bark on that rock on which the neighbouring magnif-

---

[2] Creighton: *Road*, pp. 374–5; for attempts to refer the Quebec Resolutions to the people, see *Confederation Debates*, pp. 269, 316, 327, 333.

icent union has split?" Building their nation just at the time of crisis in the United States, the Canadians reacted strongly against federalism.[3]

Yet it was confederation and not union that the Quebec Resolutions proposed. A unitary state could not be realized; the Canadians, too, were organizing a semicontinental region, with strong geographic, ethnic, and historic contrasts. It was the sectional division of central Canada that had given the impulse to constitutional experiment. George Brown and the *Globe* argued that federalism did not cause sectional conflict but, instead, might alleviate it. The sources of conflict in the United States had simply been too overwhelming for the constitutional system; no such irrepressible seeds of conflict existed in Canada. What Brown wanted was a strong central Parliament, elected on the basis of representation by population, with provinces holding just those powers that would safeguard vital sectional interests. If such a settlement could be achieved, French and English would be reconciled.[4]

The French inclination was to hold to the existing situation. It was the job of Cartier and other French supporters of the Quebec Resolutions to convince their compatriots that adequate federal powers were incorporated to satisfy the special interests of Quebec.[5] Maritime particularism also contributed to the cause of federalism, but opponents of the Quebec Resolutions in the Maritimes were divided among proponents of a unitary state, of regional union, and those of the status quo. The leading opponent of confederation in the Maritimes was Joseph Howe, who dubbed it the "Botheration" scheme. He was not reassured by the federal aspects of the scheme and feared that the general government, dominated by the French, would lord over the provinces. He too cited the American precedent but with a new slant. American federalism with its doctrine of states' rights had worked well, he argued. On the other hand, "all the misery, bloodshed and finan-

---

[3] Waite: *Life and Times*, pp. 33–4, 113; R. G. Trotter: "Some American Influences upon the Canadian Federation Movement," *Canadian Historical Review*, V (Sept. 1924), 215.

[4] Waite: *Life and Times*, pp. 127–8; Careless: *Brown*, II, 109–11, 167–9; *Confederation Debates*, p. 88; Scott: "Political Nationalism," *Canadian Journal of Economics and Political Science*, VIII, 401–3.

[5] Martin: *Foundations*, p. 325; W. M. Whitelaw: *The Maritimes and Canada before Confederation* (Toronto, 1934), pp. 124–7.

cial ruin have resulted from the attempt to over-ride the State rights, and to give to the General Government powers analogous to those which are claimed for the Government at Ottawa."[6]

Although federalism thus proved unavoidable, the framers of confederation tried to avoid just those flaws that they believed had led to the breakdown of the American Republic. The formula for dividing powers between the center and the provinces, for example, was just the opposite of the American: the central government was granted power to legislate on all matters of a general character; a list of specific federal powers was by example only and not exclusive. The provinces, on the other hand, were limited to a specified list of powers, with some powers shared between central and provincial governments. The Canadian Senate, too, was to differ from the American. To the Quebec conference, this difference was a key to the situation. The delegates denied the premise of the large state–small state compromise of Philadelphia. The Canadian Senate was to provide regional equality for Ontario, Quebec, and the Maritime provinces taken together. Having no sovereign status, the small colonies had no principle on which to base their claim for more representation in the Senate. And even then the senators were to be appointed by the central government. The powers of the provinces were derivative in other ways. The lieutenant governor was to be appointed by the central government, and provincial laws were subject to disallowance. The Quebec conference did not decide on detailed constitutions for the provinces, but many assumed that they would be glorified municipalities that would soon wither away.[7]

But there was just a note of ambiguity in the Quebec Resolutions, concerning both what had been done and how the system would work in practice. The strongest centralists and the most insistent French federalists had come to agreement because they saw different meanings in their agreement. Macdonald and others believed they had created a supreme Parliament for a fully self-governing kingdom or dominion. They hoped or assumed that the provinces would simply wither away from having nothing to do. In his first dispatch conveying the Quebec Resolutions to the

---

[6] J. Murray Beck, ed.: *Joseph Howe: Voice of Nova Scotia* (Toronto, 1964), p. 174; Morton: *The Critical Years*, p. 175.
[7] Creighton: *Road*, Chaps. v. and vi, especially pp. 144–5.

Colonial Office, the governor, Lord Monck, explained that the term confederation really did not mean anything. Within its very broad jurisdiction, the central Parliament would be supreme, and therefore, Lord Monck explained, "to the extent of that authority, the Union is not Federal, it is Legislative—Whatever the Union may be called the central government under such a system possesses to the extent of the powers given to it, and for the purposes of the execution of those powers, all the characteristics of a government representing a Legislative consolidation."[8]

These beliefs were hard to reconcile with the French view that the provincial powers would be adequate to preserve the French language, laws, and institutions. Nor were the French to be the only supporters of provincial powers. Political rivals of the central government found refuge in most provincial governments and therefore espoused provincial rights. In this sense the critics who had pointed to the divisive character of federalism were proved correct. From the 1880's on, the dissident provinces were to raise the "compact theory of confederation," the view, historically untenable but potent, that confederation had been a treaty between contracting parties, that, therefore, it could be altered by the provinces without reference to the central government. They pitted the provincial property and civil rights power against the central peace, order, and good government clause, taking a long series of cases to the judicial committee of the Privy Council.

In some of the early cases, the provincial argument was presented by Judah Benjamin, former Confederate statesman, who was still advocating states' rights. From 1883, the trend of the cases went against the central government. In *Hodge* vs. *the Queen* of that year, the judicial committee ruled that provincial powers were not delegated but were plenary and ample within the limits of their powers—a ruling reflecting the realities of politics of the 1880's more than the intentions of the founders in the 1860's.[9] The confederation of Canada was a tenuous achievement that had been possible only in the strained circum-

---

[8] Martin: *Foundations*, p. 340.

[9] Peter H. Russell, ed.: *Leading Constitutional Decisions; Cases on the British North American Act* (Toronto, 1965), pp. 2–10; A. R. M. Lower et al.: *Evolving Canadian Federalism* (Durham, N.C., 1958), p. 29; N. McL. Rogers, "The Compact Theory of Confederation," Canadian Political Science Association, *Annual Report* (1931), pp. 210–11.

stances of the Civil War and its aftermath. With the pressures of the critical 1860's removed, internal conflict began to take precedence over external challenge. It remains in the last portion of this chapter to examine the extent and nature of the external threat of the later 1860's and to demonstrate its impact on Canadian national politics.

The Canadian determination to build a strong state, sharply differentiated in its founding principles from the United States, was spurred by the specter of American annexationism. Throughout the war, newspapers such as the New York *Herald* had called for the annexation of the British North American provinces, and despite improved Anglo-American relations at the end of the war, they continued to do so. Between 1865 and 1871, in fact, speculation about the annexation of some or all of British North America to the United States was increased. The ending of the Reciprocity Treaty stirred annexation talk, for the question of economic relations was inevitably linked to the question of political relations. The attempts of the Irish-American Fenian movement to annex Canada by force stirred up the question at the same time. Finally, the American claim from Britain for damages done by the *Alabama* and other Confederate corsairs raised the hope among some senators that the compensation might be in the form of British territory in North America.

Reciprocity, Canadians believed, had brought the greatest period of prosperity the provinces had known. A few Canadians assumed, in fact, that Canada could not survive without it, and this belief was more widespread in the United States. In 1865, John Potter, the American consul general in Montreal, asserted publicly that abrogation was a useful way to force Canada to join the United States.[1] Americans interested in annexation, assuming that Canada had received all the benefits of the treaty, would thus oppose any renewal or renegotiation. The protectionist interest, victorious in the reunited Republic, would allow no backsliding without solid political or territorial gains.

There were, of course, American supporters of reciprocal free trade, and the provinces sought their help. Joseph Howe, the veteran Nova Scotian politician who was a fisheries commissioner under the treaty, went to Detroit in June 1865 to speak on the question of a new treaty. There, before 450 delegates of boards

---

[1] Warner: *Continental Union*, pp. 47–8.

of trade from American border cities, he received a good reception, and the convention adopted a resolution calling for renegotiation. But this resolution had no impact on a protectionist Congress.

That same summer, during the last year of the treaty, A. T. Galt and W. P. Howland, both members of the Canadian coalition cabinet, went to Washington to study the prospects for renewal. They were not hopeful. Early in 1866 the two men returned to Washington, accompanied by two Maritime delegates, to testify before the House Ways and Means Committee. This time the Americans were not entirely negative. They offered free trade in millstones, firewood, gypsum, and rags. Such concessions were not worth having; the Reciprocity Treaty continued for another month and finally lapsed. British North America continued to hope for the recovery of the treaty. But the triumph of protectionism in the United States made the prospect so bleak that Macdonald decided to shelve the question so as not to seem dependent on the United States. The anticipated economic collapse did not come about, and Canada found time to search for other outlets for the products of her economy.[2]

At the same time, British North America was facing a more violent and immediate threat to her existence. Canadians had long feared a collision with the United States at the end of the war. Disbanded troops might turn to filibustering raids. The Americans might try to avenge the hostility of the provinces toward the Union cause. The expansive energies of the reunited Republic might sweep over the unoccupied northwest. The Canadian government, as has been noted, believed that the first months following the war were the most critical. Members of the Canadian cabinet were on their way to London to discuss defense policy when Lee surrendered at Appomattox.

The fears of the Canadians were justified. The entire Republic did not turn on Canada, but the activities of the Fenian Brotherhood, minor as they seemed in retrospect, could have had serious repercussions in Anglo-American relations. The Fenian movement, with its blustering, inept, and faction-ridden leadership, was made dangerous by the adherence of thousands of battle-hardened veterans of the Union army. American officials, sensitive to the power of Irish voters and sympathetic with anti-

---

[2] Masters: *Reciprocity*, pp. 87, 95–7.

British causes, might have been lax in enforcing American neutrality. Then, an initial success, a Fenian foothold on Canadian soil, might have led the United States to give full support and recognition to their efforts. Had not Britain reorganized the Confederacy as a belligerent power in 1861? The Fenian cause depended on calculations such as these and on the cooperation of the large Irish element in Canada and New Brunswick.

In the event, Canadian preparedness, American propriety, and Irish loyalty in Canada combined with Fenian incompetence, and the movement was limited to a few sporadic raids. The Canadian militia was called up in November 1865 and again in March 1866, but the Fenians did not attack. The patriotic excitement began to die down, and the militia began to disperse. In early April, however, small groups of Fenians began to move into the coastal towns of eastern Maine, apparently grouping for a raid on New Brunswick. They succeeded only in stealing the flag from a customs house before they were overwhelmed by the New Brunswick militia, British regulars, and a ship from the naval squadron at Halifax.

Attention then abruptly shifted back to Canada. On the last day of May 1866 fifteen hundred Fenians crossed the Niagara River into Canada West. The province equaled and surpassed the patriotic excitement of March as militia units rushed to defend the border. At Limestone Ridge on June 1, the Fenians repulsed a small detachment of militia in a sharp engagement. With odds mounting against them, the Fenians withdrew across the border on June 3. In a poorly coordinated second attack, another large Fenian force entered Canada near Lake Champlain on June 7 but withdrew without a decisive clash. By this time Canada was thoroughly prepared, and it was becoming evident that the Irish of Canada would not rebel in support of the invasions. Furthermore, President Johnson proclaimed the neutrality of the border on June 6, too slowly to satisfy Canadian opinion but effective in destroying Fenian hopes of official support. Even with this reassurance, rumors of Fenian activities would still create enormous excitement in August 1866, when the British government sent out three regular regiments with supporting artillery.

For the next two or three years, factionalism and weakness prevented the Fenians from attempting further coups. But they maintained their goal of invading Canada. In May 1870, however, an attempt to strike into Quebec failed. The alert intelligence system, the efficiently trained militia, and the prompt reaction of the United States in cutting off supplies and reinforcements made it plain that the Fenians could not succeed. An attempt to raid Manitoba the next year was the last major Fenian threat.[3]

The blustering incompetence of the Fenians and the wide discrepancy between intention and accomplishment have made the whole episode seem a comedy, a farce but for the men killed and property destroyed. It is tempting to conclude from its failure that the movement was never really dangerous, and that its importance was minor. But if these activists had gained the slightest success, or if they had gained any open support from the Canadian Irish, then those politicians seeking Irish votes, those who passively supported annexation might have come to their support. The Fenians failed utterly, but not perhaps inevitably. The sense of jeopardy was real to contemporary Canadians, and in this fact lies the significance of the Fenian raids. The patriotic fervor aroused in Canada reinforced the confederation movement, and the common danger drew the provinces closer together. In the New Brunswick election of 1866, the Fenian issue was used effectively in turning the anticonfederates out of office. Some of the opponents of confederation said that Fenians might almost have been a confederationist plot. British North American nationalism received a great stimulus. As the *Globe* commented in 1870, "Canadians have gained more in national character during the last six years than in any previous twenty." The "outrageous proceedings of the Fenians" had produced this result.[4]

Canadian nationalism also was stimulated by agitation in the United States to annex the provinces by peaceful and legal means. The strongest and most purposeful annexation sentiment was directed against the British American west, from Red River to Vancouver Island. The commercial communities of St. Paul and San Francisco were already drawing the British territory into their economic orbits. To many of the people in the British

---

[3] C. P. Stacey: "The Fenian Troubles and Canadian Military Development, 1865–1871," Canadian Historical Association, *Annual Report* (1935), pp. 26–35; C. P. Stacey: "Fenianism and the Rise of National Feeling in Canada at the Time of Confederation," *Canadian Historical Review*, XII (Sept. 1931), 238–61.

[4] Quoted in Stacey: "Fenianism and National Feeling," *Canadian Historical Review*, XII, 252.

American west, furthermore, Canada seemed nearly as alien and quite as grasping as the United States. Annexationists hoped to gain support from the population of the territories and also to obtain the official backing of the United States government. The leaders in Congress were Senators Alexander Ramsey of Minnesota and Zachariah Chandler of Michigan. Ramsey proposed in 1867 that the United States grant reciprocity to Canada, annex the British American west, and consider all outstanding issues between Britain and the United States closed—presumably including the *Alabama* claims. Chandler, who proclaimed that "this continent is ours," proposed in 1869 that the United States negotiate with Britain for the annexation of all British North America, and called in 1870 for the appointment of representatives to approach the people of Red River. From St. Paul, in the meantime, James Wickes Taylor, an ardent annexationist, sent constant reports to the government assessing the strength of American influence in the Red River settlement and urging federal action.[5]

Some proponents of annexation aimed not only at the West but at the Maritime provinces and Canada itself. The confederation movement itself stimulated some proposals, for it aimed to establish a monarchy, incompatible with North American freedom. In response to this threat, Congressman Nathaniel Banks of Massachusetts introduced a bill in 1866 to annex the provinces. This move got nowhere, but in the next year his motion protesting the creation of a monarchy in North America passed the House, dying in the Senate.[6] The annexation movement gathered steam a couple of years later when Senator Charles Sumner proposed annexation as a means of settling the *Alabama* claims. To the claim to be compensated for the actual damage done by the *Alabama*, Sumner, with Chandler's support, added indirect claims. He asserted that the raids had checked the natural growth of American commerce, and that British support had prolonged the war by as much as two years. Sumner calculated the amount of these direct and indirect claims at over two billion dollars. Annexation hopes reached their height when Hamilton Fish, secretary of state of President Grant's new administration, took up Sumner's idea. Fish, however, soon dropped the scheme when

---

[5] Warner: *Continental Union,* pp. 105, 109–11, 121–2.
[6] Ibid., pp. 66–7.

he became convinced that the loyalty of the provinces made it unrealistic.[7]

Proposals for annexation could be taken seriously in the years just after the war for several reasons. First, the expansionist energies of the North were now released from the necessity of compromising with the slave states in Congress. To punish Britain for her attitude during the war was popular, and in the elections of 1864 and 1866 Republican candidates used Anglophobia to win Irish votes. The West was sparsely populated and possessed the flimsiest of governments. The provinces, deprived of reciprocity, apparently lacked the economic strength to survive outside the Republic. This view was held even by some people in the provinces. The backers of confederation claimed it was supposed to solve the problem of prosperity, but some Maritimers were so hostile to the scheme that they preferred annexation. Finally, the British government itself seemed to be indifferent to the future of the provinces. It was small wonder, then, that some Americans believed that only a small push would bring half a continent into the American Republic. This was a miscalculation, however, for none of these factors of weakness was as significant as the annexationists believed. The British American public was more loyal, the politicians more determined and resourceful, than American politicians believed. Furthermore, the annexation cause was actually weak in the United States. It possessed neither enough general public support nor enough congressional votes to command consistent support from the administration. The result of annexationist activity was just the opposite of the intention. It was possible for Canadian politicians to document amply their charge that the United States threatened the existence of British North America. They could stir support for confederation and build up national feeling. Five years after the Civil War British North America was stronger not only because of her new institutions but also because of this developing feeling of national identity.

Although Canada was thus greatly strengthened, any one of the several issues in dispute between the United States and Britain could still threaten the security of the dominion. Only if these issues were substantially settled could Canada rest secure.

---

[7] Ibid., pp. 94, 97–8; Maureen M. Robson: "The *Alabama* Claims and the Anglo-American Reconciliation, 1865–1871," *Canadian Historical Review*, XLII (Mar. 1961), 2–5.

Only if they were settled could fears of annexation be safely forgotten, for annexation sentiment fed on Anglo-American conflict. At issue were not only the *Alabama* claims but also the disputed boundary in the San Juan Islands. In addition, the United States wanted to secure access to the St. Lawrence waterway, which had been included in the Treaty of 1854, although the Americans did not want to concede reciprocity in return. The Canadians, for their part, wanted not only to negotiate a new reciprocity agreement but also to gain compensation for the damage done by the Fenians. They were unwilling to concede the American desires without gaining some of their claims in return. In 1870 they began to enforce the old convention of 1818 by excluding American fishermen from the inshore Maritime fisheries, their aim being, as in 1854, to wring some concession from the United States.[8]

Unfortunately for the Canadians, the British government still handled Canadian diplomatic affairs, and British priorities were quite different. The British wanted simply to eliminate the causes of Anglo-American conflict, and they were willing to compromise on many points. They were unwilling to give Canada the naval or diplomatic support needed to use the fisheries as a strong bargaining counter. When British and American plenipotentiaries met at Washington in 1871, therefore, the position of John A. Macdonald, the Canadian delegate, was particularly embarrassing. As a member of the British delegation he was bound by the agreement made at the conference; yet, as prime minister of Canada, he was politically bound to bring home a satisfactory settlement. In specific detail Macdonald was unable to gain a satisfactory settlement, but the over-all import of the Treaty of Washington of 1871 was to end the years of tension and ensure the survival of Canada. The *Alabama* claims and the San Juan Islands boundary dispute were to be placed in arbitration. Canada was forced to concede the American right to the fisheries and access to the St. Lawrence waterways without gaining for herself the coveted reciprocity, except for the single item of fish. Canada was granted free navigation on Lake Michigan and the rivers of Alaska. Having sacrificed specifically Canadian interest for imperial interest, the British undertook to pay Canada the Fenian

---

[8] Donald Creighton: *John A. Macdonald, the Old Chieftain* (Toronto, 1955), pp. 75–6, 96.

damages and to underwrite the proposed Canadian Pacific Railway. These agreements formed no part of the treaty itself but were a significant part of the settlement.[9]

The Treaty of Washington ended the period of Anglo-American tension of the war and postwar years. By conceding most of the American demands, the British seemed to be selling out Canadian interests. The British had no choice, however, but to recognize the continental dominance of the United States. The last of the British troops were leaving North America. Britain lacked the power or the will to challenge American supremacy. But by supporting the unification of Canada, Britain prevented a piecemeal disintegration and annexation of the British provinces. By conceding gracefully Britain had removed the sense of grievance that had given impetus to American hostility. By overriding Canadian desires, finally, Britain had increased the Canadian determination to remain independent. In the years to come, Canadian nationalism could be asserted not only against the United States, but also, to a lesser degree, against Britain herself. Although Canada still hoped to miraculously regain reciprocity, she turned gradually to economic nationalism in imitation of and response to American policy. In 1872 Macdonald made the "national policy" a slogan, and after 1878 he made it a policy. The national policy was partly an attempt to knit the nation together by east-west transportation development, minimizing dependence on the American railway system; it was also a policy of high tariffs for the industrial sector of Ontario. In its increasingly differentiated economy, Canada was developing metropolitan centers of its own and interests that demanded protection from American competition and that would be hostile to any renewal of reciprocal free trade.

The strongly centralized dominion was made possible by the tensions arising out of the Civil War. Internal weaknesses started to show only when the tensions were removed. But for the time being Canadian independence was secure. Canada was too weak to withstand a determined assault by the United States, but the reasons for such an assault had been removed. Whether Canada could withstand the slow pressure of American continental economic growth for the coming century remained to be seen.

---

9 Morton: *The Critical Years*, p. 256.

The Civil War
and Latin America

Harry Bernstein

---

*P*rofessor *Bernstein's earlier inquiries into Latin American history and the influence of events in the United States upon it have earned for him a wide scholarly audience.[1] In the essay that follows, the Civil War and Reconstruction are examined from this angle. So seen, familiar individuals and institutions— Lincoln, Grant, slavery, the Freedmen's Bureau, and private, Negro-centered philanthropy—take on unsuspected shadings. The summation of what a Matías Romero, a Tavares Bastos, a José Carlos Rodrígues reported on developments in the United States during the Civil War era and their analyses of related trends in their own nations in Latin America offer insights that speak to their past and to our present.*

---

[1] See also Bernstein: "South America Looks at North American Reconstruction," pp. 87–104 in *New Frontiers of the American Reconstruction,* ed. by Harold Hyman (Urbana, Ill., 1966).

The Civil War and the militant issues of that period were not the only forces radiating from North American life: there were also intellectual, scientific-scholarly, and creative contributions. The United States was already familiar with, and now became more interested in, Latin America. The Civil War did not stop or interrupt the main lines of this inter-American communication, although some of the activity was reduced. Fully civilian and scientific-scholarly, the inter-American exchange thrived during the period of the Civil War and Reconstruction.

Emancipation, of course, was more spectacular an achievement than the dawning sense of a hemisphere republic of letters. Freedom for the slaves and the bitter battles of the war were far more vital concerns. Nevertheless, the intellectual life of the hemisphere kept going. Since 1700 the notion of an all-American culture had developed and spread from one America to the other. The Civil War did not kill this idea, even while the issue of emancipation overshadowed it.

The liberation movement, political liberalism, and the rediscovery of the Americas all went separate ways. Each had its own following, and its own relative importance. Yet occasionally their lines would meet. Antislavery action and science brought many minds together. Science and political liberalism often appeared in the same person. When the Harvard geologist Louis Agassiz, the future philosopher William James, and the Cornell geologist Charles Hartt went to Brazil, the social conditions they found there, especially slavery, did not leave them unaffected.

Agassiz's enthusiasm for the emancipation of the economic opportunities in the Amazon River valley was as keen as his enthusiasm for the emancipation of both the Brazilian and North American Negro slaves. He also brought Brazilian scientists and engineers into contact with North American ideas and scientific societies.[1] The relationship to the political liberalism of that day came to the fore in the discussions between Agassiz and the noted Brazilian reformer and liberal A. C. Tavares Bastos. The North Americans, like the Navy scientists of the previous decade, were

---

[1] Harry Bernstein: *Making an Inter-American Mind* (Gainesville: Univ. of Florida Press; 1961); Carleton S. Smith: "William James in Brazil," in *Four Papers presented in the Institute for Brazilian Studies, Vanderbilt University* (Nashville: Vanderbilt Univ. Press; 1951), pp. 95–138.

very interested in the Amazon. The geologists were concerned with natural and geologic history. Tavares Bastos impressed them with his liberal and progressive plans for modernizing the Amazon region.

In the century before the Civil War, and in the century since, a Pan-American as well as an inter-American outlook became firm pillars of the North American academic and intellectual tradition. It is no surprise, therefore, that the few years of the Civil War, even if violent, should fit into this historic process. The civilian basis of the inter-American work of the decade had been laid long before. The cultural side of the United States facing Latin America was already immersed in history.

This inter-American impact went on, as it had always done, in the Latin American book trade, the work of scientists, the learned societies, and the rise of a common historiography of the Americas. This last idea, that the historians of the United States ought to know more about the Spanish period of New World history, itself had an old history. Many important North Americans had already answered by their works the question "Do the Americas have a Common History?" Authors of books and collections of documents took it for granted that there was much in common.[2]

At the opening of the 1860's, Ephraim Squier made a proposal for a *Documentary History of the Americas*, which followed the great, pioneer idea of Buckingham Smith put forth in the 1850's. Both these projects antedate the more famous effort of Hubert Howe Bancroft to write a history of those areas of the United States that were once Spanish. Both Smith the historian and Squier the ethnologist confidently believed in the mutual history of the Americas, if not the common history of the continent.

---

[2] The Civil War may have separated North from South in the United States, but it spurred the historic tie between North and South America. Lewis Hanke, ed.: *Do the Americas have a Common History? A Critique of the Bolton Theory* (New York: Alfred A. Knopf; 1964). Bolton himself, whose concept of a greater America is under continuous barrage in this book of essays, never realized how far back the inter-American interest of history went. That was because he looked to the Southwest for the Spanish substance. But the Yankee and New Yorker were Hispanists from 'way back.

The Civil War and Latin America

Neither the earlier war with Mexico nor the Civil War ended the peaceful contact between Hispanic and North American culture. Even before the war-torn decade, Buckingham Smith had predecessors, one of whom was Edward Everett, during the era of the Monroe Doctrine. After Civil War years, Squier's proposals began to bear fruit—from the time of Hubert Bancroft to Herbert E. Bolton, in the 1920's. In this period were initiated the first college courses on Latin America, with Daniel de Leon teaching at Columbia University in 1885, and Bernard Moses at the University of California in 1895.

Just as the Civil War expanded North American technology, business, and finance, so the hemisphere's cultural and educational forces got a new impulse. Buckingham Smith rallied behind his idea the greatest and most influential historians of his generation. Squier turned for support to Lewis Morgan of Rochester, New York, the most influential ethnologist of his day. Squier lacked the connections of Smith, who enlisted Francis Parkman, George Bancroft, Dr. Francis Hawks, George Folsom, Jared Sparks, and even William H. Prescott.

During this single generation from 1850 to 1870, encompassing the Civil War period, Americans moved beyond national boundaries into the hemisphere to discover and incorporate into American history the traces of Spain and Portugal. This mid-century generation was remarkable for its expansion of intellectual horizons beyond the shorelines of the Gulf of Mexico and the Caribbean. These men touched the *tierra firme,* or continent of South America; they saw both the common inter-American interest and the common inter-American historical framework, without rejecting Europe or European influences. In fact, they brought in more of Europe through Spain and Portugal. They enlarged the idea of Spain in America, as Parkman had done with France in America. The next hundred years down to the "New Frontier" of the 1960's were noteworthy for the rediscovery, even the cultural *conquista,* of Latin America.

At the opening of the Civil War period, August 1860, Ephraim Squier wrote to Lewis Morgan:

> I take the liberty of sending you herewith a Plan and Prospectus of a "Collection of Rare and Original Documents and Relations concerning the Discovery and Conquest of

America, chiefly from the Spanish Archives." Number One of this Collection is now ready for delivery in accordance with the terms of the Prospectus.

The task of getting together the Documents for this Collection and of preparing them for the Press, I need not say, has been essentially a "labor of love," and of individual gratification. The printing of them and the satisfaction of the curious must however be a matter of considerable risk; but this I am willing to undertake if I can secure among gentlemen interested in tracing American history and Ethnography to its source a sufficient number of subscribers to the series to pay the cost of paper and printing. This will require about 150 subscribers.[3]

From the earlier day of the Smith proposal through the era of Bancroft's enterprise, North Americans prepared to teach, study, and write about Latin America.

The Latin American poet was somewhat chauvinistic when he characterized the United States as Caliban and Latin America as Ariel. In the variety of its Western Hemisphere interests and purposes the United States was both Caliban and Ariel: both money-minded and culturally enlightened. Involved with civil war and slavery at home, it also turned an inter-American face toward Latin America. In addition to the magic name of Abraham Lincoln and the Emancipation Proclamation, the United States also had for export a number of scientific and scholarly interests in Latin America. The *leyenda negra,* or black legend, of Spanish inhumanity vanished from the American mind more quickly than Manifest Destiny from popular prejudice.

The Civil War in the United States meant different things to Latin America. Slavery did not interest many Latins, but those Cubans and Brazilians who favored or tolerated their own slave systems watched the outcome of the struggle over emancipation with increased anxiety. Mexico concentrated her attention on national survival while suffering the French-Habsburg intervention and occupation. For other countries such as Chile, Argentina, and Colombia, slavery and emancipation had slight importance compared with political and national questions, at least as far as the political leaders and government officials were concerned.

The Latin American masses held their gaze on Abraham

---

[3] Ephraim Squier to Lewis Morgan, Aug. 1860, Lewis Morgan Manuscripts, Rush Rhees Library, Univ. of Rochester, Rochester, New York.

Lincoln. Intellectuals often wrote about him, especially after the assassination. Lincoln became both a man and myth of the greatest importance. The United States had to share its image and opinion of Lincoln with Latin America. The democratic ideal of Lincoln, the good neighbor policy of Franklin D. Roosevelt, and the youthful force of John F. Kennedy represent different stages of American impact on Latin America. Lincoln, Roosevelt, and Kennedy meant more to the common man than did the common history of the Americas. They not only presented the picture of justice with progress but also symbolized the New World as against the Old. The tragedy of these hero figures has done something, somehow, to bring an emotional solidarity into being. Lincoln was the first of these "people's politicians" to inspire and win the affection of the Latin Americas.

None of the other contemporary institutional or impersonal issues raised by the Civil War decade had as much meaning for Latin America. The Lincoln impact was large; it was new and stirring. Slavery, federalism, the civilian versus the general were already known and bitterly fought about in Latin America. The newest and the oldest factor was the person, especially in a continent dominated by *personalismo*. The idealization of Lincoln and the Lincoln legend put Cuba, Mexico, Brazil, Chile, and Argentina into a common congregation. Only a basic human need could have brought about so uniform and widespread a hero-worship. For a while, Lincoln meant more than Bolívar. The Civil War had produced an inter-American model political man.

Most slavery in Latin America had already been abolished, without civil war or abolitionist agitation. Cuba and Brazil were the exceptions. Slavery lasted in Cuba until 1880, and in Brazil until 1888. Constitutional action and legislation brought about the end of the social evil without producing either civil war or social reform. Moreover, Spanish America did not develop any basis for abolitionist propaganda or organization that might have brought together North and South American abolitionist leaders or groups. Antislavery liberalism in the New World did not supply any inter-American impact.

Brazil, to a small degree, is an exception. However, present research and the current state of knowledge are so slight as to discourage any firm statement. In Brazil the militant Negro and the friendly white encouraged the escapes of slaves, rebellion, manumission, and a hard-fought public movement in favor of abolition. Brazil somewhat resembles the United States in this respect. Furthermore, the Brazilian abolition movement became alive and organized during and after the time that the Civil War and the Emancipation Proclamation pointed one way toward abolition. The names of Lincoln and Wendell Phillips were well known among Brazilian abolitionists after 1865. One of Theodore Parker's books was translated into Portuguese as *The Servile Element.*

A contemporary document, of the highest value for the study of comparative slavery in the Western Hemisphere, tried to separate into two parts the meaning of the Emancipation Proclamation. In this 1880 analysis addressed to Madrid, the Proclamation was declared significant in the Brazilian move for abolition but inconsequential for Spanish America or Spain's colonies. Since the document was a secretary's memorandum to the Spanish Overseas Ministry, it may be taken with some reserve. In his survey of slavery in the European colonies of the New World, the writer believed the Brazilian antislavery legislation to be inspired by the United States. "The War and North American emancipation of slaves obliged the Government [of Brazil] to present to the Senate in 1865 a project of law for emancipation, whose results are not yet known."[4]

While giving special attention, for obvious reasons, to slavery and sugar cane in Louisiana, the memorandum went on to say flatly that "the abolition of slavery in the states offers nothing of interest so far as the study of their procedure is concerned." The Spanish colonial officials saw nothing in the United States that they wished to copy or imitate for their Caribbean sugar-slave societies of Cuba and Puerto Rico.

Spanish America's own abolition preceded the Civil War decade. It was not connected with Spain's late search for solutions in Cuba and Puerto Rico. The end of slavery in Spanish America coincided for the most part with the struggles for independence and national liberty. Before 1863, the social and political goals of equality for the Negro before the law were written into the constitutions of almost all the Latin American

---

[4] *Apuntes Historicos sobre la Abolicion de la Esclavitud en Colonias y estados de civilizacion cristiana.* Manuscrito del ano de 1880, presentada al Ministerio de Ultramar en Madrid (in folio, 44 pp.).

countries. Therefore, emancipation in Spanish America came through legal and political means; there was little or no abolition and very little emphasis on the problem in speeches or literature —pamphlets, newspapers, and novels were not the vehicles for abolitionist agitation in Latin America. Latin American abolition was not influenced by the North American movement. Nor was it influenced, or derived from, English humanitarian and moral antislavery feeling. Neither nineteenth-century Spanish antislavery agitation nor the French Société des Amis des Noirs had much to do with it. Latin American emancipation derived from Spanish colonial practices and from peninsular Spanish liberalism of the Age of Enlightenment and the Spanish Constitution of Cadiz in 1812.

The Emancipation Proclamation of 1863 and the Reconstruction Amendments had little or no influence upon Spanish America. Moreover, North American abolition had much of the Christian moral argument. The moral note did not have any impact upon Spanish America. This is not surprising, in the light of the historical ecclesiastical and canonical silence about Negro slavery in the Spanish American and Brazilian church laws.

The political result of the Civil War—the success of a national-federal government—was more important than slavery to Latin America. In fact, the North American way of life—its society, public education, science, and industry—cut lines of influence as deep as the federal-liberal character of the Constitution. Political survival of the United States as a whole, the test of a republic, was the dominant issue. The Declaration of Independence of 1776 and the Constitution of 1787 rang out with much more imitation and appeal to the Spanish than the Emancipation of 1863. The two eighteenth-century landmarks were of course broader and more universal, providing for "all men . . ." They were well established in North America, and widely known and cited in South America. Moreover, for Latin America, where emancipation had been achieved in almost all countries by 1863, the Proclamation was an anticlimax.

In addition, the United States needed a different "image" in the several years following the Mexican War and the expansionist actions in Central America and Cuba. The Monroe Doctrine, a "big brother" statement of protection, had little voice and no effect. The fact is that the twenty years before Lincoln became

President were nationalistic. U.S. national interest and private gain alone determined what ought to be continental, that is, shared. Already an economic expansion toward Latin America, reflecting the centuries-old belief in an El Dorado there, attracted big thoughts and empire builders. By 1880 few Latin Americans even bothered to recall the "we the people" image of the Declaration and the Constitution. Latin America could hear only manifest destiny at work.

The Civil War, without Lincoln and the Emancipation Proclamation, would still have had its legal, constitutional meaning. The war decade signified crisis and political impact concerning the idea of federal-state powers. It also brought out another immediate and future danger for Latin America, where bloody battles had made several generals famous. Militarism was a new, more modern rival to the older caudillism or dictatorship. The political general became a factor in Latin America. But Lincoln and the struggle for the Union and the Constitution gave an important lesson to Latin America: Lincoln dominated his generals. Furthermore, Congress and party leaders upheld the civilian power, stood in the path of any wartime militarism, and controlled the postwar Reconstruction-occupation forces. Liberal and civilian Latin Americans saw an important lesson in this unqualified civilian control over the United States Army. Mexico under Juárez, Brazil under Emperor Pedro II, and Argentina in the Mitre-Sarmiento era came out of the contemporary wars in Latin America with the civilian arm at the helm. At that time the victory of civilians over generals was part of the outcome of the struggles going on throughout the New World.

Many Latin Americans stressed that Lincoln's greatest battle and victory was to maintain the Constitution while cutting down slavery. Then, in 1863, with the Emancipation Proclamation he made his purpose clear to South America. It was not only an humanitarian act, but also part of the North American national interest, not directed against a foreign power but within the constitutional structure. It enhanced the power of federal government. Lincoln never had to say a word about that publicly. The struggle over national power was clearly seen in Latin America. Intelligent Latin Americans knew that Lincoln's Republican wing, in Congress and on the battlefield, had increased the powers of the federal government.

It was also clear to many that slave power, exercised politically by a wing of the Democratic party, was being stopped in the Caribbean, Central America, and Mexico. Lincoln helped make the New World safe for commerce and business, as the forces encouraging economic progress took over from slavery and feudalism. Latin Americans understood this well, and it was written about often.

Lincoln not only ended the Latin American expansionism of the Democratic party. He also gave short shrift to the anti-Latin expansionism of such Republicans as Horace Greeley. He ended both extremisms. Latin America, in turn, looked favorably upon Lincoln's military occupation of the South. The constitutional amendments leading to the Reconstruction era were discussed and approved of in Latin America.

Latin Americans also knew that the Civil War had strengthened a free society, stimulated public education, and released the economic strength of the middle sectors of North American life. A new capitalism came out of wartime industry and prewar development. Latin America needed railways. The Civil War decade trained large numbers of military engineers, especially railway, bridge, and public works engineers. Many of these men went to Latin America to work on much-needed construction projects.

In the immediate postwar years, however, the political picture was still more important than the economic. The Civil War in the United States awakened nationalism in Latin America. No wonder the writings of Columbia College's Francis Lieber were translated into Spanish. He found much in the North American federal-national experience that appealed to the intellectuals of Latin America. Professor Lieber was a Hamiltonian federalist. His political nationalism provided arguments for Latin American nations that were then facing a similar dualism of states' rights versus federal powers in government. In President Monroe's day, the United States had recognized the nationality of the Latin American countries. Then, under the Monroe Doctrine, the United States gave priority to its own interests, only indirectly recognizing those of the other New World nations. Now, for Mexican, Argentine, Cuban, and Brazilian writers, to choose certain examples, the issues of the Civil War revealed their own national problems.

The great Argentine political writer Juan B. Alberdi realized that the struggle over nationalism in the United States was the same as the issue of nationalism and provincial rights in Argentina. Alberdi, however, paid no attention to the slavery question in the United States. He could only notice the political factors of the Civil War. However, he did prove to be very sensitive, even jingoistic, concerning the Negro aspects of Brazil, Argentina's historic and nearby rival.

Alberdi saw no great "cause" in the Civil War. He did not expect the Republican party to seek the spread of the republican system throughout the New World. In fact, he saw national interest transcending the republican system. In his *Crisis Permanente*, the sharp-tongued Argentine asserted that the United States did not care about the presence of British monarchy in Canada, Russian monarchy in Alaska, Brazilian monarchy in South America, as long as Mexico was allowed to be republican. In his *El Imperio del Brasil ante la Democracia de America* (1869), the militant Argentine wishfully declaimed: "We can say that at the Battle of Petersburg General Grant killed two eagles with one shot" (i.e., the eagle of the Habsburg Maximilian and the eagle of Brazil's Braganza).

Alberdi's great fame, however, is not in international affairs, or in his discussions of the Latin American policy of the United States. It is in his ideas for the internal development of a united Argentina. He saw the South's secession from the Union as he had earlier seen the secession of Buenos Aires from the Argentine Confederation of 1853. In Alberdi's letter to Governor Urquiza, from Paris in 1861, he wrote:

> The cause which you have defended since 1851 and which after ten years is about to owe you greater service is the same which today the Washington government is defending. The majority of the United States claims, rightly, that no State individually has the right of separation, the Union being as permanent and indissoluble as marriage. You have defended it with noble title, since among us the dissident province is but one, while in North America there are ten dissident states.[5]

He noticed that each day the party in the United States that defended national union was getting stronger and stronger. That turned out to be right. He was a poor prophet, however. He was

---

[5] Ramón J. Cárcano, ed.: *Urquiza y Alberdi. Intimidades de Una Política* (Buenos Aires: La Facultad; 1938), pp. 596–7.

also a little mistaken, at least at the beginning of the Civil War, in thinking that no European nation would favor the dismemberment of the United States.

The Argentines, who were mostly white and European, showed little interest in slavery, emancipation, or race equality. The Caribbean peoples of Latin America, on the other hand, naturally were much more interested in both Negro slavery and emancipation than in the political questions of national union, civilians versus generals, the political right of secession, and so on. The Civil War in the United States had much more personal as well as patriotic meaning for the Cubans, slavery being one of their most crucial concerns. It is both strange and noteworthy that no abolitionist argument or movement appeared in Cuba before the Civil War decade. The freeing of Cuban slaves was a delicate topic, for liberals as well as conservatives. Not until the liberal patriot-leader Carlos Manuel de Céspedes freed his own slaves and proposed island-wide abolition in 1868 did the prospect take on life. The success of the abolitionists, the Civil War, and the Emancipation Proclamation explain the belated but welcome appearance of antislavery action among the Cuban patriots.

Cuba in fact echoed some of the civil divisions of the North American Civil War. Two groups were formed on the island: one was for Lincoln, the other for the Confederacy. The friends of Lincoln included those Cubans who wanted to bring political reforms to the Spanish colony. Most of them became the patriot forces of the Ten Years' War, which lasted from 1868 to 1878. Cuban Negro slaves did not reveal their emotions or loyalties, but many of them, with colored freedmen, waited in the port of Havana for the arrival of boats from the Union to receive the latest news about the Northern cause. They exulted happily over Northern victories, because that meant to them the redemption of the African race. The North stimulated the foes of Spanish colonialism. Finally, "the image of Lincoln, in humble abodes as well as mansions, sheltering altruistic and progressive men, became the expression of the deepest Cuban aspirations." Lincoln thus awakened Cuban nationalism.[6]

---

[6] *Historia de la Nacion Cubana* (10 vols.; Havana: Editorial Historia de la Nacion Cubana, S.A.; 1952), IV, *Ruptura con la Metrópoli (desde 1837 hasta 1868)*, 31.

When news came to Cuba that "the man with the sad look"
—Cervantes's phrase for Don Quixote—had been assassinated,
there was consternation and grief. Cubans expressed their personal and moral sympathies in speeches and eulogies; some of
them went into personal mourning, as though in Lincoln a
friend or relative had passed away. (In the twentieth century,
the deaths of Franklin D. Roosevelt and John F. Kennedy produced a similar effect.) The identification with Lincoln, through
nationalism or the emancipation issue, overcame existing religious, cultural, and linguistic differences, briefly creating a
solidarity of sentiment. The story is told that the noted Cuban
doctor Juan Bruno Zayas honored the memory of Lincoln by
financing, in a gesture of personal expiation, the emancipation
of those children of Negro slaves in Cuba born on July 4, 1865.

The victory of the antislavery cause in the United States
gave rise to a new social and human issue in Cuba, and the older
political goals of independence and liberty were reactivated. How
much of this was due to the Civil War is not yet fixed by research.
But there is no doubt that the Civil War period motivated the
political crusade against Spain for Cuban liberty. There is also
no doubt that the United States both sheltered and stimulated
Cuban patriotism, antislavery action, and nationalism. The years
of Lincoln and the Northern cause helped make Cuban history.

Of course, neither Cuba nor Argentina had the special interest that Mexico had in the outcome of the Civil War: for
Mexico, bordering on the United States, was concerned with re-
covering its independence and nationality, and the United States
could possibly have a good deal to do with that effort. Working
in the Mexican legation in Washington, the young Matías Romero (1837–98) was an indefatigable proponent of Mexico's
cause.[7]

Other important and patriotic Latin Americans besides Romero were in Washington during the war period, among them
Benjamin Vicuña Mackenna from Chile and Domingo F. Sarmiento from Argentina. Sarmiento brought the impact of the

---

[7] I have completed a historical biography of Matías Romero. His diary
has been published. His personal manuscript correspondence is enormous;
his letters during the Civil War period have been printed. I have sketched
his youthful and formative years in Harry Bernstein: "Mocedades de
Matías Romero," *Historia Mexicana*, X, 4 (Apr.–June 1961), 588–612.

United States into Argentina by way of a biography of Lincoln and his interest in North American public schools, public libraries, and civic education. One of the several Latin American editors of the inter-American publishing house Appleton & Co., Sarmiento received great praise for his work in publishing. He did not look for the slavery issue, and like his contemporary, Alberdi, who stayed in Argentina, Sarmiento did not see the Emancipation Act as important in itself. He made little comment either on the Black Belt or on Black Brazil.[8]

Matías Romero was concerned chiefly with the impact of North American politics and economics upon Mexico. While Romero agitated for the North American forces of the Civil War era to get the French out of Mexico, Benjamin Vicuña Mackenna, the Chilean, propagandized to get Spain out of the Caribbean and the Pacific. Sarmiento, as already seen, had little political purpose in Washington; his primary interests were cultural.

Romero's diplomatic maneuvers during the Civil War helped save the Mexican nation. He convinced the Juárez government in Mexico that it was not Lincoln alone but also the rising Republican party that would help save the independence of Mexico. For him, the rise of new economic and political forces in the United States meant the safety of Mexico in the present and the progress of Mexico during a reconstruction and recovery period. He felt that despite extremist wings and several jingoistic figures in the Republican party, it would end territorial expansion, aggression, or annexation at the expense of Mexico. North American investors and their political friends would no longer want to annex Mexican territory and thus destroy the country's nationality. He felt they only wanted to lease and use territory, to make profits and seek protection of law. He advised his government, during the Civil War and to the end of the century, that the new leaders wanted only concessions, railway rights-of-way, leaseholds, and commercial agreements. Mexico did not need to fear loss of national domain from the new party in power. Romero was responsible for many of the investment

---

[8] D. F. Sarmiento: *Vida de Abran Lincoln, Decimo Sesto Presidente de los Estados Unidos.* (2nd edn., rev.; New York, 1866). His friend Matías Romero did not share his views about Lincoln. The great intellectual figure of Colombia, Salvador Camacho Roldan, shared Sarmiento's esteem for Lincoln, and also wrote a biography of the American President.

ideas that marked the later Porfirio Díaz era. It turned out that
the new United States, after Reconstruction, began to stir up
interest in Pan-Americanism and a Pan-American society.

Romero thought American capital and technology were
beneficial to Mexico and Latin America. A generation before the
era of Díaz and the bumptious imperialism of Theodore Roosevelt, Romero told all the Mexicans who would listen to him that
the Civil War in the United States had emancipated its capital
and had freed the North American mind from anti-Mexicanism.
The United States had begun to cluster several image-forming
influences in the hemisphere: Pan-Americanism, emancipation,
the Monroe Doctrine. Romero understood the forces behind these
influences, and he saw no evil in North American materialism
and capitalism. Unlike many Latin American poets, the more
prosaic Romero refused to depict the United States as "bad"
and Latin Ameria or the Hispanic spirit as "good." There was
no Caliban or Ariel imagery in his mind.

Romero saw the Civil War as an economic struggle—a war
against the Southern influences of feudalism and slavery waged
by the Northern forces of liberal capital and progress. He appealed to North American Protestantism to see Mexico's civil
war as one brought on by Catholic feudalism aided by hacienda
feudalism. Thus he tried to bring both civil wars together in
history and the interpretation of history.

He also tried to tie together Reconstruction in the United
States and the reconstruction of Mexico. Through the smoke
and noise of the Civil War Romero calculated its meaning for
Mexico. Through his friendships with leading Republican politicians and businessmen, he received assurances that the United
States would be in a position to help Mexico as soon as the crisis
of the Civil War was over. These assurances became reality
when, indeed, both the Republican party platforms and congressional leadership allowed Mexico to get back on its feet and restore nationalism and liberalism. So recovery from the Civil War
did go hand in hand with Mexican reconstruction.

Romero worked best among the Republicans of the state of
New York, although he also dealt directly with Congress and the
Cabinet in Washington and was a long-time personal friend of
General Grant. The New York interest in Latin America was
considerable. New York capitalists and merchants had much to
do with reconstruction and the building of railways in Mexico.

During the war years Romero remained close to those New York Republicans who sided with him against the federal administration about policy toward Mexico. He played politics with those New Yorkers who were opposed to Seward's caution and neutralism. He brought influential members of the Union League Club over to his point of view. His associates included James Beekman, some of the chief figures of the St. Nicholas Society, the president of Columbia College, Charles King, and others in the first ranks of business and finance. They became willing supporters of Benito Juárez, the Indian president and leader of the Mexican cause. Romero created strong allies in both Manhattan and Washington against the French and the Habsburg Maximilian, although he could not budge Seward and Lincoln. However, after Mexico's crisis was all over, Seward became a close friend of his. On a Mexican visit in 1872 Seward stayed at Romero's home.

Romero felt that the issues of the Civil War and the war in Mexico were similar to those of the sixteenth-century war between the Dutch republican patriots and the feudal empire of Philip II of Spain: freedom versus feudalism. These views and speeches prefigured the later sentiment for religious freedom in Mexico and for the liberty of North American Protestants to preach and teach there.

When Romero joined Juárez's cabinet as minister of the treasury in 1868 he brought these ideas of religious freedom in the United States back with him, earning the enmity of the Jesuits and later Catholic church historians. His close and lasting friendships with Grant, Garfield, and many others in New York, Washington, and later in California gave human relief to the economic map of the flow of North American money and technology into Mexico from 1865 on. Matías Romero, "a Mexican Yankee," tied together the doctrines and interests of North American economic liberalism as well as political and religious tolerance. His long friendship and correspondence with Hiram Barney, former collector of the port of New York and an important lawyer and political figure in that state, are enough to show the connection between the forces released by the Civil War in the United States and the economic evolution of the Mexican nation.

The Mexican in Yankeeland was a prophet without great public honor in his own day. Married secretly in Philadelphia to a Protestant, North American girl, Matías Romero was a bridge between North American capital and Mexican growth as long as he lived. He himself described, making allowances for his own self-esteem, how close he was to the inside of Civil War and Reconstruction history:

> I was therefore in Washington during nearly two years of Mr. Buchanan's administration, the whole of Mr. Lincoln's first and second administrations, and of his successor Mr. Johnson. . . .
>
> I feel constrained to say that my stay in Washington has been so long, and my acquaintance with the leading public men of this country so intimate that I can state with truth that I know a great deal about the unwritten history of this country, which if carefully selected would afford material for very interesting personal memoirs.[9]

Fortunately for historical writing and our better knowledge of the Civil War, Romero was one who liked to write and have his name in print. He had clear, strong views about writing history, especially history and narratives about an era in which he had a personal part. As late as 1885 he expressed these views to his friend Hiram Barney. Barney had wanted to see Romero and talk over many things, one of which was:

> . . . the question of my writing about Lincoln. If I do write it will be about matters which have not been alluded to by others. They were of a confidential nature and I am not satisfied that I have a right to publish what I know.[1]

Romero, himself a biographer of Juárez and Grant, was very conscious also of personal role in history. Romero had his own opinion of Lincoln—and it was uncomplimentary—but he did not let it interfere with the history of the Civil War era. He answered his friend entirely naturally:

> . . . If I was in your place I should write by all means my personal recollections of Mr. Lincoln. If they were confidential at the time now they cannot be so, and they are on the contrary a matter of public interest.[2]

---

[9] Matías Romero: *Mexico and the United States* (New York: G. P. Putnam's Sons; 1898), p. iii.

[1] Barney to Romero, Romero Papers, Box 74.

[2] Romero to Barney, in Copiador, No. 42.

Romero also had firm views on other contemporary matters arising during the Civil War that affected the United States and Mexico. Slavery was one of these matters. Unlike most white liberals, Matías Romero never professed any guilt feelings about slavery. He disliked the institution, whether for white, Negro, or Indian, but without emotional involvement.

Romero held long discussions with Montgomery Blair about slavery in Mexico and the United States. Blair, a member of Lincoln's Cabinet and attorney for Dred Scott, was also reputed to be the author of one early draft of the Emancipation Proclamation. Like many other Mexican liberals, Romero opposed the extension of slavery under the Confederates into Mexico and even the proposal to allow freed Negroes to migrate to Mexico. He did not favor the movement of any Africans into a country where the Indians continued to predominate. For that matter, he was also cool toward European immigration. Romero was thinking only politically and nationalistically.

Therefore, Romero opposed Blair's feeler that Southern Negroes be helped to move across the Rio Grande. Romero was already as outraged as others were at the news that the Emperor Maximilian had reinstated both the plantation system and Negro slavery in Mexico. Romero may have also felt that the "deportation" of Southern Negroes to Mexico, whether accepted by the South or ordered by Northern victors, would serve only to strengthen "the usurper" Maximilian. But the fact remained, nevertheless, that he did not wish to promote Negro immigration into Mexico.

Romero acknowledged the announcement of the Emancipation Proclamation, but he never gave it special praise or even special notice, since Mexico had already abolished slavery. His attention was concentrated on politics, diplomacy, and economic growth. Since he was one of the very few Latin Americans who disliked Lincoln, that may have added to his coolness.

If Mexicans and Mexico found such routine meaning in the slavery issues of the Civil War, because they were then fighting for Mexico's very existence, such was not the case with Brazil and the Brazilians. The issue of slavery had a very strong impact there, because it was a significant aspect of Brazilian society. Brazil's "plantocracy" and slavery were far more similar to institutions in the United States than anything Mexico had. While Romero theorized about the Civil War and Mexican feudalism, the Church, or the tyranny of Spain under Philip II, Brazil's reality closely resembled the American South in its actual social conditions, race relations, and agricultural basis. Brazil, as we have seen, already had her own antislavery history. It is true that Brazil also watched the Civil War politically, but not as much as Mexico had to. Emperor Pedro II's recognition of his fellow-Habsburg monarch, Maximilian of Mexico, pleased neither the United States nor Mexico. It may have also quickened the formation of republicanism in Brazil. The slavery question, however, had its own momentum there.

The idea, inspiration, and example of the emancipation (other than the appeal of Lincoln) had probably the largest single impact of the Civil War on Brazil. Emancipation, as has been pointed out, brought fear to the slaveowners that the North American example would be emulated in Brazil. It also triggered optimistic, enthusiastic hopes in abolitionists, liberals, and some early Brazilian republicans that free Negro labor would build up an artisan-based working class and society. Even those who defended the more "humane" conditions of Brazil's slaves, compared with those in the United States, also shared this aspect of the antislavery optimism.

The most important Brazilian thinker and writer of the Civil War period was A. C. Tavares Bastos. He drew his readers' attention to the nature of slavery in both the Americas:

> Certainly our slaveowners deserve some praise for the most part, compared to the cynical cruelty of slave breeders in Delaware, Maryland, Kentucky, or Missouri. We have no deeds here like the lamentable picture of B. Stowe, the slave hunt, the *lynch-law*, the legal prohibition of all instruction and religious education, etc.[3]

Despite such concessions to Brazilian slaveowners, Bastos condemned the system.

As for the slaves themselves, many Brazilian progressives were convinced that emancipation in the United States would

---

[3] A. C. Tavares Bastos: *Cartas do Solitário*. 3rd edn., 5th Series, Brasiliana, Vol. 115 (Rio de Janeiro: Companhia Editôra Nacional; 1938). First printed in 1862, based upon his letters to the newspaper *Correio Mercantil*. Tavares Bastos exaggerated both sides of his comparison, and conveniently forgot the centuries of "slave hunts" in Brazil.

make a free farmer out of the ex-slave. The North American example strengthened the Brazilian argument. Moreover, both Brazil and South America were influenced by the noted French geographer Elisée Reclus. Reclus had written about the Negro in Colombia and the coastal Caribbean, where he had traveled. Brazilians leaned even more upon Reclus's article in the *Revue de deux mondes* (March–April 1863), where he had drawn up a sort of prophecy of the future of the North American Negro after the Civil War and emancipation. Reclus, after tracing the continuous pressure of the abolitionists upon the "timid government" of President Lincoln, then stirred the reader with reference to the climax of the immortal act of January 1, 1863. Tavares Bastos accepted Reclus's forecast of Negro adjustment after emancipation. He was equally optimistic regarding the prospects for agriculture, labor, and the trades. Both Reclus and Bastos were sure that the Negro would be capable of great economic productivity after gaining his political freedom. Negro labor could maintain the stricken cotton plantation and the factory. Emancipation would allow the Negro to contribute to the Negro community as well as to the whole society.

The Civil War also unveiled some important political realities for Brazil. Brazilians began to realize, watching the United States, that their natural allies were to be found in the Western Hemisphere, not in France or Britain. Tavares Bastos launched his tireless efforts to reach a widely based friendship with the United States. He sought the connecting links of commerce and republicanism in addition to emancipation. He used the occasion to promote his materialist desire for steam-navigation links to New York. Living in the Amazon-Maranhão region, Tavares Bastos was also a spokesman for better utilization of the Amazon Valley.

He and other Brazilians also realized that the outcome of the Civil War meant, in a large sense, the continuation of liberal democracy and the promise of reform—these in addition to the Negro's freedom. What was better for facts and ideas, economic gains, and political liberty than the closer connection between the great power of North America and the great power of South America?

Not every Brazilian, however, was so optimistic. Nor did everyone share such a view of Brazil. Slaveowners dreaded the impact of emancipation; others saw their country as a backward, slavocrat-feudal monarchy that would suffocate. Tavares Bastos himself well knew the slaveowners' fear of abolition; and he avoided the error of putting all of Brazilian slavery together. He did not idly copy or apply emancipation without thought for Brazil's reality.

He saw that slavery in the interior provinces was different in its implications for Brazilian national security from what obtained in the coastal provinces. Slavery in the regions along the borders of Brazil was still more of a problem. Bastos then proposed immediate emancipation, with just compensation to the slaveowners, for the Negro slaves in those Brazilian border provinces that adjoined the free states of Spanish America. This meant different legislation for the slaves up near Guiana from those down near Argentina. He wanted to avoid the social turmoil created by the Paraguayan War.

In a letter to the secretary of the British and Foreign Anti-Slavery Society, Bastos, combining both his liberalism and nationalism, explained his views: he showed that slavery along the southern and southwestern border was a special danger to Brazilian security, an element that could lead to military adventures. In addition, Bastos, always a states' rights man and a federalist in the Brazilian sense, told those Brazilians who wanted to emancipate all slaves in Brazil at once that abolition could not be simultaneous; at best it could only be immediate or imminent in some of the provinces. To back up his argument he pointed out that in the United States slavery in the Northern and Western states had been abolished at different times, prior to the 1863 Proclamation.

Granted then that emancipation should be slowed down in Brazil, what about the optimistic effects of emancipation? Taking his cue from the report of the American Freedmen's Union, as annexed to the Report of the Anti-Slavery Conference, Bastos became particularly concerned with what the United States was doing to hold the Negroes near their birthplace. He found that the freed slaves became the working classes in the same vicinity where they had been born and raised. Tavares Bastos stated emphatically: let Brazil's states take notice and not forget it. It could only mean, then, that to make a man of the slave the Negro must be sent to school, as was done in the United States.

For Bastos the school provided the channel for the second American Revolution: "The world has never seen such a revolution, in the same society, in half a dozen years." Schools for every child and adult, that was the answer! Abolition, emancipation, and the achievement of personal liberty through education were all one and the same thing.

He knew of and praised the wartime protection of the freed slaves by the United States Army, followed by the work of the religious and lay Negro welfare groups and the Freedmen's Bureau. Private initiative and personal effort on behalf of the United States' freedmen were well known to him, but Brazil had no equivalent of the Peabody Fund. North American philanthropical help was not being emulated in Latin America. Nevertheless, the example of American private and public aid did make quite an impression upon Bastos and other Brazilians. Government help, from the time of the Emancipation Proclamation to the Freedmen's Bureau, was in his opinion a good beginning for Brazil to note.

Each Brazilian slave-owning generation since independence had seen with fear the gradual abolition of slavery and the ending of the African slave trade. Slavery came to an end on the continent around them, and then in nearby Guiana and in the Caribbean. First came the abolition of slavery in Spanish America, beginning with independence and slowly moving across the continent until it was achieved in Colombia in 1853. Abolition moved through the British Caribbean, in Jamaica and Guiana in 1833; the great work of the French Société des Amis des Noirs had culminated in the achievement of Schoelcher in the French Caribbean—he abolished slavery in Martinique and Guadeloupe in 1848. Only Cuba and Brazil remained slave cultures.

The abolitionist threat in the United States and the final capstone of the Emancipation Proclamation added to the fears of the Brazilian planters, especially those with large landholdings and large slave forces. The consequences were far more serious than the idea or the principle. Emancipation meant great economic and financial loss, followed almost at once by the abrupt and disastrous exodus of the emancipated slaves. The idea of emancipation and abolition in Brazil conjured up the slaveowners' fears of an immediate and wholesale extension of the *quilombo* (runaway slave community) tradition.

However, the reverse took place when emancipation occurred: the slave tended to stay in the vicinity of the master, or rather, the place where he had been born. Despite this, emancipation for the owners meant an uprooting, a break-up of the traditional economic and social rule from the "Big House." At the same time, the intelligent planters were already beginning to think at least of a white, European, tenant-farmer immigration.

The planter classes left to others those aspects of emancipation that gave rise to debates about liberty. The rural aristocracy and urban slaveholder of Brazil were not thinkers, either of the Left or the Right. They were the pragmatic descendants of Portuguese farmers and merchants, aware of two things—labor and profit. Abolition of slavery in Brazil and emancipation in the United States were a threat to these two interests. If the news about the Emancipation Proclamation had not meant the danger of migration and exodus, it is possible that the Brazilian slaveowner would have freed his mind sufficiently to let slavery, the costs of which were enormous, be replaced by cheaper, free, low-wage labor. In Brazil, where for two centuries the runaway slave in the Afro-Brazilian *quilombo* had brought out hate and fear, the thought of legalizing the voluntary departure of Negroes led to criticism of what the United States had done. Louis Agassiz gave a chapter in his book *A Journey in Brazil* (Boston, 1868) the subtitle "Effect of Emancipation in the United States upon Slavery in Brazil."

Professor Agassiz felt that Brazilians were trying by gradualism to achieve that "which was forced upon us without previous preparation," and he understood the effort involved. He considered that if slavery was more hopeful in Brazil from a political point of view, it also looked more odious than in the United States from a moral point of view. It was his opinion, shared by many travelers and observers, that the black Brazilians' moral and sexual habits were very bad, due to poor religious instruction and precept. José Carlos Rodrígues, a Brazilian in the United States, was also stating that Negro slaves in the United States were more Christian, more upright and moral, and better trained as artisans than those in Brazil.

José Carlos Rodrígues was one of the most literary and liberal Brazilian intellectuals of the later nineteenth and the early twentieth century. Unlike most of his generation, who were being attracted by Europe, whether Germany, France, England, or Italy, Rodrígues lived and worked in the United States, as a bibliographer and collector of Brazilian books and manuscripts, a journalist, and a newspaper proprietor in New York City at the end of the Civil War decade. To those who are familiar with United States-Brazilian relations during and after the 1860's, Rodrígues had many other reasons for distinction. He was making available scholarships to Brazilian boys going to Cornell to study, and, in addition, he gave financial support to Charles Hartt, pioneer in geological studies in Brazil, and was a patron of Brazilian studies in the United States.

O Novo Mundo, which Rodrígues edited and published, lasted only about two years. Since the aftermath of the Civil War and Emancipation decade in the United States coincided with the renewal of antislavery and abolitionist agitation in Brazil, Rodrígues was in the unique position of being able to see the two antislavery movements. However, not all his readers were interested in slavery or abolition. The expectation of expanded commerce between New York and the Amazon, or New York and Brazil, produced in the pages of *O Novo Mundo* mainly items and articles of commercial, agricultural, and technical value.

Rodrígues not only observed the impact of the United States upon Brazil; he also took account of the United States' domestic reaction to the announcement of Pedro II in 1867 that Brazil would soon take steps to abolish slavery as early as possible. His optimism at that time, of course, was premature, since slavery was not abolished until 1888. In 1870, writing an editorial in *O Novo Mundo* on the emancipation of slaves, Rodrígues pointed out that

> four years ago when Don Pedro 2º declared he was going to take measures to abolish the servile element in the Empire as soon as possible, all the foreign press exulted with sincere rejoicing to see Brazil receive so quickly the moral of the Civil War in the United States.

Rodrígues bent a large part of his efforts to an emphasis upon the significance of slavery, especially in the economy and in society. He was a little disturbed to have to admit (again prematurely) that Spain, in her colonies, seemed to be beating Brazil to emancipation of all slaves. It irked him that Cuba, without any antislavery movement, Negro revolts and *quilombos,* or abolitionist agitation, might get there first.

Struggle and abolitionism were part of education. That meant a great deal, and Rodrígues felt Brazil should have learned and borrowed from the experience and the progressive gains of the United States. According to him, the political history of the United States from the time of the American Revolution to the Civil War was really the history of the struggle against slavery.[4] The two countries thus had in common the struggle for civil liberty and human equality. They happened to be the only two nations in the New World *not* to have provided or declared for the abolition of slavery in their Declarations of Independence.

Developing his review of comparative slavery a little further into an ambitious article entitled "History of Slavery in the United States" (*O Novo Mundo,* August 24, 1871), Rodrígues wrote for his Portuguese-language readers an account of how slavery had died out in the United States. He then pointed out the means by which Brazil could achieve the same end: emancipation acts, constitutional amendments, congressional legislation. Tavares Bastos, in Brazil, had pointed out the role of the states in the abolition of slavery. But Rodrígues, in the United States, stressed the example of a national government taking both the lead and the follow-up in abolition.

Rodrígues was far more interested in the example of emancipation in the United States for Brazil than in the secondary question of whether one country had a more tolerant attitude toward slaves than the other. He was not interested in the question of a "gentle versus severe slavery." As a Brazilian influenced by residence and associations in the United States, he looked to the example of the United States as a model and inspiration for abolition of slavery in his own culture and political system.

There are many ways to look at the Civil War and its impact upon Latin America. Besides slavery, Emancipation, and Reconstruction there is the idea of states' rights and nationalism, the

---

4 *O Novo Mundo,* March 21, 1871.

prospects of trade, and the sense of independence from Europe, all of which the war brought up. Among the great events and great names of the Civil War period there was even a stab at establishing a monarchy. Some looked upon Maximilian of Mexico with fear or admiration. For planters and slaveowners he provided the laws and the model of a redeemer, especially when he restored slavery to Mexico. In Brazil, monarchists and slavocrats looked with a sense of solidarity toward the castles in Chapultepec (Mexico City) and in Petropolis (Brazil). Petropolis and Chapultepec had much more in common than emperors, castles, lovely views, and garden walks.

The Brazilian Tavares Bastos could see much in the Civil War period besides slavery. Politics, trade, shipping, and federalism also reflected on Brazil. The North American political and constitutional systems had begun to teach Latin American legislators, reformers, and jurists about the balance and compromise between nationalism and federalism.[5] Slavery was only one course of study; the art of government and enduring constitutions was another. We see the exchange and inter-American work of United States culture, books, history, public education, scientific societies, and individuals. The Civil War period continued to convey the examples and experience of North American science and scholarship, as well as antislavery action, commerce, and constitutions.

The Civil War evoked from Latin America the same interest in freedom and independence that the American Revolution had brought out. For the United States both eras led to great events. For Latin America the events in turn led to great expectations. But the Civil War and its aftermath proved to be more disappointing. The image of the United States in Latin America during the generation after the American Revolution was still promising and beckoning to Latin America. The thirty years after 1781 were full of the optimism of the Age of Enlighten-

---

[5] It may not be too late to point out here that federalism in Latin America means just the opposite from what it does in the United States. There, political literature, movements, and leaders identified with federalism are those that support the rights of the states as equal to or coexistent with those of the national or federal government. Federal government must thus be equal to the sum of its parts. It should not be run from the capital city outward to the parts.

ment, the strength of the republican system, and the vigor of North American freedom.

The thirty years after the Civil War era lost this spirit. By 1900 Latin America was even more disillusioned with its own failures than with the image of the United States. True, the impact of the United States had changed from the time of Independence. In both parts of the New World the achieved nationalism was no longer a patriotic, emotional goal, but a constitutional–military system of powers and institutions. The United States was not what it had started out to look like; but neither was Latin America. Between 1900 and 1914 the changing features had made both regions harder to recognize. The Civil War was the last great period before the era of the good neighbor policy and the Alliance for Progress (1933–63) when the United States was able to stir emotion and admiration in Latin America.

Index

---

i

INDEX

INDEX

INDEX

Index

A NOTE ABOUT THE EDITOR

HAROLD M. HYMAN was born in New York City in 1924. After taking his A.B. degree at the University of California at Los Angeles, he did graduate work at Columbia University, and his doctoral dissertation, *Era of the Oath: Northern Loyalty Tests during the Civil War and Reconstruction*, won the American Historical Association's Albert J. Beveridge Award in 1952. He has taught at Earlham College in Indiana, at Arizona State University, at U.C.L.A., at the University of Illinois, and is now William Hobby Professor of American History at Rice University in Texas. In 1959 he received the Sidney Hillman Award for his *To Try Men's Souls: Loyalty Tests in American History*. In 1962 he published a biography of Edwin McMasters Stanton, Lincoln's Secretary of War, begun by Benjamin P. Thomas before his death. Mr. Hyman is married, the father of two daughters and a son.

A NOTE ON THE TYPE

The Text of this book was set on the Linotype in a new face called PRIMER, designed by RUDOLPH RUZICKA, earlier responsible for the design of Fairfield and Fairfield Medium, Linotype faces whose virtues have for some time now been accorded wide recognition.

The complete range of sizes of Primer was first made available in 1954, although the pilot size of 12 point was ready as early as 1951. The design of the face makes general reference to Linotype Century (long a serviceable type, totally lacking in manner or frills of any kind) but brilliantly corrects the characterless quality of that face.

Composed, printed, and bound by The Haddon Craftsmen, Inc., Scranton, Pa. The illustrations were printed by Halliday Lithograph Corp., West Hanover, Mass.

Typography and binding based on designs by

WARREN  CHAPPELL